# THE RADICAL IMAGINATION

*An anthology from* **DISSENT** *magazine*

# THE RADICAL IMAGINATION

*Edited by Irving Howe*
*Introduction by*
*Michael Harrington*

THE NEW AMERICAN LIBRARY

Published by The New American Library, Inc.
1301 Avenue of the Americas, New York, New York 10019
Published simultaneously in Canada by General Publishing Company, Ltd.
Library of Congress Catalog Card Number: 67–14728
Printed in the United States of America by H. Wolff, New York

# CONTENTS

33645

# INTRODUCTION
## MICHAEL HARRINGTON

I had begun this introduction as an analysis of the relationship between *Dissent* and the times which the articles in this volume both depict and reflect. More or less inevitably, this led to a consideration of the revival of American radicalism in the sixties and one more essay on the gap between the generations of thc Left began to emerge. It occurred to me that America could do without another such analysis — there are entire books devoted to the subject — and it was this realization which impelled me toward a rather novel form for a preface, mixing politics and memoir.

I did not choose this approach in order to be a *laudator prius acti* and I hope that I am not pretentiously investing my own experience with large soci-symbolic significance. It is just that a brief account of my own experience with the magazine might help give a perspective on its role and importance on the democratic Left. If that can be achieved, it might provide a vantage point from which the reader can hear the individual contributors speak for themselves more clearly.

My first reaction to the magazine — it was the period when it was founded — was that the editors were selling out.

Perhaps it is inevitable that young people come to the radical movement with the fervor of catechumens and always believe that the veterans of past struggles are tired and going soft. Or perhaps this attitude is only an expression of the special American circumstances of the recent past: the decline and ideological confusion of the entire adult Left, the discontinuities created when McCarthyism all but wiped out the radical youth movement. Whatever the sociological and psychological explanation, it seemed obvious to me in 1954 that Irving Howe and company were hell-bent for liberalism, a fate worse than death. At *Dissent* conferences, I was among those who lectured the editors on the dangers of capitulating to American imperialism, of abandoning the struggle for socialist power, and so on.

It is obvious that I do not bring up this reminiscence in order to document that cruel untruth which the middle class loves so well: that a twenty-year-old cares about poverty and injustice but a thirty-year-old does not. Quite the contrary, *Dissent,* as this collection amply demonstrates, has maintained a basically critical stance toward the American and world status quo for more than a decade. And if my own view of the universe is more complex than the one I used to urge at the *Dissent* conferences, it is animated by the same spirit.

For what I had regarded as "selling out" was a profoundly radical act. By the 1950's the classic socialist dogmas had all become problematic. In the East, the hopes of October, 1917, had been destroyed by Stalinist totalitarianism. In Europe the Social Democracy had begun to accept the welfare state as a substitute for socialism. Under such circumstances, it was possible either to incant the old truths although they no longer applied (they did, however, still sound intransigeant and pure, which was their attraction for me at that time), or to strike out in search of a new relevance. And it was, of course, the latter and liberating course which *Dissent* took.

At the same time, the question of civil liberties had an extraordinary depth and range. For, as often happens, a profound change in attitudes was debated in symbolic terms. There were not a great many proclaimed Communists clamoring for the right to teach, and even the infamous Smith Act persecutions affected a much smaller group than the Palmer Raids of the twenties. Yet, there was fierce, even passionate, argument over such issues. And in general, those who said that Communists had — because they were conspirators or accomplices in subversion, or whatever — forfeited their democratic rights to be hired as teachers or to apologize for totalitarianism without fear of reprisal, also began to affirm that America was a fine society with only vestigial social problems. And those who, like *Dissent,* maintained a principled defense of the rights of Communists kept up their attack on domestic injustice.

These internal wrongs in American society were usually seen in *Dissent* as related to a foreign policy which included Chiang, Franco, Syngman Rhee, Bao Dai (and Diem and Ky), Batista, Jiminez, etc. in the "free" world. An America which still believed in laissez-faire myths and acted on the basis of the realities of corporate power could not understand a colonial world in revolutionary motion. As a result, the various nationalist and social movements all seemed to be the creatures of some evil conspiracy located in Moscow. Thus, a kind of McCarthyite view of world politics emerged; and the equation of radicalism with Communism, which so menaced civil liberties within the United States, was projected on a global scale with a devastating effect upon the nation's foreign policy.

Though *Dissent* kept up a running criticism of United States foreign policy, the focus of the magazine was increasingly American. For one of the by-products of the rejection of the "finished programs" and talmudic verities of the old faith was to make the magazine productively parochial. In the thirties, the American Communists had followed the political dictates of the Kremlin with slavish precision. And the socialists and Trotskyists, although free of such a dependence on a distant, totalitarian oracle, were also obsessed by international events. The Socialist Party split in the mid-thirties over a debate which essentially concerned the proper tactics for the Austrian Social Democracy in the struggle against fascism; and Leon Trotsky constantly taught his American followers that the international perspective came first. So it was that radicals in this country sometimes debated the "road to power" without noticing that the workers were out creating the CIO. (In all of this, I am concerned with a sectarian internationalism, and not the real thing; for there is no question that the single most tragic moment in the history of socialism occurred in 1914 when the old promise of world brotherhood was shattered and the revolutionists joined their respective armies and began to kill one another.)

In any case, when *Dissent* broke with the facile world-views and began to confront the specific problems of a socialism in crisis, there was a creative rediscovery of what was wrong with America. It was no longer possible, so to speak, to live off the European socialist inheritance. So it was that the magazine published a ranging series of analyses of the American power structure (including some notable contributions by C. Wright Mills); explored the themes of bureaucracy and alienation long before they became a commonplace of protest rhetoric; and developed a social and economic understanding of the struggle for civil rights. And so it is that this new collection of articles from *Dissent* is, if anything, weighted in the direction of a confrontation with society in the United States.

If I can return to the personal mode for a moment, there is a curious relationship between this "American" aspect of *Dissent* and the radical revival of the sixties. Most of the young activists do not think of the magazine as belonging to their generation and movement, and more than one young militant would describe it as irrelevant, old-fogeyish, establishmentarian, or whatever the fashionable put-down might be. And yet, so much of what the new radicals have discovered in a blinding moment of insight comes to them in part, whether they know it or not, as a free gift from the older generation around *Dissent*.

In my own case, a great deal of the impulse to turn to the issue of poverty in the United States derived from the critique of the American celebration inaugurated by *Dissent*. And would it be impossibly grand-paternalistic for me to speculate, at the age of thirty-eight, that some of the angry young Leftists might follow a route similar to my own? They, too, might realize that it is wrong to confuse a tough-minded and empirical willingness to face the society as it is with a lack of principle. Certainly the work of people like Paul Goodman, Bayard Rustin, Tom Kahn, Jeremy Larner, Claude Brown and the others included in this volume hardly gives aid and comfort to complacency. Indeed, I find such thoughtful essays even more subversive than the most intransigeant slogans.

Finally, lest all this have the appearance of a eulogy, let me return to the problematic areas.

It seems to me that one of the most significant failures of American democratic socialists has been with regard to foreign policy. It is not that *Dissent* and the rest of us failed to protest this or that outrage, from the glorification of Syngman Rhee to that of General Ky. It is easy enough to join the proper picket line and the most unimaginative radical can be prepared for almost all eventualities by making an all-purpose sign, "Hands Off the ——— Revolution" (it has the virtue of applying to both Communist and anti-Communist suppressions). But to what precise degree is American foreign policy a reflex of American domestic structure? Must there be a thoroughgoing transformation of the society at home before there can be genuine support to a democratic revolution abroad? Was the failure of the high purpose of the Alliance for Progress an "inevitable" consequence of the nature of the American social system?

*Dissent* has not, of course, ignored such issues. Indeed, the magazine has published excellent reportage and analysis in this area. In particular, there was a hard-headed, and quite right, refusal of most of the facile slogans about the "Third World." It would be marvelous if revolutionary elan could, by itself, transcend the heritage of backwardness in the ex-colonial world or if tribesmen and peasants could achieve the society which urban workers and intellectuals failed to create. Reality, however, is not so simple and *Dissent* has always recognized this tragic, complex fact.

But in a sense, the years between Korea and the escalation of the Vietnam war in the sixties had an ambiguous effect. On the one hand, they permitted radicals — and Negroes and eventually a majority of the society and its politicians — to rediscover and redefine domestic injustice and to begin to do a few things about it. Yet this same mood of détente which permitted a revival of social conscience and consciousness within the society (for such would never have happened under conditions of increasing Cold War) also made the enormous problems of the majority of the people of the world recede into the distance.

Here, I think, is one of the major goads to the democratic Left in the coming period. Inside of America the problem is no longer one of becoming aware of our injustices but rather of doing something about them other than making speeches, commissioning studies, writing books, and passing inadequate laws. But internationally, from 1914 to this very moment, the Left has essentially failed to develop a political program equal to its ideals and relevant to the world at the same time. Now that political independence has more or less been realized in the colonial revolution, and the infinitely more difficult issues of economic and social development are on the agenda, the challenge is even more acute. Here, I suspect, is *Dissent's* intellectual frontier for the second half of the sixties.

Then there is that summary problem which has tormented radicals so much in the recent past and which is dealt with in some of the essays in this book: What of socialism itself?

Here, the autobiographical fragments of this introduction come full circle. In 1954, when I wondered if the editors of *Dissent* were on the verge of betrayal, I "knew" precisely and exactly what socialism was: the democratization of the society through the nationalization of the commanding heights of the economy. And indeed, in the largest sense of the term, democratic socialization remains the essence of the socialist vision. But in the intervening years, the question of means has become much more crucial — and problematic. In the old days, reaction was decently straightforward. But now there are corporate Keynesians, anti-egalitarian planners, millionaire welfareists. And there have been nationalizations which have bailed out the most backward businessmen by socializing the losses of the most rundown industries. Under such circumstances, the socialist vocation becomes much more complex and nagging, with seemingly petty issues of social technique as the undramatic stuff of revolution.

Yet there remains a vision, and that is the distinctive thing about *Dissent*. For however much intellectual humility has been imposed upon socialists in the past decade, there are certain crucial convictions that remain unaltered, and neither *Dissent* nor this writer have changed their mind one whit since 1954. The democratization of concentrated economic, social, and political power is the only hope for the achievement of Western humanist ideals, and this holds true under both capitalism and Communism. Man is not necessarily condemned to inequality and subordination, either in the welfare state or under bureaucratic totalitarianism. And this liberating, democratic possibility of a new order of things in which the people actually decide their own destiny is what makes us rebels and critics.

# 1 ◄——

## *Reflections and persuasions*

# THE CHOICE OF COMRADES
## IGNAZIO SILONE

The last forty years have witnessed the collapse of most of the great politico-social myths bequeathed to us by the nineteenth century. As a result, certain kinds of people who had relied on these myths as a compass find themselves in a state of spiritual vagueness and ambiguity that is still far from being clarified. This situation is one aspect of the general crisis of capitalism and anti-capitalism. We are confronted with the need for reassessment, not only of the problems of human behavior but also of the greater question of the meaning of our existence. It is not a matter, be it said, even in its subsidiary aspects, of literary diversion. There will always be a number of perfectly respectable people who interpret in their own fashion, by their haircut or the way they knot their ties, the spirit of the age in which they live. For others less fortunate, however, times of crisis may bring graver consequences. My concern in these pages is with them.

Suicide among writers in various countries during the past thirty years has reached an unparalleled figure. It seems to me that however much they may differ outwardly, the majority of these episodes have a common source: what Nietzsche called the nihilism of modern times. The lives of writers are, I think, not less significant than the books they write. Whenever I happen to consider the sense of bewilderment, tedium, and disgust characteristic of outrage, my mind turns not to the books of Heidegger, Jaspers, and Sartre but to the suicides of Essenin, Mayakovsky, Ernst Toller, Kurt Tucholsky, Stefan Zweig, Klaus Mann, Drieu La Rochelle, F. O. Mathiessen, Cesare Pavese, and other lesser-known figures. What a flock of terrifying ghosts they seem, when one names them all together! Persecution, exile, isolation, poverty, illness, abnormality — one or the other of these external reasons has been suggested in each case to explain how a man of talent could have sought such a desperate end. But the last writings of these men before death, or their last confidences to their friends, are invariably a confession of anguish or despair at the effort and the futility of living.

These suicides are not to be easily explained away. To pin responsibility for them on any one political regime would clearly be a misrepresentation, since we know that they occurred under widely differing regimes, in Russia, America, and Western Europe. Still less can we blame the pernicious influence of some pessimistic doctrine; Mayakovsky was the poet of a victorious revolution, and the others, from Zweig to Pavese, were deeply rooted in the humanist or religious traditions of the society from which they came. (Indeed, one might well reverse the explanation and say it was precisely because they were not pessimistic enough, because they had banished *Angst* from their doctrine and their art, that some of them were to end by succumbing to it so miserably. Inhibition is more deadly than sincerity.)

The decadence of our age, however, had already begun prior to these tragic episodes. It has not merely engulfed a number of cultivated and hypersensitive individuals; it has invaded entire classes and institutions, not even sparing the people. Nietzsche was the first to define this decadence, calling it nihilism, as I said, and giving the word a new meaning that it has retained, a meaning different from that found in Turgenev's famous novel. Since then, wars and revolutions in constant succession have borne out Nietzsche's prophecy, making evident what in his day was still perhaps obscure.

Nihilism, as Nietzsche conceived it, is the identification of goodness, justice, and truth with self-interest. Nihilism is the conviction that beliefs and ideas are, ultimately, a mere facade with nothing real behind them, and that consequently only one thing really matters, really counts: success. It is nihilistic to sacrifice oneself for a cause in which one does not believe, while pretending to believe in it. It is nihilistic to exalt courage and heroism independently of the cause they serve, thus equating the martyr with the hired assassin. And so on.

:

How did we come to this pass? The First World War is generally blamed as the cause and origin of the disaster; but would that war ever have broken out in the first place had the civilized world not already been in a state of crisis? The war merely demonstrated how fragile were the myths of progress on which capitalist civilization was based. Even in the victorious countries, venerable institutions were subjected to such terrible ordeals that they began to totter like rotten scaffolding. And from them, skepticism and corruption spread and seeped downwards to the very foundation of society. Traditional moral and religious values, rashly invoked to prop up the vested interests which were being threatened, were thereby compromised.

The authoritarian restoration which followed the war — first in Italy and the Balkans, later in Germany and elsewhere — was a remedy worse than the disease. How could conservatives ever have deluded themselves into thinking that political tyranny of any kind would eliminate nihilism? On the contrary, fascism in all its forms meant that nihilism was installed in power. The dictatorships strengthened the old instruments of coercion and created new ones, but they did not create a new moral order; indeed, with their atmosphere of fear and servility, they aggravated and exacerbated the general decadence. With the collapse of these regimes, the basic nihilism remained, buried deep in peoples' consciences.

And so in many ways we are back where we were, except that we are once again free to discuss the moral situation of man without having to make concessions to a false optimism, dissimulation not being a civic virtue in a democracy.

Political regimes may come and go, bad habits remain. The big difficulty is this: nihilism is not an ideology, it cannot be legislated about, it is not a subject for school curricula; it is a disease of the spirit which can be diagnosed only by those who are immune from it or have been cured of it, but to which most people are quite oblivious, since they think it corresponds to a perfectly natural mode of being. "That's how it has always been; that's how it will always be."

We are familiar with the picture which post-Nietzschean and existentialist literature has drawn of the predicament of present-day man. It can be summarized as follows: all links between the existence and the being of man are broken; existence has no meaning beyond itself; what is human is reduced to mere vitality. Before commenting on what I consider the provisional and transient nature of this representation, I feel bound to state that in some respects I find it praiseworthy. I think sincerity is always to be admired, especially if it requires a certain amount of courage, for without sincerity neither morality nor art can exist. And moreover, at the stage to which things are now reduced, I as a writer see no other way, outside the freedom of art, of placing before the minds of men the problems which elude them, and of presenting them with a truer image of themselves than that which they see daily in the mirror. However, literature cannot take up a permanent abode in a nihilist situation, and the only way out for it, I think, is to explore courageously the entire surface of this situation. Anyone undertaking to do so with absolute intellectual honesty and an uncorrupted heart should sooner or later be able to reach its farthest limit. At that point, one of two things will happen to him: either he will find the abyss of suicide yawning at his feet, or else he will rediscover some valid meaning in human existence. This is no abstract hypothesis, but the plain truth of what has happened to quite a number of people.

The examples are far from insignificant. Here I shall mention only two: the literary path of Ernst Jünger and that of Albert Camus. The German writer reached the farthest limit of nihilism in his famous message *Der Arbeiter*. In this description of a new type of proletarian, depersonalized and standardized, without heart, soul, or brain — a living robot — he depicted the protagonist of the transformation which is taking place in modern society. The greatest freedom of this human robot would consist in being mechanically employed in the series of civil and imperialist wars on which we have already embarked and which will dominate the coming centuries. "To sacrifice oneself for a faith," wrote Ernst Jünger, "means to reach one's maximum, irrespective of whether that faith is true or false. The mere fact that men throw themselves into the fray, even though they are knotted up with a fear that no discipline and no love of country can dispel, makes them, like martyrs, bear witness to an ultra-human reality that is beyond and within them." The heroism of Jünger's proletarian robots would therefore be all the more sublime the remoter it was from the traditional human sphere and the more closely it resembled that of highly perfected machines. This was a final point beyond which it was impossible to advance. Ernst Jünger retreated from it in time, while Hitler was still in power. In his subsequent works, among which may be mentioned the pages on pain, the novel *Auf den Marmorklippen,* and the diary he kept during the invasion of France in the Second World War, his condemnation of nihilism is increasingly explicit and increasingly based on human motives.

The experience of Albert Camus is different but analogous. No reader of his books can fail to discern the sharp contrast dividing *Le Mythe de Sisyphe* and *L'Etranger* on the one hand, from *La Peste* and the book of essays entitled *L'Homme Révolté* on the other. Camus opens *Le Mythe de Sisyphe* with the concept of suicide, in order to distill from it an explanation of the meaning of life. He bluntly defines as absurd the reasons for living. "To die voluntarily," he writes, "implies that one has recognized, at least instinctively, the absurd nature of this habit, the absence of any serious reason for living, the senselessness of this daily agitation and the futility of suffering." To kill oneself means "simply to recognize that life is not worth the trouble." In compassion Camus finds the cure for this desolate sense of the absurd. "The world in which I live repels me," he wrote later, in *L'Homme Révolté,* "but I feel with its suffering inhabitants." In his novel *La Peste* the existence of the characters is presented, not as the impassive unfolding of arbitrary and meaningless facts, but as the compassionate encounter of human beings suffering and struggling against a common destiny.

At a certain point in *La Peste* one of the characters — Rieux, a doctor — meets a municipal clerk named Grand whose wife has just left him, with no ill will on either side. "From a distance he looked at Grand, who was standing almost glued to a shop window full of roughly carved wooden toys. Tears were streaming down the cheeks of the old clerk. And those tears shook Rieux, because he understood them and could feel them in the dryness of his own throat. He could even remember the day when the poor fellow had got engaged to be married; he had seen him standing in front of a shop decked out for Christmas, with Jeanne bending towards him, telling him she was happy. No doubt but that Jeanne's fresh voice was echoing now to Grand across the distant years. Rieux knew what the old, weeping man was thinking of at that moment, and he too thought that without love this world of ours is a dead world, and that there always comes a time when, weary of the prisons of work and courage, one wants the face of another human being and a heart filled with the wonder of tenderness. . . . He felt Grand's unhappiness as his own, and something gnawed at his heart at that moment — the fierce anger that comes over one at the suffering which human beings have to endure." Even the revolt born of pity alone can restore meaning to life.

André Malraux presents a more remarkable case because this French descendant of Nietzsche, through his progress from Communism back to nationalism, gives the impression of having remained a Nietzschean at heart all the time. The stormy curve of his life's journey does indeed seem the adventure of a "superman" seeking tests and opportunities for his own dreams of glorification. Nevertheless it would be unjust to consider it as a superficial movie-hero affair. Between *La Tentation de l'Occident* and *La Psychologie de l'Art* there is more than a change of scene. In 1926 Malraux was announcing the historical downfall of Europe, "this cemetery where only dead conquerors sleep." The Communist revolt of the colored peoples seemed to offer him hope; but how ambiguous was his adherence to it. The virile sense of a new brotherhood of man alternated, in the pages of *La Condition Humaine,* with the intoxication of action for its own sake. In *Le Temps du Mépris,* brotherhood was invoked more wholeheartedly as the last resort against nihilist desperation. It was an active sympathy, consecrated by the sacrifices which culminated in the act of an unknown comrade who saved Kassner, the Communist leader, from Nazi torture. But did this member act on his own initiative or by order of the party machine? And can brotherhood be founded on anything but freedom and personal responsibility? "Economic servitude is hard," old Alvear was to say in *L'Espoir,* "but if in order to destroy it we are obliged to strengthen political or military or religious or police servitude, then what does it matter to me in comparison?" Revolutions, like trees, are to be judged by their fruits, and not by the effort they cost.

I know that these are isolated examples, and that one or even two swallows do not make a summer. Still they do point to a path of salvation, a true way out of nihilism, which springs from a sure and indestructible element deep-rooted in man.

But to return to my point. The particular spiritual condition I wish to discuss has affinities with the instances I have just mentioned. However, it follows a different path and has a significance of its own. For example, it never starts from philosophical or scientific conviction, but almost always from simple instinctive revolt against family or social surroundings. One fine Sunday some of us stopped going to Mass, not because Catholic dogmas seemed to us, all of a sudden, false, but because the people who went began to bore us and we were drawn to the company of those who stayed away. A young man's revolt against tradition is a frequent occurrence in every age and every country, and his reasons are not always clear to the onlooker. According to circumstances, it can lead to the Foreign Legion, to common crime, to a film career, to a monastery, or to political extremism. What characterized our revolt was the choice of comrades. Outside our village church stood the landless peasants. It was not their psychology that we were drawn to: it was their plight. A choice once made, the rest, as experience shows, follows automatically. Without the slightest attempt at resistance, indeed with the well-known fervor of neophytes, one accepts the language, symbols, organization, discipline, tactics, program, and doctrine of the party to which one's new comrades belong. It is hardly surprising that rarely should anything learned in the catechism and schoolbooks hinder one's docile acceptance of the new orthodoxy. Indeed, one does not even feel the need of refuting them, because all of that has become part of the world one has left behind. They are neither true nor false: they are "bourgeois," dead leaves. The choice is emotional, beyond logic. And the claim of the new orthodoxy, which one has accepted so completely, to be scientific and objective — that is not the least of the inconsistencies which you will vainly seek to force on the attention of the convert.

This is the rule. I have read a certain number of biographies of anarchists, socialists, communists, and fascists, and I am more or less famil-

iar with the circumstances that led some of my acquaintances into political activity; so far I have found no exceptions to the pattern I have just
described, and if any do exist, I think they are rare. We proclaim ourselves revolutionaries or conservatives for motives, often ill-defined, that
are deep within us, and before choosing we are, unknown to ourselves,
chosen. As for the new ideology, we learn that, usually, at the schools of
the party to which we have already pledged allegiance by an act of faith.
Altogether similar — and just as it should be — is the opposite process
of abjurement. Ideology is now given the same rough treatment once
meted out to the catechism and to patriotic stories. To speak in old-
fashioned terms, the head, even in the process of relearning, is towed
along by the heart — or, according to the health of the person in question, by the stomach.

There is one duty, however, that we cannot evade: to be aware of what is
happening. What could the landless peasants of his Southern Italian village have meant to a young student, in the years immediately preceding
the First World War, that he should embrace their cause? He was certainly not thinking of politics as a career. Besides, he as yet knew nothing of the proud Marxist prophecy acclaiming the proletariat as the legitimate heir of modern philosophy. Neither did he know that, after the
Milanese revolution of 1848, Carlo Cattaneo had declared the cause of
the proletariat to be indissolubly linked thenceforth with that of freedom,
one destined to travel through the coming ages with the other, like horse-
man and rider. He had as yet heard nothing of Rosa Luxemburg's theory
of the natural impulse to revolution of the working class, or of Lenin's
theory of the forces which propel modern society on the path of progress.
Nor did he know of Sorel or other prophets of the new Messiah. But if
the new revolutionary theories of the historical mission of the proletariat
had not yet reached that remote district of Southern Italy, emigrants
returned from America were already prompting the landless peasants to
form their first resistance leagues. It is not to be wondered at that a
young man already secretly disgusted with his surroundings, witnessing
this unaccustomed ferment, should undergo a profound change of heart
and become convinced that in an old, tired, decrepit, blasé society such
as the one in which he lived, the poor represented the final refuge of
life — something real, to which it would be wholesome to attach oneself.
   Those were the declining years of an epoch in which a number of
events had seemed to prove the myth about the liberating mission of the
proletariat. The fascination of that myth spread far beyond the narrow
limits of party politics. It was the great popular alternative to the nihilist
decadence of Nietzsche's prophecy — the promise of a new earth
and a new heaven. Morals, art, philosophy were all directly influenced by
it. And events seemed to indicate that Rosa Luxemburg was right. In

those years one did not yet risk contradiction if one claimed that wherever a workers' organization was active, under whatever regime, in whatever climate or social conditions, despite its shortcomings it would move "naturally" towards freedom and renewal. Indeed, a certain episode occurred around 1905 in Moscow which has remained a classic in the history of the workers' movement and seemed to have been created for the express purpose of proving even to skeptics how well founded was the theory of Rosa Luxemburg about the liberating impulse of the working class. The Tsarist secret police, the Okhrana, decided to encourage the formation of a labor union in the hope of drawing underground agitators into it and arresting them. These, however, scented a trap and kept clear of it; but the labor union, despite its police origin, became of its own accord a revolutionary organization, so that the Okhrana was soon obliged to disband it.

Since then, as we all know, the myth of the liberating power of the proletariat has dissolved along with that other myth of the inevitability of progress. The recent examples of the Nazi labor unions, those of Salazar and Perón and, in a broader sense, all reformist and cooperative unions, have at last convinced of this even those who were reluctant to admit it on the sole grounds of the totalitarian degeneration of Communism. Now, however, the decline of that myth must be obvious to anyone who takes the trouble to inform himself of the conditions prevailing in the world beyond his own backyard. It is no longer merely a question of a few privileged workers (the so-called "proletarian aristocracy" of the imperialist countries, made possible by the exploitation of colonial peoples); nor of the inferior groups on the margin of the productive process (the so-called *Lumpenproletariat*); but of the normal working classes. Today an experiment such as the Okhrana made in 1905 would not necessarily be doomed to failure. For Marxists the moral to be drawn is clear: a similar way of living no longer determines an identical or analogous way of thinking. Class consciousness is no longer a natural product of class. Ever since this situation arose, ever since there ceased to exist a worldwide trend of the working classes towards freedom, human life has acquired a new aspect, spiritually as well as politically. The workers' world is spiritually broken up. It is multiform. The horse of Carlo Cattaneo has thrown its rider and gone wild again. The worker, as we have seen and as we continue to see, can work for the most conflicting causes; he can be Blackshirt or partisan, executioner or victim, or simply, in rich and peaceful countries, a lazy philistine with no ideals, insured against unemployment, old age, illness, and also against the risk that the insurance company might go bankrupt. But generally, in poor countries, because of his relative political simplicity, he can still be the prey of extremists. He can still be Christ, taking on himself the sins of others; and he can also be Barabbas,.

an ignoble totalitarian Barabbas, trampling on all that is most human in man. Either way, he is a protagonist on the world stage. He is the *deus ex machina* of modern politics. It is futile to think that this fact can be abolished, or that any democracy can maintain itself for very long, propped by police tribunals in the face of working-class opposition. The vital role of the workers in production, their numbers, their greater social compactness and homogeneity — the sum of these factors in every country gives them the decisive voice in politics. No other single element is so powerful. On it depends the freedom of mankind, and much else. But since it is no longer class that decides, but conscience, we are back where we started.

One need only look around one to see the state to which consciences have been reduced. Nihilism has spread from the upper classes over the entire surface of the social fabric: the epidemic has not spared the working-class districts. Today the nihilist cult of force and success is universal. And the widespread virtue that identifies History with the winning side, the ignoble cowardice that leads so many intellectuals to Communism or to McCarthy — that too is nihilism. Are the dead, are the weak always in the wrong? Was Mazzini wrong? Was Trotsky wrong only because he was defeated? Were Gobetti and Matteotti wrong? And did Gramsci begin to be right only after April, 1945? Will he cease to be right if the strength of his party declines? And is fear of the hydrogen bomb the fear of a stronger right, a right therefore more convincing than the others?

To the general feeling of personal insecurity which in our age has been engendered by the economic crisis and the intrusion of the state and politics into every field of human activity, there corresponds the anxious search by individuals for some kind of security and protection in one or other of the political mass parties. This by no means excludes, incidentally, a double game with the opposing party, which might be the winner tomorrow. If ideological criticisms and moral campaigns cannot shake the compactness of the mass parties, if they leave the majority of their members indifferent, it is precisely for the reason already mentioned: those joining the mass parties out of inner ideological conviction are very few. And to the opportunism of individuals obsessed with their own security and that of their families, there is added the usurping tendency of collective organizations. Frankly, I cannot think of a single collective organization today which could be said to be untainted by the leprosy of nihilism. Group living, it would almost seem, creates the most favorable temperature for the incubation of its germs. Human stupidity is so monotonous. The deathly mechanism is always the same: every group or institution arises in defense of an ideal, with which it rapidly comes to identify itself and for which it finally substitutes itself altogether, proclaiming its own interests as the supreme value. "Whoever injures the Party is against History." The members of the group in question are unruffled by this procedure; in fact, they find it serves their purposes. The advantages are by no means negligible, because they are completely absolved from all personal responsibility. In the deplorable event of someone having a scruple, all he need do is bring his problem to the propaganda office. If the matter is delicate, the answer will be delivered to him at home. Few people realize that the tyranny of means over ends is the death of even the noblest ends. And it is a mere mystification to claim that the reduction of human beings to the status of instruments and raw materials can ever ensure human happiness.

There is no more melancholy image than that of the persecuted who in their turn become persecutors. Here I should like to recall the terrible letter which Simone Weil wrote to Georges Bernanos in the spring of 1938 about the Spanish Civil War. The Catholic-royalist writer's vehement indictment of the excesses of the Franco repression in Majorca is countered by the anguished confession of the young revolutionary intellectual, then a volunteer on the Republican side. The letter has been published only recently. It expresses a sensitive woman's horror at the useless massacres which accompanied these events. But she had witnessed something else that had made an even more painful impression on her than brute violence. A purer-hearted witness or a more exemplary circumstance would be hard to find.

"I have never seen," she writes, "either among the Spaniards or among the French who have come here to fight or to amuse themselves (the latter often being gloomy, harmless intellectuals) anyone who expressed, even in private conversation, repugnance or disgust for, or even only disapproval of, unnecessary bloodshed. You talk of fear. Yes, fear has played a part in these killings; but where I was I did not find that it played as large a part as you ascribe to it. Men to all appearances courageous, when dining with friends, would relate with a warm, comradely smile how they had killed priests or 'fascists' — a word of elastic meaning. I felt that whenever a certain group of human beings is relegated, by some temporal or spiritual authority, beyond the pale of those whose life has a price, then one finds it perfectly natural to kill such people. When one knows one can kill without risk or punishment or blame, one kills; or at least one smiles encouragingly at those who kill. If at first one happens to feel some revulsion, one hides it, stifles it, fearing to seem lacking in virility. There seems to be in this some impulse or intoxication which it is impossible to resist without a strength of mind which I am obliged to consider exceptional, since I have not found it in anyone. On the contrary, I have seen sober Frenchmen whom I had not previously despised — men who of their own accord would never have thought of killing anyone — plunging with obvious relish into that blood-soaked atmosphere. The very aim of the struggle is blotted out by an atmosphere of this kind. Because the aim can be formulated only in terms of the public good, the good of human beings; and human beings have no value." And the letter ends: "One sets out as a volunteer, with ideas of sacrifice, only to find oneself in a war of mercenaries, with a great deal of unnecessary cruelty thrown in."

Of course there will be people foolish enough to dismiss Simone Weil's letter as defeatist; but the defeat had preceded it, as an illness precedes its diagnosis. In this worldwide moral shipwreck, what scrap of drift-wood can one clutch in order not to drown? Among the reflections of Simone Weil collected under the title *La Pesanteur et la Grâce,* we find this indirect answer, the validity of which goes far beyond politics: one must, she says, "always be ready to change sides with justice, that fugitive from the winning camp."

We have come a long way now from the very simple situation in which some of us revolted against our family surroundings and went over to the side of the proletariat. The proletariat of this world are no longer in agreement among themselves; they are no longer the incarnation of a myth, and if one were to follow them blindly and unconditionally one might find oneself where least one wants to be. The initial choice must now be followed by another. To judge men, it is no longer enough to see if they have calloused hands: one must look into their eyes. There is no mistaking the look of Cain. Do we side with the inmates of the slave-labor camps or with their jailers? This dilemma we can no longer evade, because the executioners themselves are forcing it on us. Threateningly they demand: "Are you with us or against us?" We must call a spade a spade. We are certainly not going to sacrifice the poor to the cause of freedom, nor freedom to the poor, or rather to the usurping bureaucrats who have climbed on the shoulders of the poor. It is a matter of personal honor to keep faith with those who are being persecuted for their love of freedom and justice. This keeping faith is a better rule than any abstract program or formula. In this age of ours, it is the real touchstone.

It should be apparent from the foregoing why humanism in general, literary or philosophical, means very little to us. Perhaps the time for it will come again, but at present we feel very remote from the serenity and harmony it represents. To us it seems that the self-complacency of man implicit in humanism has scant foundation nowadays. Mankind today is in poor shape. Any portrait of modern man, if at all faithful to the original, cannot but be deformed, split, fragmentary — in a word, tragic.

This confession of humility does not cost us an effort, since we have no answers to the supreme questions about man's origin and his destiny. Frankly, these traditional problems do not even trouble us. We have stopped pondering the riddle of egg-or-chicken priority, for what is perhaps a very banal reason: we are not responsible for it, and whichever way things may originally have happened, it was not our fault. That is not the sort of problem that can give us sleepless nights. The problems that beset us are those of our present existence, of our responsibility as men of today. Only within these limits can we reach a true definition of ourselves.

This amounts to saying that we are not believers, we are not atheists, and still less are we skeptics. These labels, with their conventional implications, do not concern us. Anyone who tries to attach them to us will merely increase terminological confusion. A distaste for verbalism and facile consolations holds us back from more general statements. A proper awe of the transcendental prevents us from taking its name in vain and using it as a narcotic. And if we are not too proud to confess that there have been moments of anguish and solitude when our thoughts returned with piercing nostalgia to the tradition-bound order, the peace and security, of the home we knew in childhood, we are nevertheless obliged to add that love of truth has always ended by prevailing over considerations of personal convenience.

In a situation where the premises of metaphysics and even of history are uncertain and open to question, the moral sense is forced to extend its scope, taking on the additional function of guide to knowledge. The pitfall of abstract and superficial moralism can be a real one, but only if the moral sense is operating on a *tabula rasa*. In reality, even beyond one's frontiers of awareness, one remains a creature of flesh and blood, a man of a certain region, a certain class, and a certain time. For our part, the vital resource which saves us from the extremist situation of nihilism can be easily identified: the same emotional charge which impelled us to our initial choice has not been exhausted by disillusionment. This is not an individual case. I am not using the pronoun "we" as a puffed-up form of the first person singular. Our number is an ever-swelling legion: the legion of refugees from the International. There are really a great many, belonging to no church or political party, who now bear in secret these same burning stigmata.

Does anything at all remain to us? Yes, there are some unshakable certainties. To my way of feeling, they are Christian certainties. They appear to me so deeply immured in human existence as to be identified with it. Man disintegrates when they are denied.

This is too little to constitute a profession of faith, but it is enough for a declaration of trust. The trust is founded on something more stable and more universal than the mere compassion of Albert Camus. It is founded, in the last analysis, on the certainty that we human beings are free and responsible; that we feel the need of reaching out to touch the inmost reality of our fellowmen; and that spiritual communion is possible. The fact that spiritual communion is possible — surely this is the irrefutable proof of human brotherhood? Furthermore, it contains a rule of life. Love of the oppressed is born from it as a corollary that the disillusionments of history — the love being of a disinterested nature — can never place in doubt. To be valid, it does not need success. With these certainties as a basis for existence, how can we resign ourselves to seeing man's noblest faculties stifled in so many human creatures born to poverty and wretchedness? How can we conceive of a moral life from which this fundamental concern is absent?

Need I add that this is not to be interpreted in political terms of power or tyranny? To use the oppressed as a stepping-stone to power and then betray them is undoubtedly the most wicked of all sacrileges, because of all human beings they are the most defenseless. Frankly we must confess that we have no panacea. There is no panacea for social evils. All we have — and it is a great deal — is this trust that makes it possible for us to go on living. We are forced to pick our steps beneath a sky that is, ideologically speaking, dark. The clear, ancient Mediterranean sky, once filled with shining constellations, is overcast; but this small circle of light that remains to us enables us at least to see where to place our feet for the next step.

This amounts to saying that the spiritual situation I have just described admits neither of defense nor of arrogance. Frankly, it is merely an expedient. It resembles a refugee encampment in no-man's-land, an exposed makeshift encampment. What do you think refugees do from morning to night? They spend most of their time telling one another the story of their lives. The stories are anything but amusing, but they tell them to one another, really, in an effort to make themselves understood.

As long as there remains a determination to understand and to share one's understanding with others, perhaps we need not altogether despair.

1955
*Translated from the Italian by* DARINA SILONE

# IN DEFENSE OF RADICALISM
## STUART HAMPSHIRE

One reads these days many cries of despair, rumblings of gloom, dark hints of the inadequacy of Reason (and reasoners), of the hopelessness of progress. At the best, one expects invocations of Orwell and Tocqueville, at the worst, of Burke and Kierkegaard, and certainly not an unashamed platitude about the possibilities of progress or the needs of enlightenment. I wonder why this has happened. There seems no good ground for despair or gloom, if we are really concerned with freedom in the world in general, and not only with a few particular liberties long familiar in Europe. There are more destructive bombs in the world, but there is not less freedom; it has only become more dangerous and disagreeable to defend it.

Throughout history, very few privileged societies have enjoyed that degree of personal freedom which is today enjoyed by large sections of the population of America, of most of Western Europe outside Spain, of many parts of the English-speaking Commonwealth, and of some other countries comparably prosperous and democratic. And in many parts of the East, and of Africa, there are growing demands for greater freedom of the individual, and the means of obtaining it are coming nearer. There must always be a running change in the distribution of power within States and between States; some classes of persons lose some of their liberties, others, formerly oppressed and almost left off the pages of history, gain a freedom of choice that they never had before. Those who believe in freedom must wish to see it indefinitely extended and, as far as possible, equally distributed. They will support any movement of liberation among a suppressed section of humanity, provided that it does not bring with it some greater enslavement of others. These may be called the principles of 1789; I see no reason to repudiate them. They are now often derided as illusions; but perhaps this is because of the discomfort which their application is beginning to cause, particularly to those who in Western Europe have hitherto enjoyed liberties not widely shared elsewhere. I still believe in the "illusions" of the eighteenth century — Reason, Science, Freedom — so far as one can believe in abstract slogans at all. I do not see where they have failed; I only see the difficulty of calculating at any particular time where the greatest threat to freedom is and how it ought to be resisted.

But what is freedom? And why is it always right to defend and extend it, in preference to anything else?

A man is free and feels free: (1) If he is not liable to be killed, imprisoned, or otherwise maltreated without redress under an equal and impartial law. This is a necessary qualifying condition without which there can be no freedom at all. (2) If his manner of life, his activities, and enjoyments have been chosen by himself from a wide variety of alternatives open to him. (3) If none of these many alternatives open to him was made ineligible by human threats and sanctions. An alternative manner of life may be said to have been "open" to him if he would not, in fact, have been prevented from living in that way, had he so chosen, by anything other than his own abilities. Clearly freedom, in this sense, admits of degrees correlated with the number of alternative modes of life open. (4) If those who have executive power in the society can be influenced by his preference through some regular voting procedure. No man feels free unless he can to some extent participate in forming the prohibitions to which he submits.

There are good grounds for taking the attainment of human freedom, in this sense, as the end of political action. Whatever else men may seriously desire, need, or attach value to, they will tend to agree, in spite of other differences, in wanting and needing freedom to pursue their own ends, whatever these other ends may be. There is no other equally wide basis of agreement on which mutual respect and consent could be founded. We have no reason to believe that any statements of the form "All men desire so-and-so," or "All men attach value to so-and-so," or "All men believe so-and-so," are true, where some positive end is stated; and we have every reason to believe that almost all statements of this form are either false, or too vague to be used, or too rudimentary. Therefore, either we think it is unnecessary to find an agreed basis for mutual respect in politics, or we will judge the rightness or wrongness of any political action by reference to some principle of freedom. If anyone thinks it unnecessary to find some basis of mutual respect, it may be because he repudiates the application of moral notions to politics altogether; in which case he ought in consistency to repudiate the distinction between right and wrong entirely. He could not maintain that actions are to be divided into political actions and nonpolitical actions; this would be the fallacy of confusing domains of inquiry with divisions in reality. A man must acknowledge responsibility for all his actions, if he acknowledges responsibility for any of them. Alternatively, he may deny the need of a basis of consent on the ground that a policy is right only if it promotes an end known to be good in itself, irrespective of whether this end is agreed to be good by all or most of the persons involved; freedom of choice must be disregarded in the making of policies, if the manner of life likely to be chosen is not that manner of life which is known to be best.

I do not wish to argue against this position simply on the ground that it increases the opportunities for conflict. If I did so argue, I would be implying that, like Hobbes, I take avoidance of conflict to be the end. In fact, I believe that the extension and safeguarding of every individual's equal freedom to choose his own manner of life for himself is the end of political action. Consequently I think that anyone who uses political powers in order to promote some positive end, which he believes to be the best of all ends, acts wrongly, if he at the same time restricts the freedom of choice of the adult persons affected. He is the enemy, however worthy the positive end which he pursues. Any moral standpoint whatever must involve having enemies, unless, following Hobbes, not having enemies is itself made the end of action and the basis of morality. Most of the political thinkers of the past, beginning conspicuously with Plato, were in fact enemies of freedom. One is unlikely to find many unconditional advocates of freedom between fifth- and fourth-century B.C. Athens and eighteenth-century France: at the best, only benevolent neutrals, like Machiavelli.

Moral standpoints cannot be demonstrated; they can only be explained and expanded by showing the philosophical reasoning associated with them. If a man thinks that he knows what is good for men, and knows beyond the possibility of error, he may naturally consider himself justified in overriding the freedom of choice of others. If he thinks that he can only learn by accumulated experience what is good and worth pursuing, he will claim no final certainty for himself, and therefore will at least hesitate before overruling the different decisions of others. If he thinks that nothing can be shown to be either good or bad except in its relation to the will and feeling of some individual, he will unhesitatingly admit that he has no right to override the free choices of others in pursuit of any end of his own choosing.

The first of these three philosophies seems to me definitely mistaken, in the sense that it involves logical confusions about the nature of moral judgments. But I could not *prove* that any such claim to knowledge of positive ends must involve logical confusion; it is a matter of philosophical opinion, and no such opinion could be justified except by a prolonged argument going through most of the traditional problems of philosophy. The Roman Catholic Church, many of the Protestant churches, the Communist Party, and many puritan and secular moralists would certainly claim to know what is positively good for men, beyond the possibility of error, in at least some domains of human conduct; and they are in consequence ready to disregard the freedom of choice of individuals within these domains. Relying upon revealed truth or some supernatural authority, or upon alleged demonstrations and intuitions, they will hold themselves justified in restricting someone's freedom of choice for a purpose other than the protection of someone else's freedom of choice.

The second philosophy is the tempered liberalism of J. S. Mill; freedom of choice is not in itself the end of political action, but it is indispensable to human welfare and progress, which is the ultimate end. But if the freedom of choice of some men, or of some group, was to be sacrificed in the interests of human welfare generally, could human welfare be the sole criterion by which the sacrifice was to be justified? It seems to me that it could not; but this is a moral opinion, which again I could support by arguments but could not prove.

The third philosophy is unrestricted liberalism. I shall call anyone who accepts it a radical. For a radical the right of each man to choose for himself his own manner of life, as long as he does not disregard the equal right of others to do the same, is the sole criterion in political decision. The fabric of political arrangements and institutions ought to be continuously adjusted with a view to securing the greatest possible freedom of choice to each individual equally and under an equal law. Any prohibition and assertion of power has to be justified, in the last analysis, as the extension of the area of choice open to some men so far too narrowly confined. There has always been in every society some group or class of persons who had a conspicuously narrow range of choice of different ways of life open to them. They are said to be not free, to some degree slaves, in so far as they are not in a position to choose for themselves among alternative ways of life, and in so far as this inability could be remedied by human action without any equally large loss of liberty by others. There are always ruling or privileged groups who have the power to make a wider range of choices open to the suppressed, but usually they will not yield unless they are threatened or forced. The class or group whose freedom of choice is in this way confined will, sooner or later, prepare to assert its rights, if it is sufficiently numerous and if it is not completely enslaved and ignorant. At any time in any society there will always be a more or less complicated set of tensions of this kind which will enter into the temporary politics of that society. Anyone who takes the freedom of the individual as his criterion of political decision must support the relatively suppressed groups which are claiming greater liberty for themselves at the expense of those who now have the greater power, as long as the suppressed groups are not aiming at an even greater suppression of the liberty of others. As a matter of principle, he will support any effective resistance to the predominating power of a small group in society, provided that this resistance does not itself take totalitarian forms and override the first and last conditions of freedom given above. At any time he will align himself with that group of interests which can most effectively resist the concentration of power most likely to obstruct or prevent the extending of equal liberty within the society. His enemy will always be changing, as one preponderating group succeeds another; and it is always easy for him to miscalculate the direction from which the greatest threat to the most essential liberties comes. His conception of freedom, the positive content he gives to this informal word in any actual situation, may become out of date as the pattern of society changes and new groups call for new freedoms; while still using the same good words, he may find himself, to his surprise, on the reactionary side in the dialectical process, a process which is, as far as we know, endless and irregular, freedom sometimes retreating, sometimes advancing, and always by the opportunist action of individuals.

A radical will tend always to distrust those who speak of safeguarding our liberties. He will see in this phrase the conservative assumption that the degree and distribution of liberty already existing in a society is to be taken as the permanent standard. This assumption seems to lie behind M. Raymond Aron's recent article in *Encounter,* which analyzes English politics with scarcely a reference to what has become the most serious issue of government — policy in Africa and colonial policy generally. Because the old tensions, within England, have largely disappeared or changed their form, there is the illusion of stability, and the new tensions may pass unrecognized. Any equilibrium in a society is only a temporary adjustment of groups competing for greater power and freedom; and freedom can only be served by siding with those who have so far been excluded from the full enjoyment of the liberty which the more powerful groups possess. And yet it is natural that those who at any time talk most insistently of the defense of freedom should be those who have the most freedom to lose. This is the very simple reason why radicals are apt to distrust any congresses, or other organizations, for the defense of freedom; for freedom is not something which has to be safeguarded, but rather something which has to be extended. If one tries to stand still, only defending the freedoms already established, one unavoidably finds oneself slipping backwards into repression. An attack on established freedom has to be met, not by digging in for defense, but by going forward to offer new freedom to those who now have little freedom to lose.

This was the significance of the mild and limited social revolution which resistance to the Nazis entailed in England. In the last few years radicalism has lost impetus in England, and in America and in Western Europe generally; governments have wished to stand still, digging in to defend established freedom against Communism, and consequently have fallen into mild repression. The greatest repression for which Englishmen, and other Western Europeans, are now responsible happens at a convenient distance and is not very fully reported: it happens in colonial territories. Any political and social system which can only be maintained by mass arrests without trial, withholding of the right to vote, concentration camps and movements of people away from their homes, is evil for the same reasons that Communism is evil. The bitterness and brutality of the opposition is not an excuse, but rather a condemnation of the social system which brought this bitterness into existence. Throughout Africa the advance of Africans towards greater freedom is generally obstructed; and the government of South Africa does not even pretend to believe in extending the freedom of Africans.

To notice these facts is the most obvious requirement of sincerity, if we are to talk of freedom at all. But there are others, equally well worn, which must surely be mentioned again. The Catholic Church is everywhere opposed, in principle and in practice, to the extension of each man's freedom to choose his own way of life for himself, at least in some essential domains. In the countries where the power of the Church is greatest, and conspicuously in Spain, there is always some degree of repression, not only in the legislation affecting heretics and freethinkers, but in less crude ways in policies of censorship, in university appointments and teaching, in schools, in the enforcement of a particular sexual morality, and in the suppression of dangerous knowledge. If Catholic repression is most evident and unconcealed in Spain, it also exists in less crude forms in other Catholic countries. It is impossible to pretend that the Catholic Church, taken as a whole, wishes to defend cultural freedom; it is a temporary ally against Communism, which is certainly a much greater threat to freedom than is the Catholic Church. But it is quite pointless, on such an occasion as this, to disguise an alliance of expediency as an agreement of principle. It is better to leave alliances of expediency to the moments when, as politicians, we are required to make the material calculations responsibly. We are surely required to mark

clearly the issues of principle, the lines of division, in fundamental opinions.

Lastly, there is a certain degree of poverty, a drabness and despair in the
conditions of life which still makes the poorer parts of some cities in
Europe, and also the poorer villages in the country, seem like prisons in
which all ambitions are hopeless. It seems that it would be impossible to
break out and to start again; opportunity seems dead unless there is some
sign of revolt. There are places where almost everybody does only what
he must do in order to live, and where there is no alternative, no moment
of free choice. Where such conditions exist, it seems to me that any
effective protest or movement of revolt, even including voting for allies
of the Communist Party, may be a defense of cultural freedom. The
enemies of freedom who, having the power to alter them, allow such
conditions of life to exist, are immovable unless they feel themselves
threatened by a force that is really formidable; and sometimes and in
some places it may be true that only the Communist Party is in fact
sufficiently formidable and only temporary support of the Communists
will count as an effective protest. And in some countries outside Europe,
where the great majority of people have lived at the subsistence level for
many generations, one may see two kinds of men, the two kinds seeming
almost two species: those who, having wealth, may choose their own
form of life and work, who may think for themselves and move to other
places and follow their own ambitions and curiosities, and those who are
never in a position to refuse the kind of life which circumstances impose
upon them and who cannot even reflect upon alternatives. Every serious
attempt to break out from this condition seems to me to be right, provided that it is restrained by some respect for the elementary natural
rights of those who still stand in the way, and for democratic procedures,
where these already exist.

Any revolutionary assertion of the individual's right to some share of
the means to think and choose for himself deserves sympathy and support for the same reasons that would make us sympathize with an effective revolt of scientists, peasants, or other groups in the Soviet Union.
The Communist Party will certainly crush even the most elementary liberties of its own followers whenever it achieves real power; but those who
have no freedom to lose immediately may hope to use this lever of
power, the only one they have, and then throw it away later. They may
miscalculate, and their last state of frustration may be as bad, or worse,
than their present one. But what other calculation can they make if there
exists no other power which seriously threatens those who bar the way to
improvement? They do less for freedom if they remain crushed and inert.
And so do we, if we take sides against them, from fear of Communism,
without trying to provide some alternative means of breaking out.

Freedom is only safeguarded by supporting every movement which aims at providing some greater diversity of choice for the mass of the people in any country anywhere, and which at the same time respects the right of minorities to vote, and equality before the law. Freedom of choice generally shows itself, whenever it is felt to be growing in any section of society, in public arguments, in new forms of pleasure, in travel and in movement, in experiments in building, in pride in cities, in changes of custom and morality and in the complaints of those who are dispossessed, in the new *emigré* nostalgia. These signs, still evident in America, seem to me to be becoming fewer in Western Europe as we lapse into a Restoration mood, soon to find Bonalds and de Maistres all around us and little Chateaubriands.

Most of the freedoms which we have wished to safeguard in Europe were won by rebels and radicals. Similar freedoms will be, and are being, won by rebels and radicals in Asia and Africa, largely at the expense of Europeans. If we meet to agree that the old radical ideas of enlightenment are naïve, out of date and too simple, and that some new appeal to Burke and the sanctity of tradition is needed, I think that we will have met too late, in time only to show fear. But these are questions of opinion, of moral decision supported by argument. There can be few certainties, either in judgments of practical possibility or in judgments of right and wrong. There is only the necessity of argument and of sympathy.

1956

# ON SOCIALIST REALISM

## ABRAM TERTZ

**I**

What is socialist realism? What is the meaning of this strange and jarring phrase? Can there be a socialist, capitalist, Christian or Mohammedan realism? Does this irrational concept have a natural existence? Perhaps it does not exist at all, perhaps it is only the nightmare of a terrified intellectual during the dark and magical night of Stalin's dictatorship? Perhaps a crude propaganda trick of Zhdanov or a senile fancy of Gorki? Is it fiction, myth, or propaganda?

Such questions, we are told, are often asked in the West. They are hotly debated in Poland. They are also current among us, where they arouse eager minds, tempting them into the heresies of doubt and criticism.

Meanwhile, the productions of socialist realism are measured in billions of printed sheets, kilometers of canvas and film, centuries of hours. A thousand critics, theoreticians, art experts, pedagogues, are beating their heads and straining their voices to justify, explain, and interpret its material existence and dialectical character. The head of the State him-self, the First Secretary of the CP, tears himself away from pressing economic tasks to pronounce some weighty words on the country's esthetic problems.*

The most exact definition of socialist realism is given in a statute of the Association of Soviet Writers: "Socialist realism is the basic method of Soviet literature and literary criticism. It demands from the artist a truthful and historically concrete representation of reality in its revolutionary development. Moreover, the truthfulness and historical concreteness of the artistic representation of reality must be linked with the task of ideological transformation and education of workers in the spirit of socialism." †

This innocent formula is the foundation on which the entire edifice of socialist realism was erected. It includes the link between socialist realism and the realism of the past, as well as its new and distinguishing quality. The link lies in the *truthfulness* of the representation; the difference, in the ability to seize the *revolutionary development* and to educate readers in accordance with that development, *in the spirit of socialism.* The old realists, or, as they are sometimes called, critical realists (because they criticized bourgeois society), men like Balzac, Tolstoy, and Chekhov, truthfully represented life as it is. But not having been instructed in the genius and teachings of Marx, they could not foresee the future victories of socialism, and they certainly did not know the real and concrete roads to these victories.

The socialist realist, armed with the doctrine of Marx and enriched by the experience of struggles and victories, is inspired by the vigilant attention of his friend and teacher, the Communist Party. While representing the present, he listens to the march of history and looks toward the future. He sees the "visible traits of Communism," invisible to the ordinary eye. His creative work is a step forward from the art of the past, the highest peak of the artistic development of mankind and the most realistic of realisms.

Such, in a few words, is the general scheme of our art. It is amazingly simple, yet sufficiently elastic to comprehend Gorki, Mayakovski, Fadeev, Aragon, Ehrenburg, and hundreds of others. But we cannot understand this concept at all as long as we skim the surface of the dry formula and do not penetrate into its deep and hidden meaning.

The gist of this formula — "the truthful, historically concrete representation of reality in its revolutionary development" — is founded on the concept of Purpose with a capital P. The Purpose is an all-embracing ideal, towards which truthfully represented reality ascends in an undevi-

---

* This refers to Khrushchev's speeches to Soviet intellectuals, collected and published in 1957 under the title, *For a Close Link Between Literature and Art and the Life of the People.*
† First All-Union Congress of Soviet Writers, 1934, p. 716.

ating revolutionary movement. To direct this movement towards its end and to help the reader approach it more closely by transforming his consciousness — this is the Purpose of socialist realism, the most purposeful art of our time. . . .

Our art, like our culture and our society, is teleological through and through. It is subject to a higher destiny, from which it gains its title of nobility. In the final reckoning we live only to speed the coming of Communism.

A tendency towards purpose is part of human nature. I extend my hand to receive the coins. I go to a movie to spend some time with a pretty girl. I write a novel to earn glory and the gratitude of posterity. Each of my conscious moves is purposeful.

Animals do not have such long-range intentions. They are moved by instincts. They bite to bite, and not for the purpose of biting. They don't think about tomorrow, wealth, God. They live without facing any complex problems. But man invariably wants what he has not got. This quality of our nature finds its outlet in a feverish activity. We transform nature into our own image and turn nature into an object. Aimless rivers become arteries of communication. Aimless trees become paper filled with destiny.

Our abstract thought is no less teleological. Man explores the world by attributing to it his own purposefulness. He asks: "What is the use of the sun?" and answers: "To give light and heat." The animism of primitive peoples is the first attempt to conquer senseless chaos by endowing it with many aims, and to animate the indifferent universe with a life useful to man.

Science has not freed us from the childish questions of "Why?" Behind the causal relations that it establishes we find the hidden and distorted purposefulness of natural phenomena. Science says: "Man descends from the monkey" instead of saying: "The destiny of the monkey is to become man."

However man may have originated, his appearance and purpose are inseparable from God — that is, from the highest idea of purpose which is accessible to us, if not through our understanding, then through our wish that there should be such a purpose. This is the final purpose of all that is and of all that isn't, and is the infinite — and probably purposeless — Purpose in itself. For how could Purpose have purposes?

There are periods of history when the presence of Purpose is evident, when minor passions are absorbed in the striving for God and He openly calls mankind to Himself. Thus arose the culture of Christianity which seized the Purpose in what is, perhaps, its most inaccessible meaning. Then came the era of individualism which proclaimed the freedom of the individual as the Purpose and set about worshiping this purpose with the aid of the Renaissance, humanism, superman, democracy, Robespierre, banquets, and other forms of prayer. And now we have entered the era of a new worldwide system — that of socialist purposefulness.

A blinding light pours from this summit of thought. "A world that we can imagine, more material and better suited to human needs than Christian paradise" — thus was Communism defined by the Soviet writer Leonid Leonov.

Words fail us when we try to talk about it. We choke with enthusiasm and we use mostly negative comparisons to describe the splendor that is waiting for us. Then, under Communism, there will be no rich and no poor, no money, wars, jails, frontiers, diseases — and maybe no death. Everybody will eat and work as much as he likes, and labor will bring joy instead of sorrow. As Lenin promised, we will make toilets of pure gold. . . . But what am I talking about?

> *What words and what colors are needed*
> *To describe these grandiose heights*
> *Where whores are as modest as virgins*
> *And hangmen as tender as mothers?*

The modern mind cannot imagine anything more beautiful and splendid than the Communist ideal. The best that it can do is to restore to circulation old ideals of Christian love and the liberty of the individual. But it has been unable so far to set up a new Purpose.

Where socialism is concerned, the Western liberal individualist or Russian skeptical intellectual is about in the same position as the cultured and intelligent Roman with regard to victorious Christianity. He called the new faith of the crucified God barbarous and naïve, laughed over the lunatics that worshiped the cross — that Roman guillotine — and believed that the doctrines of the Trinity, the Immaculate Conception, Resurrection, etc., made no sense whatsoever. But it was quite above his powers to advance any serious arguments against the *ideal* of Christ as such. True, he could say that the best parts of the moral code of Christianity were borrowed from Plato, just as contemporary Christians assert here and there that Communism took its noble aims from the Gospel. But could he say that God conceived as Love or Goodness was evil or monstrous? And can we say that the universal happiness, promised for the Communist future, is evil?

> *For don't I know that blindfold thrusts*
> *Will not make darkness yield to light?*
> *Am I a monster? Is not the happiness of millions*
> *Closer to me than empty luck for a few?*
>
> PASTERNAK

We are helpless before the enchanting beauty of Communism. We have not lived long enough to invent a new Purpose and to go beyond ourselves — into the distance that is beyond Communism.

It was the genius of Marx that he proved the earthly paradise, of which others had dreamed before him, was actually the Purpose which Fate destined for man. With the aid of Marx, Communism passed from moral efforts of isolated individuals — "Oh, where are you, golden age?" — into the sphere of universal history, which became purposeful as never before and turned into mankind's march toward Communism.

At once, everything fell into place. An iron necessity and a strict hierarchical order harnessed the flow of centuries. The ape stood up on its hind legs and began its triumphant procession towards Communism. The system of primitive Communism arose because it was fated to grow into slavery; slavery, to give birth to feudalism; feudalism, towards capitalism; and finally capitalism, so that it could give way to Communism. That is all! The magnificent aim is achieved, the pyramid is crowned, history at an end.

A truly religious person relates all the splendid variety of life to his divinity. He cannot understand another faith. He believes in the Purpose so that he can despise other purposes. He shows the same fanaticism — or if you prefer, *printsipialnost'* — with regard to history.* A consistent Christian views the entire history previous to the birth of Christ as the prehistory of Christ. From the point of view of the monotheist, the pagans existed only to call upon themselves the will of the only God and, after a suitable preparation, to become monotheists.

It can therefore hardly surprise us that, in another religious system, ancient Rome has become an indispensable stage on the road to Communism. Or that the Crusades are not explained by their internal dynamics, by the ardent efforts of Christians, but by the action of the omnipresent forces of production that are now ensuring the collapse of capitalism and the triumph of socialism. True faith is incompatible with toleration. Neither is it compatible with historicism, i.e. with toleration applied to the past. And though the Marxists call themselves historical materialists, their historicism is actually reduced to a desire to regard life as a march towards Communism. Other movements are of little interest to them. Whether they are right or wrong is a matter of dispute. What is beyond dispute is that they are consistent.

If we ask a Westerner why the French Revolution was necessary, we will receive a great many different answers. One will reply that it happened to save France; another, that it took place to lead the nation into an abyss of moral experiments; a third, that it came to give to the world

* *Printsipialnost'* is a Russian word with no English equivalent. It describes the mental habit of referring every matter, however small, concrete, or trivial, to lofty and abstract principles.

the great principles of Liberty, Equality, and Fraternity; a fourth, that the French Revolution was not necessary at all. But if you ask any Soviet schoolboy — to say nothing of the beneficiaries of our higher education — you will invariably receive the correct and exhaustive reply: the French Revolution was needed to clear the way to Communism.

The man who received a Marxist education knows the meaning of both past and future. He knows why this or that idea, event, emperor, or military leader was needed. It is a long time since men had such an exact knowledge of the meaning of the world's destiny — not since the Middle Ages, most likely. It is our great privilege to possess this knowledge once more.

The teleological nature of Marxism is most obvious in the works of its latest theorists. They brought to Marxism the clarity, strength, and rigor of military orders and economic decrees. A good example is Stalin's judgment on the role of ideas, taken from the fourth chapter of the *Short Course of History of the Communist Party of the Soviet Union:*

"There exist different ideas and theories. There are old ideas and theories which have outlived their time and serve the interests of outdated forces of society. Their significance lies in their hampering the growth of the society and its forward march. There are also new, advanced ideas and theories which serve the interests of the advanced forces of society. Their significance lies in facilitating the growth of the society and its forward march."

As long as its famous author lived, the *Short Course* was the bedside book of every Soviet citizen. The entire literate population was constantly urged to study it and in particular its fourth chapter, containing the quintessence of the Marxist creed and written by Stalin himself. A quotation from V. Il'enkov's novel *The Great Highway* illustrates the universal validity that was attached to the *Short Course:*

"Father Degtyarev brought in a small volume and said: 'Everything is said here, in the fourth chapter.' Vinkentii Ivanovich took the book and thought: 'There is no book on this earth that contains everything that a man needs. . . .' But Vinkentii Ivanovich [a typical skeptical intellectual] soon realized that he was wrong and accepted Degtyarev's view, which was that of all advanced people: This book 'contains everything that a man needs.' "

Every word of this quotation is pervaded by the spirit of purposefulness. Even the ideas that do not favor the movement towards the Purpose have their destiny: to hamper the movement towards the Purpose (once, no doubt, the destiny of Satan). "Idea," "superstructure," "base," "law of nature," "economics," "forces of production" — all these abstract and impersonal concepts suddenly come to life, are covered with flesh and blood and become like gods and heroes, angels and devils. They create purposes and suddenly, from the pages of philosophical treatises and scientific investigations, there resounds the voice of the great religious Mystery: "The base produces the superstructure so that it can serve the base." *

This is not the only happy turn of phrase by Stalin which the author of the Bible might envy. The specific teleology of Marxist thought consists in leading *all* concepts and objects to the Purpose, referring them all to the Purpose, and defining them all through the Purpose. The history of all epochs and nations is but the history of humanity's march towards Communism, and the history of the world's thought happened, so to say, in order to bring forth "scientific materialism," i.e. Marxism, i.e. the philosophy of Communism. The history of philosophy, proclaimed Zhdanov, "is the history of the birth, rise, and development of the scientific world view and its laws. As materialism grew and developed in the struggle against idealism, so the history of philosophy is the history of the struggle between materialism and idealism." † These proud words seem like the voice of God Himself exclaiming: "The whole history is My history, and since I assert myself in the struggle with Satan, world history is also the history of My struggle with Satan."

And so it rises before us, the sole Purpose of all Creation, as splendid as eternal life and as compulsory as death. And we fling ourselves towards it, breaking all barriers and rejecting anything that might hamper our frantic course. We free ourselves without regret from belief in an afterlife. From love of our neighbor, from freedom of the individual and other prejudices, by now rather shopworn and looking all the sorrier by comparison with the great Ideal before us. Thousands of martyrs of the revolution gave up their lives for the new religion and surpassed the first Christians by their sufferings, their steadfastness, and their holiness:

> *Polish commanders*
> *Branded our backs with*
> *Five-pointed stars.*
> *Mamontov's bands*
> *Buried us alive*
> *Up to our necks.*
> *The Japanese*
> *Burned us in fireplaces*
> *Or railroad engines*
> *And poured lead and tin*
> *Into our mouths.*
> *They all roared:*
> *"Abjure!"*

* J. Stalin, *Marxism and Linguistic Questions.*
† A. A. Zhdanov, "Contribution to the Discussion of G. F. Aleksandrov's *History of Western European Philosophy,*" June 24, 1947.

> *But from our burning throats*
> *Only three words came:*
> *"Long*
> *Live*
> *Communism!"*
>
> MAYAKOVSKI

To our new God we sacrificed not only our lives, our blood, and our bodies. We also sacrificed our snow-white soul, after staining it with all the filth of the world.

It is fine to be gentle, to drink tea with preserves, to plant flowers and cultivate love, nonresistance to evil, and other philanthropies. But whom did they save and what did they change in this world, these ancient virgins of both sexes, these egoists of humanism who bought themselves an easy conscience penny by penny and rented themselves a cozy corner in the heavenly almshouses?

We did not want salvation for ourselves but for all of humanity. Instead of sentimental sighs, individual perfection, and amateur dramatics for the benefit of the hungry, we set about to correct the universe according to the best of models, the shining model of the Purpose which we approached ever more closely.

So that prisons should vanish forever, we built new prisons. So that all frontiers should fall, we surrounded ourselves with a Chinese wall. So that work should become a rest and a pleasure, we introduced forced labor. So that not one drop of blood be shed anymore, we killed and killed and killed.

In the name of the Purpose we turned to the means that our enemies used: we glorified Imperial Russia, we wrote lies in *Pravda* [Truth], we set a new Tsar on the now empty throne, we introduced officers' epaulettes and tortures. . . . Sometimes we felt that only one final sacrifice was needed for the triumph of Communism — the renunciation of Communism.

O Lord, O Lord — pardon us our sins!

Finally, it was created, our world, in the image and likeness of God. It is not yet Communism, but it is already quite close to Communism. And so we rise, stagger with weariness, encircle the earth with bloodshot eyes, and do not find around us what we hoped to find.

Why do you laugh, scum? Why do you claw with your well-cared nails the spots of blood and dirt that have stuck to our jackets and uniforms? You say that this is not Communism, that we took the wrong turning and that we are further from Communism now than when we started. Well then, where is *your* Kingdom of God? Show it! Where is the free personality of the superman that you promised?

Achievements are never identical with the original aim. The means used to reach the aim change its original appearance into something unrecognizable. The stakes of the Inquisition helped to establish the Gospel; but what is left of the Gospel after the stakes have done their work? Yet all of them — the stakes of the Inquisition and the Gospel, the night of Saint Bartholomew and Saint Bartholomew himself — add up to one great Christian culture.

Yes, we live in Communism. It resembles our aspirations about as much as the Middle Ages resembled Christ, modern Western man resembles the free superman, and man resembles God. But all the same, there is *some resemblance,* isn't there?

This resemblance lies in the subordination of all our actions, thoughts, and longings to that sole Purpose, which may have long ago become a meaningless word but still has a hypnotic effect on us and pushes us onward and onward — we don't know where. And, obviously, art and literature could not but get caught in the meshes of that system and become, as Lenin predicted, "a small wheel and a small screw" of the gigantic state machine. "Our magazines, both scientific and artistic, cannot be apolitical. . . . The strength of Soviet literature, the most advanced in the world, is that it is a literature for which there can be no other interests than those of the people and of the State." *

It must be remembered, when reading this decree of the Central Committee, that the interests of the people and of the State — which, incidentally, are exactly the same from the point of view of the State — have but a single aim: the all-pervading and all-absorbing Communism. "Literature and art are part of the whole people's struggle for Communism. . . . The highest social destiny of art and literature is to mobilize the people to the struggle for new advances in the building of Communism." †

When Western writers deplore our lack of freedom of speech, their starting point is their belief in the freedom of the individual. This is the foundation of their culture, but it is organically alien to Communism. A true Soviet writer, a true Marxist, will not even know what they are all about. What freedom — if the comparison be permitted — does the religious person require from God? The freedom to praise God still more ardently?

Contemporary Christians, who have broken their spiritual fast and accepted the spirit of individualism, with its free elections, free enterprise, and free press, occasionally abuse the phrase "freedom of choice" that Christ is supposed to have bequeathed us. This sounds like a dubious borrowing from the parliamentary system to which they are accustomed, for it bears no resemblance to the Kingdom of God, if only because no president or prime minister is ever elected in paradise. Even the

* Decree of the Central Committee of the CPSU(b), August 14, 1946.
† N. S. Khrushchev, "For a Close Link Between Literature and Art and the Life of the People," *Kommunist* magazine, No. 12, 1957.

most liberal God offers only one freedom of choice: to believe or not to believe, to be for Him or for Satan, to go to paradise or to hell. Communism offers just about the same right. If you don't want to believe, you can go to jail — which is by no means worse than hell. And for the man who believes, for the Soviet writer to whom Communism is the purpose of his own and humanity's existence (and otherwise there is no place for him either in our literature or in our society), there can be no such dilemma. For the man who believes in Communism, as Khrushchev correctly noted in one of his latest cultural pronouncements, "for the artist who truly wants to serve his people, the question does not arise of whether he is free or not in his creative work. For him, the question of which approach to the phenomena of reality to choose is clear. He need not conform or force himself; the true representation of life from the point of view of Communist *partiinost'* * is a necessity of his soul. He holds firmly to these positions, and affirms and defends them in the work."

It is with the same joyous facility that this artist accepts the directives of the Party and the government, from the Central Committee and its First Secretary. For who, if not the Party and its leader, knows best what kind of art we need? It is, after all, the Party that leads us to the rules of Marxism-Leninism, the Party that lives and works in constant contact with God. And so we have in it and in its leader the wisest and most experienced guide, who is competent in all questions of industry, linguistics, music, philosophy, painting, biology, etc. He is our Commander, our Ruler, our High Priest. To doubt his words is as sinful as to doubt the will of God.

These are the esthetical and psychological concepts the knowledge of which is indispensable to anyone who would penetrate the secret of socialist realism.

## II

Works produced by socialist realists vary in style and content. But in all of them the Purpose is present, whether directly or indirectly, open or veiled. They are panegyrics on Communism, satires on some of its many enemies, or descriptions of life "in its revolutionary development," i.e. life moving towards Communism.

Having chosen his subject, the Soviet writer views it from a definite angle. He wants to discover what potentialities it contains that point to the splendid Purpose. Most subjects of Soviet literature have in common a remarkable purposefulness. They all develop in one direction, and a direction well known in advance. This direction may exhibit variations in

* *Partiinost'* is the point of view that considers everything in terms of the correct Party line.

accordance with time, place, conditions, etc.; but it is invariable in its course and its destiny: to remind the reader once more of the triumph of Communism.

Each work of socialist realism, even before it appears, is thus assured of a happy ending. The ending may be sad for the hero, who runs every possible risk in his fight for Communism; but it is happy from the point of view of the superior Purpose; and the author never neglects to proclaim his firm belief in our final victory, either directly or through a speech of his dying hero. Lost illusions, broken hopes, unfulfilled dreams, so characteristic of literature of other eras and systems, are contrary to socialist realism. Even when it produces a tragedy, it is an *Optimistic Tragedy,* the title of Vishnevski's play in which the heroine dies at the end but Communism triumphs.

A comparison between some representative titles of Soviet and Western literature is revealing. *Journey to the End of the Night* (Céline); *Death in the Afternoon* and *For Whom the Bell Tolls* (Hemingway); *Everyone Dies Alone* (Fallada); *A Time to Live and a Time to Die* (Remarque); *Death of a Hero* (Aldington), are all in minor key. *Happiness* (Pavlenko); *First Joys* (Fedin); *It is Well!* (Mayakovski); *Fulfilled Wishes* (Kaverin); *Light over the Earth* (Babayevski); *The Victors* (Bagritski); *The Victor* (Simonov); *The Victor* (Chirikov); *Spring in the Victory Collective Farm* (Gribachev), and so on, are all in a major key.

The splendid aim towards which the action develops is sometimes presented directly at the end of the work. This method was brilliantly used by Mayakovski. All his major works after the Revolution end with passages about Communism or with fantastic scenes describing life in the future Communist State (*Mystery Bouffe; 150,000,000; About This; Vladimir Il'ich Lenin; It is Well!; With a Full Voice*). Gorki, who during the Soviet era wrote mainly about the days before the Revolution, ended most of his novels and plays — *The Artamonov Affair; The Life of Klim Samgin; Egor Bulichev and Others; Dostigaev and Others* — with a vision of the victorious Revolution, which was a stage on the way to Communism, and the concluding gesture of the old world.

Even when the book does not end with such a grandiose denouement, it still exists implicitly and symbolically, commanding the development of characters and events. For example, many of our novels and stories deal with the work of a factory, the building of an electricity work, the application of an agricultural decree, and so on. An economic task is carried out in the course of the action (e.g. the start of building introduces the plot; the end of building — the denouement). But the task is presented as an indispensable stage on the way towards a higher purpose. In such a purposeful view, even technical processes acquire dramatic tension and can be followed with great interest. The reader finds out step by step how, against all kind of obstacles, the plant was put to work, the "Victory" collective farm gathered a good crop of corn, and so on. He closes the book with a sigh of relief and realizes that we have made yet another step towards Communism.

Since Communism is for us the inescapable outcome of the historical process, many of our novels have made the impetuous course of time the mainspring of their action. The course of time, working its way towards the Purpose, works for us. The Soviet writer does not think in Proustian terms. He does not search for lost time; his motto is rather: "Time, march on!" He hastens the course of life and affirms that each day lived is not a loss but a gain for man — because it brings him closer to the desired ideal, even if only by one millimeter.

This purposefulness of the historic processes is linked with the great interest our writers show in history, both recent and remote. Recent historical events like the Civil War and collectivization are landmarks on the road we chose. In more remote eras it is, alas, harder to find the movement towards Communism. But if the writer concentrates hard enough he will uncover, even in the most remote of times, some phenomenon that might be called progressive because, in the final account, it aided in some way our victories of today. The writers merely anticipate somewhat and give these events the Purpose that they did not yet have. And so the leaders of the past like Ivan the Terrible, Peter the Great, or the peasant rebel Stenka Razin, though they did not know the word "Communism," still know quite well that our future will be brilliant. They never cease to celebrate this future from the pages of our historical novels, and they constantly gladden the heart of their readers by their astounding perspicacity.

Another subject is offered to our literature by the internal world of man's psychological life. This internal world moves towards the Purpose by dynamics of its own, fights against "the traces of the bourgeois past in its conscience," and reeducates itself under the influence of the Party and of surrounding life. A large part of Soviet literature is an "educational novel" which shows the Communist metamorphosis of individuals and entire communities. Many of our books turn around the representation of these moral and psychological processes, which aim at producing the ideal man of the future. One such is Gorki's *Mother,* where an ignorant woman, defeated by life, is transformed into a conscious revolutionary. Written in 1906, this book is generally considered the first example of socialist realism. Or there is Makarenko's Pedagogical Poem about the young criminals who take the road to honest work, or Ostrovski's novel *How the Steel Was Tempered,* i.e. how the steel of our youth was tempered in the fire of the Civil War and the cold of early Communist construction.

As soon as the literary character becomes fully purposeful and conscious of his purposefulness, he can enter that privileged caste which is universally represented and called "positive heroes." This is the Holy of Holies of socialist realism, its cornerstone and main achievement.

The positive hero is not simply a good man. He is a hero illuminated by the light of the most ideal of all ideals. Leonid Leonov called his positive hero "a peak of humanity from whose height the future can be seen." He has either no faults at all or else but a few of them — for example, he sometimes loses his temper a little. These faults have a twofold function. They help the hero to preserve a certain likeness to real men and they provide something to overcome as he raises himself ever higher and higher on the ladder of political morality. However, these faults must be slight or else they would run counter to his basic qualities. It is not easy to enumerate these basic qualities of the positive hero: ideological conviction, courage, intelligence, will power, patriotism, respect for women, self-sacrifice, etc., etc. The most important, of course, are the clarity and directness with which he sees the Purpose and strives towards it. Hence the amazing precision of all his actions, thoughts, tastes, feelings, and judgments. He firmly knows what is right and what is wrong; he says plainly "yes" or "no" and does not confuse black with white. For him there are no inner doubts and hesitations, no unanswerable questions, and no impenetrable secrets. Faced with the most complex of tasks he easily finds the solution — by taking the shortest and most direct route to the Purpose.

The positive hero first appeared in some books of Gorki written in the first decade of the twentieth century. He started by proclaiming to the world: "One must say firmly yes or no!" Many were shocked by the self-assurance and straightforwardness of his formulations, by his tendency to preach at everyone around him and by his pompous monologues celebrating his own virtues. Chekhov, when he managed to read through *The Petty Bourgeois,* frowned with embarrassment and advised Gorki to soften the loud proclamations of his hero. Chekhov feared pretentiousness worse than fire: he viewed such purple passages as a boastfulness foreign to the Russian character.

But Gorki was deaf to such advice. He did not fear the reproaches and sneers of the shocked *intelligentsia* and its repeated assertions that the new hero was dull-witted and narrow-minded. He knew that his hero was the man of the future and that "only men as pitiless, straight and hard as swords will cut their way through." *

Since then the positive hero has gone through many changes and presented himself in many guises. He unrolled his positive qualities in many ways, grew big and sturdy, and finally drew himself up to his full stature. This happened already in the 1930's, when the Soviet writers dropped

* *The Petty Bourgeois,* 1901.

their little cliques and their literary tendencies, and accepted, almost unanimously, the best and most advanced trend of all: socialist realism.

To read the books of the last twenty or thirty years is to feel the great power of the positive hero. First he spread in every direction, until he filled all our literature. There are books in which *all* the heros are positive. This is but natural, once we are coming ever closer to the Purpose. So that if a book about the present deals not with the fight against the enemies but with, say, a model collective farm, then all its characters can and must be positive. To put negative characters in such a situation would, to say the least, be strange. And so we get dramas and novels where all moves smoothly and peacefully. If there is a conflict between the heroes, it is a conflict between good and better, model and super-model. When these books appeared, their authors — men like Babaevski, Surkov, Sofronov, Virta, Gribachev, etc — were highly praised and set up as examples for others. True, since the Twentieth Congress — one hardly knows why — our attitude towards them changed somewhat and we apply to them the contemptuous adjective "conflictless." Once Khrushchev came out in defense of these writers, such reproaches were stilled somewhat but they are still leveled here and there by intellectuals. They are unjust.

Since we don't want to lose face before the West, we occasionally cease to be consistent and declare that our society is rich in individualities and embraces many interests. And that it has differences of opinion, conflicts, and contradictions, and literature is supposed to reflect all that.

True, we differ from each other in age, sex, nationality, and even intelligence. But whoever follows the Party line knows that these are heterogeneities within a homogeneity, differences of opinion within a single opinion, conflicts within a basic absence of conflict. We have one aim — Communism; one philosophy — Marxism; one art — socialist realism. This was well put by a Soviet writer of no great literary gifts but politically irreproachable: "Russia took its own road — that of unanimity. . . . For thousands of years men suffered from differences of opinion. But now we, Soviet men and women, for the first time agree with each other, talk one language that we all understand, and think identically about the main things in life. It is this unanimity that makes us strong and superior to all other people in the world, who are internally torn and socially isolated through their differences of opinion." *

Beautifully put! Yes we really are all alike and we are not ashamed of it. Those of us who suffer from superfluous differences of thought we punish severely by excluding them from life and literature. There can be

* V. Il'enkov, *The Great Highway,* a novel which appeared in 1949 and was awarded the Stalin Prize. One cannot but recall in this connection Khrushchev's *cri de coeur* against the Jews: "They are all individualists and all intellectuals. They want to talk about everything, they want to discuss everything, they want to debate everything — and they come to totally different conclusions!"

no substantial differences of opinion in a country where even the anti-Party elements confess their errors and wish to rectify them as soon as possible, and incorrigible enemies of the people ask to be shot. Still less can there be such differences among honest Soviet people, and least of all among positive heroes who think only of spreading their virtues all over the world and of reeducating the few remaining dissidents into unanimity.

True, there are still disagreements between the vanguard and the backward and there is still the sharp conflict with the capitalist world that does not let us sleep in peace. But we do not doubt for a single moment that all these contradictions will be resolved, that the world will become unified and Communist and that the last, by competing with each other, shall become the first. This great harmony is the final Purpose of Creation, this beautiful absence of conflict is the future of socialist realism. And so we can hardly reproach those overharmonious writers who have indeed withdrawn from contemporary conflicts but only to glance at the future, i.e. to find out how they can best pay the debt which, as writers, they owe to socialist realism. Babaevski and Surkov have not deviated from the sacred principles of our art, but have rather developed it logically and organically. They embody the higher stage of socialist realism and the embryo of the coming Communist realism.

The growing strength of the positive hero is shown not only in his incredible multiplication — he has far surpassed other kinds of literary character in quantity, put them into shade, and sometimes replaced them altogether. His qualitative growth has also been remarkable. As he approaches the Purpose, he becomes ever more positive, great, and splendid. He also becomes more and more persuaded of his own dignity, especially when he compares himself to contemporary Western man and realizes his immeasurable superiority. "But our Soviet man has left *them* far behind. He is now close to the peak while they are still wandering in the foothills" — this is the way simple peasants talk in our novels. And the poet runs out of words when he tries to describe this superiority, this incomparable positiveness of our positive hero:

> *Nobody rose so high*
> *For centuries and centuries.*
> *You are above all glory,*
> *You are beyond all praise.*
> M. ISAKOVSKI

The novel *Russian Forest* by Leonid Leonov, the first writer to be awarded a Lenin prize — which replaced the Stalin prize — is the best work of socialist realism for the last five years or so. It contains a remarkable scene. The brave girl Polya, entrusted with a dangerous mission, makes her way to the rear of the enemy — the action takes place during the Patriotic War. As a camouflage she is supposed to collaborate with the Germans. She plays this part for a while in talking to a Nazi officer, but with great difficulty: it is morally painful to her to talk the enemy's language. Finally she cannot stand it any more and reveals her true self and her superiority to the German officer: "I am a girl of my time . . . maybe just an ordinary girl, but I am the world's tomorrow . . . and you should stand up, yes, stand up when you talk to me, if you have a trace of self-respect left! But there you sit, only because you are nothing but a horse that the Chief Hangman puts through its paces. . . . Well, don't just sit there, do something! . . . Get up and show me the place where Soviet girls are shot!"

The fact that by this pompous tirade Polya betrays herself and moreover harms the mission with which she has been entrusted does not disturb the author in the least. He finds an easy way out of the resulting situation. The noble purity of Polya's heart converts a *starosta* * who happened to listen to the conversation. His conscience suddenly awakens, he shoots at the German, loses his life and saves Polya's.

But this is not what matters. It does not matter so much that the *starosta* moved, within the batting of an eyelid, from the rearguard to the vanguard. What matters very much more is that we have here the straight and immutable determination of the positive hero raised, we might say, to the second power. Polya's behavior may seem stupid from the point of view of common sense. But it is filled with an immense religious and esthetic significance. Under no circumstances, even to further his task, does the positive hero dare so much as to look negative. Even in the face of the enemy who must be outwitted and cheated he must demonstrate his positive qualities. They cannot be hidden or camouflaged: they are written on his brow and they sound in his every word. And so he defeats the enemy not by cleverness, wits, or physical strength but by his proud attitude alone.

Polya's deed is the key to much that to the nonbeliever appears grossly exaggerated, stupid, and false — especially the positive hero's propensity to pontificate on elevated themes. He makes Communist assertions at home and at work, in friends' homes and on lonely walks, on the love couch and on the death bed. But this is not a contradiction; positive heroes were created to present to the world, on every suitable and unsuitable occasion, a model of purposefulness:

> *Measure*
> > *Each detail*
> > > *By the great*
> > > > *Purpose*
> > > > MAYAKOVSKI

* A peasant official put in charge of the village by the Germans.

*Only men who are as straight and hard as swords will cut their way through.*

GORKI

Never before have there been heroes like this. Though Soviet writers are proud of the great traditions of nineteenth-century Russian literature which they want to follow in every possible way and sometimes actually do follow (even though they constantly upbraid Western writers for slavishly imitating outworn literary canons) the positive hero of socialist realism is a break with the tradition, not its continuation.

A very different type of hero prevailed in the last century, and Russian culture lived and thought differently then. Compared with the fanatical religiosity of our time, the nineteenth century seems atheist, tolerant, disoriented. It was soft and shriveled, feminine and melancholy, full of doubts, inner contradictions, and pangs of conscience. Chernyshevski and Pobedonostsev, the great radical and the great reactionary, were perhaps the only two men of the century who really believed in God. Of course, an incalculable number of peasants and old women also believed in God; but they were not the makers of history and culture. Culture was made by a handful of mournful skeptics who thirsted for God simply because they had no God.

But you might object: How about Tolstoy and Dostoevsky, how about the thousands of other "seekers after God," from the Populists to Merezhkovski, whose search of God has lasted well into the middle of *our* century? I assume that to search means not to have. He who has, who really believes, does not search. And what should he search for, if everything is clear and all that he has to do is to *follow* God? God is not found; He finds us and comes upon us. When He has found us, we cease to search and start to act, doing His will.

The nineteenth century was a century of searching, of ardent or calm aspirations, unwilling or unable to find a solid place under the sun, torn by uncertainties and dualism. Dostoevsky regretted that the Russian was so broad — he should be narrowed, he felt. But Dostoevsky was so broad himself that he could embrace within himself both Orthodoxy and nihilism. He could find room in his soul for all the Karamazovs — Alyosha, Mitya, Ivan, Fedor (some would add Smerdyakov). We don't know to this day which of them predominated. For breadth excludes faith: no wonder we narrowed ourselves down to Marxism, thus fulfilling Dostoevsky's wish. Dostoevsky fully understood the temptations of breadth, eternally disputed with himself and passionately wished to end these disputes, offensive to the one God.

This thirst for God, this wish to believe, arose — as did the search — in a spiritual desert. It was not yet faith, and if the wish preceded faith — Blessed are they who thirst! — it is like hunger preceding a meal. . . . The great hunger of the nineteenth century perhaps conditioned us Russians to throw ourselves so greedily upon the food prepared by Marx and to devour it even before we had time to analyze its taste, smell, and consequences. But this hundred years' hunger was itself caused by the catastrophic absence of food: it was a hunger of godlessness. That is why it proved so exhausting and felt so unbearable, making us "go among the people," turn radical and renegade, and suddenly remember that we are, after all, Christians . . . But there was no relief anywhere:

> *I want to make peace with heaven,*
> *I want to love, I want to pray,*
> *I want to believe in the good.*

But who is it that cries so anxiously for faith? None other than the *Demon* of Lermontov's poem.* It is the very "spirit" of doubt that has torn us so long and so painfully. He confirms that it is not the saints that thirst for God but those who have no God and have left Him.

It is a very Russian Demon. He is too inconsistent in his passion for evil to figure as a full Devil and too inconsistent in his repentance to make his peace with God and rejoin the obedient angels. His tone is not straightforward but ambiguous — "not day and not night, not light and not dark." There are only semi-tones, the secret glitter of twilight that was later glimpsed by the symbolist poet Blok and the symbolist painter Wrubel.

A consistent atheism, an extreme and inflexible denial of God, resembles religion more than this vague incertitude. For this is the crux of the Demon's problem: he has no faith and he suffers from lack of faith. His is the eternal motion upwards and downwards, backwards and forwards, between heaven and hell.

Remember what happened to the Demon? He fell in love with Tamara, that divine beauty incarnated in a ravishing woman, and decided to believe in God. But as soon as he kissed Tamara she died, killed by his touch. She was taken from him, and he was once more alone in his anguished unbelief.

For a century this was also the story of Russian culture, which had been possessed by the Demon even before Lermontov. Russia went into a frenzied search for an ideal; and no sooner did she touch heaven than she fell. The slightest contact with God led to denying Him, and with the denial came the anguish of unrealized faith.

The universal genius of Pushkin took note of this collision in *The Prisoner of the Caucasus* and other early poems; but it was only in *Eugene Onegin* that he unfolded the theme in its full amplitude. The plot of *Onegin* is a simple anecdote: as long as Tatiana loves Onegin and is willing to belong to him, he is indifferent to her; but when she marries

* Lermontov, the great Romantic poet, wrote this work in 1842.–TRANSLATOR

another, he falls in love with her passionately and hopelessly. Embedded in this banal story are contradictions on which Russian literature has dwelled to the days of Chekhov and Blok: contradictions of a spirit without God and of a Purpose irrevocably lost.

The central hero of this literature — Onegin, Pechorin of Lermontov's *Hero of Our Time,* Beltov of Herzen's *Whose Fault?,* Lavretski of Turgenev's *Nest of Gentlefolk,* and Rudin of his novel of that name — is usually called "the superfluous man." For all his generous impulses he is unable to find a destiny and he presents a lamentable example of a purposelessness that is of no use to anybody. He is, as a rule, a reflexive character, with tendencies to self-analysis and self-flagellation. His life is full of unrealized projects, and his fate is sad and slightly ridiculous. A woman usually plays a fatal part in it.

Russian literature is full of love stories in which an inadequate man and a beautiful woman meet and part without achieving anything. The fault, of course, lies with the man, who does not know how to love his lady as she deserves, actively and with a purpose. Instead, he yawns with boredom, like Onegin and Rudin, or else he kills his beloved, like Aleko in Pushkin's *Gypsies* or Arbenin in Lermontov's *Masquerade.*

If only the hero were at least a low fellow, incapable of higher feelings! But no, he is a noble creature and the most attractive woman boldly offers him her heart and hand. But instead of rejoicing and taking life with a song, he commits some irresponsible acts and, against his own desires, does everything he can to ensure that his beloved shall not become his.

Judging by the literature of the time, all hearts were broken in nineteenth-century Russia and no children were born for a while. But the writers were not describing the actual life and customs of the Russian nobility; they were engaged in depth metaphysics of an aimlessly agitated spirit. In this literature, woman was the touchstone of man. His relations with her bare his weakness, and, compromised by her strength and beauty, he descends from the stage on which a heroic action was to be played, bows to fate, and sneaks out into nothingness with the shameful cry of a base, useless, superfluous man.

The women, those innumerable Tatianas, Lizas, Natalias, Bellas, and Ninas [Tatiana is the heroine of *Eugene Onegin;* Lisa of *A Nest of Gentlefolk;* Bella of *A Hero of Our Time*], shine like an ideal, chaste and beyond the reach of Onegins and Pechorins, who love them so clumsily and unsuccessfully. For Russian literature they served as a synonym of the ideal, as symbol of a higher Purpose.

For woman is generally considered a beautiful, pure, and nebulous creature. Not too much is asked from her: she need not be concrete and definite to save man; it is enough that she be pure and beautiful. And since she occupies, like every Purpose, a passive and waiting position, her beautiful, magical, mysterious, and not too concrete nature permits her to represent a higher stage of the ideal and to serve as a substitute for the absent and desired Purpose.

This was the woman that the nineteenth century found most to its liking. She impressed it by her vagueness, her mysteriousness, and her tenderness. Pushkin's dreamy Tatiana opened up an age; the "Beautiful Lady" to whom Blok dedicated his first collected poems closed it. Tatiana was indispensable so that Onegin should suffer *through the absence of somebody*. And, concluding a love story that lasted for a century, Blok took the Beautiful Lady as his Bride, only to betray Her and to lose Her and to torment himself all his life by the purposelessness of his existence.

Blok's poem *The Twelve* — a work at the boundary between two hostile and mutually exclusive cultures — contains an episode that puts a full stop to the love theme of the nineteenth century. The Red Guard Petka kills, against his will and in a fit of anger, his sweetheart, the prostitute Katka. The tragic murder and the sorrows of lost love resuscitate the old drama, known to us from the days of Lermontov's *Masquerade* and *Demon*. Blok himself used it in many variations — did not the fool Petka and big-mouthed Katka, with her new boyfriend Harlequin-Vanka, issue from Blok's own Pierrot and Columbine? But if the old heroes, the Demons and Arbenins, just turn their emptied soul inside out and freeze into a hopeless sorrow, Petka, who followed in their footsteps, is not allowed to do it. His more politically conscious comrades rouse him and reeducate him:

> *You sure go on and on, you bastard,*
> *What are you? A little girl?*
> *Sure, you want to turn your soul*
> *Inside out for us to see? O.K.*
> *Come on, snap out of it, look smart,*
> *Get yourself under control!*
>
> . . . . . . . . . . . . . . .
> *And Petrukha soon slowed down*
> *His hurried steps*
>
> . . . . . . . . . . . . . . .
> *He threw back his head*
> *And became gay once more.*

Thus a new hero was born, never seen before. In bloody battles against the enemy — "I will drink blood for my black-browed beauty!" — and in the works and pains of the new era — "This is no time for babying!" — he cures himself of sterile reflections and useless pangs of conscience. He lifts his head proudly, cheers himself up and enters Soviet literature under the flag of the new God whom Blok, from old habit, calls Jesus Christ:

> *Forward, forward*
> *Working people!*

The superfluous man of the nineteenth century became even more superfluous in the twentieth. To the positive hero of the new era he was strange and incomprehensible. The superfluous man seemed to him much more dangerous than the openly negative enemy. After all, the enemy was like the positive hero — clear, straightforward, and, in his own way, purposeful. Only his significance was negative — to hinder the movement to the Purpose. But the superfluous man was a creature of different psychological dimensions, inaccessible to computation and regimentation. He is neither for the Purpose nor against the Purpose — he is outside the Purpose. Now this simply cannot be, it is a fiction, a blasphemy. While the whole world, having defined itself with regard to the Purpose, is divided into two antagonistic camps, he feigns not to understand this and keeps mingling his colors in vague and ambiguous schemes. He proclaims that there are no Reds and no Whites but simply people, poor, unfortunate, superfluous people:

> *They all lie in a row —*
> *No line between them.*
> *Look: soldiers!*
> *Who's ours? Who's theirs?*
> *He was white and now he's red —*
> *The blood reddened him.*
> *He was red and now he's white —*
> *Death whitened him.*
>            M.  TSVETAYEVA *

In the religious struggle, the superfluous man proclaimed his neutrality and expressed his sympathy with both parties, as in these verses of the symbolist poet Voloshin:

> *Both here and there, among the ranks*
> *One voice alone can be heard:*
> *"Who is not for us, is against us.*
> *There are no neutrals. Truth is with us."*
>
> *And I stand alone among them*
> *In the roaring flame and smoke*
> *And with all the strength that I have*
> *Say a prayer for them both.*

Such words, as blasphemous as a simultaneous prayer to God and Satan, could not possibly be permitted. It was more correct to proclaim them to be a prayer to the Devil: *"Who is not for us, is against us."* And

* Marina Tsvetayeva returned to Russia in 1940 after a long exile and committed suicide two years later. She has been posthumously "rehabilitated" recently and her work republished.–TRANSLATOR

this is what the new culture did. If it turned again towards the superfluous man, it was only to prove that he was not at all superfluous but rather harmful, dangerous, and negative.

Naturally, the leader of the new crusade was Gorki. In 1901 he sketched the first model of the positive hero and attacked those "who were born without faith in the heart," who "never felt that anything was true," who "forever wandered between yes and no."

Gorki roared "No!" at these superfluous men, who roused his ire by their indefiniteness, and called them "petty bourgeois." Later he extended the concept of "petty bourgeois" far and wide and cast into it all who did not belong to the new religion: property owners large and small, liberals, conservatives, hooligans, humanists, decadents, Christians, Dostoevsky, Tolstoy. Gorki was a man of *printsipialnost';* G. Chulkov called him the only truly believing writer of his time. He knew that all that is not God is Devil.

The literary revaluation of the superfluous man and his rapid transformation into a negative figure was intensified in the 1920's, the formative years of the positive hero. When they were placed side by side, it became obvious to everybody that there are no heroes without Purpose, but only heroes who were for or against the Purpose and that the superfluous man was, when all is said and done, a camouflaged enemy, a base traitor who should be unmasked and punished as quickly as possible.

Thus wrote Gorki in *The Life of Klim Samgin,* Fadeyev in *The Debacle,* and many others. In *The Towns and the Years* Fedin purged his heart of the last drop of pity for the superfluous hero, formerly so enchanting. The only dissonant note was perhaps struck by Sholokhov in his *Quiet Flows the Don.* Having shown the tragic fate of that superfluous man, Grigori Melekhov, he bade him an affectionate farewell. Since his hero belonged to the simple people and not the intelligentsia, it was possible to close an eye to Sholokhov's behavior. Today his novel is considered a model of socialist realism. But it is a model that, for obvious reasons, has found no imitators.

Meanwhile, other superfluous men, wishing to save their lives, renounced their past and duly transformed themselves into positive heroes. One of them recently said: "There is nothing in the world more disgusting than fence-sitters. . . . Yes, yes, I am a Red. A Red, the devil take you." * The curse was addressed, of course, to the Whites.

Thus did the hero of nineteenth-century Russian perish ingloriously.

## III

In its content and spirit, as in its central figure, socialist realism is much closer to the eighteenth century than to the nineteenth. Without realizing

* Fedin's *An Extraordinary Year,* 1949.

it, we jump over the heads of our fathers and revive the tradition of our grandfathers. Like ourselves, the eighteenth century had the idea of political purposefulness, the feeling of its own superiority and a clear consciousness that "God is with us":

> *Hark, hark, O Universe*
> *To vict'ries beyond human power;*
> *Listen, O astounded Europe*
> *To the exploits of these Russians.*
> *Peoples, know and understand,*
> *Believe ye that with us is God;*
> *Believe that, aided by His hand,*
> *A single Russian can defeat*
> *All your abysmal evil forces.*
> *Peoples, know this dread Colossus:*
> *God is with us, so honor ye the Russian.*

These verses of the eighteenth-century poet Derzhavin have a very contemporary ring, though the language would, of course, need modernizing. Like the socialist system, so eighteenth-century Russia conceived of itself as the center of Creation. Inspired by the plenitude of its virtues — "self-created and self-fortified" — it proclaimed itself as an example to all peoples and all eras. Its religious self-conceit was so strong that it did not even admit the possibility of the existence of other norms and ideals. In his *Portrait of Felitsa,* Derzhavin, praising the ideal reign of Catherine II, expressed the desire that

> *Peoples savage and remote,*
> *Covered still with wool and scales,*
> *Dressed only with leaf and bark,*
> *And adorned with wings of birds,*
> *Should all gather at Her throne,*
> *Hear the gentle voice of Law,*
> *So that tears should run in torrents*
> *Down their swarthy, sunburned faces.*
> *They should cry and understand*
> *The bliss of living in our time,*
> *Should abandon their equality,*
> *And all subject be to Her.*

Derzhavin simply cannot imagine that these "savages," the Huns, Finns, and other peoples that surrounded the Russian throne somewhat in the manner of the Internationale, should reject this flattering offer and not wish to submit at once to Catherine, who is, after all, "celestial grace incarnate." For him, as for our writers, anyone who does not wish to become like the model proposed to him and does not hasten to forget his barbarous "equality" and accept the proffered gift of "bliss" falls into one of two categories. He either is so stupid that he does not understand his own interests, in which case he must be reeducated. Or he lacks virtue and is, to use one of our words, a "reactionary," in which case he must be liquidated. For in our world there is nothing finer than this state, this faith, this life, and this Empress. So Derzhavin believed, just as a contemporary poet who celebrates the new reign in Derzhavin's language:

> There is no country like vast Russia,
> No flowers grow as bright as ours,
> Great is our people, free and deathless,
> Our proud, eternal Russian people.
> It stemmed attacking hordes of Batu
> And broke all chains that held it down,
> It made Russia and it raised her
> To heights of stars and crests of time.
>
>                                    A. PROKOFIEV

Eighteenth-century literature produced its own positive hero. He is "the friend of common good"; he "strives to surpass all in courage," etc.; i.e. he constantly raises the level of his political morality, possesses all the virtues, and tells everybody just what to do. This literature knew nothing of the superfluous man. Neither did it know the destructive laughter that was the chronic disease of Russian culture from Pushkin to Blok and reached its climax among the decadents. "All the most lively and sensitive children of our century are stricken by a disease unknown to doctors and psychiatrists. It is related to the disorders of the soul and might be called 'irony.' Its symptoms are fits of an exhausting laughter which starts with a diabolic mockery and a provocative smile and ends as rebellion and sacrilege." *

Seen in this way, irony is the laughter of the superfluous man who divides both himself and everything sacred in this world. "I know men who are ready to choke with laughter when they learn that their mother is dying, that they are starving to death, that their fiancee has betrayed them. Through this accursed irony, everything is the same to them: good and evil, the blue sky and the stinking pit, Dante's Beatrice and Sologub's Untouchable Lady. [Fedor Sologub, a poet of the turn of the twentieth century, with decadent tendencies.] Everything is confused, as in a tavern or a fog." †

Irony is the faithful companion of unbelief and doubt; it vanishes as soon as there appears a faith that does not tolerate sacrilege. There was no irony in Derzhavin, nor in Gorki — except for a few early tales. In Mayakovski there are a few examples, mostly from prerevolutionary

* A. Blok, *Irony*, 1908.
† Blok, *ibid.*

times. Mayakovski soon found out what he could and what he could not laugh about. He could not permit himself to laugh at Lenin, whom he praised to the skies, any more than Derzhavin would laugh at his Empress. Pushkin, by contrast, addressed indecent verses even to the chaste and modest Tatiana. Pushkin was the first to taste the bitter joys of self-negation, even though he was gay and had a balanced character. As for Lermontov, he almost seems to have imbibed the poison in his childhood. In Blok himself and in his contemporaries Sologub and Leonid Andreev, destructive laughter became an elemental force sweeping everything before it.

As in the eighteenth century, we became severe and serious. This does not mean that we forgot how to laugh; but laughter ceased to be indecent and disrespectful; it acquired a Purpose. It eliminates faults, corrects manners, keeps up the brave spirits of youth. It is laughter with a serious face and with a pointing finger: "This is not the way to do things!" It is a laughter free from the acidity of irony.

Irony was replaced by pathos, the emotional element of the positive hero. We ceased to fear high-sounding words and bombastic phrases, we were no longer ashamed to be virtuous. The solemn eloquence of the ode suited us. We became classicists.

When Derzhavin, in his old age, wrote the ode "To the great boyar and military commander Reshemysl," he gave it a subtitle "or the image of what a great lord should be." The art of socialist realism might be given the same subtitle: it represents the world and man as they should be.

Socialist realism starts from an ideal image to which it adapts the living reality. Our demand "to represent life truthfully in its revolutionary development" is really nothing but a summons to view truth in the light of the ideal, to give an ideal interpretation of reality, to present what should be as what is. For we interpret "revolutionary development" as the inevitable movement towards Communism, towards our ideal, in the light of which we see reality. We represent life as we would like it to be and as it is bound to become, when it bows to the logic of Marxism. This is why socialist realism should really be called "socialist classicism."

Some theoretical books and articles by Soviet writers and critics use the terms "romanticism" and "revolutionary romanticism." Gorki wrote much about the links between romanticism and socialist realism. He longed for "the illusion that exalts" and defended the artist's right to embellish life and to present it as better than it is. These calls did not remain unheeded, though many of Gorki's formulas are now veiled by an embarrassed silence or interpreted pharisaically: it is obviously not easy to admit that what we really need are some pretty lies. No, no, God forbid! We are against illusions and against idealization, we write only the truth and at the same time present life in its revolutionary development. . . . Why should we embellish life? It is quite beautiful as it is, we are not out to embellish it, we just want to show the germs of the future it contains. . . .

All this talk is merely our usual literary politics. In reality — as Gorki knew — romanticism suited our tastes only too well. It gravitates towards the ideal, makes our wishes pass for the truth, likes pretty knick-knacks, is not afraid of bombast. This is why it had its well-known success among us. Yet romanticism has played a less important part in our art than might have been expected. It made its presence felt mostly in the prehistory and initial period of socialist realism. In its mature period — the last twenty, thirty years — socialist realism has had a comparatively slight romantic tinge.

Romanticism is intimately connected with the *Sturm und Drang* period of Soviet literature, the first five years after 1917, when life and art were flooded with sentiment, when the blazing elan towards a happy future and the worldwide significance of the Revolution were not yet regimented by a strict political order. Romanticism is our past, our youth for which we long. It is the ecstasy of swollen banners, the explosions of passion and rage, the rattling of sabers and the neighing of horses, the shootings without judgment and without consequences, the "On to Warsaw!", the life, sleep, and death under the naked sky lit by the fires of regiments as nomadic as the Tartars of old:

> *Youth that led us*
> *To the march of sabers,*
> *Youth that threw us*
> *On the ice of Kronstadt.*
>
> *Battle horses*
> *Carried us off,*
> *On city squares*
> *They massacred us.*
>                    E. BAGRITSKI

These are not just the sentiments of revolutionists who have survived and grown fat. The memory of the Revolution is as sacred, both to those who took part in it and those who were born after it, as the image of a dead mother. It is easier for us to grant that everything that happened after the Revolution was its betrayal than to insult its memory by reproaches and suspicions. Unlike the Party, the State, the Ministry of State Security, collectivization, Stalin, etc., the Revolution needs no justification by the Communist paradise that awaits us. It is self-justified and justified emotionally, like love or inspiration. And even though the Revolution was carried out in the name of Communism, its name does not sound less sweet to us for that. Maybe even sweeter. . . .

We live between past and future, between the Revolution and Communism. And if Communism promising us golden mountains and representing the inevitable logical outcome of all human history imperiously pulls us forward, the past too pushes us in the back. For it is we who accomplished the Revolution. How then can we blame it or blaspheme against it? We are caught in this psychological squeeze. In itself, we may like it or not. But both before us and behind us stand temples so splendid that we could not bear to attack them. And when we remember that, should our enemies win, they would make us return to the prerevolutionary mode of life (or incorporate us in Western democracy, it hardly matters), then, I am sure, we will start once more from where we started. We will start from the Revolution.

While working on this article I have caught myself more than once dropping into irony — that unworthy device! I caught myself trying to avoid the phrase "Soviet power." I preferred to use its synonyms, like "our State," "the socialist system," and so on. No doubt this was due to the fact that when I was young, the words of one of our Civil War songs went straight to my soul:

> *All of us into the fight*
> *For Soviet power*
> *And as one man we'll die*
> *Fighting for it.*

It is enough for me to pronounce the words "Soviet power" to make me see the Revolution with my mind's eye. I see the taking of the Winter Palace, the cracking motion of machine-gun belts, the bread cards for one eighth of a pound, the defense of Red Petersburg. In a strictly logical judgment, "Soviet power" and "the socialist state" are the same thing. But if I have a few things against the socialist state — trifles, all of them — I have absolutely nothing against the Soviet power. Ridiculous? Maybe. But this is also romanticism.

Yes, we are all romantic with regard to our past. But the further away we are from our past and the closer we come to Communism, the weaker becomes the romantic halo that art has bestowed upon the Revolution. This is understandable: romanticism is, indeed, part of our nature; but it is not all of it. Sometimes it even violates our nature.

Romanticism is too anarchical and too emotional, while we are becoming ever more disciplined rationalists. It is at the mercy of turbulent feelings and diffuse moods, forgetting logic, common sense, and law. "The folly of the brave is the wisdom of life," the young Gorki assured us. This advice was timely when the Revolution was made: fools were necessary then. But can we call the Five Year Plan "folly of the brave"? Or the guidance of the Party? Or, indeed, Communism itself, inevitably prepared by the logical course of history? Here every point is thought through, rationally foreseen, and subdivided into corresponding paragraphs. What folly is this? Hm, comrade Gorki, you obviously haven't read your Marx!

Romanticism is powerless to express our clarity and precision. Composed gestures and even moderately solemn speech are foreign to it. It waves its arms, gets excited and dreams distant dreams of the time when Communism is all but built and will be seen any moment.

In affirming an ideal, romanticism is not binding enough. It takes the wish for the reality. This is not bad in itself, but it smells of subjectivism and lack of self-restraint. The wish is the reality, because it must be. Our life is beautiful not only because we want it to be beautiful but also because it must be so: it has no choice.

All these arguments, mostly voiceless and unconscious, gradually dried up the hot current of romanticism. The river of art was covered with the ice of classicism. As art became more precise, rational, and teleological, it squeezed out romanticism.

The cold breath and ponderous heaviness of classicism was felt by us long ago, but few men dared to be outspoken on this subject. "The spirit of classicism blows upon us from all directions. All breathe it; but they either cannot distinguish it or don't know its name or simply are afraid to speak about it." *

The most daring of all was N. Punin, a fine art critic. At that time he was connected with futurism; he is completely forgotten now. Already in 1918 he noted "the marked classicism of Mayakovski's verses." He declared that in his *Mystery Bouffe* — his first major postrevolutionary work — Mayakovski "ceased to be a romanticist and became a classicist." He forecast that "much as he would like to, Mayakovski will never again rebel as impetuously as he did in the past."

Although his forecast proved remarkably correct — and not only as regards Mayakovski — the term "classicism" did not take hold in a Soviet literature that kept becoming more clearly classicist. It was, perhaps, too embarrassingly frank. Also, it recalled certain undesirable associations that seemed to lower our dignity. We preferred to call ourselves modestly "socialist realists" and hide our name under this pseudonym. . . .

Beginning with the 1930's, the passion for solemnity finally imposes itself and a pompous simplicity of style, the hallmark of classicism, becomes fashionable. We call our state "the Power"; the mujik — "cultiva-

* A. Efros, *The Messenger on the Doorstep*, 1922.

tor of the bread"; the rifle — "saber." We capitalize a great number of words. Allegorical figures and personified abstractions invade our literature, and we speak with slow solemnity and grandiose gestures.

> *Yes, we believe, we must believe*
> *That truth exists — this is our stand;*
> *And that the good is not defenseless*
> *And conquers evil in the end.*
>
> A. TVARDOVSKI

> *The time has come! In vain with cruel fate*
> *The Fascist Lord has Moscow threatened long.*
> *But to victorious Moscow fell Berlin.*
>
> M. ISAKOVSKI

The first heroes of Soviet literature stormed the fortresses of capitalism with torn bast shoes on their feet and sexual oaths on their lips. They were coarse and unrestrained: "Vanka! Put some paper rubles in your shoes! You can't scoot barefoot to the meeting!" (Mayakovski). But now they acquired good looks, elegant clothes, and refined manners. If they are sometimes lacking in taste, this is the national and social trait of our classicism, born as it was of Russian democracy. But neither the heroes nor their authors ever suspect that they are in bad taste. They try with all their power to be beautiful, polite, and cultured. They present every detail "correctly" and "in the best of tastes."

"Under the white ceiling sparkled an elegant chandelier, fringed with transparent glass pendants, as with icicles. . . . Tall silvery columns supported a blindingly white cupola, decorated with necklaces of electric bulbs."

What is this? A Tsar's palace? No, an ordinary club in a provincial town.

"On the stage, by the polished wing of the grand piano stood Rakitin, dressed in sober gray. Like a blue river, a necktie flowed down his breast."

A singer? A fashionable tenor? No, a simple Party worker.

And now let's look at the people. It does not curse, it does not fight, it does not drink itself senseless the way the Russian people used to do. And if it takes a drink at a wedding table covered with exquisite foods, it is only as an accompaniment of toasts:

> Terentii raised his eyes, looked at the round of guests, rumblingly coughed into his fist, caressed the silver flow of his beard with a trembling hand, and said:
> "First of all let us congratulate the young couple, may they be happy and embellish the earth by their presence."
> The guests followed him with their toasts, among the melodious clinking of the wine glasses:

"May they honor their parents!"
"May they have healthy children!"
"And not injure the glory of the kolkhoz!"

The quotations are taken from the novel *From the Whole Heart* by E. Maltsev, published in 1949. It is like dozens and hundreds of other novels. It is a sample of classicist prose of average literary quality. The style has long become a commonplace of our literature, and passes from author to author without undergoing any substantial change.

Every style has its distinctive quality. But classicism is more prone than other styles to impose its mark, to observe pedantically definite canons and norms, to be conservative as to form. It is among the most stable of styles. It brings and accepts new elements mostly in its formative period, but later tries to follow established models faithfully and is hostile to researches in form, experimentalism, and originality. This is why it rejected the talents of many poets who wanted to embrace it but retain their personality: V. Khlebnikov, O. Mandelshtam, and N. Zabolotski among them.* Even Mayakovski, whom Stalin called "the most talented poet of our Soviet era," remained in it a tragically solitary figure.

Mayakovski was too much of a revolutionary to become a traditionalist. To this day he is accepted politically rather than poetically. For all the paeans written to his glory, his rhythms, images, and language seem overbold to most of our poets. Those who want to follow in his footsteps copy his mannerisms but are unable to grasp what is essential in him — his boldness, inventiveness, and passion. They imitate his verses but don't follow his example. . . .

Geniuses, of course, are not born every day, and the state of art rarely seems satisfactory to contemporaries. Still I must sadly confess, with other of my contemporaries, that our literature has become progressively impoverished in the last two or three decades. Fedin, Fadeev, Ehrenburg, Ivanov, and many others have written worse and worse with the years. The twenties, of which Mayakovski wrote that "Only poets, alas, we have none," now seem to be the years in which poetry flourished. Since the writers accepted socialist realism en masse — the beginning of the thirties — literature has gone down and down. Some few glimmers of light during the Patriotic War did not save it.

In this contradiction between the victory of socialist realism and the low quality of literary production, many are inclined to blame socialist realism. They say that great art cannot be written under it and even that it is the death of all art. But Mayakovski provides a refutation, to start with. For all the originality of his talents he remained an orthodox Soviet

* A. F. Khlebnikov, who died in 1922, was one of the founders of Russian futurism; Mandelshtam, who rebelled against the symbolists, died after deportation; Zabolotski is among the most talented Soviet poets today.—TRANSLATOR

writer, perhaps the most orthodox Soviet writer — and this did not stop him from writing good poetry. He was an exception to general rules, but mostly because he observed these rules more strictly than others. In his poetic practice he carried out the demands of socialist realism more radically and more consistently. For the contradiction between socialist realism and literary quality, the blame must fall on literature, i.e. on the writers who accepted the rules of socialist realism but did not have sufficient artistic consistency to embody them in deathless images. Mayakovski had that consistency.

Art is not afraid of dictatorship, severity, repressions, or even conservatism and clichés. When necessary, art can be narrowly religious, dumbly governmental, devoid of individuality — and yet good. We go into esthetic raptures over the stereotypes of Egyptian art, Russian icons, and folklore. Art is elastic enough to fit into any bed of Procrustes that history presents to it. But there is one thing it cannot stand: eclecticism.

Our misfortune is that we are convinced socialist realists but not convinced enough. Submitting to its cruel rules, we are yet afraid to follow to the end the road that we ourselves have chosen. No doubt, if we were less educated, it would be easier for us to attain the integrity that is indispensable to a writer. But we went to school, read all kinds of books, and learned only too well that there were great writers before us — Balzac, Maupassant, Tolstoy, and, yes, what's his name? — Chekhov. This is what has undone us. We wanted to become famous and to write like Chekhov. This unnatural liaison produced monsters.

It is impossible, without falling into parody, to produce a positive hero in the style of full socialist realism and yet make him into a psychological portrait. In this way, we will get neither psychology nor hero. Mayakovski knew this and, hating psychological analysis and details, wrote in proportions that were larger than life. He wrote coarsely, poster-style, homerically. He avoided like a plague descriptions of common life and rural nature. He broke with "the great traditions of the great Russian literature" and, though he loved Pushkin and Chekhov, he did not try to imitate them. All this helped Mayakovski to lift himself to the level of his epoch and to express its spirit fully and clearly, without alien admixtures.

But the writing of so many other writers is in a critical state right now precisely because, in spite of the classic nature of our art, they still consider it realism. They do it because they base their judgments on the literary criticism of the nineteenth century, which is farthest away from us and most foreign to us. Instead of following the road of conventional forms, pure fantasy and imagination which the great religious cultures always took, they try to compromise. They lie, they maneuver, and they try to combine the uncombinable: the positive hero, who logically tends towards the pattern, the allegory — and the psychological analysis of character; elevated style, declamation — and prosaic descriptions of ordinary life; a high ideal — and truthful representation of life.

The result is a loathsome literary salad. The characters torment themselves not quite like Dostoevsky's, are mournful not quite like Chekhov's, found their happy families not quite like Tolstoy's, and, suddenly becoming aware of the time they are living in, scream at the reader the copybook slogans which they read in Soviet newspapers, like "Long live world peace!" or "Down with the Warmongers!" This is neither classicism nor realism. It is a half-classicist half-art, which is none too socialist and altogether not realism.

It seems that the very term "socialist realism" contains an insoluble contradiction. A socialist, i.e. a purposeful, a religious, art cannot be produced with the literary method of the nineteenth century called "realism." And a really faithful representation of life cannot be achieved in a language based on teleological concepts. If socialist realism really wants to rise to the level of the great world cultures and produce its *Communiad,* there is only one way to do it. It must give up the "realism," renounce the sorry and fruitless attempts to write a socialist *Anna Karenina* or a socialist *Cherry Orchard.* When it abandons its effort to achieve verisimilitude, it will be able to express the grand and implausible sense of our era.

Unfortunately, this is unlikely to happen. The events of the last few years are dragging our art on a road of half-measures and half-truths. The death of Stalin inflicted an irreparable loss upon our religiously esthetic system; it cannot be resuscitated through the now revived cult of Lenin. Lenin is too much like an ordinary man and his image is too realistic: small, bald, dressed in civilian clothes. Stalin seemed to be specially made for the hyperbole that awaited him: mysterious, omniscient, all-powerful, he was the living monument of our era and needed only one quality to become God — immortality.

Ah, if only we had been intelligent enough to surround his death with miracles! We could have announced on the radio that he did not die but had risen to Heaven, from where he continued to watch us, in silence, no words emerging from beneath the mystic moustache. His relics would have cured men struck by paralysis or possessed by demons. And children, before going to bed, would have kneeled by the window and addressed their prayers to the cold and shining stars of the Celestial Kremlin.

But we did not listen to the voice of our conscience. Instead of intoning devout prayers, we set about dethroning the "cult of personality" that we ourselves had created. We thus blew up the foundations of that classicist colossus which, if we had waited but a little, would have joined the Pyramid of Cheops and the Apollo of Belvedere in the treasury of world art.

The strength of a theological system resides in its constancy, harmony, and order. Once we admit that God carelessly sinned with Eve and, becoming jealous of Adam, sent him off to labor at land reclamation, the whole concept of the Creation falls apart, and it is impossible to restore the faith.

After the death of Stalin we entered upon a period of destruction and reevaluation. It is a slow and inconsistent process, it lacks perspectives, and the inertia of both past and future lie heavy on it. Today's children will scarcely be able to produce a new God, capable of inspiring humanity into the next historical cycle. Maybe He will have to be supplemented by other stakes of the Inquisition, by further "personality cults," and by new terrestrial labors, so that after many centuries a new Purpose will rise above the world. But today no one yet knows its name.

And meanwhile our art is marking time between an insufficient realism and an insufficient classicism. After the loss it suffered it is no longer able to fly towards the ideal and to sing the praises of our life in a sincere and high-flown style, presenting what should be as what is. In our works of glorification resound ever more openly the notes of baseness and hypocrisy. The most successful writers are those who can present our achievements as truthfully as possible and our failings as tactfully, delicately, and untruthfully as possible. This is what happened with Dudintsev's novel *Man Does Not Live by Bread Alone,* which stirred up a lot of noise and was publicly anathemized for blackening our bright socialist reality.

But is the dream of the old, good, and honest "realism" the only heresy to which Russian literature is susceptible? Is it possible that all the lessons that we received were taught in vain and that, in the best of cases, all we wish is to return to the naturalist school and the critical tendency? Let us hope that this is not so and that our need for truth will not interfere with the work of thought and imagination.

Right now I put my hope in a phantasmagoric art, with hypotheses instead of a Purpose, an art in which the grotesque will replace realistic descriptions of ordinary life. Such an art corresponds best to the spirit of our time. May the fantastic imagery of Hoffmann and Dostoevsky, of Goya, Chagall, and Mayakovski (the most socialist realist of all), and of many other realists and nonrealists teach us how to be truthful with the aid of the absurd and the fantastic.

Having lost our faith, we have not lost our enthusiasm about the metamorphoses of God that take place before our very eyes, the miraculous transformations of His entrails and His cerebral convolutions. We don't know where to go; but, realizing that there is nothing to be done about it, we start to think, to set riddles, to make assumptions. We may thus invent something marvelous? Perhaps; but it will no longer be socialist realism.

1960
*Translated from the Russian by* GEORGE DENNIS

*The preceding essay, one of the major intellectual documents of the twentieth century, was written by the distinguished Russian critic and novelist whose work appeared in the West under the name of Abram Tertz and whose real name was later revealed to be Andrei Sinyavsky. "On Socialist Realism" appeared in several European journals and then received its first American publication in the pages of* Dissent *in 1960. Its author was sentenced in 1966 by a Russian court to seven years of hard labor — still another in the line of writers to suffer in behalf of freedom of opinion and speech. —Ed.*

# NEW STYLES IN "LEFTISM"
## IRVING HOWE

There is a new radical mood in limited sectors of American society: on the campus, in sections of the Civil Rights movement. The number of people who express this mood is not very large, but that it should appear at all is cause for encouragement and satisfaction. Yet there is a segment or fringe among the newly blossoming young radicals that causes one disturbance — and not simply because they have ideas different from persons like myself, who neither expect nor desire that younger generations of radicals should repeat our thoughts or our words. For this disturbing minority I have no simple name: sometimes it looks like kamikaze radicalism, sometimes like white Malcolmism, sometimes like black Maoism. But since none of these phrases will quite do, I have had to fall back upon the loose and not very accurate term, "New Leftists." Let me therefore stress as strongly as I can that I am not talking about all or the majority of the American young and not-so-young who have recently come to regard themselves as radicals. Much should be said about the positive aspects of youthful radicalism, as in part I have said in an essay, "Berkeley and Beyond" in the May 1, 1965, *New Republic*.

The form I have felt obliged to use here — a composite portrait of the sort of "New Leftist" who seems to me open to criticism — also creates some difficulties. It may seem to lump together problems, ideas, and moods that should be kept distinct. But my conviction is that this kind of "new leftism" is not a matter of organized political tendencies, at least not yet, and that there is no organization, certainly none of any importance, which expresses the kind of "New Leftism" I am here discussing. So I would say that if some young radicals read this text and feel that some of it is relevant to them but the rest is not, I will be delighted by such a response: the more any of them feels that parts of my portrait don't apply to him, the better it is. I do, however, believe that through this composite portrait I am touching upon an observable reality, a noticeable trend.

## Some Background Conditions

A

The society we live in fails to elicit the idealism of the more rebellious and generous young. Even among those who play the game and accept the social masks necessary for gaining success, there is a widespread disenchantment. Certainly there is very little ardor, very little of the joy that comes from a conviction that the values of a society are good, and that it is therefore good to live by them. The intelligent young know that if they keep out of trouble, accept academic drudgery, and preserve a respectable "image," they can hope for successful careers, even if not personal gratification. But the price they must pay for this choice is a considerable quantity of inner adaptation to the prevalent norms: for there is a limit to the social duplicity that anyone can sustain.

But the society not only undercuts the possibilities of constructive participation, it also makes very difficult a coherent and thought-out political opposition. The small minority that does rebel tends to adopt a stance that seems to be political, sometimes even ideological, but often turns out to be an effort to assert a personal style.

Personal style: that seems to me a key. Most of whatever rebellion we have had up to — and even into — the Civil Rights movement takes the form of a decision as to how to live individually within this society, rather than how to change it collectively. A recurrent stress among the young has been upon differentiation of speech, dress, and appearance, by means of which a small elite can signify its special status; or the stress has been upon moral self-regeneration, a kind of Emersonianism with shock treatment. All through the fifties and sixties disaffiliation was a central impulse, in the beatnik style or the more sedate Salinger way, but disaffiliation nevertheless, both as a signal of nausea and a tacit recognition of impotence.

I say, recognition of impotence, because movements that are powerful, groups that are self-confident, do not opt out of society: they live and work within society in order to transform it.

Now, to a notable extent, all this has changed since and through the Civil Rights movement — *but not changed as much as may seem*. Some of the people involved in that movement show an inclination to make of their radicalism not a politics of common action, which would require the inclusion of saints, sinners, and ordinary folk, but rather a gesture of moral rectitude. And the paradox is that they often sincerely regard themselves as committed to politics — but a politics that asserts so unmodulated and total a dismissal of society, while also departing from Marxist expectations of social revolution, that little is left to them but the glory or burden of maintaining a distinct personal style.

By contrast, the radicalism of an earlier generation, though it had numerous faults, had at least this advantage: it did not have to start *as if* from scratch, there were available movements, parties, agencies, and patterns of thought through which one could act. The radicals of the thirties certainly had their share of Bohemianism, but their politics were not nearly so interwoven with and dependent upon tokens of style as is today's radicalism.

The great value of the present rebelliousness is that it requires a personal decision, not merely as to what one shall do but also as to what one shall be. It requires authenticity, a challenge to the self, or, as some young people like to say, an "existential" decision. And it makes more difficult the moral double-bookkeeping of the thirties, whereby in the name of a sanctified movement or unquestioned ideology, scoundrels and fools could be exalted as "leaders" and detestable conduct exonerated.

This is a real and very impressive strength, but with it there goes a significant weakness: the lack of clear-cut ideas, sometimes even a feeling that it is wrong — or even "middle class" — to think systematically, and as a corollary, the absence of a social channel or agency through which to act. At first it seemed as if the Civil Rights movement would provide such a channel; and no one of moral awareness can fail to be profoundly moved by the outpouring of idealism and the readiness to face danger which characterizes the vanguard of this movement. Yet at a certain point it turns out that the Civil Rights movement, through the intensity of its work, seems to dramatize . . . its own insufficiency. Indeed, it acts as a training school for experienced, gifted, courageous people who have learned how to lead, how to sacrifice, how to work, but have no place in which to enlarge upon their gifts. There may in time appear a new kind of "dropout" — the "dropout" trained by and profoundly attached to the Civil Rights movement who yet feels that it does not, and by its very nature cannot, come to grips with the central problems of modern society; the "dropout" who has been trained to the fine edge of frustration and despair.

The more shapeless, the more promiscuously absorptive, the more psychologically and morally slack the society becomes, the more most candidates for rebellion seek out extreme postures which will enable them to "act out" their distance from a society that seems intent upon a maliciously benevolent assimilation; extreme postures which will yield security, perhaps a sense of consecration, in loneliness; extreme postures which will safeguard them from the allure of everything they reject. Between the act of rebellion and the society against which it is directed, there remain, however, deeper ties than is commonly recognized. To which we shall return.

B

These problems are exacerbated by an educational system that often seems inherently schizoid. It appeals to the life of the mind, yet justifies that appeal through crass utilitarianism. It invokes the traditions of freedom, yet processes students to bureaucratic cut. It speaks for the spirit, yet increasingly becomes an appendage of a spirit-squashing system.

C

The "New Leftism" appears at a moment when the intellectual and academic worlds — and not they alone — are experiencing an intense and largely justifiable revulsion against the immediate American past. Many people are sick unto death of the whole structure of feeling — that mixture of chauvinism, hysteria, and demagogy — which was created during the Cold War years. Like children subjected to forced feeding, they regurgitate almost automatically. Their response is an inevitable consequence of overorganizing the propaganda resources of a modern state; exactly the same sort of nausea exists among the young in the Communist world.

Unfortunately, revulsion seldom encourages nuances of thought or precise discriminations of politics. You cannot stand the deceits of official anti-Communism? Then respond with a rejection equally blatant. You have been raised to give credit to every American power move, no matter how reactionary or cynical? Then respond by castigating everything American. You are weary of Sidney Hook's messages in *The New York Times Magazine?* Then respond as if the talk about Communist totalitarianism were simply irrelevant or a bogey to frighten infants.

Yet we should be clear in our minds that such a response is not at all the same as a commitment to Communism, even though it may lend itself to obvious exploitation. It is rather a spewing-out of distasteful matter — in the course of which other values, such as the possibility of learning from the traumas and tragedies of recent history, may also be spewed out.

D

Generational clashes are recurrent in our society, perhaps in any society. But the present rupture between the young and their elders seems especially deep. This is a social phenomenon that goes beyond our immediate subject, indeed, it cuts through the whole of society; what it signifies is the society's failure to transmit with sufficient force its values to the young, or perhaps more accurately, that the best of the young take the proclaimed values of their elders with a seriousness which leads them to be appalled by their violation in practice.

In rejecting the older generations, however, the young sometimes betray the conditioning mark of the very American culture they are so quick to denounce: for ours is a culture that celebrates youthfulness as if it were a moral good in its own right. Like the regular Americans they wish so hard not to be, yet, through wishing, so very much are, they believe that the past is mere dust and ashes and that they can start afresh, immaculately.

There are, in addition, a few facts to be noted concerning the relationship between the radical young and those few older people who have remained radicals:

> 1) A generation is missing in the life of American radicalism, the generation that would now be in its mid-thirties, the generation that did not show up. The result is an inordinate difficulty in communication between the young radicals and those unfortunate enough to have reached — or, God help us, even gone beyond — the age of forty. Here, of course, *our* failure is very much in evidence too: a failure that should prompt us to speak with modesty, simply as people who have tried, and in their trying perhaps have learned something.
> 2) To the younger radicals it seems clear that a good many of the radicals of the thirties have grown tired, or dropped out, or in some instances, sold out. They encounter teachers who, on ceremonial occasions, like to proclaim old socialist affiliations, but who really have little or no sympathy with any kind of rebelliousness today. They are quick — and quite right — to sense that announcements of old YPSL ties can serve as a self-protective nostalgia or even as a cloak for acquiescence in the status quo. But it must also be said that there is a tendency among the "New Leftists" toward much too quick a dismissal of those who may disagree with them — they are a little too fast on the draw with such terms as "fink" and "establishment."

All this may describe the conditions under which the new political outlook appears, but it does not yet tell us anything about the specific culture, so to say, in which it thrives. Let me therefore indicate some of the political and intellectual influences acting upon the "New Leftism," by setting up two very rough categories:

## Ideologues and Desperadoes

### IDEOLOGUES, WHITE

The disintegration of American radicalism these last few decades left a good many ideologues emotionally unemployed: people accustomed to grand theorizing who have had their theories shot out from under them; people still looking for some belated evidence that they were "right" all along; people with unexpended social energy and idealism of a sort, who desperately needed new arenas in which to function.

1) *The Remains of Stalinism.* The American Communist Party was broken first by McCarthyite and government persecution, and second by an inner crisis following Khrushchev's revelations and the Hungarian revolution. Those who left out of disillusionment were heartsick people, their convictions and sometimes their lives shattered. But those who left the Party or its supporting organizations because they feared government attack were often people who kept, semi-privately, their earlier convictions. Many of them had a good deal of political experience; some remained significantly placed in the network of what might be called conscience-organizations. Naturally enough, they continued to keep in touch with one another, forming a kind of reserve apparatus based on common opinions, feelings, memories. As soon as some ferment began a few years ago in the Civil Rights movement and the peace groups, these people were present, ready, and eager; they needed no directives from the CP to which, in any case, they no longer (or may never have) belonged; they were quite capable of working on their own *as if they were working together,* through a variety of groups and periodicals like *The National Guardian.* Organizational Stalinism declined, but a good part of its heritage remained: people who could offer political advice, raise money, write leaflets, sit patiently at meetings, put up in a pleasant New York apartment visitors from a distant state, who, by chance, had been recommended by an old friend.

2) *True Believers.* On the far Left there remains a scatter of groups still convinced that Marxism-Leninism, in one or another version, is "correct." What has failed them, however, is the historical motor provided by Marxist theory: the proletariat, which has not shown the "revolutionary potential" or fulfilled the "historical mission" to which it was assigned. Though the veteran Marxists cannot, for fear of shattering their whole structure of belief, give up the *idea* of the proletariat, they can hardly act, day by day, as if the American working class were indeed

satisfying Marxist expectations or were the actual center of revolutionary ferment. Thus, in somewhat schizoid fashion, they have clung to their traditional faith in the proletariat as the revolutionary class, while in practice searching for a new embodiment of it which might provide the social energy they desire. And in the Negro movement they seem to have found it.

That this movement, with great creative flair, has worked out an indigenous strategy of its own; that it has developed nonviolent resistance into an enormously powerful weapon; that the Negro clergy, in apparent disregard of Leninist formulas, plays a leading and often militant role — all this does not sit well with the old Marxists. They must therefore develop new theories, by means of which the Negroes become the vanguard of the working class or perhaps the "true" (not yet "bought-off") working class. And, clustering around the Negro movement, they contribute a mite of wisdom here and there: scoffing at nonviolence, employing the shibboleth of "militancy" as if it were a magical device for satisfying the needs of the Negro poor, etc. They are experienced in "deepening the struggle," usually other people's struggles: which means to scorn the leadership of Dr. King without considering that the "revolutionary" course they propose for the Negro movement could, if adopted, lead it into a *cul de sac* of isolation, exhaustion, and heroic blood. Understandably, they find allies in Negro nationalists who want not so much to deepen as to divert the struggle, and among young militants who dislike the idea that Negroes might, if successful in their struggle, come to share some of the American affluence and thus become "middle class."

3) *Authoritarian Leftists.* In figures like Isaac Deutscher and Paul Sweezey we find the true intellectual progenitors of at least part of the "New Leftism"; the influence they exert has been indirect, since they are not involved in immediate struggles, but it has nevertheless been there.

Sweezey's *Monthly Review* is the main spokesman in this country for the view that authoritarianism is inherent or necessary in the so-called socialist countries; that what makes them "socialist" is simply the nationalization of the means of production; that democracy, while perhaps desirable in some long-range calculation, is not crucial for judging the socialist character of a society; that the claim that workers must be in a position to exercise political power if the state can in any sense be called "theirs," is a utopian fallacy. At times this technological determinism, put to the service of brutal dictatorship, has been given a more subtle reading by Sweezey: namely, that when the conditions supposedly causing the Communist dictatorship — economic backwardness and international insecurity — have been overcome, the Soviet regime would in some unspecified way democratize itself. In November, 1957, after the Khrushchev revelations, *Monthly Review* printed a notably frank editorial:

The conditions which produced the [Soviet] dictatorship have been overcome. . . . Our theory is being put to the crucial test of practice. And so far — let us face it frankly — there is precious little evidence to confirm it. In all that has happened since Stalin's death we can find nothing to indicate that the Communist Party or any of its competing factions, has changed in the slightest degree its view of the proper relation between the people and their leadership . . . there is apparently no thought that the Soviet people will ever grow up enough to decide for itself who knows best and hence who should make and administer the policies which determine its fate.

And finally from Sweezey: "Forty years is too long for a dictatorship to remain temporary" — surely the understatement of the Christian Era!

One might suppose that if "our theory is being put to the crucial test" and there "is precious little evidence to confirm it," honest men would proceed to look for another theory, provided, that is, they continued to believe that freedom is desirable.

Eight years have passed since the above passage appeared in *Monthly Review,* the "precious little evidence" remains precious little, and Sweezey, once apparently dismayed over the lack of democracy in Russia, has not moved to Titoism or "revisionism." No, he has moved toward Maoist China, where presumably one does not have to worry about "the proper relation between the people and their leadership. . . ." Writing in December, 1964, the *MR* editors declared with satisfaction that "there could be no question of the moral ascendancy of Peking over Moscow in the underdeveloped world." They agreed with the Chinese that Khrushchev's fall was "a good thing" and they wrote further:

The Chinese possession of a nuclear potential does not increase the danger of nuclear war. Quite the contrary. The Chinese have solemnly pledged never to be the first to use nuclear weapons . . . and their revolutionary record of devotion to the cause of socialism and progress entitles them to full trust and confidence.

The logic is clear: begin with theoretical inquiry and concern over the perpetuation of dictatorship in Russia and end with "full trust and confidence" in China, where the dictatorship is more severe.

There is an aphorism by a recent Polish writer: "The dispensing of injustice is always in the right hands." And so is its defense.

IDEOLOGUES, NEGRO

1) *Black nationalism.* Here is a creed that speaks or appears to speak totally against compromise, against negotiating with "the white power structure," against the falsities of white liberals, indeed, against anything but an indulgence of verbal violence. Shortly before his tragic murder Malcolm X spoke at a Trotskyist-sponsored meeting, and listen-

ing to him I felt, as did others, that he was in a state of internal struggle, reaching out for an ideology he did not yet have. For the Negroes in his audience he offered the relief of articulating subterranean feelings of hatred, contempt, defiance, feelings that did not have to be held in check because there was a tacit compact that the talk about violence would remain talk. Malcolm declared that he would go, not unarmed, to Mississippi, *if* the Negroes there would ask him to come: a condition that could only leave him safely North, since the last thing the Negroes of Mississippi needed or wanted was Malcolm's military aid. For both the Negroes and whites in the audience there was an apparent feeling that Malcolm and Malcolm alone among the Negro spokesmen was authentic because . . . well, because finally he spoke for nothing but his rage, for no proposal, no plan, no program, just a sheer outpouring of anger and pain. And that they could understand. The formidable sterility of his speech, so impressive in its relation to a deep personal suffering, touched something in their hearts. For Malcolm, intransigent in words and nihilistic in reality, never invoked the possibility or temptations of immediate struggle; he never posed the problems, confusions and risks of maneuver, compromise, retreat. Brilliantly Malcolm spoke for a rejection so complete it transformed him into an apolitical spectator, or in the language his admirers are more inclined to use than I am, a pure "cop-out."

2) *Caricature.* If, nevertheless, there was something about Malcolm which commands our respect, that is because we know his life-struggle, his rise from the depths, his conquest of thought and speech. LeRoi Jones, by contrast, stands as a burlesque double of whatever is significant in Malcolm.

In his success as both a New School lecturer and prophet of "guerrilla warfare" in the U.S.; in his badgering of white liberal audiences; in his orgies of verbal violence committed, to be sure, not in Selma, Alabama, but Sheridan Square, New York; in his fantasies of an international race war in which the whites will be slaughtered, Jones speaks for a contemporary sensibility. But he speaks for it in a special way: as a distinctively American success, the pop-art guerrilla warrior.

He speaks at that center of revolutionary upsurge, the Village Vanguard. He explains that the murder of Negroes in the South does not arouse the kind of horror and indignation that the murder of white civil rights workers does. *He is absolutely right,* the point cannot be made too often. But Jones cannot stop there: it would be too sensible, too humane, and it would not yield pages in the *Village Voice.* Instead, responding to a question, "What about Goodman and Schwerner, the two white boys killed in Mississippi, don't you care about them?" Jones continues, as quoted in the *Voice:*

> "Absolutely not," rapped out Jones. "Those boys were just artifacts, artifacts, man. They weren't real. If they want to assuage their leaking

consciences, that's their business I won't mourn for them. I have my own dead to mourn for."

Is this not exactly the attitude Jones had a moment earlier condemned in regard to killings in the South, but the same attitude in reverse? And is it really impossible for the human heart to mourn for *both* Negro and white victims? Not, to be sure, for ordinary whites, since they, we all know, are "white devils"; but at least for those who have given their lives in the struggle?

3) *Desperadoes, white.* In effect, I have already described this group, so let me here confine myself to a few remarks about one of its central battle-cries, "alienation."

The trouble with the current use of alienation as a mode of social analysis is that it explains almost everything, and thereby almost nothing. The term has become impossibly loose (like those other handy tags, "the Establishment" and "the Power Structure"). As used by Marx, alienation had a rather precise reference: it pointed to the condition of the worker in the capitalist productive process, a condition in which "the worker's deed becomes an alien power . . . forcing him to develop some specialized dexterity at the cost of a world of productive impulses." This kind of analysis focuses upon the place of the proletarian within the social structure, and not upon the sediment of malaise among those outside it.

Since Marx wrote, the term has acquired an impossible load of signification. During most of the bourgeois era, the European intellectuals grew increasingly estranged from the social community because the very ideals that had animated the bourgeois revolution were now being violated by bourgeois society; their "alienation" was prompted not by Bohemian willfulness but by a loyalty to Liberty, Fraternity, Equality, or to an induced vision of pre-industrial society which, by a twist of history, came pretty much to resemble Liberty, Fraternity, Equality. Just as it was the triumph of capitalism which largely caused this sense of estrangement, so it was the expansion of capitalism which allowed the intellectuals enough freedom to release it. During the greater part of the bourgeois era, intellectuals preferred alienation from the community to alienation from themselves. Precisely this choice made possible their boldness and strength, precisely this "lack of roots" gave them their speculative power.

By now the term "alienation" frequently carries with it a curious reversal of moral and emotional stress. For where intellectuals had once used it as a banner of pride and self-assertion, today it tends to become a complaint, a token of self-pity, a rationale for a degree of estrangement from the society which connotes not an active rebellion against — nor even any active relation to — it, but rather a justification for marginality and withdrawal.

Somewhere amid the current talk about "alienation" an important reality *is* being touched upon or pointed to. There *is,* in our society, a profound estrangement from the sources of selfhood, the possibilities of human growth and social cohesion. But simply to proclaim this estrangement can be a way of preserving it. Alienation is not some metaphysical equivalent of the bubonic plague which constitutes an irrevocable doom; it is the powerlessness deriving from human failure to act. It is neither a substitute for thought, nor a dissolvent of human will, not even a roadblock in the way of useful work. To enter into the society which in part causes this estrangement and by establishing bonds with other men to transform the society, is one way of partially overcoming alienation. Each time the Civil Rights movement brings previously mute Negroes into active political life, each time a trade union extends its power of decision within a factory, the boundaries of alienation are shrunk.

Meanwhile, there is truth in Harold Rosenberg's remark that:

> The sentiment of diminution of personality ["alienation"] is an historical hypothesis upon which writers have constructed a set of literary conventions by this time richly equipped with theatrical machinery and symbolic allusions. . . . By all evidence, the hollow-man tradition has completely captured our "serious" prose [and some of our serious youth]. . . . Once vanguardist, this tradition . . . has lately come to dominate popular literature and feeling. The individual's emptiness and inability to act have become an irrefrangible cliché, untiringly supported by an immense phalanx of latecomers to modernism. In this manifestation, the notion of the void has lost its critical edge and is thoroughly reactionary.

4) *Desperadoes, Negro.* A new kind of young Negro militant has appeared in the last few years, and he is a figure far more authentic and impressive than any of those I have thus far mentioned. He is fed up with white promises. He is proud to be estranged from white society. He has strong, if vague, "nationalist" inclinations. He is desperate — impatient with the tactics of gradualism, nonviolence, and passive resistance. He sees few, if any, allies upon whom he can count; few, if any, positive forces in society that might stir people into action. In effect, he decides that he must "go it alone," scornful of the white liberal and labor groups, as well as of those Negro leaders who choose to work with them. He seeks to substitute for a stagnant history his own desire and sacrifice.

Let me suggest a very limited comparison. This kind of young Negro militant, though not of course interested in any kind of individual terrorism, acts out of social motives somewhat like those of the late nineteenth-century Russian terrorists, who also tried to substitute their intransigent will for the sluggishness of history. And the consequences may be similar: the best cadres exhausted in isolation and defeat.

Such a response may well be the inevitable result of an abrupt and painful coming-to-awareness on the part of young Negro militants who had previously suppressed their suffering simply in order to survive but now feel somewhat freer to release it. Their devotion is beyond doubt, as their heroism is beyond praise; yet what I'm here tempted to call kamikaze radicalism, or what Bayard Rustin calls the "no win" outlook, can become self-defeating in political life.

## The "New Leftist"—A Sketch

We can now venture a portrait of the "New Leftist," not as one or another individual but as a composite type — with all the qualifications I stated at the outset.

### CULTURAL STYLE

The "New Leftist" appears, at times, as a figure embodying a style of speech, dress, work, and culture. Often, especially if white, the son of the middle class — and sometimes the son of middle-class parents nursing radical memories — he asserts his rebellion against the deceit and hollowness of American society. Very good; there is plenty to rebel against. But in the course of his rebellion he tends to reject not merely the middle-class ethos but a good many other things he too hastily associates with it: the intellectual heritage of the West, the tradition of liberalism at its most serious, the commitment to democracy as an indispensable part of civilized life. He tends to think of style as the very substance of his revolt, and while he may, on one side of himself, engage in valuable activities in behalf of civil rights, student freedom, etc., he nevertheless tacitly accepts the "givenness" of American society, has little hope or expectation of changing it, and thereby, in effect, settles for a mode of personal differentiation.

Primarily that means the wish to shock, the wish to assault the sensibilities of a world he cannot overcome. If he cannot change it, then at least he can outrage it. He searches in the limited repertoire of sensation and shock: for sick comics who will say "fuck" in nightclubs; for drugs that will vault him beyond the perimeters of the suburbs; for varieties, perversities, and publicities of sex so as perhaps to create an inner, private revolution that will accompany — or replace? — the outer, public revolution.

But the "New Leftist" is frequently trapped in a symbiotic relationship with the very middle class he rejects, dependent upon it for his self-definition: quite as the professional anti-Communist of a few years ago was caught up with the Communist Party which, had it not existed, he would have had to invent — as indeed at times he did invent. So that for all its humor and charm, the style of the "New Leftist" tends to become a rigid anti-style, dependent for its survival on the enemy it is supposed to panic. To *épater le bourgeois* — in this case, perhaps, to *épater le père* — is to acquiesce in a basic assumption of at least the more sophisticated segments of the middle class: that values can be inferred from, or are resident in, the externals of dress, appearance, furnishings, and hairdo's.

Shock as he will, disaffiliate as he may choose, the "New Leftist" discovers after a while that nothing has greatly changed. The relations of power remain as before, the Man still hovers over the scene, the "power structure" is unshaken. A few old ladies in California may grow indignant, a DA occasionally arrest someone, a *Village Voice* reporter arrange an interview; but surely that is all small change. And soon the "New Leftist" must recognize that even he has not been greatly transformed. For in his personal manner he is acting out the dilemmas of a utopian community, and just as Brook Farm had to remain subject to the laws of the market despite its internal ethic of cooperation, so must he remain subject to the impress of the dominant institutions despite his desire to be totally different.

Victimized by a lack of the historical sense, the "New Leftist" does not realize that the desire to shock and create sensations has itself a long and largely disastrous history. The notion, as Meyer Schapiro has remarked, that opium is the revolution of the people has been luring powerless intellectuals and semi-intellectuals for a long time. But the damnable thing is that for an almost equally long time the more sophisticated and urban sectors of the middle class have refused to be shocked. They know the repertoire of sensationalism quite as well as the "New Leftist"; and if he is to succeed in shocking them or even himself, he must keep raising the ante. The very rebel who believes himself devoted to an absolute of freedom and looks with contempt upon any mode of compromise is thereby caught up in the compulsiveness of his escalation: a compulsiveness inherently bad enough, but rendered still more difficult, and sometimes pathetic, by the fact that, alas, each year he gets a year older.

Let me amend this somewhat. To say that the urban middle class has become jaded and can no longer be shocked, is not quite correct. No; a kind of complicity is set up between the outraged and/or amused urban middle class and the rebels of sensation. Their mutual dependency requires that each shock, to provide the pleasures of indignation, must be a little stronger (like a larger dose . . .) than the previous one. For the point is not so much that the urban middle class can no longer be shocked as that it positively yearns for and comes to depend upon the titillating assaults of its cultural enemies. So that when a new sensation (be it literary violence, sexual fashion, intellectual outrage, high-toned pornography, or sadistic denunciation) is provided by the shock troops of culture, the sophisticated middle class responds with outrage, resistance, and anger — *for upon these initial responses its pleasure depends.*

But then, a little later, it rolls over like a happy puppy on its back, moaning "Oh baby, *épatez* me again, harder this time, tell me what a sterile impotent louse I am and how you are so tough and virile, how you're planning to murder me, *épatez* me again, baby. . . ."

Thus a fire-eating character like LeRoi Jones becomes an adjunct of middle-class amusement and, to take an enormous leap upward in talent and seriousness, a writer like Norman Mailer becomes enmeshed in his public conduct with popular journalism and publicity.

The whole problem was anticipated many years ago by Trotsky when, writing about the Russian poet Yessenin, he remarked that the poet thought to frighten the bourgeoisie by making scenes but as it turned out, the bourgeoisie was delighted, it adored scenes.

One thing alone will not delight the bourgeoisie: a decrease in income, a loss in social power, a threat to its property.

There is another sense in which cultural style dominates the behavior of the "New Leftists." Some of them display a tendency to regard political — and perhaps all of — life as a Hemingwayesque contest in courage and rectitude. People are constantly being tested for endurance, bravery, resistance to temptation, and if found inadequate, are denounced for having "copped out." Personal endurance thus becomes the substance of, and perhaps even a replacement for, political ideas.

Now this can be a valid and serious way of looking at things, especially in extreme situations: which is, of course, what Hemingway had in mind. Among Civil Rights workers in the deep South such a vision of life reflects the ordeal they must constantly face; they *are* under extreme pressure and their courage *is* constantly being tested. Yet their situation cannot be taken as a model for the political life of the country as a whole. If one wants to do more than create a tiny group of the heroic, the tested, and the martyred, their style of work will not suffice. If one wants to build a movement in which not everyone need give "the whole of their lives," then the suspicion and hostility such an outlook is bound to engender toward the somewhat less active and somewhat less committed can only be damaging. For in effect, if not intent, it is a strategy of exclusion, leaving no place for anyone but the vanguard of the scarred.

It is, at times, a strategy of exclusion in a still more troubling sense: it reduces differences of opinion to grades of moral rectitude. If, for example, you think Martin Luther King or Bayard Rustin was wrong in regard to certain tactical matters; if you disagree with what Rustin proposed at the Democratic national convention and what King did in Selma, then you call into question their loyalty and commitment: you may even charge them with "copping out" or "fooling with the power structure." This approach makes it impossible to build a movement and, in the long run, even to maintain a sect.

DOMESTIC POLITICS

A division of opinion, still incipient and confused, has appeared among people in the radical, student, and Civil Rights movements. There are those who, in effect, want to "go it alone," refusing to have anything to do with "the Establishment," and those who look forward to creating a loose coalition of Negro, labor, liberal, and church groups in order to stretch the limits of the welfare state. To an inexperienced eye, this may suggest a division between the more and less radical; but it is not. Radicalism is not a quantity.

The "go it alone" tendency in the Civil Rights movement starts from a recognition that the obstacles to success are enormous. It sees no forces within the society that could provide a new social dynamic. It shares with the liberals the questionable assumption that everyone in our society, except perhaps the bottom-dog poor, is bound to it by ties of material satisfaction. The labor movement is mired in its own fat; the ministers are Sunday allies; the liberals are two-faced, unreliable, perhaps cowards. What remains is a strategy of lonely assault, which must necessarily lead to shock tactics and desperation.

For if the above estimate of the American situation is valid, if there is so little possibility of a new social dynamism arising from or within its major social segments, then the outlook of the Black Muslims has to be acknowledged as persuasive. For obviously an estimate which sees major reforms as unlikely makes a traditional revolutionary overthrow seem still more unlikely; and the talk among irresponsibles about "guerrilla warfare in America" is mere self-indulgence, since guerrilla warfare can succeed only when a large portion or a majority of the population is profoundly disaffected, something certainly not true in the United States. Consequently — the logic of this argument moves inexorably — there is nothing left for American Negroes but the separatism of the Muslims.

Unless, of course, one turns to the tactic of shock, inducing such misadventures as the stall-ins at last year's World's Fair or the Triboro Bridge fiasco. Neither of these demonstrations had a precise objective, neither had any way of measuring achievement, accumulating allies, registering victory. Such methods, born of desperation, could only cut off the dedicated minority of Civil Rights activists from their white allies and much more important, from the mass of Negroes.

Now it is not our business to give advice to the Civil Rights movement on tactical issues or to rush into taking positions about its inner disputes. It is not the business of anyone except those directly engaged. But about some larger aspects of its problem we can speak.

One issue has been posed simply but conveniently by a *Village Voice* reporter, Jack Newfield, who writes that Dr. King's "basic goal is integration, and SNCC's is a revolution." Earlier Newfield had described this revolution as being not against capitalist society but "against Brotherhood Weeks, factories called colleges, desperation called success, and sex twice a week."

> *An aside:* I think it is a totalitarian invasion of privacy for a political or social movement to concern itself with the frequency its adherents or anyone else engage in sexual relations. For the right to make love to whomever you wish, of whatever sex you choose, in whatever posture you prefer, I will fight . . . well, almost . . . to the death; but beyond that, the frequency of your encounters, like the quality of your orgasms, is no one's business but your own.

What the people who talk about integration vs. revolution don't see is that to achieve integration, even in the limited terms presumably favored by Dr. King, would indeed *be* a revolution, greater in consequence and impact than that effected by the rise of industrial unionism in the thirties.

But for the sake of argument let us accept the issue as "integration vs. revolution." Naturally enough — it's an old habit — we then opt for revolution; there remains only the detail of who is going to make it.

Clearly, the vast majority of whites are in the grip of the Establishment. The liberals? Establishment. The churches? Establishment. The unions? Establishment. Intellectuals? Establishment.

But not only the whites, also the Negroes. Wilkins, Young, Powell, King, Farmer? The black Establishment. Rustin? He sold out to it.

Where then does that leave us? Well, some students . . . but can we be so sure of *them?* May they not in time decide to go back to graduate school, perhaps after discovering that the people, in refusing to heed the revolutionary missions from the campus, are a rather hopeless quantity? What is left, then, is a handful . . . and where that handful must end is in despair, exhaustion, burning themselves out in the all-too-characteristic rhythm of American radicalism, which too often has tried to compensate for its powerlessness in reality by ferocity in words.

At this point I hear a voice crying out: "No, not just a vanguard of the desperate! We are going to organize the poor, the millions beneath the floor of society, those who have been mute and unrepresented for too long . . . and it is they who will form the basis of a new movement, beyond the pale of Establishment politics."

Good. The poor need to be organized, and more power to those who try. Every such effort, big or small, deserves the approval and support of socialists and liberals. But some problems remain. I leave aside the fact that twentieth-century history indicates a high rate of failure in previous efforts of this kind; that the unstructured, atomized, and often demoralized "underclass" has been the most resistant to organization. After all, history need not repeat itself, and perhaps this time the effort will succeed. No, the questions I would raise have to do not with failure but success.

Imagine a campaign to organize the poor in a large city, undertaken by young people who will have no truck with the Establishment. Through hard work and devotion, they build up a group of, let's say, 150 people in a slum of mixed racial composition — a notable achievement. What happens next? The municipal "power structure" begins to pay some attention and decides either to smash the group as a dangerous nuisance or to lure away some of its leading members. If the local organization of the poor must now face attack, it would seem to have no choice but quickly to find some allies — in the unions, among churchmen, perhaps even in the American Jewish Congress, "establishmentarian" as all of these may seem. Suppose, however, the "power structure" decides to offer various inducements — jobs, improved housing — to some of the Negro members, and various other organizations, like the reform wing of the Democrats and certain trade unions, also enter the picture. What will the uncompromising, anti-Establishment leaders of the poor do now? Does not the reality of the situation require them to enter negotiations, formally or informally, and thereby become involved in the socio-economic life of the city? Can they remain exempt from it? And if so, how long do you suppose their followers will remain with them? For that matter, why should they? The goods and services that, with enough pressure, the "power structure" can be made to provide, the poor need, want, and deserve. Can one seriously suppose they will be exempt from such "temptations"? There is only one way to be certain the poor will remain beyond the temptations of our society, and that is to keep them hopelessly poor.

The idea of coalition or realignment politics as advanced by socialists is not a rigid formula, or a plot to deliver our souls into the hands of the Establishment. It is meant as a strategy for energizing all those forces within the society that want to move forward toward an extension of the welfare state. In some places, such a loose coalition might take the form of politics outside the established institutions, like the Freedom Democratic party of Mississippi — though that movement, if it is to succeed, must begin to find allies within the white community. In other places, as in Texas, there is a coalition of labor, liberal, intellectual, and minority groups (Negro, Mexican) within the Democratic Party — and by all accounts a pretty good coalition. Can one say, as if all wisdom were bunched into our fists, that such a development should not be supported simply because it grows up within the framework of a major party?

If we are serious in our wish to affect American political life, we must learn to see the reality as it is. We have to seek out and prod the forces that exist. And I think it is a gross error — the kind of deep-seated conservatism that often alloys ultra-radicalism — to say that everything in the major sectors of American society is static, sated, "Establishment." Who, twenty-five or thirty years ago, could have foreseen that Catholic priests and nuns would be marching into Montgomery? Who could have foreseen the more thoroughgoing ferment in the American churches of which this incident is merely a symptom? Instead of scoffing at such people as Civil Rights "tourists," we ought to be seeking them out and trying to get them to move a little further, up North too.

And a word about the labor movement. Its failures, ills, and decline have been documented in great detail by American socialists — perhaps because we ourselves have not quite understood what its nature and possibilities are, preferring instead to nag away when it did not conform to our preconceptions. Right now, to be sure, the unions look pretty sluggish and drab. Still, two leaders named David MacDonald and James Carey have just been toppled by membership votes (and when something like that happens to a trade union leader in Russia, China, Cuba, Algeria, or Zanzibar, please let me know).

Bayard Rustin says: "The labor movement, despite its obvious faults, has been the largest single organized force in this country pushing for progressive social legislation." That is true, but not enough. What seems the static quality of the trade unions may be a phase of rest between the enormous achievements of the past forty years and possible achievements of the future. If the Civil Rights movement succeeds, may it not also enter such a phase? And do you suppose that the struggles of only a few decades ago to organize unions were any the less difficult, bloody, and heroic than those in the South today? And if it's a revolution in the quality of American life that you want, then have not the industrial unions come closer to achieving that for millions of people than any other force in the country?

We are speaking here partly of speculations, partly of hopes. None of us has any certain answer or magic formula by which to overcome the painful isolation of the radical movement: if there were such a thing, someone would by now have discovered it. We are all groping to find a way out of our difficulties. I don't wish to draw a hard-and-fast line between "realigners" and "go-it-aloners." There is room for both disagreement and cooperation. You want to organize the poor? Splendid. We propose certain sorts of coalitions? An essential part of such a coalition ought to be drawn from the poor you propose to organize. And in turn, if you're to keep them organized, you will have to engage in coalitions. Right now — let's be candid — you don't have very many of the poor and we don't have much of a coalition. Disagreements of this kind are fraternal, and can be tested patiently in experience.

The true line of division between democratic socialists and Left authoritarians concerns not tactics, but basic commitments, values, the vision of what a good society should be. It concerns

## POLITICS AND FREEDOM

The "New Leftists" feel little attachment to Russia. Precisely, as it has turned away from the more extreme and terroristic version of totalitarianism, so have they begun to find it unsatisfactory as a model: too Victorian, even "bourgeois." Nor are they interested in distinguishing among kinds of anti-Communism, whether of the Right or Left.

When they turn to politics, they have little concern for precise or complex thought. (By contrast, the more reflective among the younger radicals, such as some leaders of Students for a Democratic Society, have made a serious effort to develop their intellectual and political views; they understand the sterility to which a mere "activism" can lead, in fact, the way it must sooner or later undermine the possibilities even for activity.) A few years ago the "New Leftists" were likely to be drawn to Communist China, which then seemed bolder than Khrushchev's Russia. But though the Mao regime has kept the loyalty of a small group of students, most of the "New Leftists" seem to find it too grim and repressive. They tend to look for their new heroes and models among the leaders of underdeveloped countries. Figures like Lumumba, Nasser, Sukarno, Babu, and above all Castro attract them, suggesting the possibility of a politics not yet bureaucratized and rationalized. But meanwhile they neglect to notice, or do not care, that totalitarian and authoritarian dictatorship can set in even before a society has become fully modernized. They have been drawn to charismatic figures like Lumumba and Castro out of distaste for the mania of industrial production which the Soviet Union shares with the United States; but they fail to see that such leaders of the underdeveloped countries, who in their eyes represent spontaneity and anarchic freedom, are themselves — perhaps unavoidably — infused with the same mania for industrial production.

Let me specify a few more of the characteristic attitudes among the "New Leftists":

1) *An extreme, sometimes unwarranted, hostility toward liberalism.* They see liberalism only in its current versions, institutional, corporate and debased; but avoiding history, they know very little about the elements of the liberal tradition which should remain valuable for any democratic socialist. For the "New Leftists," as I have here delimited them, liberalism means Clark Kerr, not John Dewey; Max Lerner, not John Stuart Mill; Pat Brown, not George Norris. And thereby they would cut off the resurgent American radicalism from what is, or should be, one of

its sustaining sources: the tradition that has yielded us a heritage of civil freedoms, disinterested speculation, humane tolerance.

2) *An impatience with the problems that concerned an older genera-tion of radicals.* Here the generational conflict breaks out with strong feelings on both sides, the older people feeling threatened in whatever they have been able to salvage from past experiences, the younger people feeling the need to shake off dogma and create their own terms of action.

Perhaps if we all try to restrain — not deny — our emotions, we can agree upon certain essentials. There are traditional radical topics which no one, except the historically minded, need trouble with. (Anyone who compares the files of radical journals of the thirties with those of *Dissent* this past decade can see for himself how large our own break from Marx-ist scholasticism and polemic has been.) To be unconcerned with the dispute in the late twenties over the Anglo-Russian Trade Union Com-mittee or the differences between Lenin and Luxemburg on the "national question" — well and good. These are hardly burning problems of the moment. But *some* of the issues hotly debated in the thirties do remain burning problems: in fact, it should be said for the anti-Stalinist Left of the past several decades that it anticipated, in its own somewhat con-stricted way, a number of the problems (especially, the nature of Stalin-ism) which have since been widely debated by political scientists, sociol-ogists, indeed, by all people concerned with politics. The nature of Stalinism and of post-Stalinist Communism is not an abstract or esoteric matter; the views one holds concerning these questions determine a large part of one's political conduct; and what is still more important, *they reflect one's fundamental moral values.*

No sensible radical over the age of thirty (something of a cut-off point, I'm told) wants young people merely to rehearse his ideas, or mimic his vocabulary, or (heaven forbid!) look back upon his dusty old articles. On the contrary, what we find disturbing in some of the "New Leftists" is that, while barely knowing it, they tend to repeat somewhat too casually the tags of the very past they believe themselves to be tran-scending. But we do insist that in regard to a few crucial issues — above all, those regarding totalitarian movements and societies, there should be no ambiguity, no evasiveness.

So that if some "New Leftists" say that all the older radicals are equally acceptable or equally distasteful or equally inconsequential in their eyes; if they see no significant difference between, say, Norman Thomas and Paul Sweezey such as would require them to regard Thomas as a comrade and Sweezey as an opponent — then the sad truth is that they have not at all left behind them the old disputes, but on the con-trary, are still completely in their grip, though perhaps without being quite aware of what is happening to them. The issue of totalitarianism is neither academic nor merely historical; no one can seriously engage in politics without clearly and publicly defining his attitude toward it. I deliberately say "attitude" rather than "analysis," for while there can be a great many legitimate differences of analytic stress and nuance among democratic socialists in discussing the totalitarian society, morally there should be only a candid and sustained opposition to it.

3) *A vicarious indulgence in violence, often merely theoretic and thereby all the more irresponsible.* Not being a pacifist, I believe there may be times when violence is unavoidable; being a man of the twentieth century, I believe that a recognition of its necessity must come only after the most prolonged consideration, as an utterly last resort. To "advise" the Negro movement to adopt a policy encouraging or sanctioning violence, to sneer at Martin Luther King for his principled refusal of violence, is to take upon oneself a heavy responsibility — and if, as usually happens, taken lightly, it becomes sheer irresponsibility.

It is to be insensitive to the fact that the nonviolent strategy has arisen from Negro experience. It is to ignore the notable achievements that strategy has already brought. It is to evade the hard truth expressed by the Reverend Abernathy: "The whites have the guns." And it is to dismiss the striking moral advantage that nonviolence has yielded the Negro movement, as well as the turmoil, anxiety, and pain — perhaps even fundamental reconsideration — it has caused among whites in the North and the South.

There are situations in which Negroes will choose to defend themselves by arms against terrorist assault, as in the Louisiana town where they have formed a club of "Elders" which patrols the streets peaceably but with the clear intent of retaliation in case of attack. The Negroes there seem to know what they are doing, and I would not in any way fault them. Yet as a matter of general policy and upon a nationwide level, the Negro movement has chosen nonviolence: rightly, wisely, and heroically.

There are "revolutionaries" who deride this choice. They show a greater interest in ideological preconceptions than in the experience and needs of a living movement; and sometimes they are profoundly irresponsible, in that their true interest is not in helping to reach the goals chosen by the American Negroes, but is rather a social conflagration which would satisfy their apocalyptic yearnings even if meanwhile the Negroes were drowned in blood. The immediate consequence of such talk is a withdrawal from the ongoing struggles. And another consequence is to manufacture a cult out of figures like Malcolm X, who neither led nor won nor taught, and Robert Williams, the Negro leader who declared for violence and ended not with the Negroes in Selma, or at their strike in the hospitals of Westchester County, or on the picket line before the Atlanta Scripto plant (places where the kind of coalition we desire between Negro and labor was being foreshadowed), but by delivering short-wave broadcasts from Cuba.

4) *An unconsidered enmity toward something vaguely called the Establishment.* As the term "Establishment" was first used in England, it had the value of describing — which is to say, delimiting — a precise social group; as it has come to be used in the United States, it tends to be a term of all-purpose put-down. In England it refers to a caste of intellectuals with an Oxbridge education, closely related in values to the ruling class, and setting the cultural standards which largely dominate both the London literary world and the two leading universities.

Is there an Establishment in this, or any cognate, sense in the United States? Perhaps. There may now be in the process of formation, for the first time, such an intellectual caste; but if so, precise discriminations of analysis and clear boundaries of specification would be required as to what it signifies and how it operates. As the term is currently employed, however, it is difficult to know who, besides those merrily using it as a thunderbolt of opprobrium, is *not* in the Establishment. And a reference that includes almost everyone tells us almost nothing.

5) *An equally unreflective belief in "the decline of the West"* — apparently without the knowledge that, more seriously held, this belief has itself been deeply ingrained in Western thought, frequently in the thought of reactionaries opposed to modern rationality, democracy, and sensibility.

The notion is so loose and baggy, it means little. Can it, however, be broken down? If war is a symptom of this decline, then it holds for the East as well. If totalitarianism is a sign, then it is not confined to the West. If economics is a criterion, then we must acknowledge, Marxist predictions aside, that there has been an astonishing recovery in Western Europe. If we turn to culture, then we must recognize that in the West there has just come to an end one of the greatest periods in human culture — that period of "modernism" represented by figures like Joyce, Stravinsky, Picasso. If improving the life of the workers is to count, then the West can say something in its own behalf. And if personal freedom matters, then, for all its grave imperfections, the West remains virtually alone as a place of hope. There remains, not least of all, the matter of racial prejudice, and here no judgment of the West can be too harsh — so long as we remember that even this blight is by no means confined to the West, and that the very judgments we make draw upon values nurtured by the West.

But is it not really childish to talk about "the West" as if it were some indivisible whole we must either accept or reject without amendment? There are innumerable strands in the Western tradition, and our task is to nourish those which encourage dignity and freedom. But to envisage some global apocalypse that will end in the destruction of the West is a sad fantasy, a token of surrender before the struggles of the moment.

6) *A crude, unqualified anti-Americanism, drawing from every possible source, even if one contradicts another: the aristocratic bias of Eliot and Ortega, Communist propaganda, the speculations of Tocqueville, the* ressentiment *of postwar Europe, etc.*

7) *An increasing identification with that sector of the "third world" in which "radical" nationalism and Communist authoritarianism merge.* Consider this remarkable fact: In the past decade there have occurred major changes in the Communist world, and many of the intellectuals in Russia and Eastern Europe have reexamined their assumptions, often coming to the conclusion, masked only by the need for caution, that democratic values are primary in any serious effort at socialist reconstruction. Yet at the very same time most of the "New Leftists" have identified not with the "revisionists" in Poland and Djilas in Yugoslavia — or even Tito. They identify with the harder, more violent, more dictatorial segments of the Communist world. And they carry this authoritarian bias into their consideration of the "third world," where they praise those rulers who choke off whatever weak impulses there may be toward democratic life.

About the problems of the underdeveloped countries, among the most thorny of our time, it is impossible even to begin to speak with any fullness here. Nor do I mean to suggest that an attack upon authoritarianism and a defense of democracy exhausts consideration of those problems; on the contrary, it is the merest beginning. But what matters in this context is not so much the problems themselves as the attitudes, reflecting a deeper political-moral bias, which the "New Leftists" take toward such countries.

> *A few remarks:* a) Between the suppression of democratic rights and the justification or excuse the "New Leftists" offer for such suppression there is often a very large distance, sometimes a complete lack of connection. Consider the case of Cuba. It may well be true that U.S. policy became unjustifiably hostile toward the Castro regime at an early point in its history; but how is this supposed to have occasioned, or how is it supposed to justify, the suppression of democratic rights (including, and especially, those of all other left-wing tendencies) in Cuba? The apologists for Castro have an obligation to show what I think cannot be shown: the alleged close causal relation between U.S. pressure and the destruction of freedom in Cuba. Frequently, behind such rationales there is a tacit assumption that in times of national stress a people can be rallied more effectively by a dictatorship than by a democratic regime. But this notion — it was used to justify the suppression of political freedoms during the early Bolshevik years — is at the very least

called into question by the experience of England and the U.S. during the Second World War. Furthermore, if Castro does indeed have the degree of mass support that his friends claim, one would think that the preservation of democratic liberties in Cuba would have been an enormously powerful symbol of self-confidence; would have won him greater support at home and certainly in other Latin American countries; and would have significantly disarmed his opponents in the United States.

b) We are all familiar with the "social context" argument: that for democracy to flourish there has first to be a certain level of economic development, a quantity of infrastructure, and a coherent national culture. As usually put forward in academic and certain authoritarian-Left circles, it is a crudely deterministic notion which I do not believe to be valid: for one thing, it fails to show how the suppression of even very limited political-social rights contributes, or is *in fact* caused by a wish, to solve these problems. (Who is prepared to maintain that Sukarno's suppression of the Indonesian socialists and other dissident parties helps solve that country's economic or growth problems?) But for the sake of argument let us accept a version of this theory: let us grant what is certainly a bit more plausible, that a full or stable democratic society cannot be established in a country ridden by economic primitivism, illiteracy, disease, cultural disunion, etc. The crucial question then becomes: can at least some measure of democratic rights be won or granted? — say, the right of workers to form unions or the right of dissidents within a single-party state to form factions and express their views? For if a richer socio-economic development is a prerequisite of democracy, it must also be remembered that such democratic rights, as they enable the emergence of autonomous social groups, are also needed for socio-economic development.

c) Let us go even further and grant, again for the sake of argument, that in some underdeveloped countries authoritarian regimes may be necessary for a time. But even if this is true, which I do not believe it is, then it must be acknowledged as an unpleasant necessity, a price we are paying for historical crimes and mistakes of the past. In that case, radicals can hardly find their models in, and should certainly not become an uncritical cheering squad for, authoritarian dictators whose presence is a supposed unavoidability.

The "New Leftists," searching for an ideology by which to rationalize their sentiments, can now find exactly what they need in a remarkable book recently translated from the French, *The Wretched of the Earth*. Its author, Frantz Fanon, is a Negro from Martinique who became active in the Algerian revolution. He articulates with notable power the views of those nationalist-revolutionaries in the underdeveloped countries who are contemptuous of their native bourgeois leadership, who see their revolution being pushed beyond national limits and into their own social structure, who do not wish to merge with or become subservient to the

Communists yet have no strong objection in principle to Communist methods and values.

Fanon tries to locate a new source of revolutionary energy: the peasants who, he says, "have nothing to lose and everything to gain." He deprecates the working class: in the Western countries it has been bought off, and in the underdeveloped nations it constitutes a tiny "aristocracy." What emerges is a curious version of Trotsky's theory of permanent revolution, concerning national revolts in the backward countries which, to fulfill themselves, must become social revolutions. But with one major difference: Fanon assigns to the peasants and the urban declassed poor the vanguard role Trotsky had assigned to the workers.

What however, has really happened in countries like Algeria? The peasantry contributes men and blood for an anti-colonial war. Once the war is won, it tends to disperse, relapsing into local interests and seeking individual small-scale ownership of the land. It is too poor, too weak, too diffuse to remain or become the leading social force in a newly liberated country. The bourgeoisie, what there was of it, having been shattered and the working class pushed aside, what remains? Primarily the party of nationalism, led by men who are dedicated, uprooted, semi-educated, and ruthless. The party rules — increasingly an independent force above the weakened classes.

But Fanon is not taken in by his own propaganda. He recognizes the dangers of a preening dictator and has harsh things to say against the Nkrumah type. He proposes, instead, that "the party should be the direct expression of the masses," and adds, "Only those underdeveloped countries led by revolutionary elites who have come up from the people can today *allow* the entry of the masses upon the scene of history." (Emphasis added.)

Fanon wants the masses to participate, yet throughout his book the single-party state remains an unquestioned assumption. But what if the masses do not wish to "participate"? And what if they are hostile to "the" — always "the!" — party? Participation without choice is a burlesque of democracy; indeed, it is an essential element of a totalitarian or authoritarian society, for it means that the masses act out a charade of involvement without the reality of decision.

The authoritarians find political tendencies and representative men with whom to identify in the Communist world; but so do we. We identify with the people who have died for freedom, like Imre Nagy, or who rot in prison, like Djilas. We identify with the "revisionists," those political *marranos* who, forced to employ Communist jargon, yet spoke out for a socialism democratic in character and distinct from both Communism and capitalism. As it happens, our friends in the Communist world are not in power; but since when has that mattered to socialists?

In 1957, at the height of the Polish ferment, the young philosopher Leszek Kolakowski wrote a brief article entitled "What Is Socialism?" It consisted of a series of epigrammatic sentences describing what socialism is not (at the moment perhaps the more immediate concern), but tacitly indicating as well what socialism should be. The article was banned by the Gomulka regime but copies reached Western periodicals. Here are a few sentences:

Socialism is not:

> A society in which a person who has committed a crime sits at home waiting for the police.
> A society in which one person is unhappy because he says what he thinks, and another happy because he does not say what is in his mind.
> A society in which a person lives better because he does not think at all.
> A state whose neighbors curse geography.
> A state which wants all its citizens to have the same opinions in philosophy, foreign policy, economics, literature, and ethics.
> A state whose government defines its citizens' rights, but whose citizens do not define the government's rights.
> A state in which there is private ownership of the means of production.
> A state which considers itself solidly socialist because it has liquidated private ownership of the means of production.
> A state which always knows the will of the people before it asks them.
> A state in which the philosophers and writers always say the same as the generals and ministers, but always after them.
> A state in which the returns of parliamentary elections are always predictable.
> A state which does not like to see its citizens read back numbers of newspapers.

These negatives imply a positive, and that positive is the greatest lesson of contemporary history: the unity of socialism and democracy. To preserve democracy as a political mode without extending it into every crevice of social and economic life is to make it increasingly sterile, formal, ceremonial. To nationalize an economy without enlarging democratic freedoms is to create a new kind of social exploitation. Radicals may properly and fraternally disagree about many other things; but upon this single axiom, this conviction wrung from the tragedy of our age, politics must rest.

1965

# THE PRIEST AND THE JESTER
## LESZEK KOLAKOWSKI

We have done all we could to keep alive in our minds the main problems that in the course of centuries have troubled theologians, although today we formulate them in a somewhat different way. Philosophy has never freed itself from the heritage of theology, which means that theological questions were only awkward attempts to solve riddles that are still haunting mankind.

Riddles? It may be that what is involved is not really a riddle but, frequently, a situation into which we read a riddle because the most self-evident facts appear unacceptable to us.

Nothing is as deeply rooted in man as the belief in a moral law of equalizing temperatures, that is, the belief that the world eventually will reach a state where our merits and rewards, our crimes and punishments are leveled out, where evil is avenged and goodness rewarded — in other words, a world in which human values attain their complete realization. Whatever happens, man ought to rejoice, because the rewards which await him in heaven are generous.

*From* The Modern Polish Mind *by Maria Kuncewicz. By permission of Little, Brown and Co. Copyright © 1962, by Little, Brown and Co. (Inc.)*

I

And thus, the first question which contemporary philosophy has inherited from the theological tradition is the problem of the possibility of eschatology itself. We pose it differently: can the human values we accept attain complete realization? Does history evolve in the direction of final equalization and justice? One ought not to wonder that we do pose such questions to ourselves. Reflection on history has its main *source* in our dissatisfaction with history's results; the most common *hope* of historiosophy is to bring into harmony the essence of man with his existence, that is, to create a situation in which the inalienable aspirations of human nature are fulfilled in reality. Because the attainment of such a state would put an end to dissatisfaction with the results of history, it might be said that historiosophy has adopted as the main object of its hope a situation which leads to its own extinction. At any rate, every optimistic historiosophy must inevitably, by its very nature, be a victim to suicidal tendencies.

It is not difficult to see that secular eschatology, that is, the belief in an eventual elimination of the disparity between human essence and human existence (the belief in the deification of man), naturally presupposes that "essence" is a value; that the realization of essence is desirable; and it relies on the wisdom of history to bring about this realization. Secular eschatology places its confidence in the final judgment of history. We do not laugh at it, for who does not defer to this belief? For instance, every time someone believes that the unhappiness and torment of people already dead may be avenged by history, or that centuries-old accounts of wrongs eventually may be settled justly, he demonstrates his belief in the last judgment. Every time man expects that some day the requirements of his nature will be satisfied, he professes his belief in eschatology, in the end of the world, and thus also in the finiteness of man. Since the eighteenth century, that is, from the very moment when "History" or "Progress" in Europe made their way to the throne of the violently deposed Jehovah, it transpired that they could substitute for him successfully in his basic functions. From the day that historical eschatology demonstrated its possibilities, human history became an argument for atheism: a different force took upon its shoulders the labor of God and, as He had done in the past, it could lull its unhappy subjects with the vision of a happy end.

Yet the belief in progress does not necessarily mean that one must indulge in chiliastic visions; the latter require additional presuppositions, namely, the assumption that current history can be characterized by its striving toward a lasting result, one which can be defined and which will end all conflict. It is irrelevant whether we call this result the end of history or its beginning: for every eschatology the end of the history of the earth is the end of human suffering and the beginning of the life of the blessed about which we know nothing except that it will be a state of permanent contentment.

The problem of the possibility of eschatology is one of the central issues of a discipline which may be called philosophical anthropology, and which today deals with the majority of vital philosophical questions. But theology has always been a projection of anthropology on nonhuman reality. In regard to the antagonisms between the natural aspirations of human essence and man's entanglement in his external fate, philosophical anthropology today may still search for solutions either in terms of transcendency, as do the Christian existentialists (Jaspers, Marcel), or in terms of history, as do the Marxists, or, finally, it may recognize the conflict as insoluble; the last eventuality was at one time formulated by Freud, and existentialist atheists have since put it in a different way. Independently of the arguments expressed in more or less "technical" tongues, the question itself has become common currency; and almost everyone, acting under the combined or conflicting pressures of tradition and personal experiences, has a more or less ready answer to it. In this popularized version, answers need not be theses; most often they are attitudes to life which express, if only unconsciously, a solution to the following problem: is the existence of each of us merely a collection of facts, one following another and exhausting itself within its duration, or is every fact something more than the mere content of the time which comprises it — namely, an anticipation, a hope for other facts to come, the revelation of a fragment of the final perspective of fulfillment? Is each fact an absolute reality, or is it a section of the road at whose end peace awaits us? The answer to the question is of highly practical value, for it determines whether we consider our daily chores a means of saving pennies toward a retirement pension in eternity for ourselves and mankind and therefore, perhaps, disregard current facts and such values as cease to matter when the now passes; or whether, on the contrary, we see in them only their empirical and immediately given content, and therefore tend to ignore those possibilities which may be realized only after certain preparations are made, but which require transcendent interpretation via assigning sense to each fact by relating it to something outside it. Risking the loss of current values in exchange for final values, illusory though they may be, and risking, on the other hand, the loss of greater values by pursuing current values — what, indeed, could be more banal than these two extremes between which our daily life oscillates? But this is exactly what philosophy concerns itself with, having inherited the problem from theological tradition.

:

The next matter, directly related to the first, is theodicy, also a part of theological heritage. In its modern version, theodicy deals with the rationality of history, that is, it tries to discover whether the unhappiness and suffering of the individual can find sense and justification in the universal reasons on which history rests. Traditional theodicies tell us that in the poverty of the condemned shines infallible divine justice, and that human misery reflects the glory of ultimate goodness. There is a difference between the problem previously formulated and the one posed by theodicy: eschatology assigns sense to all facts by relating them to a perspective of ultimate completion; theodicy justifies partial evil by invoking the order of a wisely construed whole, while the question of whether the ultimate completion is a justification of partial evil remains unanswered.

The problem of theodicy in its modernized version treats of "the wisdom" of history, that is, the problem of conceiving such an intellectual organization of the world in which evil, known to, or experienced by, us, discovers its "sense" and value enmeshed in the wise plans of history. Ideologies based on theodicy do not necessarily have to be conservative, although the majority of historical examples might make us think so. Strictly speaking, theodicy is always conservative where it justifies evil experienced by people independently of their own decisions; it is not necessarily conservative where it justifies evil resulting from someone's free choice. In the first instance, it is simply the ideology of the helpless; in the other, it may be an ideology sanctioning our active participation in human conflict — regardless of whether on the side of good or evil.

Theodicy belongs to the department of popular philosophy, the philosophy of everyday life; and although it is sometimes practiced in the form of historiosophical abstractions, its acceptance or rejection expresses itself also in daily common attitudes, in that semi-conscious practical philosophy which influences human behavior. On this level, its action varies. Someone who has suffered an irreversible misfortune can find solace in the thought that God has used his suffering for some (undefined) good in the world's order; or else that nothing is wasted in human affairs, and the suffering of the individual is recorded in the bank of history, thereby adding to the account from which future generations will draw dividends. Anyone able to nurture such beliefs can certainly derive advantages from them, and there would be no reason to discourage him so long as he does not resort to them in the face of an evil or a misfortune which can still be opposed. But theodicies mostly do serve the following: the belief that, by an act of God or history, nothing in human life happens in vain is so powerful a stimulus to our inborn inertia and such a justification of our conservatism and laziness that, in practical life, it inevitably becomes a shield protecting human inertia against the pangs of conscience and rational criticism.

"Ultimately," one may say to oneself, "our fate is only a part of the universe, a fragment of the enormous whole where the suffering of the individual serves to enrich the universal good, where everything influences all, while the general order of things is maintained. Whatever evil happens, it is a sacrifice on the altar of the whole, and sacrifice is not borne in vain." Although sober observation does not support this optimism and points rather to the fact that no wages of history can balance the fate of an individual man, that the suffering of some contributes to the well-being of others, while the suffering of others serves no purpose and is simply what it is — bare suffering, that much of our life is ultimately spent in vain and there is no proof that it amounts to anything else; although, then, this unifying and balancing vision of the world finds no support in our knowledge of it, the belief is so deeply rooted in our desires for compensation that it appears to be one of the truly irresistible intellectual superstitions known to man. The critique of this superstition would not be — we repeat — of great importance if it acted solely as a tranquilizing interpretation of matters past and irrevocable, and not as an apology for situations that are, and whose inevitability can hardly be proved.

*Theodicy, therefore, is a method of transforming facts into values:* a method thanks to which a fact is not only what it appears to be to an empirical imagination, but an element of special meaning in a teleologically arranged order. This transforming of facts into values is no doubt a vestige of magical thinking, older than the speculative theologies, and presupposes the belief in the sanctifying or damning power of certain events, a belief which has no connection with the empirically given data, while relating to intangible qualities. The assumption that our present suffering must find compensation in some good in the future presupposes faith in the secret good qualities of unpleasant events, qualities connected with the all-wise order of the universe. This belief is of the same nature as any trust in the efficacy of magical practices. Our purpose here is to point to those essential elements in which modern secular thought is also compelled, either in negative or positive terms, to answer questions inherited from theological and pretheological, that is, magical, tradition. Every belief or disbelief in a God-less history, or a God-less universe organizing its elements in a teleological unity while assigning them values independent of human notions — is a belief or disbelief in theodicy. The question about the existence of an immanent order in the universe is not futile, a fact we accept silently any time we agree to reply to it, even in the negative; this is so because a question fit to be answered presupposes a certain *raison d'être* of that sphere of knowledge from which it derives. Theodicy is thus part of contemporary philosophy; it may be called the metaphysics of values, or speculation on man's position in the cosmos, or, even, a discussion of historical progress. In all three departments, each of them a part of nonreligious contemporary philosophy, the patronage of theodicy, and through it the patronage of magic, has not become obsolete.

The belief in eschatology, as well as the belief in theodicy, is an attempt to find for human life a support and validity outside that life — an absolute validity, a super-reality which any other reality lends meaning to and, in itself, does not require further interpretation by reference to something else. The absolute usually becomes a moral support because of being a metaphysical support; because, in a metaphysical structure of the world, *individua* appear as its manifestations, or its accidents, and only as such become understandable. But the role of the absolute manifests itself more directly in other matters, whose importance in the history of theology is well known and, in its modernized form, is still troubling not only philosophers, but all those who seek a rationale for their behavior.

First of all, the matter of nature and grace. In Christian history, this was one of the central preoccupations (Pelagianism, the Reformation, Jansenism), along with the question of theodicy (Manicheans, the Cathari), and the idea of redemption (Monophysites, Arians, Socinians). It is not difficult to see that the problem of the relation between the responsibility of the individual and the determinants acting upon him from the outside is, in all its complexity, as much alive today as it was at the time of the Council of Trent. In its most general version, this is the problem of determinism and responsibility, i.e.: in what sense and to what degree the human individual "can" or "cannot" resist the influence of forces which, independently of him, are shaping his behavior; and in what sense is he then morally responsible for himself, or, to what degree can he place responsibility on other forces over which he has no power? There are many varieties of the problem — biological, sociological, historiosophical, metaphysical; and yet the sources of social interest in it are similar to those in the past; some of the varieties have become questions to be studied and solved empirically, losing thereby their philosophical character. Others have remained within the bounds of historiosophical or metaphysical speculation, with no great chance of being solved otherwise. In considering them, man wishes to discover to what degree certain elements, independent of him — physiological or historical — can justify him *ex post,* and to what extent they can supply him with an infallible guide to his future decisions. Above all, there has grown up around historical determinism a multitude of complex questions which compel attention as the most vital in contemporary philosophical thinking.

"We have no freedom to do this or that, but only freedom to do nothing at all. And the task which historical necessity has posed is being solved with, or against, the individual." This attitude clearly summarizes the idea of historical predestination, against which all rebellion is doomed in advance to failure; it is, at the same time, the idea of justifying acts undertaken in accordance with the inherent inevitability of history. The words quoted above are from the closing chapter of Spengler's *The Decline of the West,* but they may serve as a terse formula for a more universal tendency. All concepts pertaining to natural cycles of civilizations, such as Arnold Toynbee's, are analogous repetitions of that world vision we know from *De Civitate Dei.* The opponents of historical determinism — Isaiah Berlin, Karl Popper — are continuing, in this sense, Pelagian soteriology. Marxist literature on the matter presents various motifs, usually revolving around solutions resembling those of the Council of Trent, which can be summarized as follows: acts that are contained within the framework of determinants derived from it; nonetheless, there is no irresistible grace, and the individual is responsible for accepting or rejecting the offer to cooperate tendered by the absolute to everyone; redemption is a possibility open to all, although, on the other hand, it is anticipated that not everybody will make use of it; thus, human kind is fatally divided into the chosen and the rejected; in the absolute's plans, this division is irrevocably established, and the results are determined, and yet individuals voluntarily accede either to this or the other category.

We draw these analogies not in order to ridicule an actually vital topic in philosophy, but rather to uncover the hidden rationality of theology's subject matter which, in the old version, has lost its vitality. For there is nothing surprising in the fact that certain central difficulties of any and all world concepts have a stubbornly persisting character as to their basic problems, while the actual degree of culture and the richness of vocabulary at our disposal determines the way in which we express them. Our explanations are thus directed, if at all, against that attitude of contempt which free thinkers and rationalists adopt in regard to problems that were flesh for past ages, as if we ourselves were not engaged in solving the very same questions by means of a different technique; this haughtiness is as unreasonable as derisive laughter at medieval man would be because he transported himself from one place to another by means of the horse and not the jet plane. Airplanes now serve more effectively the purpose that horses once served, just as historiosophical reflections deal more effectively with the very problems once dealt with by the medieval disputes on the Trinity and irresistible grace. Why should anyone wonder at the fact that humanity wants to realize the role which independent forces play in man's behavior? Neither is there anything strange in the desire to know not only the forces which act upon us in the form of energy transferers, but also the elementary and autonomous forces, that is, the absolute. If the absolute is a historical process, secular historiosophy simply takes over the tasks of theology which, in its old version, had

become all too obviously anachronistic. Probing into the problem of nature and grace can serve a manifold purpose: it may aim at finding in the
world a principle in whose authority one is able to have total confidence,
and which relieves man of his responsibility and solves all conflicts for
him; what is aimed at may be the highest tribunal on whose justice one
relies without fear, and which will allow no harm to be done to us if we
adhere to its guidance; it may also be that we want to acquire the certainty
that in our lives we have chosen the better side and thus all we do is just.
Some solutions to the enigma of nature and grace serve as ways of shed-
ding responsibility, which the absolute takes upon itself; this is the Calvinist solution. Another doctrine accepts responsibility, but only under
the condition that acts are performed in accordance with clearly defined
rules whose acceptance inevitably must lead to effective results; this is
the Catholic solution. Still others accept the principle of unconditional
responsibility to the absolute, but coupled with uncertainty as to the leg-
islator's intentions; this is the Jansenist solution. In all cases, it is assumed that the absolute possesses both the legislative and the judicial
power. The object of another argument is to determine whether the absolute's decrees can be well known to man, how exactly they are known,
whether — if they are known — they can be carried out, and whether
the transgressor can claim ignorance of these decrees if they are not fully
known. Roughly speaking, these were the questions that served as focal
points for all theological discussions in the sixteenth and seventeenth centuries — debates on nature and grace, predestination and justification of
one's faith and acts. The very existence of a principle which is the source
of all obligation and simultaneously a tribunal deciding in each case
whether the law was observed, was not a subject of controversy at that
time; those who today reject the existence of such a principle altogether,
reply in simple negative to a question theology has solved in a positive
way so unequivocally that it sometimes was deemed unnecessary to spell
it out.

If we put aside social conflicts bearing on the controversy over nature
and grace, we can see, from the point of view of individual motivation,
two contradictory tendencies: on the one hand, there is the desire to
find outside oneself support for one's own existence, the desire which
denotes fear of an individual, isolated life, a life relying exclusively on
man's own decisions, and thus, in final terms, the desire to rid oneself of
oneself, to jump out of one's skin; on the other hand, we observe fear of
the unreality of one's behavior and decisions, fear of harboring within
oneself an alien force that not only carries out human intentions, but is
also a will undertaking them instead of man. The conflict between striving for individual self-affirmation and striving for self-annihilation — in
other words, the conflict between fear of getting rid of one's self and fear
of one's self — may be considered the most universal subject matter of

philosophical thinking; more precisely, the history of philosophy confirms that such conflict really exists.

Let us remark in passing that the problem of original sin, very closely connected with the idea of nature and grace, also has its contemporary, although modified, form since it treats of the satanic element in man and thus also of rebellion against absolute power. In its modern version, it is the problem of utopia, that is, an attempt to break the historical absolute — power — against which any rebellion is seemingly condemned in advance to failure. The problem of redemption and incarnation also lends itself to a *sui generis* secular interpretation: it is the matter of the individual's role in history, that is, of that mechanism which allows the historical absolute to become incarnate in exceptional individuals, or, in more general terms, the question as to whether those individuals really draw their energy from transcendent sources, or rather are in themselves a spontaneous "principle of creativity" in history.

All the above-mentioned matters bear on the relationship between man and the absolute, something historiosophy has inherited from theology. However, many important questions in the theory of knowledge also originate in the very same sources, although they are not connected with historiosophy.

The most vital among them is the problem of revelation. Capricious divinity never reveals its secrets fully, yet a dimmed reflection of its wisdom does sometimes fall on mortals, depending on how much their owlish eyes can stand before being struck blind. Revelation is simply the absolute in the order of perception; it is a collection of unquestionable data; it is a way of communicating with the absolute. We need revelation not so much for learning what the world is really like, as for being able to appraise other's opinions about the world. Thus, revelation is, in terms of usage, the textbook of the inquisitor. It is a granite throne from which we can mete out verdicts without risk of error, and without which our rickety skeletons could not sustain us. Propped up by revelation, we can do more than move the earth; we can stop its motion.

Revelation is the eternal hope of philosophy. And so we see that the so-called philosophical "systems" which are supposed to give us certainty in the final stage of their investigation, give it to us always at the very beginning: by force of an almost automatically accepted succession, they begin by establishing sure knowledge, the absolute beginning of all reasoning. It would seem that once the absolute of the beginning was given, so would be its end; that, once we managed to stand on solid ground, moving forward would cease to be interesting. Since we have at our disposal what is most certain and unshakable, all further thinking would be as smooth and easy as the motion of a glass ball on ice. Revelation is "the first push" given to thought, after which thought moves onward automatically; yet it is only an apparent motion, for automatism is precisely the antithesis of thinking. Thinking, in its narrow sense which interests us here — that is, creative thinking — is a function which cannot be performed by an automaton. Philosophy is an effort to question incessantly all that appears evident, that is, to disavow existing revelations. Nevertheless, the untiring temptation to possess one's own revelation keeps on laying traps for critics; every philosophy aspiring to become "a system" questions the revelations of other systems only to establish immediately its own; there are few methods of thinking which do not tacitly subscribe to the Thomist principle whereby the aim of all motion is rest. (*"Impossibile est igitur quod natura intendat motum propter seipsum. Intendit igitur quietem per motum. . . ."*) The premise of this assumption is that the essence of motion is its opposite, namely, absence of motion. Motion realizes itself by annihilating itself or, in other words, motion is an infirmity or insufficiency of that which moves; motion reveals need, whereas need is the negative component of nature; therefore, the nature of all things realizes itself in fulfillment. In philosophical thinking, this principle appears as the conviction that thought moves only because it is imperfect, and only to attain perfection, immobility. Thought, as every motion, attains satisfaction and fulfills itself only when it ceases to be motion, that is, when it ceases to be. But the urgent need for finality, the need for revelation, is one of the needs most easily satisfied; that is why its seekers find it almost as soon as they become aware of the need. Once the revelation has been found and thought has reached its much desired fulfillment, philosophy begins to construct what it thinks is a "system"; in fact, however, the alleged beginning is already the end, and the structure has been given a roof at the moment when it seemed to us that we had just laid the cornerstone. Any philosophic finality is nothing but a substitute for revelation which, being allegedly the starting point for theologians, is, in truth, all that is needed; for, indeed, theology begins with the conviction that truth has already been given to us and its intellectual effort lies not in pitting it against reality but in assimilating the essence of something that has been totally completed.

The original key formula of secular revelation is the *Cartesian cogito:* an attempt to question all that is obvious, and all the traditional finalities, in such a way as not to allow the act of criticism and destruction to be completed before a new finality — the self-knowledge of man's own thinking process — has been attained. Descartes undertook his act of criticism fully aware that there must be a limit to criticism; that sand is usually removed to enable people to stand on solid ground. To him, critique would have been without meaning if it were not to stop at a static point, and so his critical task was to reach a point above all criticism; the goal of criticism was self-annihilation, the goal of motion was the absence of motion, a point of immobility. The exposure of the short-comings of successive revelations was to lead to the discovery of a rev-elation free of shortcomings. The progress of post-Cartesian philosophy was, to a considerable degree, a succession of imitations of the same procedure; philosophers accepted *in toto* Descartes' question, thereby half-accepting his answer, while the persistent work of modifying the *cogito* formula has lasted until the present century. In particular, the entire evolution of European idealism has brought to light the basic qual-ity of the Cartesian revelation which it shares with other revelations. Its starting point is also the point of attainment; since the awareness of the thought process is the ultimate datum of cognition, the whole of reality cannot go beyond the thought process or, to use Gilson's words, "as we begin with the immanent world, so we end with it." This seems natural: reality will always have in man's vision such nature as is inherent in the ultimate data from which he tries to reconstruct it. For to declare that certain data have the privilege of being final, is to deny the reality of everything that cannot be in some way reduced to them. If, then, the immanent world is the absolute of knowledge, it is, at the same time, all that knowledge can achieve; just as Spinoza's *causa sui,* being the starting point of the thought process, is inevitably its point of attainment, the only world whose reality can be defended. So also people for whom the physical objects of daily reality constitute the only collection of absolute data must recognize that those data necessarily exhaust all possible data, while people who assign this character to sensory phenomena will con-struct the world exclusively on the basis of sensory phenomena. In the motion of philosophical thought, the absolute starting point predeter-mines everything else, and he who attains the absolute ceases to move; any further motion on his part is illusory, as is the motion of a squirrel running up a rotating drum.

And yet the nostalgia for revelation lives at the heart of philosophy, while the need for ultimate satisfaction has still not been extinguished in its faithful. Taine's positivism had to find satisfaction in the "ultimate law" or the "eternal axiom" of reality, which discovers the unity of the universe, and to which all our knowledge must finally be reduced in some way. The great ambition of phenomenology was to present reality in the absolute and final sense, and since reality thus conceived could not be anything but immanent reality, the idealism of Husserl's late work seems to be the result of the previously mentioned inborn logic of a doctrine whose main task originally was to overcome subjectivism. The inner an-tinomy of this search for revelation was, in the case of Husserl, an illustra-tion of all such analogous searches; the statement that ultimate data can have only an immanent character, whereas transcendent reality is pro-vided, as Husserl said, with an epistemological zero indicator, presup-poses that the ultimate data cannot be established without a clear concept of transcendency, while opinions about it were left in abeyance. However, the very concept of transcendency could only have resulted from that natural, precritical cognitive attitude, no results of which were to be considered. Yet it appeared now and again that the verbal definition of the original principle, which attributed an ultimate character to pure phenomena, had required an earlier use of a concept derived from outside these phenomena, thereby also requiring borrowing from certain data of natural knowledge; without them nothing could be achieved. The epistemological absolute appeared then to be as burdened with the dead weight of nonabsolute knowledge as the Cartesian *cogito,* which is nothing else but a presumption of a fictitious thinker, a distilled intellectual substance, totally independent of all such content as experience and acquired knowledge have left to it. This is so because the absolute is impossible to describe without simultaneously describing its opposite, and by this very fact it betrays its fictitiousness. Every critique presupposes an object to be criticized; a thought process in which we "put in brackets" transcendent reality presupposes that the latter was given to our thought, regardless of how many "distingua" are added to the word "given."

Modern positivism has not saved itself, at least in its first phase, from the pursuit of the epistemological absolute; in declaring that finality is the proper word for the character of observation sentences, Moritz Schlick presented us with another version of the same maneuver which, in so many other doctrines, was to provide us with secular substitutes for revelation.

The problem of revelation is the problem of the existence of ultimate data. It is accompanied by another question: to what extent is conceptual thinking able to encompass and express ultimate data? This is the problem of mystery which, in contemporary philosophy, belongs as much as the former ones to the heritage of theology. In its modernized version, mystery is identical with the limits of rationalism; it covers all the questions that primarily concern the rationality of certain elementary components of perception, and certain indivisible fragments of reality itself. The deliberations of the personalistic doctrines about the noncommunicable character of personality are a projection into the human world inquiry of the questions which theology addressed to divinity; personalism in its metaphysical version, that is, the monadology of the human world, did not attack theology, but borrowed its troubles. In this case no more than in the previous instances do we want to imply that the troubles were illusory; the question about the rationality of the indivisible whole which human personality is, is a real question. If, at one time, it was a question about the mystery of the divine personality, it was formulated in sufficiently general terms for the theoretical priority to remain in the hands of theologians; in the evolution of the very word "persona" — the mask —

there took shape a difficulty which has tripped philosophers ever since. This difficulty usually is solved by means of a rather simple slogan, "personality is inexpressible"; but the slogan itself, even if true, is just as sterile as the statement that God is a mystery to mortals.

The problem of the relation between faith and reason has also appeared in a modernized form. We concern ourselves with it every time we try to find out to what degree experience and rational thought can unequivocally resolve conflicts and what the role is of unprovable factors in our image of the world. The controversy over the unprovable assumptions of empirical knowledge on the one hand and, on the other, the existence of preferential criteria in regard to conflicting sets of experience, has inherited much from the old tradition. If certain facts cannot be integrated with a previously accepted coherent set of principles which explain our past experiences, how much within our rights are we to ignore these facts or to advance interpretations whose purpose is to align them, sometimes falsely, with the system? These are the daily troubles of scientific thinking, similar to those that occurred in the past when revelation was the skeleton which organized all our knowledge into one compact "system." At the bottom of these controversies, there lies the antagonism of the same two tendencies which were present in nearly all the above-mentioned problems: on the one hand, the integrationist and monistic inclinations, a hope, in ultimate terms, of containing the world in one formula, or at least to discover a principle that would explain the whole of reality; and on the other hand, the pluralistic urge to disregard coherence in knowledge, a lack of ambition to construe a forest out of single trees, a readiness to accept single facts as absolute even if, when confronted, they should contradict each other. It was William James who, in radical formula, expressed the anti-monistic attitude toward knowledge: if the facts contradict each other, we still can accept each of them separately, since there is no reason to suppose that one inflexible elementary law rules the universe and arranges its history. We have the right to assume that the way in which things happen varies, and that the effort to reduce variety to uniformity is most frequently futile and artificial. Let every fact be its own explanation and the general knowledge elastic enough to react separately to any situation. If, in a series of experiences, the world crumbles before our eyes like a heterogeneous mass thrown together accidentally, we have the right to assume that the world's structure is precisely what it seems — chaotic, free of uniformity and order, full of accidents, more akin to a garbage heap than a library where every item has its clearly defined place and where everything has been inventorized.

And yet this obsession with monism, the stubborn passion to arrange the world in accordance with a single unifying principle, this search for a magic formula to make reality decipherable, proves to be more lasting than all the other adventures of man's intellectual development. Philosophy itself favors it; each epoch which prides itself on having created a great scientific synthesis seems to reveal more and more of an orderly world — while presenting us with more and more general principles, compared to which all those known before appear incidental. Thus philosophy, especially since it has developed the aspirations of a scientific discipline, eagerly calls upon science to bear witness to its ventures. But when it tries to renounce its monistic hopes, it does just the opposite — it denounces science and explains that a scientific vision of the world is not a reconstruction of an organization actually inherent in the world, but the result of just such natural propensity of the human mind.

All the above-mentioned examples are nothing but attempts to justify theology not by rebuilding its whole structure systematically, but by illustrating some of its subjects; these examples were drawn from the speculative theology of scholasticism. But the wealth of mystic theology was not lost either, and it retains its splendor in contemporary thought.

The problems of mystic theology are particularly alive in the following four departments of modern philosophy: the practical interpretation of knowledge; dialectics; the explanation of the world in terms of the whole; and finally, in matters relating to the substantial character of the first reality.

With regard to the first, one ought to note that the mystics were pioneers in the field of the pragmatic approach to knowledge. Because the qualities of the absolute elude the investigation of the instruments at the disposal of human speech, which is used only for describing finite things, the only concept our knowledge has of the absolute is of a practical nature. In the strict sense of the word, this knowledge does not say what the qualities of God are, but instructs us as to the best way of paying homage to Him and how, by self-renunciation, one can approach His glory. Moreover, this knowledge is not so much a series of prescriptions one can learn by heart before applying them in practice, as the actual application of them; reason does not precede will but rather the acts of will become simultaneously acts of understanding; our knowledge of God is as great as the love we give Him.

Advanced by the first pragmatists and still retaining its force, the practical interpretation of knowledge is a generalized version of the mystics' program: let us ignore the question of what the world looks like "in itself" and accept instead scientific theories as practical guidance for our behavior under certain circumstances. Pragmatism rejects as irrelevant all queries about the nature of reality, and substitutes for them practical questions.

The second guardian of the properties taken over from mystical theology is dialectics. We know that the attempts to apply everyday concepts to the absolute existence have led to antinomies, hence the mystics became masters of a thinking which proceeds by thesis and antithesis; to say that no categories of human speech apply to God is to say that every time we speak of Him all categories apply to Him; thus God is and is not, He is all and nothing, maximum and minimum, affirmation and negation. In the mystical texts we also find the modern idea of alienation, as well as the idea of the world's development through its own negation. Alienated from its source, the world, an emanation of God, being finite, is the negation of its source. But in its reverted motion it tends to annihilate itself, and again become identical with its genesis; this vision of Erigena contains in itself almost all the rudiments of dialectical logic. As in Hegel's logic, alienation in mystical theology did not have to be a negative phenomenon: the absolute secretes its theophanies by force of the fatality of its own nature, and by secreting them becomes, so to speak, enriched because it can regain them anew. Likewise, original sin and the fall of man can be considered a necessary phase previous to man's future happiness to which he can look forward because of his Savior's act of redemption: *"O felix culpa quae talem ac tantum meruit habere redemptorem"* — thus speaks the well-known medieval song; blessed be the sin which deserves such a savior.

Historiosophical reflections on progress which fulfills itself through its "negative aspects," and on alienation by which man is enriched as he overcomes it, are variations on the same theme.

As the third accomplishment of mystic theology from which contemporary thought has borrowed, we mentioned questions dealing with the unifying interpretation of existence. Thus the theory of "Gestalt" appears in mystical texts in an almost perfect, although somewhat generalized, form, the modern equivalent of which can be found in Bergson's speculations rather than in the methodology of the "Gestaltists." A really independent existence is the prerogative of the absolute only; all the finite fragments we distinguish in the universe, and the differences between separate things, are either a kind of pathological alienation which awaits its end in the universal return of the world to the absolute's womb, or else a deformed product of our imagination, which tries to impose upon an indivisible whole a principle of multiplicity and differentiation completely alien to it.

Also the mystical problem of applying the concept of substance to the absolute has begun to flourish anew in our century. The question as to whether the original reality has the character of substance, or whether its substantialness is a secondary phenomenon, an attribute of our perception, or even its creation, whereas the original reality is something not substantial — event, relation, act — this question is obviously of theological origin. The questioning of the idea of substance in favor of the metaphysical priority of other principles which were traditionally considered secondary predicates, has, in our century, appeared in theories which are otherwise completely different: Giovanni Gentile's actualism, Alfred Whitehead's and Bertrand Russell's theory of events, and Natorp's theory of relation — to mention only three cases each of a different origin — all meet at a certain, quite distant, point in their genealogy, a point which, to each of these philosophers, would seem totally alien to his thought. But every one of us has spiritual ancestors whose portraits he prefers not to display in the family dining room, though much malicious gossip goes on about them among the neighbors. Besides, we ourselves do not deny that our deliberations at this moment are somewhat reminiscent of the famous *Liber Chamorum;* in this case, however, the author has no intention of removing himself from the disreputable register.

## II

Our list so far has been merely a loose collection of cases with one common feature; this was to show that many basic problems which are today considered by various philosophical doctrines — sometimes diametrically opposed to each other — as well as by "everyman's" philosophy which always revolves around the same questions as "technical" philosophy, are a continuation of theological controversies, or rather a new version of the same propositions which, in the original and less elegantly phrased version, we have known from the history of theology. And yet, led by the same instinct which, as was said, lies at the bottom of the monistic tendencies of the human mind and gives birth to monistic interpretations of reality, we also want to formulate a coordinating principle which will permit us to span the conflicting views of the world in a systematic way.

The majority of the cited examples revealed that there exists in philosophy an antagonism centering on the same scheme: for or against eschatology, that is, for or against the ordering of the facts of current life by reference to the absolute which eventually is to be realized; for or against theodicy, that is, for or against seeking justification in the absolute for every individual evil in this world; for an interpretation of man in the categories of grace, or rather, in the categories of nature, that is, for or against assigning to the absolute all responsibility for our actions; for or against revelation, that is, for or against seeking a principle of knowledge that is permanent and inaccessible to criticism, and which gives us the guarantee of infallible thinking; for or against the monistic concept of knowledge, and thus, for or against striving for intellectual power over reality by way of possessing a code of supreme and elementary laws explaining everything; for or against the unifying interpretation of the world, and thus, for or against such vision as lends every thing a meaning by referring it to the absolute, a manifestation, a part, or an accident of which it constitutes. In short: for or against the hope of finality in existence and knowledge, for or against seeking support in absolutes.

We have tried to present the nature of this conflict as a constant struggle between two summarily defined but essential tendencies to which philosophy tries to lend a discursive character; a situation in which the human individual can rely only on himself, a situation in which he cannot "define" himself and identify himself absolutely with anything else. Such a situation breeds fear which finds expression in man's seeking support in the absolute reality, and thus in self-annihilation; in man's seeking for himself and his acts a definition which refers him to something he is not; on the other hand, there is the affirmation of the individual existence as an irreducible fact, and thereby the rejection of all reasons justifying individual existence, the refusal to accept any absolute reality, the refusal to recognize immobility as the genuine nature of something that is mobile, the refusal to consider the prospect of finality.

And to what peculiarities of human nature — to use this much abused term — ought one to ascribe that indestructible tropism towards absolutes, that hope for the revelation of one, ultimate principle which would explain the whole world and shoulder the burden of man's existence, behavior and thought?

There are various doctrines explaining the hunger for self-definition by reference to the absolute, a feeling which may well be hunger for nonexistence. Theologians have long tried to convince us that it is the creator-given-and-oriented gravitation that rules man's thought; they call it natural religious feeling. This, however, is equivalent to justifying one's own doctrines by facts whose acceptance must be preceded by the acceptance of the same doctrine you try to justify. And anyway, by what right are we to call religious feeling something that may just as well manifest itself outside all that which both in our daily life and in science we commonly term religion? I think we ought to define religion before we speak of *homo religiosus;* otherwise we may fall into a trap — a common one, to be sure — and define religion through religious feeling, characterizing the latter in a way which presupposes the knowledge of what religion is. It would be simpler, would it not, to view religion as we know it in its historical formulae, as an instance of a more universal phenomenon which may also occur outside religion.

But even if we disregard this one, we still have at our disposal a whole series of other explanations which are merely different ways of expressing the same thought, and which, unfortunately, give rise to all too many doubts to be satisfactory. Let me mention four such attempts:

One of them, formulated by Freud, and later ignored on the whole by his disciples, is the theory of the death instinct, i.e., the theory in accordance with which there exists in animated matter a constant nostalgia for reverting to the inorganic state, a constant tendency to reduce tensions and, ultimately, to liquidate them entirely — in other words, to discontinue organic processes altogether. The death instinct thus would be hostile to the libido, and at the same time explain the striving of the mind to discover in the world such principles as would reduce personal forms of existence to impersonal ones.

Another doctrine has long been known in its methodological (Ockham), as well as theological (Malebranche) and physicalist (Maupertuis), version; Avenarius and the empirio-critical group have investigated it in detail; it is the principle of economy. In its summary metaphysical shape, this principle implies that in nature — and thus also in the behavior of organisms and in thinking — there is a latent tendency to maximal reduction of effort and the use of the simplest means. Freud's theory may be considered as the economy principle specifically applied to the organic world. The principle of economy, as the principle of the natural tendency of all systems to equalize tensions and differences, might also help to interpret man's thinking in an attempt to reduce *individua* to an undifferentiated absolute, an attempt to explain monistic realities.

The third possibility, one formulated in the "Gestalt" theory, is the principle of simplification, according to which all "Gestalt" systems or entities have an inborn tendency to acquire forms as simple, regular, and symmetrical as possible. This principle is again another version of the principle of economy, and can be used in this case for similar purposes.

As the fourth possibility on the list, we quote Sartre's formula maintaining that existence "*for itself*," that is, human existence — defined as pure negativity in relation to the rest of the world, freedom but a freedom-*privatio* — is imbued with a constant and contradictory desire to be transformed into an existence "*in* itself"; it would like to shed the nothingness which torments it, but nothingness, that is, freedom, is at the same time precisely what defines human existence; to want to shed nothingness, to return to the world "in itself," is therefore tantamount to annihilating one's self as individual existence, and thus simply annihilating the existence itself.

All the explanations above represent, as one can see, translations of the same thought into four different tongues. They all give rise to doubts and difficulties. Both the theory of the death instinct, and the principle of economy, as well as its kindred versions, are attempts to raise (or, if one prefers, to lower) the principle of increasing entropy to the dignified level of a universal metaphysical theory, applicable not only to all forms of energy that are known and presumed, but also to human behavior, feeling, and thinking. If this principle of universal tendency to equalize tensions and liquidate irregularities and differences were to be accepted, it would be possible to interpret the history of philosophy within the principle's framework, and all the previously mentioned forms of nostalgia for the absolute which have given substance to philosophical life for centuries would simply be individual cases of its line of action. The very essence of philosophical research could be derived from the same propensity human thought shares with all the other systems of energy. The content of the different metaphysical doctrines would have its basis in the processes of energy transformation on which the human brain depends. And the strong links between conservative thought in the philosophic sense, and social conservatism and that inertia of public life which we call reaction, would be still another individual illustration of the said principle.

However, had such a principle governed human thought exclusively, it never would have caused the previously mentioned chronic conflict in philosophy which, to our mind, effectively directs its course: a conflict between the search for the absolute and the urge to escape from it, between the fear of oneself and the fear of destroying oneself. As things now stand, thought which is subject to the process of increasing entropy, that is, conservative thought, has been opposed in the course of intellectual history by a mode of thinking which exemplifies reverse processes, processes of increasing tension. In all fields of culture, in philosophy as much as in art and custom, there always has been present an antagonism whereby everything that is new derives from an unceasing need to question the existing absolutes. Although every new form of thinking that tries to disassociate itself from the accepted absolutes, establishes, sooner or later, its own final absolutes, and although every rebellion against accepted truth eventually passes into a conservative state, it prepares the ground for a new phase in which its own absolutes become in turn the object of criticism. Can any mode of thinking, even the most radical, escape this fate? All historical examples make us doubt it; besides, the hope of formulating such a mode of thinking would mean a hope of achieving an ultimate method contrary to its very premises. In this regard, the history of ancient skepticism provides a highly revealing example: a doctrine which assumed the function of questioning all accepted truths and dogmas became itself an atrophied and barren dogma of questioning; the critique of the immobility of all accepted principles became the immobility of universal criticism; for no principle of universal criticism is safe from the antinomy of the liar.

And so we do not know of any absolutely elastic ultimate method which history could not threaten with ankylosis. We know only of methods which retain vitality because they have managed to develop instruments of self-criticism. It is our opinion that there is more than one method which creates instruments to criticize itself over a relatively long period of time: in our century, we believe that this has been attained by Marxism and by phenomenonology and psychoanalysis. To state this is not tantamount to accepting the various and contradictory propositions these methods contain. The statement is only meant as a recognition of the ability of these methods to go beyond the absolutes they advance, and to detect the hidden premises of their own radicalism; in this lies their chance to live not only as congregations of perennially acquiescing believers, but also as thinking organisms capable of further evolution. Although within each of them there exists a current of orthodoxy and a group of people who know only how to repeat invariably the original formulae, each one of them has also produced offspring capable of life. The other "great doctrines" of the twentieth century, such as the philosophy of Bergson, for instance, never went beyond this initial phase and have remained in history as closed systems that may claim admirers but no offspring.

The antagonism between a philosophy consolidating the absolute and a philosophy questioning the accepted absolutes, appears to be incurable, as incurable as the existence of conservatism and radicalism in all areas of human life. It is the antagonism of a priest and a jester; and in almost every historical epoch, the philosophy of the priest and the philosophy of the jester have been the two most general forms of intellectual culture. The priest is the guardian of the absolute who upholds the cult of the final and the obvious contained in the tradition. The jester is he who, although an habitué of good society, does not belong to it and makes it the object of his inquisitive impertinence; he who questions what appears to be self-evident. The jester could not do this if he himself were part of the good society, for then he would be, at the most, a drawing room wit. A jester must remain an outsider; he must observe "good society" from the sidelines, for only then can he detect the nonobvious behind the obvious and the nonfinal behind what appears to be final. At the same time, he must frequent good society so as to know what it deems holy, and to be able to indulge in his impertinence.

The jesting role of philosophy was mentioned by Georges Sorel in connection with the Encyclopedists — but in pejorative terms; a jester was merely a toy of the aristocrats. Yet, although it is true that philosophers entertained monarchs, their antics had their effect in earthquakes. There can be no agreement between a priest and a jester, unless, as it sometimes happens, one becomes transmuted into the other. (It happens more often to a priest; so Socrates became Plato.) The philosophy of the jester is a philosophy which in every epoch denounces as doubtful what appears as unshakable; it points out the contradictions in what seems evident and incontestable; it ridicules common sense and reads sense into the absurd — in other words, it undertakes the daily toil of the jester's profession along with the inevitable risk of appearing ludicrous. Depending on time or place, the jester's thought can oscillate between the various extremes of thinking, for what is holy today was paradoxical yesterday, and absolutes revered at the Equator may be a sacrilege at the

Pole. The jester's attitude is an endless attempt to reflect on the various arguments of contradictory ideas: an attitude dialectical by its very nature; simply to overcome what is because it *is*. A jester does not jeer out of sheer contrariness; he jeers because he mistrusts the stabilized world. In a world where allegedly everything has already happened, the jester's contribution is an always active imagination which thrives on the resistance it must overcome.

It was Fichte's admirable observation that thought cannot function without overcoming obstacles, just as a car cannot start on ice, or an airplane in a vacuum. For the same good reason, a philosophy must be regarded as illusionary if it is reduced to pure auto-reflection or else contained in the closed world of a monad. The assumption that the subject can be identical with the object in the act of perceiving, is contradictory; to presuppose such an identity is tantamount to presuming immobility, a situation where no perception is possible. If, then, philosophy undermines the absolute, if it rejects the uniformity of the principles to which reality can be reduced, if it affirms the plurality of the world and the mutual nonreducibility of things, thereby affirming human individuality, it does not do so in the name of monadology, or in the name of the concept of the individual as a self-sufficient atom; because the affirmation of individuality is possible only in contradistinction to the rest of the world, in its relation to the world: relations based on factual dependence, responsibility, resistance.

A philosophy which tries to do without the absolute and without the prospect of completion cannot, by its very nature, be a consolidating structure, for it has no foundations and desires no roof; its function is to undermine the existing foundations and pull down the roofs. In the intellectual life it has all the vices and virtues of an indiscreet person whose sense of respectability has not developed. That is why in certain epochs the conflict between the philosophy of the jester and that of the priest resembles a contest between the irritating features of adolescence and the irritating features of senility. The difference is this: only the former are curable.

Someone might say that our reasoning tends to submit to the temptation of the very same monistic thinking it criticizes, that it betrays a tendency to submit a multitude of facts to one ordering principle. But it is not the ordering of facts that is contrary to the anti-absolute philosophy. Order can be a handy slogan for the police as well as for a revolutionary. There is only one kind of order hostile to an anti-absolutist philosophy: an order which has formulated fully the plurality of existing worlds; an order which has tasted the satisfaction of a fully accomplished task. A policeman's ideal is the order of a comprehensive dossier; while the ideal of the philosopher is the order of an active imagination. Both the priest and the jester violate the mind: the former by strangling it with catechism, the latter by harassing it with mockery. At a royal palace there are more priests than jesters, just as in a king's realm there are more policemen than artists. It does not seem possible to change this. The preponderance of the believers in mythology over the critics seems inevitable and natural: it is the preponderance of a single world over the many possible worlds; it is the preponderance of the simplicity of fall over the complexity of climbing to the top. We have observed the validity of this preponderance when, with astonishing speed, new mythologies replace old ones. In the intellectual life of societies, wherever the machinery of traditional beliefs has gone rusty, new myths flock into being, created *en masse* from technological progress and scientific achievements. Thousands find consolation in imagining friendly inhabitants of other planets one day coming to the earth to solve the problems human kind cannot cope with; for others, "cybernetics" raises the hope of solving all social conflicts. A rain of gods is falling from the sky on the funeral rites of the one God who has outlived himself. The atheists have their saints and the blasphemers are erecting chapels. Perhaps the desire for the absolute, the striving to equalize tensions, must embrace a disproportionately larger number of units in the system than the increase of tensions, if the whole is not to blow up. If this is so, then the existence of priests is justified, although this is no reason for joining their ranks.

Priesthood is not merely the cult of the past as seen through contemporary eyes, but the survival of the past in unchanged shape. It is thus not only a certain intellectual attitude to the world, but, indeed, a form of the world's existence, namely, a factual continuation of a reality which no longer is. In the attitude of the jester, on the other hand, there materializes that which is only a possibility and which, in him, becomes real before it becomes factual. For our thought of reality is also part of it, no worse than the other parts.

We declare ourselves in favor of the philosophy of the jester, that is, for an attitude of negative vigilance in the face of any absolute. We do not do this because we want to argue; in these matters, a choice is an appraisal. We declare ourselves in favor of the nonintellectual values inherent in an attitude the perils and absurdities of which we know. It is the option for a vision of the world that provides prospects for a slow and difficult realignment of the elements in our human action that are most difficult to align; goodness without universal toleration, courage without fanaticism, intelligence without apathy, and hope without blindness. All other fruits of philosophy are of little importance.

1962

*Translated from the Polish by* PAUL MAYEWSKI

LESZEK KOLAKOWSKI *was born in 1927 in Radom. After studying philosophy at Lodz University he held various teaching positions at Lodz and Warsaw Universities. In 1954 he became professor of history of modern philosophy at the latter, and concurrently taught at the Institute for Training of Scientific Workers, a secondary school maintained by the Central Committee of the Polish Workers' Communist Party. During this time he also edited* Po Prostu, *a weekly for young Communist intellectuals. In 1955 the magazine was officially censured for its deviation policy — it had been especially critical of the "new class," the bureaucracy, and its police methods. In 1957 the magazine was suspended and was never revived. Kolakowski became editor in chief of the bimonthly* Studia Filozoficzne *(which succeeded* Myśl Filozoficzna*) but gave up this post in 1959 though he remained on the editorial board. His essay, "The Priest and the Jester," originally appeared in* Tworezosc *and gave rise to much critical discussion among Communist thinkers. He is also author of* On Karl Marx and the Classical Definition of Truth *(1959), delivered as a lecture at Tubingen University, West Germany;* The Individual and the Infinite; World Outlook and Daily Life; Responsibility and History *(published in the French* Les Temps Modernes*). He is presently living in Warsaw.*

# SOCIALISM WITHOUT MARX

## BEN B. SELIGMAN

**I**

One of the more ironic incidents in the history of economic thought was the development of a theory of socialism utilizing the very ideas employed to attack Marx. Dismayed by the sharply critical turn he had given to classicism, economists in the late nineteenth century resorted to the psychological notions of utility as an escape from the radical implications he had underscored. Beginning with W. Stanley Jevons (an interesting theoretician in spite of his silly sunspot business cycles notions) and the Austrian economists, Carl Menger, Friedrich von Wieser, and Eugen von Böhm-Bawerk, a new approach to economics was worked out. This was known as marginalism, and it is one of the dominant themes in economics today. Seeking to create a sound psychological basis for economic science, the marginalists concentrated on the behavior of individual firms rather than the totality of economic action. As suggested, one of their many noteworthy ventures was a broadside attack on Marxism. The Austrians particularly were determined to root out this alien influence in Western economics and they chortled approvingly when Eugen von Böhm-Bawerk announced the complete and utter demise of the Marxian heresy and the end of socialist doctrine.* Yet, it was the very

* Eugen von Böhm-Bawerk, *Karl Marx and the Close of His System*, New York, 1949.

marginalism that stemmed from Austrian theory which provided the building blocks with which a non-Marxian socialist theory could be constructed.

Marginalism sets up conduct models of the *firm*. In more modernistic terminology, it attempts to delineate a decision-making procedure. The behavior of firms is concerned fundamentally with purchases of labor and other resources, conversion of these into products, and the sale of what is put out. Since these can be expressed as "schedules of quantitative relationships" it becomes logically feasible to subject these patterns to a kind of mathematical treatment. Implicit in this is the assumption that the businessman always wants to maximize his profit. Within this framework, marginalism becomes a rather powerful analytical tool. The process of finding a maximum is precisely what is involved in the concept of allocating scarce resources to alternative uses. What the theory says is that economic behavior has a large and significant rational component which, revolving as it does about measurable pecuniary quantities, is subject to analysis. Cost, revenue, and productivity in their marginal form are said to simplify economic thinking.

From the vantage point of marginalism, Böhm-Bawerk could be extremely critical of Marxism. He derided it because the transformation of value into prices was a logical mishmash. He argued that the theory of market exchange in Vol. III of *Das Kapital* contradicted the theory of Vol. I. He insisted that the subjectivist marginal approach was logically superior to cost of production notions such as the labor theory of value. Moreover, marginalist theory was capable of much greater theoretical generality and could be employed to evaluate extra-market phenomena. The Marxist response, however, was that Böhm-Bawerk was asking the wrong question: the basic economic problem was to analyze the social process of production. Marginalist theory merely substituted psychology for the facts of economic life.

Yet the subjectivism of the Austrians provided a rational, logical set of ideas which could be used to describe the proper functioning of a socialist society. The Austrians began their theorizing with the case of Robinson Crusoe. They did this in order to facilitate outlining certain fundamental patterns of economic behavior which were supposedly universal. Questions of value, cost, and returns were appropriate to any society, they said: in the long run, neither history nor sociology were really necessary for economic analysis. In fact, the more one could abstract from an historically determined system, be it capitalism or socialism, the purer the economics.

Friedrich von Wieser, a leader of the Austrian group, was one of the first to suggest that a general economic theory could be evolved to describe a socialist regime, for the problem of allocating scarce resources to alternative ends in order to maximize satisfactions was evident in any social order, whatever its political form.* Wieser had worked out the notion of opportunity cost, a concept which measured the *real* cost of a venture in terms of next best alternatives. This is, of course, an allocation problem and lends itself to analytic maximizing techniques. Incorporated into his treatment of economic calculation (the key question in a non-Marxian socialist theory) the basic ideas were couched in terms of comparing the economics of the household, business enterprise, and government. From this it was easy to derive the notion that a capitalist and socialist economy were governed by the same basic "economic laws." The legal and political superstructures were put to one side, on the supposition that these reflected the "ends of existence," something supposedly irrelevant to pure economics.

The argument is basically simple: those who control the socialist economy have to account for used-up resources, assuming that the objective of rational behavior has meaning for such a society. The labor theory of value cannot be used for this allocation task. It is rather in the market that the required economic calculation is established. Surprisingly enough, Wieser has some doubts about the efficacy of capitalism's market. Competition, he thought, could be a risky affair, "where the stronger would too often find opportunities of mercilessly exploiting the weaker." His preference was for a mixed economy.†

## II

The major attack on socialism as a practicable notion was leveled by Ludwig von Mises, a Viennese economics professor (now at NYU) for whom all the world's ills can be traced to a political disease called statism. A great adept at rather careless invective, Mises' opus *Socialism*‡ purports to be a massive sociological compendium on the subject. In it he speaks of chiliastic urges, collectivism, guild socialism, speculation, free love, the disutilities of labor as well as economic calculation. The latter point is, of course, central to Mises' position, and there is no doubt that he raised the question more sharply than anyone else. In fact, he's made a career of it.

Mises' main point is that markets in which prices are set for land, labor, and capital, do not exist under socialism. But, economic calculation requires pricing. How, asks Mises, can it be carried on in the absence of markets? Economic activity would be absolutely chaotic, for without a pricing mechanism the central authority would have no data for allocating resources or determining consumer demand. Means of production would be applied to frivolous uses or entirely wasted.

* Friedrich von Wieser, *Natural Value*, New York, 1956.
† *cf.* Wieser's *Social Economics*, New York, 1927, espec. pp. 185 *ff.*
‡ Second edition, New Haven, 1951.

This view was supported by Friedrich A. von Hayek, whose name is frequently associated ideologically with Mises.* Hayek interprets the problem a bit more subtly, however. He too sees the choice between socialism and capitalism revolving about the ability to distribute resources among alternative uses. Granting that a collective economy might approach a solution by ordering the community's needs in some preordained way, he does not believe, however, that it could account for the costing problem. Costs are "advantages to be derived from the use of given resources in other directions." In capitalism, such a decision is brought to fruition in the market without any conscious action on the part of particular personalities. Decision-making stems from the way in which prices are structured, and this in turn is rooted in the many acts of many people. At the same time, Hayek sought to reply to the welfare economists' approach, whose views we shall shortly examine. The latter implies a calculus of utility and it was the validity of this that he rejected. Individual utility scales could not be added to create a kind of social utility, for there is no way, said Hayek, in which interpersonal comparisons could be legitimately validated. Therefore, the only approach to a theory of resource allocation was through choice as reflected in the determination of market price under capitalism.

Hayek persisted in his view that a socialistic solution to the problem of resource allocation was impracticable simply because complete knowledge of all the relevant data would be unavailable to the authorities.† This must be so, since economic knowledge is of the bits and pieces variety, existing in but scattered parts, in a dispersed and incomplete form in the minds of many individuals. Such knowledge, he agrees, would have to be transferred to the central authorities under socialism. But it is not viable, communicable, scientific knowledge; it is rather, knowledge of time and place and is not the kind of information that can be subject to testing and measurement by a single agency. Such knowledge — of a particular skill, of the existence of some surplus stocks, of a sudden need for roofing — cannot enter into statistics and therefore cannot be conveyed to the planners.

Yet Hayek must admit that the capitalist market does transmit such information, since businessmen do react to bits and pieces knowledge in a way in which he would approve. But, he insists, central planning could employ only scientific or statistical data and such information is mainly technological in nature. The conclusion is obvious: only knowledge of time and place, mysteriously entering the price system, provides the basis for economic decisions, something that central planning cannot accomplish. Hayek's refusal to concede that planning might be an effective in-

* cf. F. A. von Hayek, ed., *Collectivist Economic Planning*, London, 1935.
† cf. idem, *Individualism and the Economic Order*, Chicago, 1948, espec. Chapter IV.

strument for overcoming conditions of imperfect knowledge is odd, for businessmen more and more seek through such methods as market and motivation research to reduce bits and pieces information to measurable form. In actuality, efforts are always made to get behind forces that influence prices, for no businessman wishes to consign his future to the realm of total ignorance. There seems no logical reason why a central planning authority could not adopt similar devices.

Hayek's approach is rooted in a concern with economic structure. For example, a central planning authority, he avers, would have to treat two similar machines located in different places as distinct means of production. Should the equipment have been installed during different time-periods, there certainly would be no question as to the need to characterize these as dissimilar units, each of which must appear in the "equations" a central planning body must solve. This would make the problem of calculation insuperable. As Vilfredo Pareto once remarked, if with 100 people and 700 commodities there would be 70,699 equations, what happens when there are several million inhabitants and several thousand commodities? And when account is taken of goods in progress and those transported, it appears obvious that not all the relevant data can be made available to even formulate the necessary equations. Changes in climate, population, and the consumption package itself make it dubious that rational "ideal" planning is a practicable proposition.

At the same time that Hayek was developing these seemingly devastating arguments against the collective society, Mises came up with the further notion that socialism, by sundering distribution from production, would compound its inner difficulties. Said he: "It is irreconcilable with the nature of the communal ownership of productive goods that [socialism] should rely even for a part of its distribution upon the economic imputation of the yield to the particular factors of production." That is to say, without a market, a socialist order would have no way of connecting the value of consumer goods with the process of production. Just why this should be so is not made clear although it is evident that to Mises the problem lies in the inability, in the absence of a market, to relate values of output to rewards of factors: in technical terms, so the argument runs, imputed values cannot be calculated without market prices. Mises, however, can only assert that "it is in the very nature" of socialist production that the shares of land, labor, and capital are indeterminate. While there may be an exchange of consumer goods under socialism and it may be that money will be utilized as a kind of *numéraire,* his only important point is that production goods cannot be evaluated, making genuine economic calculation impossible. But when Mises admits in the same breath the possibility of socialist productive requirements being affected by demand, one begins to wonder whether his entire argument can really stand up! Clearly, if this is possible there must be a more intimate economic value relationship between the various sectors of the economy, even in a socialist system.

It should be obvious that the Mises-Hayek approach purports to make socialism a logical impossibility. When the Austrian utility analysis is adopted, valuation of consumer and producer goods take place through exchange value based on psychic entities. This must be so since it is the degree of participation and utilities that determines value. However, the transactions are entirely objective in themselves and they abstract from any utility comparisons. In fact, the latter is anathema to many economists. However, the economic calculations that come out of this process are short-run ones, avoiding price variability over the long haul or factors outside the cash nexus of the exchange equation. All that Mises and Hayek are interested in is the market itself and the wonderful job it does, for no human mind can encompass the "bewildering mass of intermediate products and potentialities of production." Socialism can't work because under socialism there is no exchange of production goods. Therefore, socialism is not a real economic system, at least not in the Mises-Hayek meaning.

## III

Curiously enough, the proper response to this seemingly devastating argument was available during the century's first decade in the writings of Vilfredo Pareto and some of his followers. Pareto had some rather sharp things to say about socialism in his *Les Systèmes Socialistes*.* Yet there stemmed from his ideas the notion that the general economic principles worked out for a capitalism could apply to socialism equally as well. Every society, whether it is Crusoe's, Jefferson's, or Carnegie's, has but limited resources which must be distributed efficiently among competing needs. The economic problem is to do this in a way that will bring about maximum results in productivity, in profits, in taxes, in sales, in satisfaction. The economic theorist is unconcerned with ultimate social ends: he leaves that to the philosopher. His realm is that of resource decision-making, wherein the correct apportionment of limited resources is the major objective.

Pareto's hint was developed further in a genuinely remarkable way by an Italian economist, Enrico Barone. An army colonel and later professor of political economy who also wrote film scripts, Barone was "a prodigy of speed in assimilation and simplification." A superb mathematician, he developed in greater detail the Paretian optimum idea, especially as it might be applied to the planning of production in a collective society. His analysis, presented in an unfinished article, "The Ministry of

* Paris, 2 volumes, 1902–03. *cf.* also Pareto's *Manuel d'Economique Politique,* Paris, 1907.

Production in a Collective State," developed socialist equilibrium equations somewhat analogous to Léon Walras' general equilibrium system for a free enterprise economy.* While in the latter the simultaneous answer for all the variables yields a solution for both production and distribution, a socialist economy would have to decide on distribution in advance. Only then might the decisions regarding production be worked out. The purchasing power distributed by the Ministry would provide the basis for constructing the necessary supply and demand schedules leading to the allocation of labor and savings. Investment decisions would have to be decided upon by the central authority.

The basic data essential for establishing the equilibrium conditions of the socialist equations include information on available capital, productive capacity, and coefficients of consumer tastes. The last merely implies that with a given set of prices, consumers distribute their income as between spending and saving in a certain way: it does not suggest an inquiry into utility or satisfaction. Four sets of equations are developed by Barone: the first relates to the physical basis of production; the others successively to new capital; the final cost of goods and services (which equals the prices of the factors of production); and the cost of production, which equals the prices of the final product plus the services of new capital. Given these equations as the basic economic model for production, there is no reason why a socialist Ministry cannot solve them as effectively as the free market. The basic precondition is simply that a pattern of income distribution be enforced which will maximize welfare in the Paretian sense. This suggests that in Barone's view production equilibrium in a socialist society depends on income distribution. Saving, interest, and net investment will all have to be provided for. But to dictate what proportion of income should be saved might detract from "welfare," hence it may be preferable to employ a system of premiums in order to bring saving into balance with investment. By deducting a part of income, it would be possible for the authorities to produce new capital in excess of amortization, that is, to engage in economic expansion.

The significant point in Barone's model is that the individual is left free to make his own choices among consumption goods. The only guiding rule the Ministry should observe is to "maximize welfare." This can be done by so adjusting production as to reduce the need for individual movement; that is, to order the economy in a way that would make everyone satisfied with his current situation. When cost of production is minimized and the value of the output corresponds to such minimum cost, then equilibrium will have been achieved. Thus, quite subtly, Barone has brought us to a point where there is no distinction between the system of equations in a collective society and that in free enterprise. As Paul Samuelson has said: "It is a tribute to his work that a third of a

* Reprinted in *Collectivist Economic Planning,* pp. 245 *ff.*

century after it was written there is no better statement of the problem in the English language to which the attention of the students may be turned."

Yet Barone felt that the equations could be tested only by an experimental approach, for they do not lend themselves to easy calculation. He thought that there were practical difficulties in establishing on paper the necessary numerical equivalents. However, should it be possible to process such data — and in this day of the electronic calculator this is no wild notion — there would be no serious analytical problems to face. The only hesitation that Barone expressed involved the enormous variability of the economic factors, rather than the technical ones. That is to say, as a theoretical matter, socialism was entirely feasible.

## IV

The definitive response to the Hayek-Mises broadside was given in the modern welfare approach beginning with Fred M. Taylor's famous 1928 presidential address to the American Economic Association.* The principles of this counterattack are relatively uncomplicated. In a socialist society the prices of finished goods as well as those of the factors of production are to be set by a process of trial and error. Equilibrium is reached by so adjusting the prices of these commodities as to eliminate surpluses or deficits. Decisions on output and investment are to be made by plant managers on the assumption that resources will be utilized up to the point at which the cost of producing an additional unit will just be covered by the prevailing unit return. The premise here is that marginal cost will increase with further output, so that production beyond the equality of marginal cost to price would merely incur losses. This is, of course, the short run view: in the long run new investment would be undertaken if the return from the added output would be equal to or even greater than the long period cost incurred.

The objective of this so-called "welfare" approach is to avoid centralizing investment and output decisions. All the Central Planning Board need do is to decide on the total amount to be invested, while the managers guide the direction of investment and output in consonance with the principle just outlined. The demand and supply of capital could be adjusted by the Central Planning Board by altering the rate of interest which, contrary to Marxist theory, would become part of long period cost.

Taylor's excellent essay argued that production in a socialist state would be guided in quite the same way as under private enterprise. The State would give its citizens a money income and authorize them to spend it in any way they desired. This assures independence of consumer

* Reprinted in *On the Economic Theory of Socialism,* Minneapolis, 1938.

choice. Taylor, however, makes no comment on the pattern of income distribution, merely assuming that the State, in the interest of maximizing welfare, would so distribute income as to benefit the entire citizenry. The purchases of the citizens would in effect constitute a social judgment. Commodity prices would be based on cost, defined as the "drain on the economic resources of the community," an unfortunately none too clear concept (which becomes even more obscure when Taylor hints that what he has in mind is the drain on primary materials). Capital goods, however, are fully amenable to evaluation by imputation, or derivation from the value of consumer goods. The socialist authorities, said Taylor, should be able to work up "factor valuation tables" which should give satisfactory results in costing items such as sewing machines or drill presses. Argued Taylor: "It would be necessary to multiply the valuation of each factor used in producing that machine by the quantity of that factor so used and add together these different products." The implication was that such a procedure could be easily stated in monetary terms.

An ideal socialism would be impelled by its very nature to guide its actions in accordance with consumer decisions. If prices of output were set at levels higher than the cost of the resources absorbed in their manufacture, the citizenry would in effect suffer a diminution of income. Too low a price would lead to shortages. A trial and error solution of price determination would result in a clearing of the market (the economist's equilibrium) and at the same time solve the problem of imputed value for capital goods. Whatever knowledge was available would supply the information for the factor valuation tables; enterprises would conduct their affairs as if the tables were correct; they would observe carefully the results of their decisions and make adjustments as needed. Too high a valuation would induce sparse utilization and lead to factor surplus; a low valuation would create shortages. Taylor concluded confidently that "if the economic authorities of a socialist state would recognize the equality between cost of production on the one hand and the demand price of the buyer on the other as being . . . adequate proof that the commodity in question ought to be produced, they could . . . perform their duties . . . with well-founded confidence that they would never make any other than the right use of the economic resources placed at their disposal."

Oskar Lange, a brilliant theoretical economist who spent some years in the U.S. before returning to postwar Poland, supported Taylor's argument with a persuasive series of articles in the *Review of Economic Studies* in 1936 and 1937.* Lange categorically rejected the contention that economic calculation is impossible in a socialist society. The fact is, said Lange, Mises-Hayck were confused by misreading the function of

* Reprinted, *op. cit.* pp. 57 *ff*.

prices, which are not only ratios of exchange but also general propositions for judging the economic terms on which alternatives are offered. It
is the latter concept that has meaning for a socialist society, for it is
precisely this notion which has relevance for the problem of allocation.
There is no reason why socialism cannot provide the institutional setting
for guiding choice and selecting alternatives. The latter would require
information regarding how inputs relate to outputs, or what is known as
the production function, in order to judge alternatives. But this should
not be difficult in a socialist state.

The argument about having to "solve" hundreds of these equations is
otiose, says Lange, for Hayek and Mises solve these equations every time
they buy a newspaper, as do millions of consumers, and doubtless there
are few mathematicians among them. The fact is, that even under capitalism, trial and error underlies the business of satisfying consumer needs
and allocating resources. In a theoretical sense consumers "maximize
total utility" by spending their income so that the marginal utility derived
from all applications is equal. Producers maximize their profits through
achieving an optimum scale of output, which is reached at the point
where marginal cost equals price. The fact is that in the competitive
situation price must be regarded as a parameter, that is, a variable constant, over which the individual producer has no direct influence. Since it
is only in such circumstances that the textbook version of the market
really comes into existence, it may be said, somewhat paradoxically, that
perfect competition can exist only in a socialist society.

If socialism begins its economic functioning with free consumer choice
in the selection of both goods and employment, then the Central Planning Board's "artificial" price system represents exactly the same sort or
parameter to which producers and consumers would have to react under
capitalism. Naturally, different behavior patterns would induce altera-
tions in the parametric set. Producers, instead of pursuing a course
which under capitalism is intended to maximize profit, now follow the
instructions of the Planning Board. The only rules they must obey are
those which require a proper combination of factors so that the scale of
production set by the equality of marginal cost to price will be achieved.
Furthermore, the lowest average cost of production can be assured if the
distribution of resources is such as will make the marginal productivity
of inputs equal in all possible uses. The prices of capital goods — again
the imputation problem — can be worked out by starting with the historical costs available to the Planning Board when it is created and subsequently working out trial and error adjustments. Errors can be quickly
corrected since they would be localized rather than distributed throughout the economy.

Lange does concede that arbitrary decisions regarding the rate of in-

terest would be a disadvantage, since this would not necessarily reflect
consumer wishes. The Planning Board, in other words, would have to decide for itself an appropriate rate of capital accumulation. Another thorny
question stems from the apportionment of labor among the different occupations. Here, the need to balance rewards with "disutilities of work"
would lead to unequal incomes, an outcome directly in conflict with the
objective of an equal income distribution. Lange would overcome this
anomaly by supplying suitable doses of free incomes — leisure, parks,
social services, and the like — all of which would create the effect of
equal income.

Insofar as the political framework was concerned, Lange at that time
did not suggest that the institutional changes he was advocating would
abolish private property. In small industry and farming, where competition was still effective, there would be no need to alter property relationships, for all that a socialistic economy should do is to assure, at the very
least, a formal competitive system. Where competition already exists
there is no need to disturb the situation. However, socialism cannot be
brought about by gradual means, argued Lange. It must be done all at
once in those areas where it will operate most effectively, or else the
"withdrawal of efficiency" by opponents will ensue.

Lange's views on these matters reveal a certain naïveté regarding the
complexities involved in achieving a political and economic transformation. The admission that rationing might be employed to supplement the
efforts of the Central Planning Board must certainly vitiate the applicability of his rules for governing the economy, for this would necessitate
the utilization of output quotas in order to achieve a given production
goal. This gives his system an uncomfortable resemblance to the Soviet
economic order.

The central problem in the new society, says Lange, is the growth of
bureaucracy, which can easily become ossified and inflexible in dealing
with subtle matters of economic planning. But he insists, no civilized
people would tolerate such a situation (thus quite underestimating the
extreme limits to which the human being can be pushed). However, he
does score a point in his debate with Mises-Hayek when he argues that to
measure the efficiency of a socialist bureaucracy one ought to compare it
with the work of corporation officials rather than a capitalist civil service. Socialism, we are told, can create a democratic administrative machinery if it develops an atmosphere of publicity and responsibility.

There were other economists who developed interesting variants of the
Taylor-Lange model, among them Abba P. Lerner, H. D. Dickinson,
and E. F. M. Durbin. Even Gustav Cassel, the noted Swedish economist
and a rather strong opponent of socialism, was able to demonstrate how

a socialist economy might function in his classic *Theory of Social Economy*.* Abba Lerner's original ideas were developed in 1936, when he still considered himself to be a socialist and was quite anxious to develop marginal analysis for the solution of economic problems in a socialist society. His view was that prices must be so set that resources freed by reduced output would be sufficient to produce an equal sum of another good. That is, no commodity should be produced unless its importance is greater than the alternative which had been foregone. While Lerner acknowledges that the technique for achieving this aim might at best be an approximate one he doubts that this would represent any real impediment.†

It was in his *Economics of Control* that Lerner first set forth a positive statement of his views.‡ (The earlier articles were somewhat pedantic quarrels with other writers on definitions of overhead cost, prime cost, and which significant marginal concepts should apply in a socialist state.) The book was begun as a treatise on socialist economics, but in the process of composition Fabian socialist ideas were displaced by New Dealism. Although the work discusses the economics of socialism, the major emphasis is on the theory of control in a capitalist society. Lerner's major objective became an attempt to reveal those operations of the price mechanism which would be applicable to laissez-faire as well as collectivism.

The marginalist rules that are worked out are intended to control both price and output. A basic prerequisite, as in all these systems of diffused control, is freedom of action and choice in both commodity and factor markets. The guiding rule is a simple one: factory managers are to be instructed to increase output so long as the value of the marginal product of any factor is greater than its price. In actuality, the problem would be a good deal more complicated than Lerner's rule suggests, for in putting the matter this way the operational difficulties were simply pushed to one side. Furthermore, combining the factors of production and establishing rules for setting price policy are really distinct matters, but in Lerner's guide book these were subsumed in a single set of "instructions."

Lerner argues that his is a middle of the road economics, quite neutral in its political implications. The economics of control suggest, however, that governments have the responsibility to see to it that all resources are properly employed, that monopoly is minimized, and that income is dis-

* Originally published 1918, translated New York, 1924. Other noteworthy discussions may be found in James E. Meade, *Planning and the Price Mechanism*, New York, 1949; E. F. M. Durbin, *Problems of Economic Planning*, London, 1949; W. A. Lewis, *Principles of Economic Planning*, London, 1949; Carl Landauer, *Theory of National Economic Planning*, Berkeley, 1944; and B. P. Beckwith, *Marginal Cost Price — Output Control*, New York, 1955. Space limitations do not permit a detailed discussion of these writers.
† A. P. Lerner, *Essays in Economic Analysis*, London, 1953, pp. 38 *ff.*
‡ New York, 1944.

tributed in the most efficacious manner. The latter, it is said, will be at an optimum when it is no longer possible to increase welfare or satisfactions by further shifting goods among the citizenry. At this point the marginal substitutability of goods would be equal for all. It is not clear how goods would be exchanged in Lerner's scheme, although barter arises as a possibility. A money economy might be instituted through the distribution of a proper *numéraire*. Again, satisfactions could be increased by shifting incomes about from those whose usefulness for money is less to those whose utility is greater.

Now, the Central Planning Board would doubtless discover how intricate the task is to compare the value of marginal products, presumably necessary to judge relative efficiencies. The best way out of the dilemma is to simply allow plant managers to price output according to ordinary markets procedures. The planning board would still have enough work to do, says Lerner wryly, in supervising managerial operations. But the main point, he avers, is that individuals would be induced to pursue those economic measures that in themselves result in social gains. This gets quite close to Adam Smith's invisible hand. Says Lerner, ". . . every individual in trying to minimize his own sacrifice of alternatives when he spends his money income to his own best advantage is led automatically and even unconsciously to minimize the social sacrifice in producing what gives him most satisfaction." Yet Lerner does acknowledge that private enterprise as constituted today cannot fulfill the requirements of "optimum allocation"; monopoly, advertising, and product differentiation set up barriers which impede the attainment of welfare. The objective of the controlled economy therefore would be to work toward the conditions necessary for achieving an optimum. This, then, brings Lerner around to the very "competitive solution" from which he originally demurred, for only by assuring that market impediments would not arise could the Central Planning Board point toward a welfare goal.

Perhaps the final word on the kind of socialism we are discussing was given by Joseph A. Schumpeter.* He begins by asking, "Can socialism work?" and his answer is: "Of course it can." "No doubt is possible about that," he continues, "once we assume, first that the requisite stage of industrial development has been reached and second, that transitional problems can be successfully resolved." Schumpeter's institutional setup includes a Central Planning Board, although there might be a parliament or other elective body to set basic policy. He also assumes that plant managers would need some degree of freedom to decide on production: in fact, a socialist economy could not function effectively until a *modus vivendi* had been established between managerial latitude and central

* cf. his *Capitalism, Socialism and Democracy*, New York, 1942, pp. 167 ff.

control. Yet of all the writers on this problem, Schumpeter, whose ab-
horrence for socialism was well known, was the only one to realize that
the new society had to be more than a matter of the full stomach: socialism, he held, implied a new kind of human being, toward the development of which economics was no great help. In fact, he said, reflecting
his concept of economics as neutralist mechanics, the principles of a
socialist economy could hold for any kind of society, so long as the marginalist rules were observed.

Technically speaking, the basic question is whether the economic data
of socialism would permit the formulation of equations which are consistent and sufficient in number to permit a solution of all the un-
knowns. To Schumpeter there is no question but that this is entirely possible. Insofar as the Lange-Mises debate is concerned, it is the latter who
is in error. Schumpeter grants that under socialism political decisions
will guide the initial distribution of income. In a completely egalitarian
society income will be divided evenly: but a less than completely egalitarian socialism is also conceivable. Whatever the pattern is, the Central
Planning Board need only see to it that all the vouchers distributed are
equal to the total available consumer goods. The Central Planning Board
would allocate basic resources to individual plants on condition that
managers pursue economical means and follow marginal principles in
their pricing policies. Enterprises will know what their production schedules should be as soon as prices are announced and consumer demand is
known. The Central Planning Board has only to set prices at that level
which would clear the market; naturally, this would be in accordance
with the marginalist rule, for "as long as this rule is being observed no
element of productive resources can be devoted to any other line of production without causing destruction of as much consumer's values, expressed in terms of consumer's dollars, as that element would add to its
new employment."

Schumpeter stressed the point, often voiced by nineteenth-century socialists, that a socialist society, to be successful, ought to inherit from its
capitalist predecessor a full endowment of skills, experience, and techniques. That is to say, a socialist society should follow a mature capitalism. Again, as did Lange, Schumpeter saw bureaucracy as a major problem. It is inevitable that such a society would require a large number of
administrators. But despite the serious administrative problems stemming from a flowering of government staff, socialism could still function
more effectively than capitalism, for the very element that absorbs the
full energy of the capitalist, uncertainty, will have been abolished. No
longer would plant operations have to be predicated on the probability of
rival operations, for these would be known through the Central Planning
Board. There would be no waste of resources or delays in timing, and the
reserves for conducting economic warfare, so characteristic of a capital-

ist economy, would be eliminated. The Central Board could also adjust its investment program so that the trade cycle would become an archaic phenomenon. In fact, the ". . . socialist management could attain [its goal] with less disturbance and loss without necessarily incurring the disadvantages that would attend attempts at planning progress within the framework of capitalist institutions." It is Schumpeter's contention that socialism could be as superior to big business capitalism as the latter is to the eighteenth-century competitive system.

Socialist rationality, continued Schumpeter, is superior to capitalist rationality: technological improvements in a capitalist society must simmer through the economy via gradual adoption by individual firms, while under socialism such improvements can be adopted simultaneously by all enterprises. But above all, the saving in cost through the elimination of economic strife would be enormous. In fact, society might very well spare the work of some occupations, such as that of lawyers, for in the absence of private property and capitalism's typically complex tax structure, what would they have to do? There would be no demigods about, only ordinary citizens. The clerk would still look at a Sunday football game through socialist TV while experts, professionals, and politicians would abound. It is even possible that a socialist bureaucracy might develop useful incentives that would not hamper the proper functioning of the economy. But the chief merit of a socialism rooted in welfare concepts lies in its clear revelation of the true nature of economic phenomena, something all too obscure in capitalism.

## V

One might have thought that Schumpeter's approach would have met with the approval of even those for whom Marx has always had the last word. But this, unfortunately, is not the case. Marginalism, opportunity cost, and consumer choice have always exemplified mere bourgeois prejudice to orthodox Marxists. Such writers as Maurice Dobb, Paul Baran, and Paul Sweezy, knowledgeable as they are in the ways of ordinary economics, reject welfare theorems as thoroughly unsuitable to a socialist economy. For them, the assumption of consumer sovereignty is somewhat silly, since lopsided distribution of income makes "voting" in the market a patently uneven affair. Welfare socialism could not overcome this condition since some trades would be receiving more income by virtue of a higher social valuation of their output or because of greater relative scarcity. This would merely perpetuate uneven income distribution, they say. In fact, equal incomes, say these critics, would simply distort the cost structure unless a system of bounties and taxes were instituted. For these reasons, says Dobb, competitive socialism is an illusion. The determination of priorities in production through marginalist analysis, he insists, is unnecessary, for it may be essential for socialism to invest as heavily as possible in capital goods. What Dobb suggests is that the socialist economy forego present needs in the interest of building up future satisfactions; there is no other meaning which can be given to his advice than that the planning authorities "violate the principle of equimarginal returns and apply a different time discount to different sections of an industry." *

That this is a theoretical justification for Soviet experience is inescapable. Paul Baran's reaction to welfare socialism is even sharper, if less subtle. He simply dismisses it as irrelevant, for it is an unwarranted assertion to say that the kind of "welfare" stemming from capitalism is equivalent to that of a socialist state.† The values and aims, he argues, which determine economic choice, are conditioned by the features of a particular social system. Hence, no purpose can be served by establishing socialist optimums which are borrowed almost in their entirety from an individualistic economics.

In Baran's view, a socialist economy will not be based on consumer sovereignty. Since he takes the Soviet economy as a model, it is necessary to grant him this premise. One can only question whether sovietism is genuine socialism, for as Baran concedes, the State would have to mold consumer choice ". . . in the interest of the community as a whole." Change, he insists, requires compulsion. Opportunity cost is of no aid in working up major decisions regarding the proper choice "among the few technological alternatives involving large indivisibilities and fixed coefficients." Unfortunately for Mr. Baran's thesis, some leading Russian economists have been stumbling toward opportunity-cost notions. The systems of priorities could not be worked out via the labor theory and they have had to devise techniques which can only be described as virtually marginalist. The Baran-Dobb attitude merely explains why economic theory has progressed so little in the Soviet Union.

Dobb is even more centralist in his views than Baran. In an early essay he insisted that socialist economics could be discussed only in terms of the Soviet scheme of things.‡ Since capitalist class relations are done away with, the coordination of production must be more direct than the market allows. Welfare socialism means a diffusion of decisions and consequently a diffusion of results so that the old tendency to disequilibrium would be simply carried over. But why this should be so, Dobb seldom makes clear. His concern is to justify the Soviet crash program and to this end he develops a theory of investment saturation. Decisions must be made centrally, for action by individual enterprises would only lead to

* Maurice Dobb, *On Economic Theory and Socialism,* London, 1955, pp. 38 *ff*.
† *cf.* Baran's essay on economic planning in *Survey of Contemporary Economics,* Homewood, 1952, Vol. II, pp. 355 *ff*.
‡ *cf.* his *Political Economy and Capitalism,* London, 1937, p. 273.

uneven development. Ordinarily, saving, consumption, and income are the outcomes of disconnected acts, but with planning these are all "separate facets of a single decision." Thus, there is no need for the Central Planning Board to follow the competitive solution, for this would only duplicate capitalist calamities. Consumer choice, argues Dobb, is not a reliable guide, for individual desire may easily conflict with social requirements. Moreover, he says, the presumption that consumer choice would be any more rational under welfare socialism than under capitalism is unwarranted. Choice under competitive conditions, says Dobb, reveals a bias toward a greater variety of goods than is necessary for the collective interest. The result is a kind of Gresham's law of taste in which the base satisfactions begin to dominate the social outlook. Thus, consumer sovereignty does not necessarily imply the development of desirable goals, it is averred.

But as Abba Lerner remarked, Dobb seems to be searching for a transcendental optimum in which an attempt would be made to create an ethic of social behavior based on some kind of undefined collective consensus. Why such collective choices should be superior to individual action is not made clear. Nor is Dobb able to specify the nature of economic law in his centralist socialism, unless it be *diktat* from the top administrative body, as with the Soviets. At best, we learn only that economic law is concerned with how man handles materials, a trite and none too informed proposition. The analysis of the relation of wage income to the value of consumer goods is little more than a restatement of Marx's surplus value theory in the phraseology of receipts and costs. Dobb's main point is that production requires a proper balance between component elements at different points of time, so that each stage of production is defined as part of the process of making a finished commodity in the distant future. Aside from the fact that this is as much a technological as it is an economic problem, it also offers a neat justification for a policy of applying up to one-fourth of national output to gross investment. Needless to say, the kind of socialism which Dobb found so attractive before the war has hardly come up to the expectation that its primary concern would be humanity.

Dobb's version of the socialist scheme begins with a set of equations in which wages equal consumption goods and "profit" is equal to a certain share of consumer goods. The Central Planning Board is concerned mainly with technological decisions: the size of plants, their number and location, the labor input, and the like. Investment, says Dobb, can be self-financing, for when a price is set for investment goods, wages will tend to increase because of the resulting increased demand, causing prices to rise. The consequent "profit" can be used to finance further investment. But the Planning Board cannot follow the marginalist principle in doing all this, he says, for then the amount of employment would be governed entirely by the investment process. This would mean that adjustments in the labor force would depend solely on the operation of impersonal marginalist relationships rather than on the will of the Planning Board and consequently would be "clearly irrational." Decisions on alternate investment possibilities should be made by inspection. All the board need do is to work out the ratio of productivity to the cost of a project and in this way work up a list of priorities which would enable it to plan investment over the long period. This would eliminate uncertainty; control would be maintained over key decisions rather than diffused through the economy; high standards of production can be established; new plants would produce new goods rather than duplicate old ones; and "unnecessary" products would be forbidden.

Quite obviously, Dobb and Baran prefer a "command economy." In their view socialism cannot function unless it is highly centralized with all the decisions predetermined by some planning board. No choice is to be allowed to people, and the putative higher requirements of the State are to dominate even unto the exclusion of the rights of the public to decide for itself its own fate. The subtlety of the argument is not denied and the technical effectiveness of a command economy has been well demonstrated by Russian industrial achievements. But it is an argument for totalitarianism nevertheless. That it has anything to do with socialist ethics and socialist values is doubtful. Simply enough, socialism can no longer be discussed purely in economic terms. In fact, it seems reasonable to suggest that the way in which a socialist economy works must be in consonance with the moral and political aims that socialists seek to attain. In such a framework the competitive solution of market socialism seems by far the more desirable objective. Even the economic arguments in its favor are impressive: freedom of choice to consumers; a minimum of controls over plant managers; the utilization of pecuniary incentives for socialist purposes; the minimizing of failures through "trial and error" procedures; the reduction of inequality of income; and above all, the elimination of instability and unemployment. The recent history of Britain and Scandinavia suggests that there is validity in these arguments.

1959

# THE RIGHT TO BE LAZY

## HENRY PACHTER

What the Lord did on the eighth day the Bible does not state; it is permitted to speculate that He continued to rest and, for all that the last million years' record shows, never returned to the hectic working spree of the first six days. And when, after another million years, He will be sitting gloriously on His throne, with angels leisurely winging around Him, He will behold His arrangement with satisfaction and say: All is as it should be. By definition, anyone who can offer Himself such a long vacation must be God; by the same token, the lesser breeds are eating their bread in the sweat of their brow. He will muse upon the sorry fate of the Devil, busily running the world, rushing hither and thither to aggrandize his little kingdom and really leading one hell of an existence. And He will take pity on the damned — Sisyphus rolling his stone up hill, Tantalus hopping for his apples, the Danaides pouring water into the bottomless barrel.

For it's labor that is Hell and leisure that is Paradise. Mankind knew that even when it was very young. We never got over that first and most effective of all curses which was the punishment for the first sin. The curse has worked well indeed; we still think it's a sin to revive that blissful state which existed before the Fall. But the wisdom of the peoples has never forgotten; it imagines Heaven as the absence of pain and effort; it exalts royalty ("The king was in the counting house . . .") as representatives of the gods on earth — clearly because leisure is the measure of distinction and pleasure is divine.

Anyway, the people have always been wiser than the textbooks; they never believed that wealth makes no man happy. Neither do they believe that riches are usually come by the hard way. Experience shows that the harder the work, the less the pay. The dirtiest jobs are not paid in proportion to the marginal "disutility" or distaste of their execution, but in accordance with the disrepute in which a person stooping to them is held by his equals and betters. Society may teach children that work never dishonors anybody, but when they grow up they would rather work less and receive higher honors.

This, Aristotle would say had he lived to see it, is as Nature would have it; for it is debatable whether those who do the menial work have a soul, whereas those who have leisure to enjoy the pleasures of life, must of necessity have richer experience and a larger scope of soul. The more leisure the higher the rank on the social scale. On the other hand, the most effective slogan of revolutionary class hatred has been: he that does not toil neither shall he eat.

That terrible revolution did happen, though the exact time of its happening is not quite clear. Sociologists generally credit the Reformation with bringing about a complete change in people's attitudes toward work. Dr. Martin Luther, it will be remembered, rejected "good works," apparently because they interfere with works *tout court,* good or bad; he taught that the rich and mighty would go to heaven despite their bad works and the poor to hell for their good works; he also admonished the princes to keep the peasants in their place, and if failing, to quarter, wheelbreak, blind, whip, and hang them. An even gloomier chap was Calvin. When he governed Geneva he declared it a sin against God and a burden on the city's treasury if any man were idle; he sent the spiritual and terrestrial police into every household to make sure every man was working. He was one of the first churchmen to condone a modest amount of usury (by calling it interest; stinginess he called thrift, and hoarding — diligence). His defense of the usurer was echoed by that staunch churchman, Mellon, who never foreclosed properties unless the tenants were "weakened by bad habits and extravagant living" — which unfortunately he found to be the case fairly regularly. Calvin never married and he forbade his followers all pleasures, luxuries, and above all, idleness, which gives a man ideas. Before Freud he discovered that frustration can be converted into furious work. His friend Zwingli thought that "labor is a thing so godlike . . . in things of life, the laborer is most like to God."

Their later followers, however, found it difficult to persuade sensible men that this could be true, if only because the Catholics were having a good time and still expected God's forgiveness. Therefore they invented Calling. It is difficult to explain Calling if you can't say it's another word for work. Calling means work as a crusade; it means that a man has been identified with his work so intimately that his life no longer consists of hours of work and hours of play or rest: it is all work. If he does rest, it is to restore his energy for work; his recreation, too, must be usefully employed; his play must exercise his mental or physical powers. *Kraft durch Freude* was not invented by the Nazis; this mentality had been there all along waiting to be topped off with the usual German instinct for turning all-too-seriousness into ridicule. The Americans are only slightly behind the Germans; however, as is fitting, our example comes not from government propaganda but from commercial advertising. A maker of foam rubber tells us to "rest efficiently" on his mattresses. Now, I like foam rubber and using it for rest should be a pleasure, but that ad man has spoiled it for me. If I feel that even in my sleep I am being efficient I don't enjoy it anymore.

Even Calvin's universe had its rewards, however. In the first place, work was pleasing to God; then, to follow one's Calling brought recognition among men. Some people's Calling did not call them to great deeds, nor to great riches either; but just to fill one's place as ordained from on high. Doing one's job well was satisfaction in itself. Finally, a man could look with pride at his work. Whatever he did was completely his own and even if done in cooperation with others, he still had insight into the whole process. Our language has retained a reminiscence of this bliss: we still say "work" for both the act of creating and the product. By contrast, we say "labor" for the expenditure of human energy and for the supply of same. In the English language (and in none other, so far as I know), the word "job" can be set aside to name the social and economic relationship between the worker and his working place. Since language is prefabricated thought, a worker referring to his "job" is revealing a truth about modern society; he is "class-conscious." But if he naïvely says "my work," forgetting that he neither owns his product nor controls the process of its production, he atavistically uses conceptions from the craftsman's age. His parlance beclouds the fact that under the conditions of industrial capitalism the worker is separated from his product, first by a huge apparatus of machinery which does not belong to him, second by his contract which deprives him of the fruit of his labor, third by the market. All he knows is that for the time being he has a job requiring him to supply a specified amount of labor and to cooperate in the production of some merchandise which his boss thinks he can sell. Usually he specializes in some phase of production and has very little insight into the whole process. He cannot possibly feel the satisfaction of an artisan looking at his work; he is not asked to be "creative" and has very little chance even to show ingenuity. All his pride is concentrated on the work process, which he can speed up, even improve, but which never leads to any fulfillment or end.

The more efficient the worker is, *qua* worker, the greater his estrangement from his product. So much of it passes over his work bench; he boasts of his inventiveness in cutting corners, getting out more production in a given time, making more money to take home.

The myth of Productivity has driven out the friendly gods of old. In their place we have enthroned the religion of efficiency. We love efficiency, paradoxically, for two reasons: it saves "labor," but on the other hand it makes working more efficient. If efficiency were used only to speed up our working hours and extend our leisure time, it would be all to the good. But this is not the case at all, or very rarely so. My hero in technology always was that attendant boy who was too lazy to turn by hand all the valves on Newcomen's first primitive steam engine; he connected the various faucets with rods which later were attached to the flywheel, and thus invented the feedback. This invention really was meant to save "work"; but when his employers later used it, they did so to save "labor." Now here is the paradox: as a human being, the worker should be glad that machinery was being invented to relieve him of (at least some of) the drudgery; as an employee he had to fight hard not to be relieved entirely by the machine. Under capitalistic conditions he had to fight on two fronts — on the one hand for his "right to work," on the other hand for his "right to leisure." Fortunately, both flies could be caught with the same swatter — the long history of class strife in the nineteenth century is the story of a gradual shortening of the working day. With this device, workers have assured themselves a place among human beings; they have won recognition for their desire to rest and play beyond the call of duty, while at the same time they have stretched the need for labor.

The price of better working conditions was the division of labor, or the acceptance of, and acquiescence in, the conditions of factory work by the worker, his integration into a huge organization of well laid out production processes, his subservience to the requirements of machine production. In this organization, the worker no longer has control over his product; at best, he may have control of his machine, but in most cases the machine will have control of him. Only the top management has control of production and the sales manager has control of the product. The worker often does not even see his product, he even may have little insight into the production process. When the first news of the atomic bomb was published, the most shocking revelation, to me, was not its enormous power of destruction, but the report that thousands of people had been employed in its production without knowing what they were doing. Here all the traditional notions of "workmanship," "pride in one's work," "calling," were voided of any meaning. Professional prowess no longer lies in "creativeness" nor in anything that refers to the product. The satisfaction is not in creating the product; it is in productivity. The worker is completely estranged from his product, and in fact, any opinion research probing a little beneath the surface will reveal that workers love their machines but are indifferent to what they produce. (Foundations please take note; this is a really worthwhile project which also might be interesting to management.)

Marxist critics of capitalism first considered "alienation" as a purely economic estrangement of the worker from his product. No amount of worker participation will overcome this condition, for the simple reason that even under the most favorable conditions, the employers don't have control over the verdict of the market either. The condition, however, also is inherent in modern mass production as such; even an entirely state-controlled or cooperative enterprise cannot escape it. The remedy is trade union action which gets for the worker as much out of the proceeds as the market will carry — a remedy which does not remedy the situation, but makes it less obnoxious. The enterprise can give the worker a very decent or even a very high (monopolistic) wage and make working conditions for him really pleasant with MUZAK, air conditioning, coffee break, and other devices of "human engineering," all justified as conducive to higher efficiency, of course; still, we are even more deeply entangled in the basic contradiction — that work and leisure are two very different things; the devices of personnel management only help to underline the basic fact that labor is measured by its disutility to the worker, that he strives to exert himself less, to spend less time inside the factory, has no pride in his work and gets little satisfaction out of a job well done — except perhaps the promotion which enables him to spend more time outside the factory and enjoy it better. This condition transcends capitalism; it is characteristic of all industrial societies, including a socialist economy based on industrial production. Isn't it significant that travelers to Utopia usually find themselves in garden cities suggesting a precapitalist society?

All the devices of human engineering and personnel relations are just so many acknowledgments of the fact that work generally is unpleasant, that office hours are a nuisance, and work discipline is degrading. This unpleasantness is overcome by morale-building ideologies, such as "work ennobles the worker," "common interest goes before self-interest," "duty before pleasure," "there is a war on." Sportsmanlike nations can be persuaded to stage productivity competitions, warlike nations can be asked to outproduce the enemy. Totalitarian governments particularly have developed techniques of combining war ideology with racing images; they constantly organize battles of the grain, battles of production, battles of the cradle, etc. Failure to increase production unfailingly results in a charge of "sabotage," but the most potent device of totalitarian imposition is the myth of Productivity which persuades the worker that his job is his duty, and that Duty, or one's job, stands higher in the hierarchy of values than one's personal needs.

At best, such verbalizations are the results of utter confusion; when the philosophers speak of *homo faber,* they mean the inventor, the creator, the playful explorer, the craftsman perhaps, but never the industrial worker. Man is free and creative only when he plays; he transcends himself only when his work serves no purpose; he fulfills himself only when he has no "job" to do. He develops his personality only when he throws off the thraldom of labor. He creates "works" only where he is not in the position of a "worker." The nihilistic, fascist ideologist, Ernst Juenger, went as far as to "suggest the question, whether workers are not of a third sex"; a robot need not be human.

That workers are people was most forcefully asserted by Marx's son-in-law, Paul Lafargue, in his slogan "The Right to be Lazy." His pamphlet under this title tells the story of a hundred years' fight for shorter hours; but there was more to it. Lafargue had not been brought up in the Calvinist virtues and did not believe in the pseudo-socialist philosophy that work alone redeems man from this vale of miseries. He felt that man needed very much to be redeemed from the obligation to work, and saw that industrial machinery might help him to get rid of the drudgery. Much as he welcomed this opportunity, he also saw the danger of man's enslavement by the machines. The bold speculations of his eminent father-in-law on the all-pervasiveness of labor made him uneasy; he did not deny that socialists should fight for "the right to work," but he was not so sure that they also should fight for the duty to work. To him, it was just as important to fight for the right not to work. He was a brave man who truly believed in freedom, and when he felt that his life had been played out, he allowed no duty to retain him; he quit, even in his last action asserting a man's right to take his life into his own hands.

Lafargue was thirty years younger than Marx, and in the meantime two more generations have passed. To say that I disagree with Marx amounts to saying that today I can see where Marx was a child of his age. He believed in work as man's salvation from exploitation. His enemies were the leisure classes which were monopolizing consumption. The streak of the Jewish prophet and chiliast in Marx blinded him to the virtues of luxury and pleasure; his own life was that of a zealot; he poked fun at Lassalle's suggestion that the workers ought to increase their desiderata. So deeply was he steeped in the idea of productivity that he even proposed labor service, and his idea of progressive education was to

merge the factories with the schoolroom. Marx was a Victorian gentleman and a Prussian scholar, besides being an Apostle of Justice; in neither
capacity did he understand the workers. He had made himself such a
high image of the ideal proletarian (with arms growing thinner and fists
erected higher) that the specimens whom he met in real life usually annoyed him. Philosophical materialist, he liked them best when they were
least concerned with the good life; and he honestly expected them to
sacrifice their consumer interests to the beauties of the socialist society of
pure producers.

Under the conditions of capitalism, the worker tries to welsh on his
contract and delivers less labor than he is expected to; the employer, on
the other hand, holds the union responsible for the delivery of an honest
day's work. Under state socialism or state capitalism, the worker's interest in his "job" is supposed to wax to enthusiastic proportions; it's "his"
state he is working for and the benefit is supposed to accrue to all. As a
consumer and taxpayer, the worker certainly should tell himself, as his
own employee, to work harder; but unless he develops a split personality
it does not happen that way. His participation in management is only
vicarious; he may be his boss in the abstract; but this abstract personality
confronts him in the alienated shape of a supervisor, and the conflict can
be resolved only by institutionalizing the split of personality — free
trade unions must bargain as his representatives (*qua* worker) with
management as his representative (*qua* consumer). Management still
will insist on labor-saving devices to cut costs, while the union will ask
for work-saving devices even if they are costly. This applies notably to
jobs which are dirty and demand great exertions, but give little or no
satisfaction psychologically.

I simply do not believe that "socialist conscience" will drive anybody
to volunteer for the job of a groundhog. Lowly jobs can be filled only by
one of four devices: higher wages; special honors and/or some sense of
adventure that may be connected with them; labor service or some other
form of forced labor; finally, the presence of a lower class or race whose
members are prevented from rising to better positions. I reject the last
two and consider the second as too rare to be generalized. Groundhogs
must be paid higher wages or given longer vacations after the first enthusiasm of exerting themselves for their own government has worn off. The
same, however, though less drastically demonstrable, is true of all government efforts to increase productivity. A socialist government wishing
to stay clear of compulsion must recognize the freedom of trade unions
and cooperatives. I cannot imagine a socialist society in which all is eternal harmony; least of all can I accept the ideal of a docile labor force,
bent on furiously fulfilling its duty toward the socialist fatherland and
enthusiastically improving its productivity. If capitalism were to be criticized only because it is wasteful and inefficient, I would have little quar-

rel with it; but it is wasteful with human happiness and economical only with material goods. I expect socialism to be rather wasteful with material resources but thrifty with unpleasantness imposed on human beings. The most efficient, i.e., cost-saving, economical way of producing merchandise may not always be the best from the standpoint of the worker's comfort. Our technology has advanced efficiency to provide for everybody; we can well afford to be inefficient wherever it suits us better. There was a time when "monopolies" were accused of sabotaging technological progress for the sake of profit. Today, automation is precipitating a new industrial revolution before society has made the necessary adjustments to use the new efficiency for the benefit of all mankind. We have become slaves of Progress; we have not dared to stop the development of atomic power as long as the nations cannot agree on disarmament. Marx was right against the Luddites: industrialism and capitalism could not be arrested but had to be digested. The atom, however, is right against Marx, and we have not digested its implications yet. The age of the robot is here; mankind can sit back and relax; the need for efficiency no longer worries us; productivity no longer is the measure of human contribution to the process of production; our needs can be filled by push-button operations.

Our problem is rather to increase our ability to enjoy our leisure time. We need to develop our creative ranges of play; we need to learn what it means to be free from the drudgery of work. Up to now our play has been modeled after the image of our work; even in consuming we maintained producer attitudes, or even worse — the dull and dutiful attitudes of factory work. We have to forget, to un-learn the producer attitudes; we have to renounce efficiency and productivity as human attributes. We have to insist on our right to be lazy and just human.

Indeed, why efficiency? It is generally agreed that socialism will be a very cumbersome way of providing administration and planning. If we admit, with Engels, that the cook ought to have a go at ruling the state, I am afraid we shall not only eat less well but also have more serious reasons to gripe (by the way, I think this is absolutely necessary and healthy; people under socialism must have some outlet for their natural aggressiveness). If we rotate labor from town to country, from manual to clerical, from executing to executive, out goes the expert and the efficiency. Not that I believe in these silly devices; I only refer to them for two purposes: first, to show that even the fathers of socialist thought, who introduced them, must have been aware that socialism is not a way to organize society more efficiently. Second, they show how much they were aware of the problem of human values which I am discussing here. But in those days they could only think of making work more "humane"; they had to organize their ideas of socialism around man the producer. It was only natural that they had to come to ridiculous conclusions. I suspect it might even be shown that the idea of totalitarian dictatorship is inherent in their conception of productivity. Now we can make the Copernican turn: not by thinking of better devices of organizing *homo faber* shall we liberate him from the realm of necessity, but by resolutely acknowledging his human ability to enjoy life and to act creatively in purposeless play.

Once labor has been recognized as something to get away from and leisure has been recognized as the legitimate and significant sphere of human endeavors, we even might expect those psychological changes which are just utopian dreams in the classical theory of socialism. The founding fathers all imagined that socialist production habits would create community spirit and other virtues which would prevent the recurrence of acquisitiveness and of war. There was neither proof in theory for such possibilities, nor did experiment bear these hopes out, except where communities were founded on a strictly religious basis. If we succeed, however, in substituting a religion of laziness for the worship of industriousness, the acquisitive instincts, while they still cannot be killed, might find no cultural and social nourishment and no economic sphere in which they could become active. Indeed, Fourier's paranoiac conjecture of a new animal might for the first time be rationally discussed. Those who might find some of his suggestions strange are asked to consider that he believed in play, too.

• •

P.S.: My attention is drawn to the following passage from *Das Kapital*, Vol. III, Pt. 2, ch. 48: "The realm of freedom does not begin until work stops being determined by need and external necessity; by nature it lies beyond the realm of material production proper . . . [even under socialist planning, labor] always remains in the realm of necessity. Beyond this begins that humane development of human energy which finds its end in itself, the true realm of freedom. . . ." Marx indeed here seems less orthodox, from the standpoint of alienated philosophy, than I suspected, while I seem less heretical, from the Marxian point of view, than I fondly believed. But there is a Marx quotation for every occasion, and overlooking the whole trend of his thinking, I would agree with Erich Fromm that Marx more than other socialist writers was influenced by the ideas of his time. Incidentally, I regret a difference of terminology with Fromm's fine discussion of the same problem in his new book *The Sane Society;* I read it after this essay had been set, otherwise it would have been easy to coordinate my language with his.

1956

# THE THIRD DIMENSION OF GEORG LUKACS

## HAROLD ROSENBERG

". . . everlasting uncertainty and agitation distinguish the bourgeois epoch from all earlier ones. All fixed, fast-frozen relations . . . are swept away, all new-formed ones become antiquated before they can ossify. All that is solid melts in the air . . ."

*The Communist Manifesto*

"I have tried to show that these [*angst* and chaos] form the essential content of modernism. This vision of the world as chaos results from the lack of a humanist social perspective."

GEORG LUKACS, *The Meaning of Contemporary Realism*

I remember Lukacs from the thirties as a Marxist literary critic who all agreed was a great, original thinker, though no one I knew had read more than one or two of his pieces. My own assent to his reputation was based on Lukacs's theory of "intellectual physiognomy," which explained what made characters in novels and plays profound or trivial. "Intellectual physiognomy" seemed to me the answer to a deep riddle of fiction: how an Othello or Lear could deliver wonderful utterances yet be convincingly stupid or raving, while a personage in an "intellectual" novel, e.g., one by Aldous Huxley, might philosophize brilliantly about abstruse issues yet produce an effect of shallowness. "Intellectual physiognomy" went boldly into the relation of intellect to insight, instead of the usual dodge of pitting them against each other. That Othello was endowed with an impressive intellectual physiognomy had nothing to do with his education, his "ideas," or even his mental capacity; it was a quality that descended to him from his author as a kind of family resemblance. Given a Shakespeare or a Tolstoy for his fictional father, an idiot becomes a genius without ceasing to be an idiot.

I don't know how accurate a description this is of Lukacs's idea. I am not even sure, after these decades, that I actually read the article in which it was contained. Perhaps someone told me about intellectual physiognomy and I decided that that's what it meant. Nor did I ever try to figure out what intellectual physiognomy had to do with Marxism, unless it implied that the proletariat as conceived by Marx had, despite its illiteracy, a more profound character than the bourgeoisie and the intellectuals. But the bourgeoisie, too, since they sprang out of Marx's mind would be deeper than they appeared in ordinary experience. . . . At any rate, I have long admired the theory of intellectual physiognomy and its author with it. This admiration was not lessened by hearing from time to time that Lukacs was resisting Stalin's "socialist realism" and that during the Hungarian uprising he was at the age of seventy thrown into prison by the Russians.

The Lukacs who now comes forward in *The Meaning of Contemporary Realism,* written seven years ago and just published in England and in the United States (under the title of *Realism in Our Time*),* has nothing to say about intellectual physiognomy nor any concept of comparable originality. He takes his stand as a Marxist foe of modernist literature — Joyce, Proust, Kafka, Musil — or of modernism in literature, and defends as an alternative "realism" and the realistic tradition.

Much in the Lukacs we are presently privileged to read cannot be taken seriously; it requires an effort to believe that it was meant to be, though indubitably it was. Such statements as, "Our starting point is really the point of convergence of two antitheses: the antithesis between realism and modernism and the antithesis between peace and war," which line up literary modes on the two sides of current political struggles (are the Chinese modernists or realists?), wake one up to the distance that today separates one's thinking from what has come to constitute Marxism. Given this distance it is futile to dwell on the absurdities, exaggerations, and misstatements of fact in *The Meaning of Contemporary Realism;* its very texture is made up of them — e.g., that with Thomas Mann "from *The Magic Mountain* onwards, socialism never ceases to be a central intellectual and compositional [!] element."

Lukacs, it turns out, has also failed to surmount the insensibility of Marxist criticism to the processes by which a work of literature actually comes into being. Creation, he believes (or his critical vocabulary compels him to say), takes place through the "translation" of a "consciousness of reality" into "adequate esthetic form." Thus he complains of the "selective principle which apparently underlies modernist writing" that "it is not a selection applied to the totality of the reality to be described" — as if it still needed to be demonstrated that works of art do not "describe reality" and that their "selective principle" is not "applied" but is an effect of imagination, temperament, and the works the author has chosen as his tradition. Lukacs's mechanic's approach to literary creation as the

* New York: Harper & Row Publishers, Inc., 1964.

analytical manipulation of facts and situations — "the realistic writer must seek the nodal points of these [social-individual] conflicts, determine what they are at their most intense and most typical, and give suitable expression to them" — raises the suspicion that his good (i.e., cleared of Stalinist perversions) socialist realism would result in no better writings than the worst.

It ought to be added that with all due reverence for the pathos of Lukacs's resistance to Stalinism, some of his statements fall short of rudimentary honesty. In his Preface to the German Edition of *The Meaning of Contemporary Realism,* written in Budapest in 1957, he declares his joy at being able at last to speak "openly," then calls for "relentless criticism" with the argument that "only on the basis of such criticism, *as with Rosa Luxemburg's complex legacy,* can Stalin's positive achievements be seen in perspective" (my italics). This abominable coupling of the inspired martyr of German Socialism with the sordid tyrant could have had no other purpose than to display orthodoxy in regard to strains of Marxist thinking condemned by the Party. It took another five years for Lukacs to permit himself a direct thrust at "the disastrous legacy of Stalinism." And though he still gets into trouble, it is for belonging to a wing of Party opinion. Our sympathies for this side in the inner struggle of Soviet development ought not to mislead us into considering him a free mind or into overlooking the weight of intellectual backwardness in his literary opinions.

Lukacs thus turns out to be a thorough disappointment; one did not expect to encounter this much "Marxism" in the great Marxist thinker. The sole interest in the present collection of essays is the angle of Lukacs's attack on vanguard literature, the fact that this attack is made from a premise that welcomes the revolution of the twentieth century. Other anti-modernist critics, say, Bernard Berenson or certain academic "humanists," simply discard this century and its works and glut themselves on the art of other times. As a Marxist, Lukacs is obliged not only to see this radical period as a culmination, he must hold its upheavals to be a good thing. He is stuck with change, and in literature he must ask for more rather than less emphasis on the derangements of the time. If he is to judge modernist works as inferior he must do so not for their failure to measure up to the masterpieces of other centuries but for their inadequacies in dealing with the novelties of this one. That Marxism, like the polemical varieties of traditionalist criticism (for example, that of F. R. Leavis) measures the value of contemporary works by the degree of historical consciousness displayed in them, including the historical significance of their esthetic modes, is of itself almost a guarantee of its pertinence. Criticism by fiction of the historical drama in which we are all cast as actors or as victims, and of which there are no disinterested spectators, is what keeps the novel and the play going in our time above their

commercial, academic, and propaganda functions. Works deficient in conscious response to this drama, and the psychological, political, cultural,
technical issues mixed together in it, are doomed to tiresomeness and
triviality regardless of freshened-up mannerisms. We are thus at one with
Lukacs to the extent that he examines modern styles from the standpoint
of today and tomorrow rather than as incidents in an esthetic totality
standing apart from or above time.

In substance Lukacs's objections to modernist productions are familiar to us from other sources. He plays the customary themes on disintegration in Joyce, the nihilism of Kafka and Beckett. The evils of
modernist literature he finds to be abstraction, distortion, subjectivism,
formalism — traits objected to by all antimodernists from Eisenhower to
Pius XII. Lukacs's thesis that "the essential content of modernism is
*angst* and chaos" (a thesis which can be refuted without much trouble —
where is the chaos in Valéry or Mondrian?) parallels the opinion concerning contemporary *society* held by swarms of elegists of cultural decline, most of them reactionaries who hate the industrial age. The distinction of Lukacs is that his notion of the downward movement of
literature is fitted into a coherent theory of social development. He condemns modern art in the name of progress, and in so doing exposes more
fully than does any political pronouncement of the Communists what the
Communist conception of progress is. And not only the Communist, for
as a *liberal* form of Communism, Lukacs's criticism also reflects fairly
accurately the cultural outlook of the Left generally and particularly its
attitude toward modern art.

In the postwar novel and theater, despair, the "void," "loss of self,"
have become clichés used to organize episodes, language, images. One
can hardly help sharing Lukacs's impatience with glib intimations of an
underlying "human condition" that turns real events into mere illustrations of an irresistible sickness. As literary criticism, however, rather
than metaphysics, Lukacs's condemnation of philosophies of *angst* and
chaos is beside the point; he is obliged to distinguish between panto-
mimes of despair and its genuine poetry. You do not dispose of Kafka
through refuting Heidegger nor through finding a comparable "message"
in a grade B movie. This is another way of saying that the issues of
criticism cannot be stated, much less solved, in terms of mere abstract
disputation. If Marx was right and "everlasting uncertainty" is a trait of
the epoch, the effect after a hundred years would inescapably be to deposit a widespread tinge of *angst* in almost every feeling, and "continuous agitation" would have made "chaos" an element of contemporary
sensibility. In finding forms for these states *as they are actually experienced,* modernist literature and art would represent not a timeless condition but the condition of the time. Lukacs submerges this problem in
the very title of his chapter directed against modern art: it is called "The

Ideology of Modernism." As with antimodernists of the Church, the State, the Rotary Clubs, the "distortion," etc., of vanguard forms is seen by him as owing not to the revolutionary character of present-day reality but to the errors or perversity of writers, their faulty "perspective." Adjust this perspective and the social equivalents of distortion (official lies, mass-communication fantasies), abstraction (alienated people, empty relations, things devoid of quality), subjectivism (the collapse and betrayal of ideals), formalism (the regulation of public and private life by impersonal systems) would presumably be overcome. Lukacs's version of dialectical materialism demands that conditions be cured in literature before they are changed in life. Art that takes its shape from the "everlasting uncertainty" is, regardless of its character, mere "naturalism" to Lukacs and inferior to "realistic" works issuing from the mental constructions of "the humanist social perspective." For Marx all that was solid was melting in the air; for Lukacs it has no right to do that in the novel.

Faced with extremist art, all antimodernists raise the banner of "realism," whether it be Catholic realism, the common-sense realism of the liberals and the Left, the "socialist realism" of Khrushchev, the taken-for-granted realism of the mass media and of 95 percent of U.S. thinking and practice in fiction. Lukacs's discussion of "perspective" reveals that as an alternative to modern styles, "realism" means not the representation of contemporary reality, subjective or social, but its correction through ideological imperatives. For this descendant of the materialistic interpretation of history, social reality has become contingent on thought. In a situation that generates *angst, angst* itself must be driven out by defeating the "ideology of modernism."

What is marvelous about Lukacs is that he has developed a philosophy of resistance to change on no other ground than change itself. "The fact that in the midst of this 'permanent revolution,' this endless 'revaluation of all values,' there were [twentieth-century] writers of major talent who clung to the standards of nineteenth-century realism is, therefore, of ethical as much as of artistic significance. These writers' attitudes sprang from the ethical conviction that though changes in society modify human nature, they do not abolish it." With permanent revolution set in quotation marks, Lukacs has discovered in "human nature" the key for turning Marxism into a species of traditionalism which shores up literature as a trans-historical order against the dissolving processes of twentieth-century development. Whereas in *The Communist Manifesto* the nineteenth century leaps forward into the twentieth, with Lukacs the twentieth century crawls back toward the nineteenth. Reality, Old Faithful, is still there in the streets and drawing rooms if only the novelists would put themselves in a position to see it.

All antimodernists, we said, pine for realism. Lukacs wants two: bourgeois critical realism and "socialist" (though not Stalinist). These realisms, he contends, represent the truths of successive historical epochs, but they are connected with and depend on one another. Bourgeois critical realism needs to turn toward socialism as its goal in order to be able to face the present without sinking into *angst;* "socialist realism" needs to be aware of bourgeois realism behind it in order to be guided by its models and esthetic standards. Both realisms are continuations of the supreme works of earlier epochs; they hold the line of narrative and dramatic art through Shakespeare to Homer.

The test for Lukacs of the realist novelist or playwright is his ability to create solid, three-dimensional characters in contrast to the "shadowy blurs," stylized puppets, or unlocated mystics of modernist fiction. Lukacs quotes approvingly the contrast noted by Camus between a character of Dostoyevsky and one of Tolstoy as "like that between a film and stage character" (as silly a distinction as one between a character on a page and one on a stage). Lukacs believes that the malady of shadowiness is getting more serious: already in the time of Zola, he observes, it had become extremely difficult to create lasting human types, "the real criterion of literary achievement." Today matters are far worse. But the third dimension can still be achieved through correct perspective: here Lukacs once more recalls Bernard Berenson and his opinion that what made Giotto a great painter was the solidity given to his figures by the new science of perspective. Like Berenson he harks back to the Renaissance for "tactile values" which, Berenson said, will enable us to "realize his [the artist's] representations more quickly and more completely than we should realize the things themselves." If everything solid has melted in the air, it is the job of the artist to put it together again through "the creative role of perspective." "Perspective, in this concrete form," Lukacs assures us, "is central to our problem."

Still, "lasting human types" are getting harder and harder to find in fiction, as on the street. This circumstance weighs heavily on Lukacs's literary judgments. The writers he praises as "major talents who clung to the standards of nineteenth-century realism" include Eugene O'Neill, the late Thomas Wolfe, the late Brecht, early Norman Mailer, who are either not "realists" or something less than "major talents." To oppose, as he does, Thomas Mann as a realist to James Joyce as a modernist is both theoretically absurd and esthetically obtuse. Disregarding the analogical and symbolic structure of *Ulysses* he states that in it "the stream of consciousness technique . . . is itself the formative principle governing the narrative pattern and the presentation of character." Mann's *Lotte in Weimar,* on the other hand, is superior because in it "the *monologue intérieur* is simply a technical device" (what becomes of the unity of form and content?) for exploring "aspects of Goethe's world which would not have been otherwise available," once more the mechanic's conception of the artist's technique as a tool for working on "reality." But the sum of the contrast is Lukacs's cultural conservatism, as revealed in his praise of Mann for upholding literary tradition: "However unconventional the presentation . . . the ancient rules of epic narration are faithfully observed."

Since Mann is the only first-rate twentieth-century writer Lukacs can even pretend to have on his side, and thus the sole ground for believing that "bourgeois realism" is in the running as an important tendency (a chapter in *The Meaning of Contemporary Realism* is entitled "Franz Kafka or Thomas Mann?"), it may be worth pausing on the latter's qualifications as a Lukacs "realist." The very physical setting of *The Magic Mountain* is intended to produce that "chaos" of time and values which Lukacs reprehends as "modernist." Lukacs bends his dialectical ingenuity to separate Mann from his contemporaries on the grounds that he differentiates between characters ruled by subjective and objective time. For Mann, however, the different senses of time represent opposing moral states, neither of which is superior to the other. Mann's organic-mechanical dichotomy corresponds to Bergson's view, which Lukacs repugns, and to the metaphysical split which governs the conversion of data into symbols in *Ulysses* (e.g., an old woman passing by makes Bloom think of the Dead Sea and salt as against a list representing the *élan* of growing things).

As for the solidity of the characters in *The Magic Mountain,* Lukacs's ultimate test of realism, Castorp and Ziemssen, Settembrini and Naphta (said to be a portrait of Lukacs himself) perform not as single figures "in the round" like characters in Balzac or Flaubert; they do their act in antithetical pairs; and they are composed of patterns of "naturalistic" details doubling as symbols, e.g., Castorp's cigars. Frau Chauchat is the personification of disorder — note the rattle of small panes of glass with which she enters the dining hall of the sanatarium and the consciousness of Castorp. The "flatness" of these personae is purposely emphasized by contrast with Peeperkorn, who is blown up to larger than life-size, a kind of lumbering deity bumping against the clouds.

To make matters worse for Lukacs and the "third dimension," Mann's other great work, *Joseph in Egypt,* is set in the land of the frieze, and its protagonists are modeled on the serial figures of Egyptian wall painting. Mann makes his intention explicit in the first volume of the novel through a discourse on how the personality of the young Joseph shades into the images in his gallery of ancestors, so that the hero does not know where his history leaves off and those of Jacob, Isaac, and Abraham begin. The "realism" thus attained is not Lukacs's "meaning of everyday life" but what Mann calls the "god story." In their indefinite dimensions his characters are closer to those of myth than to Lukacs's nineteenth-century egos, and by the same quality they are affiliated with HCE and Harold-or-Humphrey of *Finnegans Wake* and with Kafka's K — that is, with quintessential modernism.

Having once left the nineteenth century,* Lukacs's "realism" is no longer a descriptive category but an ideological wish (even Gorky possesses too many expressionist facets to fit in without doctrinal squeezing) — the wish common to all contemporary "realists," regardless of philosophical, political, or esthetic differences, to believe that something is immune to alteration and is *there* to be described, without needing to be constituted anew in terms of its changing relations. Lukacs is seeking in literature what he misses in life: the firmly planted "complete" type. But what is this type except the class man of social formations now in distress? Solidity of character belongs to class society: the solid person of fiction is none other than the solid citizen. A character acquires three dimensions through being set permanently in social space in the role of the aristocrat on the hill, the merchant in the marketplace, the peasant in the field. The density of the Balzacian or Tolstoyan protagonist is the effect of his being cut from a hardened lump of class soil.

Only the members of one social class lack thickness; the proletariat, Marx has informed us, is "denuded." Lukacs sees fictional types as national in substance. "Modern industrial labor," Marx replies, "modern subjection to capital, the same in England as in France, in America as in Germany, has stripped him [the proletarian] of every trace of national character." There is another group that is perhaps in an even worse state: the revolutionary intellectuals. But what if the typical condition of man in the mid-twentieth century is that of workers and intellectuals? Instead of the citizen surrounded by his possessions, his family, the stable social landscapes, there appears the fellow employee or the professional who comes and goes. Things are no longer in place and the people seen by the novelist no longer pose against a static background. In that case, to be truly a realist he cannot duplicate the character scaffoldings of *The Human Comedy* (admired by Marx, we might remind Lukacs, for its radical insights into the social formations of the time and not because Balzac was conserving Western literary tradition or belief in "human nature"). The novelist of contemporary social fact achieves imaginative veracity through devising formal equivalents of the *multiple* perspective in which his experience appears: that in which "film" figures flash by in city crowds; in which varying densities of people are established through dealing with them in conferences, cocktail parties, love affairs, the family; that of the self in its metamorphoses and

* Lukacs's *Studies in European Realism* also published recently in America (New York: Grosset & Dunlap, 1964), with an introduction by Alfred Kazin, comprises such authors as Balzac, Stendhal, Zola, Tolstoy.

its absence of space which prevent its being grasped except through myth-making. The complexities and discontinuities of modernist fiction are accompaniments of the breakdown of class fixity. Lukacs recognizes this (though again blaming on ideology what has occurred in reality, like Stalin blaming on saboteurs and oppositionists a breakdown in wheat production) when he complains that the wispy personages of contemporary literature "presuppose the elimination of all social categories." A strange complaint for a Communist! Will not the literature of the classless society be populated by ghosts? In which case, ought we not trade in Socialism for Dame Quickly's tavern?

Lukacs has set himself against the transitional person of modern democracy. His "realism" is a literary version of the Leninist program of building the future upon planes of social differentiation which are to be gradually lowered toward a common level under a system of controls, like the locks of a canal. Unlike the medievalist, Lukacs accedes to change in the structure of individuals and their relations; but he accepts it only under the regulation of inherited modes of consciousness in which the class formations of yesterday, or their equivalents, subsist for as long as possible. The anonymous person and anonymous groups struggling for visibility in modern mass society are to be overlooked by literature until a place has been delineated for them by political authority. The mold of man is to be set from above rather than be the product of man's own actions. Similarly, new esthetic possibilities are to be fitted into antique modes — "the ancient rules of epic narration" — rather than be developed as instruments of vision.

Lukacs is unable to see that massively contoured social identities ("lasting types") have been rendered obsolete by the emergence of a world culture beyond folkways or cult, and that modern *angst* is precisely the ambivalent response to the slipping away of established emblems of self. For this Marxist the issue for literature is not its capacity to enter into the range of new human potentialities opened up by the continuous loosening of social forms; as with the metaphysicians of despair whom he condemns, the issue is that beyond the solid types there exists for him nothing but emptiness and chaos.

The fear of nothingness cuts Lukacs off from the grand tradition he is so eager to see continued. It was evident to the author of Ivan Ilych, as to the author of *Oedipus,* that the three-dimensional occupant of social space was a fictional construction, a hollow dummy contrived for the eyes of others, and that in action this made-up shape would crumble — bringing a reversal of the situation and revealing a self belonging to a new order of being. To the dramatic poet individual identity has always been precarious and a pathos. In bringing Ilych, the solid, lasting type, to the fictional execution block Tolstoy was something more than a "realist" —

as was Marx when he explained that class societies produce "abstract individuals" under which the real individuals are "subsumed"; in other words, that the social type is the not-self of the individual appearing as a positive shape, while the real self is unknown and awaits disclosure through action. On this theme Kafka would seem to be saying more than any of Lukacs's human-nature-preserving literary emigrants to the nineteenth century.

It worries Lukacs that "socialist realist" dogmatism may cause modernist critics to cover up "the deeply problematic nature of modernism itself." No doubt the problematic is the distinguishing trait of a consciousness truly of this time; this puts new art and ideas at a disadvantage in coping with disciplinarians of proper "perspective." To define modernism as a solution or as a worthy cause is, of course, ridiculous. Yet Lukacs himself introduces into art the war of dogmas when he writes: "We see that modernism leads not only to the destruction of traditional forms; it leads to the destruction of literature as such.* And this is true not only of Joyce, or of the literature of expressionism and Surrealism." Such opinions are aimed at banishing the incentive to study the masterpieces of our age. They cause the mirror of modern literature to be turned to the wall, so that events take place blindly, while art becomes a copying of monuments in the oversized scale of the "humanist perspective." The net effect is a pervasive Philistinism. For Lukacs modern fiction is an esthetic and moral aberration that has somehow gotten in between the masterpieces of the past and the future. In time, he hopes, this distortion will be straightened out and the familiar proportions be restored. Then reality will be back in force. It is merely a matter of canceling an epoch of error. Or shall we say, an epoch (our own) of human history?

1962

---

* Compare the conservative Academician, Kenyon Cox, writing about The Armory Show fifty years ago: "The real meaning of this Cubist movement is nothing else than the total destruction of the art of painting." Poor humanity! To be compelled to endure this same empty threat for decade after decade, from all countries and from all ideologies.

# SO WHO'S NOT MAD?
## On Marat/Sade and Nihilism *
### LIONEL ABEL

It was Susan Sontag, I think, who first pointed up the extreme theatricality of *Marat/Sade*. Susan Sontag was right, *Marat/Sade* is theatrical.
Is the play dramatic, though? About this there seems to be some question
even in Miss Sontag's mind. When she discussed the work in her *Partisan
Review* article (Spring, 1965), the word "dramatic," scarcely used in her
text, came up in this sentence: ". . . *Marat/Sade* is far from being the
supreme masterpiece of contemporary dramatic literature, but it is scarcely
a second-rate play." From which I infer that Miss Sontag herself has
some doubt as to the value of *Marat/Sade* as drama. My own opinion —
which has the virtue at least of being settled — is that the play is indeed
a "director's play," and owes most of its values of excitement and bravura
to the staging and direction of Mr. Peter Brook. Whatever life *Marat/
Sade* has on the stage comes, in my finding, from the devices of its director,
not its author.

One could not say this were the play truly compelling. For certainly a

* *The Persecution and Assassination of Marat as Performed by the Inmates of the
Asylum at Charenton under the Direction of the Marquis de Sade*. By Peter Weiss.
Directed by Peter Brook. Martin Beck Theater, New York.

play not soundly dramatic can do little more than hold its audience; the devices of a director can merely make a play bearable. To me, *Marat/ Sade* was certainly bearable, but little more than that, except for a few moments. The first part was often tedious, and the second part a repetition of what is boring in the first. But what concerns me here is a general point, the difference between the theatrical and the dramatic.

When we find Marat on the Martin Beck stage, half of his body is enclosed in a metal bathtub, and the naked flesh of him that we do see is covered with large red spots. There he is, immobile, frail, and blotched in his bath, stained by his disease. Now the effect is electric. But this effect lasts only for a moment, for Marat is going to speak. We want to hear what he says. And as we listen, we tend not to look at his red spots; but what he says is less interesting than the red spots, much less interesting humanly, much less interesting dramatically. His voice, which often rises to an orator's shout, somehow erases the strong effect the sight of his body first gave us. His is a theatrical presence, not a dramatic one.

To point up the contrast between the theatrical and the dramatic, one has only to think for a moment of Danton in Buechner's play, *Danton's Death*. The real Danton, the Danton of history, was pockmarked, but Buechner in the directions for his work never insisted on representing him as such. For what interests us in the Danton of Buechner are the things Danton says, and were he presented with a pockmarked visage, the force of his lines would limit, make one forget, or even quite destroy, I think, any theatrical value his appearance with a pitted skin might have, just as the feebleness and platitudinousness of Marat's lines in *Marat/Sade* tend, as that play goes on, to destroy the theatrical effect our first sight of Marat, spotted and in his bathtub, gave. I suggest that the theatrical is something very different from the dramatic, and that it is finally dependent on the dramatic. A play in which the first is substituted for the second will tend to lose whatever value, as it goes on, it had at the start. This is what happens in *Marat/Sade*. Highly theatrical at the outset, never becoming dramatic, as it progresses it loses its theatricality. And not because the theatrical is contrary to the dramatic or in some sense its opposite. The theatrical sums itself up in one moment of time whereas the dramatic links into a culminating action many moments of time. When we speak of a *coup de théâtre* we have in mind an event which combines the theatrical with the dramatic, but the *coup de théâtre* simply cannot take place if some dramatic development has not prepared it. Now there is no *coup de théâtre* in the utterly theatrical play of Peter Weiss. In fact, the most theatrical thing about this play is its full title, which takes up about a minute's reading time. Read it: *The Persecution and Assassination of Marat as Performed by the Inmates of the Asylum at Charenton under the Direction of the Marquis de Sade.*

The idea that Sade might put on a play to be performed by the inmates of a lunatic asylum, and that in this play he and Marat might be the lead-ing characters, is certainly a fascinating one suggesting a real drama. But no drama takes place in Peter Weiss's play. Sade tries to convert Marat, who does not listen to him. Why would he listen to the platitudes of sadism? Marat, totally unresponsive, declaims, in his turn, the political platitudes to which he remains committed. There is no yielding of one to the other, consequently there is no dramatic play between them. The author has said that the center of his play is an argument. Now I heard none. For in any true argument there is always a moment of wavering on the part of the one or the other. But in *Marat/Sade,* the Marquis is scarcely beguiling, and Marat never gives any indication of being be-guiled.

Some, including Miss Sontag, have found a great theatrical interest in the fact that almost everyone on the stage is mad. I am inclined to think that this reveals in those who take such a view an ideological interest in the mad rather than an aesthetic or even psychologically normal response to madness. Anyone who has ever had a discussion with another person and noted or suspected at some point that the other was mad, must recall that with that thought or suspicion there was an immediate tendency to break off discussion. For one cannot know what a lunatic is thinking or feeling and the normal impulse is to detach oneself from any considera-tion of what may go on in his mind. And so it follows, however surpris-ing this may be to some people, that madmen, though theatrical, are fundamentally undramatic and do not properly belong on the stage. A moment of madness, yes, particularly as expressed by someone whom we have seen as sane before, can have dramatic interest, and of course a sane man pretending madness is interesting. But real madmen, or per-sons presented as really mad, do not belong in any theater attended by people with a taste for drama.

Yet I must admit that the audience at the Martin Beck Theater did not reason as I do, and did not feel as I do. During the last moments of *Marat/Sade,* when the inmates at Charenton threw off all restraints and went berserk, there was an unmistakable feeling of solidarity with them on the part of the audience, so that for some moments I half expected whole groups to get up on stage and add their own versions to the outra-geous "twist" Peter Brook designed. Why this fellow feeling for the mad? In answering this question, one can perhaps find some reason for the very great success of Peter Weiss's play.

Now the play is quite devoid of any intellectual meaning. Is Weiss trying to say that the content of history is sadism? This judgment might indeed make a play, and a challenging play, though I think the judgment false. In any case, Weiss has denied that this is his judgment. He asserts, "Everything irrational and absurd is foreign to me." He claims, also, to side with the platitudinous opinions uttered by Marat. Of course, none of Weiss's statements about his play need be taken seriously. In public interviews he has on the one hand described himself as a socialist, and on the other hand said that he considers socialism a failure. Such indecisiveness of judgment is hardly the sign of a superior sensitiveness to what, after judging, may remain ambiguous. Very probably, we can only learn about what is unresolvably ambiguous in politics and morals from someone whose moral and political position is clear. Certainly it would be unfair to confront Weiss's play with masterpieces like Dostoevsky's. Nevertheless, the art of the Russian novelist did settle one question (there are some questions that have been settled) now being brought up by the partisans of *Marat/Sade,* notably its director, Mr. Peter Brook. What Dostoevsky's work proved, to those, of course, who know how to read him, is that one can choose finally — Dostoevsky chose Christ as against science and socialism — and yet acknowledge with full awareness all that is valid in what one rejects. No reader can be in doubt of Dostoevsky's judgment; he denies no reader a taste of the ambiguous. Bad or inconclusive thinking is hardly the best, or even a good way, to apprehend ambiguities.

But why the enthusiasm for *Marat/Sade?* Here, I think, we have to turn aside from the aesthetics of drama and look to the ideological motives of the play.

Let me go back to the frenetic response of certain members of the audience to the final scene of *Marat/Sade.* In that response there was a clearly articulated sympathy for madness. What sustains so peculiar, and to my mind unnatural, a sympathy?

Do people tend to think now that history is a madhouse? Or, to cite again Joyce's much-quoted phrase, a nightmare? In that case, why would they not want to wake up from it? I must also point out that, when any strikingly leftist remark was made on the stage, the very same members of the audience who solidarized themselves with the stage's madmen again came to life with clapping and cheers. So there was a feeling in the theater for leftism plus madness, and I think this feeling is expressed in the play itself, whose two chief protagonists have the names Marat and Sade.

I suggest that the play appeals generally to those who have violent leftist notions and yet, like the author, think socialism a failure. In madness, one can combine such ideas.

However, the interest in madness presently expressed, and by a good many talented and intelligent people, may go far beyond the need to conciliate political leftism with despair of socialism. The frantic, the frenetic, the wild and outrageous, are continually being stated as positive values nowadays, in literature, in the films, and on the stage. I recently saw an extremely clever French film in which the goal of the hero — he achieves it — is schizophrenia. The film is light, intelligent, ironical, and in that way pays tribute to French rationality, but it is an ironic tribute, for the real appeal of the film is in the figure of its protagonist finally at home in the white walls of an asylum. And if one correlates with a film of this kind, the various expressions of hysteria, irrational violence, homosexual hatred, and sheer nuttiness regularly expressed by our youngest writers, one has to look more deeply into what may have caused or promoted what now amounts to a powerful trend.

I have in mind *The White Negro,* that wacky though powerful essay by Norman Mailer, in which our genial friend and Marxist gone haywire singled out psychopaths as the bearers of future values. In this piece, he also defended the courage of some tough young kids who beat up a weak old man. Now there was a time when courage was understood very differently. Not a few French knights in feudal times thought it unmanly to engage in combat when not outnumbered. I also have in mind Mailer's recent novel, *An American Dream,* in which the protagonist, Rojack, kills his wife and then immediately afterwards buggers their maid. I must note here that the deed is a variant of one in Jean Genet's *Querelle de Brest.* In that novel the young sailor Querelle, having killed a man, feels that he ought to pay for his crime, and has himself buggered by the local pimp. Thus buggered, Querelle becomes a marked man, an *enculé,* and for all eternity. So Querelle does not entirely escape the mark of Cain. Except that the mark Cain had to bear on his forehead is kept hidden by Genet's hero in his ass. Now Mailer's American hero, who kills as if Cain had never existed, appears, after his crime, like an innocent abroad; he has no feeling of guilt, no need for expiation. And how was Mailer's novel understood? When Philip Rahv attacked the book insofar as its hero is without any kind of conscience, his objection was met with derision, as if it were absurd to judge a fictional character morally! As if the best of our critics had not done just that, and ever since the novel came into being.

Or take Leslie Fiedler's article, *The Mutants,* published in the Fall, 1965 *Partisan Review.* I heard Mr. Fiedler give that essay as a lecture at a conference at Rutgers University and so I can supply some additional data which may throw light on Mr. Fiedler's purposes; these, from his essay as published, may be unclear. In his essay, and also in his lecture, Mr. Fiedler quoted a contemporary kid as having said to him: "Freud is a fink." Now what interested Mr. Fiedler was not whether this judgment was true or false. What interested him was that a kid should say this, and I submit that if you look at Mr. Fiedler's article you will see that he is inclined to accept the kid's judgment. Why? At Rutgers Mr. Fiedler said

in so many words, though I quote from memory — but there is a transcript of the discussion which may be checked —: "I myself have become as tired of the rationalism of Freud as of Marx." Is Freud then
really a fink? And why did the young man Fiedler cited say so? The
answer to this is not hard to find. Norman Brown, who has had a very
great impact on many of our very young men, says in his now famous
book that the insistence of many conventional American males on satisfying women sexually is a form of repression stemming from Freud, and
something to be rejected in the name of freedom. So even fucking, in
other words, is to Mr. Brown and to the young enlightened by him a bit
too classical, just too upstanding!

I want to say something further about Mr. Fiedler's essay. According
to him, the taking of drugs by the young is their expression, and main
expression, of dissatisfaction with a boring and spiritually flat society. I
will not go so far as to say that Mr. Fiedler recommends that the young
take drugs, but I suggest that no one whose children are engaged in taking drugs should call on Mr. Fiedler to dissuade them from doing so. To
take drugs, according to him, is to be an adventurer, and in a society in
which little adventure is possible. It is to travel inwards, something very
up-to-date, like the up-to-dateness of the cosmonauts who go towards
outer space. Once again, I do not want to charge Mr. Fiedler with rec-
ommending the taking of drugs, but I think his whole essay is a confession that he cannot call upon one value in whose name he could oppose
it. Why?

When there is a real trend, and I think I am talking about a real trend
here, one has to look for something deeper to explain it than the views of
those who represent it verbally, even with cleverness. It is not enough to
call names as Philip Rahv did in his review of Norman Mailer's *An
American Dream*. Nor is it enough to argue politically with the youth, as
Irving Howe did in his article on the "New Left." Call Mailer foolish or
a bad novelist — the last he is not — and the young will still listen to
him. Call the "New Left" ahistorical, as Irving Howe did in his essay,
and the young will reply — they already have replied — with violence.
Philip Rahv and Irving Howe are perfectly right, of course, but I can't
help remembering Hegel's remark about Rome in its decadence. The philosophers were right, Hegel said, but the people were right not to listen to
them.

Once again, what can be understood to lie behind the not always clear
inclination of the contemporary youth for all forms of the irrational?

More than fifteen years ago, in Alexandre Kojève's extraordinary
book, *An Introduction to the Reading of Hegel*, a work which has influenced all French thought, including Sartre's and Merleau-Ponty's, I read

the following remarkable passage, the full meaning of which I confess
not to have understood at the time and which I am here translating
rather freely:

> Philosophy has no sense or reason for being unless it can lead to Wis-
> dom, or at least to the Sage, that is to say, to the Man of Wisdom. On
> the other hand, to believe that the Sage or Man of Wisdom is possible
> is to necessarily accept philosophy, understood as a means of attaining
> Wisdom, of realizing the Sage. . . .
>
> Now on the question of the Sage the only fundamental disagreement
> is between Plato and Hegel. . . . Let us see what their disagreement
> amounts to. One can of course, with Plato, deny that Wisdom can be
> realized. Then we have an either/or. Either the ideal of the Sage is
> never and nowhere realized, and the Philosopher is simply a madman
> who pretends to be what he *knows* it is impossible to be. Or he is not a
> madman; and then his ideal of Wisdom is or will be realized, and his
> definition of the Sage or Man of Wisdom is or will be a truth.

But to deny that wisdom is realized in God, as Plato held it is, or that
it can be realized in man, as Hegel claimed, amounts, according to
Kojève, to calling the philosopher a madman — for then there is no difference between the madman and the philosopher. (One might add, between the philosopher and the criminal, and between the philosopher and
the dope addict.) The point of view expressed here, and which is so
pertinent, in my opinion, to our contemporary problems, may be
summed up as follows: either God exists and perfection on earth is not
required, or God does not exist and human life can be perfected. That is,
philosophy is a reasonable pursuit. But if God does not exist (contrary
to Plato), and if wisdom cannot be realized (contrary to Hegel), then
the madmen, the criminals and dope addicts, are as reasonable as the
philosophers, and even more reasonable insofar as they do not attempt
to philosophize.

Now, the final deliverance of this epoch is that God does not exist and
that human life cannot ever be perfected and hence that the madman, the
criminal, and the dope addict are not inferior to the philosopher. That is
why it is so difficult to argue with a young student against taking drugs,
not to speak of dissuading him from doing so. Can one say to him that
God exists? No. Can one say to him that society can be perfected? No.
(It will not do, according to Kojève, to say that society can be somewhat
improved.) Then can one say that the philosopher is better than the drug
addict? No. Or better than the criminal or the madman? Again no. It is
the vague recognition, I will not call it knowledge, that no one to be
respected can answer these questions affirmatively which emboldens our
contemporary youth and makes them so rash and so sad.

Obviously our dilemma was not new in the Russia of the 1860's. What is new, though, is the impact on a mass society of the issue of belief which Dostoevsky raised. Do we today believe in God or in man? And by "we" I mean the masses, I mean the many, the millions. For there are many Raskolnikovs among us and many more Rojacks. In fact, to appreciate fully the effect on the masses of our spiritual dilemma and the receptivity of present-day society to any and all answers, no matter how drastic, one has only to think of a contemporary Dr. Raskolnikov giving a seminar on the Double Meaning of Killing Two Pawnbrokers, or of a Dr. Rojack lecturing at an honored university on Why It Is Not Wrong to Kill One's Wife. Say that Norman Mailer is no Dostoevsky — who's going to say he is? But to say that he is not is to discriminate, and the whole question now is whether discrimination is valid. As for Mailer, his excesses in thinking were prophesied, I believe, in James Joyce's *Ulysses*. When Bloom, about to fall asleep, plays with variations on the name Sindbad, calling up Ninbad the Nailer, Tinbad the Tailor, and Binbad the Bailer, he suddenly becomes less lethargic, somewhat more caustic, and gets to the name we know and he didn't: our contemporary to him is Mindbad the Mailer.

But never mind Mindbad. The question is not whether Mailer is intelligent, but whether intelligence counts anymore. The argument for intelligence, that is for philosophy — and by philosophy I mean the taking up of any topic, art, morals, or politics, with a sincere intent to be reasonable — was, I once thought, stated forever by Aristotle. He said: if you want to philosophize, then let us philosophize; and if you don't want to philosophize, you still have to philosophize. But who in philosophy feels he has to philosophize nowadays?

In fact, our young philosophers are dulled, I believe, by their aim, which is only to be bright, that is brighter than other philosophers. And the brightest and most intolerable of all philosophers in recent times was Ludwig Wittgenstein, who said against philosophy what no philosopher ever said before him: Philosophy is Hell. For why undertake the great labor of reasoning if reason is futile, if wisdom is unrealizable, and if the philosopher is no better than the madman, the criminal, or the addict? Why? Genet is a problem to Sartre, the philosopher, who devoted a book of over 600 pages to explaining him. Sartre, as all the young know now, is no problem to Genet.

But to get back to Weiss's play. It is my assumption that the depth of the contemporary situation is there and present whenever the least conscious members of the audience at *Marat/Sade* respond to that work as they do and empathize with its moments of madness. I know I could argue with them about the aesthetics of drama, dispute and even refute their notions of taste, but how am I going to refute their spontaneous identification with the mad figures tumbling convulsively at the play's end across the stage?

1966

# 2 ←———

# *American society: reports and criticism*

# SOME PROPOSALS FOR THE SIXTIES

## MICHAEL D. REAGAN

Like other dissenters, I can go along with a number of the specific proposals of the major party platforms (particularly the Democratic document) for meeting the domestic needs of the sixties. But socialists and radicals, it seems to me, must challenge liberalism's assumption that ameliorative measures are enough. We must go beyond liberalism to begin the task of reshaping the social structure so that it will be compatible with the goals of Liberty, Equality, and Fraternity.

American liberalism is a straddle between democracy and plutocracy: it assumes that a society of political and social equality can be erected upon an economic base of flagrant inequality. It asserts that the formal political equality of one man—one vote is in itself sufficient to ensure the responsiveness of public policy to the needs and demands of the majority, ignoring both the direct political power of wealth and the barriers to social and cultural equality that it inexorably creates. But democracy is more than a procedure for discussion and voting; it is a way of life, the way of sufficient equality of condition so that, as G. D. H. Cole said, "No one is so much richer or poorer than his neighbors as to be unable to mix with them on equal terms."

Most liberals assume that competitive individualism and private initi-

ative provide an adequate base for community life. I assume that industrial democracy must make decisive inroads upon the managerial hierarchy of modern capitalism, that the goal of individual fulfillment today
requires a community-provided base of much expanded proportions, and
that the optimum human use of our economic resources can only be
attained through overhead planning. Paul Johnson's words, although
written with Britain in mind, are equally applicable here:

> The function of Socialism is not to improve, but to change society.
> Having consented to operate within the framework of nineteenth-cen-
> tury society, Labour now finds that it has accomplished most of the
> tasks which this limitation allows. It therefore has the choice of becom-
> ing a party of government, concerned primarily with administering a
> social structure to which it has become reconciled, or attempting to
> change the structure.

To give concreteness to these differences in assumptions, I submit a
group of proposals — illustrative and tentative rather than exhaustive
and firm — that might stir further discussion toward a platform for a
dissenters' political movement.

## Integration

The Negro, the Puerto Rican, the Mexican, are all discriminated against
in their political, economic, and social rights. While there is general sentiment for the breaking down of the most egregious barriers to treatment
of members of minority groups as individuals, an effective program must
go beyond what many liberals are prepared to advocate. Specifically,
dissenters should propose:

1. *Permanent federal registration of voters for all elections.* This can
help overcome the obstacles to Negro registration in the Deep South.
Plans involving the filing of suit or the exhaustion of state administrative
remedies subject the Negro to coercion and delay, and are too complex
for all but the well-educated.

2. *National FEPC and Fair Housing Practices legislation.* To rely
upon state action is to leave the problem untouched in exactly those
states and communities where it is most serious. Fair employment and
housing practices would mean a great increase in freedom and dignity for
all minority groups — racial, ethnic, and religious.

3. *Giving priority to integration when it conflicts with other social
goals.* Liberals have let integration go by the board when it interfered
with other goals in housing, education, etc. We must put integration first,
for segregation is the deepest blot on the national conscience. If this
means no federal aid to education, then so be it. The "pragmatic" approach, which separates the segregation issue from all other issues,

means separating the issue from all the most effective tools of persuasion. When federal funds of all kinds are withheld from segregated projects and from institutions and communities permitting segregation, the hard choice will be made for integration.

4. *Ending the proletarian-outcast status of farm workers, particularly migrants.* Because these families are excluded from most protective legislation (though they need it most) and are largely unorganized (though an Agricultural Workers Organizing Committee of the AFL-CIO is at last making an attempt), they are in a position as bad as that of textile workers in the early 1800's. Application of minimum wage, child labor, and unemployment compensation programs to farm workers, plus special requirements for housing and education, are essential first steps toward helping these most disadvantaged of Americans.

## Distribution of Income and Wealth

On April 15, 1960, the *Wall Street Journal* carried a story on the newly released income distribution figures for 1959, reporting that average family income had risen 4 percent to $6,520. The *Journal* did not report that the government statistics also showed that the *median* income (half the nation earned more, half less) for 1959 was $5,300; or that the *modal* income (the most frequent or usual family income) was only $4,600, and this before taxes. The median and modal incomes, however, are much the more meaningful figures in providing a picture of the degree of general well-being, and $4,600 presents a slightly different picture from $6,520.

Just as the commonly presented, and commonly accepted, picture of "average" income is distorted upward, so also is the assumption of continuing redistribution of income from top to bottom. The facts are, however, that redistribution has been a top-to-middle phenomenon; that the tax system does little to dent the pre-tax disparities in income; and that the distribution of personally held wealth (as distinct from current income) remains almost as unequal now as in 1922, and the inequality has been *increasing* since 1949.

The overall picture for 1959 is that 7.5 million families and unattached individuals had incomes below $2,000, their collective share of income being 2 percent; 11.6 million families in the income range of $2,000–$3,999 received 10 percent of personal income while constituting 21 percent of the population; and the top 5 percent of income receivers with incomes over $15,000 received 21 percent of total income.

To understate the matter, it is clear that ours remains a most unaffluent society for at least three-fifths of the families. The consequences of poverty include above-average sickness, both physical and mental; below-average — even below-minimum — housing; and, in the lowest fifth, permanent conditions of squalor, ignorance, and total lack of opportunity for the children of such families to break the vicious circle.

The direction of policy in which we must move is clear: a revitalization of the redistributive mechanisms — particularly the Federal income tax — that have largely broken down. While rapid economic growth and full employment must underlie our efforts, they are not in themselves sufficient, for the most disadvantaged groups do not gain enough from general raising of the national income to lift them out of the vicious circle of despair and lack of opportunity. As Moses Abramovitz has written, "Whereas only a rise of average income could eliminate the widespread poverty of a century ago, only redistribution of income can alleviate the poverty of relative deprivation."

## Industrial Democracy

The phrase "industrial democracy" is generally used with reference to relationships within the plant community. The need for democratization, however, is just as great at the level of "macroeconomic" decision making, and both areas are referred to here.

Despite the mandate of the Employment Act of 1946, we continue to suffer from inflation and unemployment — which we now ingeniously manage to bring about simultaneously. We have done little to assure integrated planning toward the goals of maximum employment, production, and purchasing power, and nothing to relate the composition of production to the priorities of human need. The result is that we are, as Robert Heilbroner states, ". . . in the unpleasant position of watching our society change under the impact of its own technology while we stand impotently by to suffer the consequences for better or worse."

It is time to back up the Employment Act with an effective planning process, while also enlarging the scope of national economic goals to include substantive targets for income distribution and public sector goods and services. To leave economic performance to "the market" is, in the modern, concentrated economy, to leave it to the interplay of powerful, hierarchically organized interest groups — and to the corporate-Defense Department elite of the Cold War economy. We already have planning — private planning. We need to make it public so the planners will be accountable to the electorate, and the planning will serve public ends. A set of public expectations as operational standards needs to be worked out (through the party-political process, which has at least the formal equality of one man–one vote) and brought to bear upon economic allocation through a central planning agency under Presidential direction to produce the broad diffusion of ultimate authority which democracy implies. A first step in this direction would be the passage of the Clark-Reuss bill, which calls for public hearings on price increases that might cause inflation, and for the setting of precise goals for employment, productivity, and growth in the President's *Economic Report*. In time, control over private investment, both its rate and its areas of application, would be needed also.

Because the inflation-recession cycle continues to plague the economy, and attempts at stabilization have frequently suffered from split authority (President-Congress-Federal Reserve) over monetary and fiscal control, we need to do with tax, spending, and monetary policy what we have done with tariff policy since 1934: put the initial power of decision in the hands of the President, and give the veto power to Congress, thus reversing existing arrangements in order to secure prompt and coherent action.

In the micro-policy area, the needs are for democratization of the workplace, a guaranteed annual wage, and controls over corporate power. Frank Marquart has written of the "sole prerogative" principle, by which management alone determines

> what is to be produced, how it is to be produced, how much is to be produced, what plants are to be built and where, how much capital is to be invested, what kinds of machinery are to be installed, when workers are to be hired and when they are to be laid off, and how production operations are to be rationalized.

Behind this authoritarian system, and despite all the "human-relations-in-industry" literature, lies the assumption that the worker is but a "factor of production." Even the unions, as Marquart says, do not challenge the system; in fact, they further it by the leadership's disapproval of internal opposition and critical discussion.

Restructuring of the corporate world requires breaking through the sole prerogative principle to a recognition of the social character of the work process, of the legitimacy of the worker's claim to a voice in the decisions that affect his life more intimately than those of political government. But it also calls for internal union democracy. The role of public policy is not to impose democracy from above, but to encourage the strengthening of unions so that their bargaining power may produce managerial concessions to worker participation, and to ensure the openness of union processes to internal opposition.

Wage employment in a fluctuating economy means that the cost of business downturns falls most heavily on the class least able to bear it, the hourly wage-worker, while the corporation escapes its share of the burden by treating labor as a variable cost rather than as part of overhead. Supplemental unemployment benefits and guaranteed wage plans should be encouraged, to give additional impetus to the technological forces that are gradually shifting employment from blue- to white-collar status. The discrepancy in dignity between the insecurity of an hourly wage employee subject to sporadic lay-offs and the security of the monthly or yearly salaried employee who is assured full time income is one of the sorest injustices of the industrial economy.

Our system of business regulation is in need of complete overhaul — not only because of bribery, lying, inefficiency, and stupidity in the regulatory commissions, but because we are regulating what could be controlled by the market (e.g., much of the transportation industry) while not regulating the more significant power of the non-utility industrial giants and not doing the important job of policy formulation.

We regulate railroad rates (when truck and air competition might do the job as well) but leave General Motors free to make investment and price choices that may spell inflation or deflation for the whole economy. We manipulate the credit supply so that the consumer, the home-buyer, the small businessman, and school construction bear the burden while the large corporation continues to spend whatever it likes through internal financing. Of all the "independent" regulatory commissions the Federal Reserve is the only one with powers of fundamental importance to the maintenance of full employment, and yet it is the farthest removed from Presidential direction. And so on, and so on, and so on.

The regulatory commissions need abler appointees and a code of ethics, but they need something more drastic: they need to be abolished. Their policy-making and operating functions should be placed in a federal line department under direct Presidential supervision. (They are now, by law, largely outside Presidential jurisdiction.) Their quasi-judicial functions (rate-setting, allocation of routes or broadcasting channels, e.g.) do call for some insulation from partisanship, but this can be provided within the administrative process at least as well as by the present system of *in*dependence from the Presidency with a consequent *de*pendence upon the regulated industries and the goodwill of Rep. Oren Harris. With an end to independence, and the policy guidance of a National Resources Planning Authority, business regulation could perhaps begin to operate in the public interest. If it did not, after a reasonable trial period, then the straddle of regulation — which leaves initiative in private hands and the public without a positive policy — should be abandoned in favor of de-regulation of what can be left to market control, and public ownership of the remainder.

### Housing, Education, and Health

If the social balance is to be redressed, public expenditures must rise. And these expenditures must be largely federal, for only the national government has the tax capacity to do the job. The major party platforms recognize the need, but fail to establish priorities for public sector programs. Since everything can't be done at once, selection of the crucial areas is necessary. To my mind, these are housing, education, and health.

To start with housing, we need much more of it (population growth is expected to exceed 35 million by 1975), much better (the 1950 census classified 10 percent of our housing as unhealthful and unsafe), and much faster (the pace of slum creation appears to outrun the pace of slum clearance).

A national housing goal of 2,000,000 units per year has been widely suggested, of which one million would be for population growth; 300,-000 for replacement of houses destroyed or otherwise withdrawn from use; and 700,000 to make some dent in the backlog of substandard units. Why can't the private sector take care of this? The best answer is that it manifestly does not. Average construction of new housing units per year is closer to one million than to two. In 1959 housing starts were 1.3 million; in 1960 the pace was slower. Even if there were more of it, private housing is far too expensive for those in greatest need. The national median price for a new house in 1958 was reported by the National Housing Conference to be $10,990. Using the rule of thumb that housing expenditure should not exceed one-fifth of income, the conference figured that an income of $6,409 would be required to carry the minimum house — and less than 30 percent of families had incomes this high.

If seven out of ten families can't buy new houses, let them buy those older houses that "trickle down," we are told. The trickle-down theory, however, unfortunately requires a surplus of houses at each price level in order to operate — and there has been no surplus in the postwar years.

How about apartment rental then? The National Housing Conference reports that three-bedroom apartments are generally more expensive than ownership, and that in most cities there are few or none to be had. The result is a situation familiar to any reader of the metropolitan press: entire families occupying one- and two-room apartments in converted single-family dwellings at rents higher per room than many luxury apartments on Park Avenue.

Since the private housing industry, even with subsidies, has demonstrated its inability to design and construct homes or apartments within the reach of low income families, and since nothing trickles down until already dilapidated, the only solution to the housing disgrace is a vastly increased and improved public housing program. The celebrated American standard of living — and the non-material quality of life — could be balanced and raised perhaps more by a housing program than by any other single measure. But to achieve its full value, a public housing program must create participation, varied communities, not the urban "poorhouses" of earlier programs.

The public housing program's size might well be measured by the gap between needed housing and the private rate of construction: about 700,000 units per year. This would be somewhat of a change from the declining rate of public housing starts in recent years: 134,000 in 1946, 64,000 in 1953, and 10,515 in 1957!

A second crucial area is the educational system. The starting point of our thinking must be the recognition of a *national interest* in the quality of schooling received by *all* children *everywhere* in the nation. It is not a merely personal or merely local tragedy that Mississippi spends only $123 per pupil annually while New York can spend $362, and still have its educational budget a lower proportion of state income than Mississippi's. As with families, so with the states: those who have the least need the most. If vast inequalities in educational expenditure are allowed to continue for lack of significant national aid — and no amount of bootstrap self-help can overcome the hard fact of wide variations in state tax bases — then a heavy price will be paid in corresponding inequalities in chances for individual development and economic opportunity, and in political and cultural alienation. Just as no community can afford, ethically or practically, to give a second-rate education to the children of its less affluent families, so the nation cannot afford the waste of talent and the human frustration caused by our failure to use national wealth to bring the educational systems of the poorer states up to the level of the best now known — and then to improve the best.

The most obvious needs are to improve existing schools and build new ones, so that a third of a million students can receive full-time education, and to raise the quality of teaching by the simple device of paying salaries adequate to compete with commercial occupations in the recruitment of well-trained, liberally educated graduates.

As these immediate inadequacies are remedied, more subtle challenges should bring forth additional efforts. One such is the need for "enrichment" programs. By this I do not mean only or primarily that the most advanced students are given sufficiently challenging experiences, but that culturally underprivileged children are given the supplemental aid by which their natural capacities can be released from the constrictions imposed by educationally inadequate home and neighborhood environments. One experiment in a New York City junior high, in which slum-area children were exposed to museums, natural scenery, and other taken-for-granted experiences of middle-class children — and, perhaps most important of all, received attention that assumed they were worth helping — has already shown dramatically favorable results. Educational equality of opportunity includes specifically the problem of creating motivation that will break the pattern of apathy and despair, and make capable children of educationally apathetic parents aware of higher education possibilities.

In the impending age of increased leisure, the quality of life can be improved by the development of adult education programs. We need to escape the vocational confines of existing programs to provide openings into the world of liberal culture for adults who, in their maturity, regret their failure to explore the liberal and fine arts in their formal education. And our children — *all* children; not just the "college-prep" contingent — deserve not less than their parents, and should be educated for a life-time, not just for the first job. The two-class system in education must go: not all children can reach the same level of understanding in philosophy, art, science, and literature, but all deserve to partake of their common cultural heritage so far as their capacities permit. If anything, as W. H. Ferry has argued, those who are *not* college-bound should receive the greater emphasis in their high school years upon a basic understanding of man and society than those who will have four more years' exposure.

The third focus of a social balance program should be on health — the creation of a national health service. Not just hospitalization, and not restricted to the aged, but a system universal in eligibility and cover-age as in Britain and the Scandinavian countries. Medical care for the aged is indeed, as the American Medical Association charges, but an entering wedge for a larger program. The trouble is that it is *only* an entering wedge when we should have the whole program.

Housing, education, health — these are not the only areas in which expansion of the public sector can compensate in part for the inequities of class privilege generated in the private sector, but they are all "key" measures because they would provide, collectively, the necessary founda-tions for individual achievement.

## The Media and the Marketplace of Ideas

Our chances of accomplishing any significant changes in institutions de-pend heavily upon prior changes in attitudes and ideology. These rest in turn upon the openness of the marketplace of ideas. And it is here that the most dangerous accretion of corporate power has been developing. Not content with its economic power, the modern corporation is branch-ing out into education, community development, and politics. Though business has long had disproportionate weight in the legislative process, corporations such as General Electric, Ford Motor, and Gulf Oil have now taken the plunge into electoral persuasion as well — with all of us subsidizing the effort to the extent that corporate expenditures are con-sidered tax-deductible. Through its charitable-contributions deduction, again the corporations are attempting to exercise a trusteeship over edu-cation and cultural development. And all of this manipulating of the climate of opinion is done in the name of the corporate "conscience"! The best immediate way to diminish this push of the economically domi-nant institution into other areas of life appears to be to pull the corporation back to its goods-producing function by ending the tax-deductibility of political and cultural expenditures, and perhaps writing federal charters for the largest five hundred firms, restricting them to economic functions. Then businessmen could compete in the marketplace of ideas on the same basis as the rest of us — with their own personal funds and talent.

Thanks to the less direct, but even more pervasive, influence of the corporations upon the "public" media of press and broadcasting, we are bombarded with stereotypes of the nineteenth century put forward as descriptions of the mid-twentieth: "individual enterprise," in a society over 90 percent wage and salaried; "peoples' capitalism" as a label for a corporate ownership structure in which over 90 percent of adults have no share and in which, in any case, shareholding bears little relation to control of industrial property.

Given the monolithic tone of the large-circulation media when they do enter the world of public policy, and given their entertainment orientation and consequent lack of attention to the real world, how can ideas, facts, proposals, pointing the way to an alternative to the Cold War–business culture obtain free entry to the arena? Given the middle-class, business-based sponsorship and management of the media, how can the needs and aspirations of the lower-middle and working class majority of the population be articulated?

The answer to these questions, as well as to that of realizing the cultural potential of broadcasting media, lies in the creation of noncommercial institutions, and the imposition of clearer public responsibilities upon the commercial media (whose continued existence must be assumed in this country). When the producer of a quiz show can defend rigging, deception, and lies by pleading the "terror and panic that besieged us," something is wrong with the system. That something is of course monolithic commercialism, based on a concept of broadcasting as a service to advertisers: "The public," said another producer of rigged shows, "wasn't paying any admission price to watch these programs." The advertiser pays (though of course we pay the advertiser in inflated prices), therefore the advertiser calls the tune.

> The economic organization of the television industry is in conflict with the intent of the law, which is to use this valuable and essential monopoly for the public benefit . . . we shall be compelled, it seems to me, to establish alongside commercial television . . . another network founded on the principle of public benefit and moved by noncommercial motives.
>
> Such a network, which could be governed by disinterested citizens and operated by the frustrated and unhappy professions of the existing networks, could become a powerful competitor, and by the competition

of its example a powerful regulator, of the existing commercial networks.

The new network could be financed — and a nice ironic twist this would be — by a percentage-of-profits charge upon the commercial networks, as John Fischer has suggested. And it seems to me that it would be worthwhile also to impose separation of advertising from programming (the "magazine concept") upon the commercial networks. These changes would not of themselves usher in a new era of cultural creativity; but they would provide an institutional basis to encourage rather than stifle free discussion and free art.

## The Reconstruction of Democratic Politics

Political commentators as diverse in viewpoint as Charles A. Beard and John Strachey have been united in seeing the problem of democratic politics as the problem of concentrated economic power versus the diffused power of numbers. But while Beard sees universal suffrage as embodying an impossible dream of political equality, Strachey sees one man–one vote as an essential and partially successful force for countervailing the push of monopoly capitalism toward ever-increasing inequality. The existence of a progressive income tax and the emergence of health care for the aged as a prime issue in a Presidential election year demonstrate the connection between the suffrage and the direction in which public policies are formulated. Conversely, the retention of the 27½ percent depletion allowance for the oil industry and the failure of federal wage, hour, and child labor legislation to protect the retail clerk, the cannery worker, or the migratory family illustrate the strength of minority and property-oriented elements in our political system.

Our need is more accurately characterized as the creation rather than the maintenance of democracy. We began in 1789 with a constitutional structure explicitly designed to throw obstacles in the way of majority rule (See Madison's Federalist Papers Nos. 10 and 51) and then, as all texts in American government point out, we modified this system in the direction of greater democracy by the development of national political parties, the direct election of senators, and the abolition of the property qualification to voting, and the development of a *de facto* system for direct election of the President. But what the texts ignore is the gradual, and I suspect increasing, development of a counter-trend of vulgar Madisonianism.

What I mean by this is that we have not been content with the separation of power and checks and balances established in the Constitution, but have added to these a host of additional roadblocks which make more difficult the creation of effective government. Examples include ideas such as Calhoun's "concurrent majorities" doctrine, which in its modern form means that action is taken only when almost every organized group is willing to accept a program, and the attitude that a party split between President and Congress is a good thing because it provides a further check on power. Part of the pattern also are the establishment of autonomous agencies outside the sphere of Presidential control, the excessive judicialization of the administrative process, the seniority system of congressional chairmanships, the irresponsible power of the House Rules Committee, and the denigration of party discipline and responsibility in the name of "independence."

The result of these anti-majoritarian accretions to an anti-majoritarian Constitution is a system celebrated in contemporary political science as "pluralism": public policy will be determined by the free interplay of opposing groups, slowly, without leadership, without planned objectives, without stepping on anybody's toes. One defect in such a system is that, to operate equitably, it must assume a balance of power among groups. Because such a balance does not exist, the forces of property and industrial power have made full use of the system's openness to organized group demands. *Their* toes do not get stepped on. The 1958 election and the passage of Landrum-Griffin in the 1959 Congress illustrate the size of the gap between the electoral factor — one man–one vote — and the wealth factor in our politics.

An anti-action, weak-government structure inevitably hurts the "have-nots," for their welfare requires change while that of the "haves" generally requires only that the status quo remain undisturbed. But the stronger government I want to see must also be a more accountable government, and a second significant by-product of this spurious pluralism is its destruction of governmental accountability to the electorate. Without party discipline and relative homogeneity, with an emphasis instead upon undisciplined narrow-interest groups, there is no way for a national majority of voters to hold their representatives to the program upon which they have been elected. So long as the determination of policy in Congress is free of party control, so long will we have an irresponsible government reflecting the will of economic power blocs rather than the will of the majority.

A dissenter's program of political reform, therefore, must have as its twin objectives the removal of Madisonian and pseudo-Madisonian obstacles to action, and the strengthening of the party-electoral process. The two being interdependent, what helps in one area will help in the other. For example, establishing full Presidential authority over the agencies of economic regulation would increase the degree of electoral control because, of all the parts of our national system, it is the Presidency that can come closest to expressing the sentiment of a national majority. The party reform proposals of Stephen K. Bailey and James M. Burns provide the needed outlook and program: mass-based national party financing; simultaneous election every four years of the President, House, and half the Senate; repeal of the 22nd Amendment; revision of the seniority system; strengthening of party policy committees in Congress; and a focus on the Presidential candidate as the policy leader for the whole party. Without structural changes toward a more majoritarian system, a liberal-radical program will be badly blunted, if not smothered, by the conservative coalition to whom the leaderless process of group pluralism is so supremely suited.

But politics is as much a matter of social as of governmental structure: it is as much a matter of building a social movement as of revised political mechanics. Only a strong national party of industrial and farm labor, Negroes, and the liberal segment of the middle class can provide the power base for the "Coming Political Breakthrough" that Bowles and Schlesinger have been predicting. The earlier proposals of this paper — for civil rights, redistribution of income, economic democracy, and social balance programs — will have as an important by-product the strengthening of popular political capacity — in awareness, skills, wealth. Only as the organizations of *people* are given the support of public policy will they be effective counterweights to the organizations of *capital* that threaten to recombine political and economic power in a new elite. As Daniel Bell has suggested, political action by labor can do more, and more equitably, than collective bargaining to raise substandard wages and assure full employment and full purchasing power by affecting fiscal and monetary policies. The NAACP's judicial politics also need to be followed up by Negro participation in other arenas of social change. The sit-in movement — spontaneous in origin and with widespread personal involvement — points the way to effective political action as well. The conviction that radical change is necessary and possible, it has now been demonstrated, can itself be the spark to ignite a significant social movement.

1960

# THE NEGRO MOVEMENT: WHERE SHALL IT GO NOW?*

## BAYARD RUSTIN,
## TOM KAHN, et al.

*1*) Would you care to speculate about the next stages of the equal rights movement? Several facts seem to converge to produce a stalemate or near-stalemate: a) the "era of good feeling" between Negroes and liberal whites, which reached a climax at the March on Washington, seems to have come to an end, at least for the moment; b) the Negro campaigns in the South have in a number of crucial instances run into a stone wall of opposition, effectively maintaining the Jim Crow structure; c) the pattern of repeated demonstrations, often without precise objectives, leads to exhaustion, demoralization, loss of interest, when there are no visible results; d) it becomes more and more apparent that the demand for Negro rights is deeply related to problems of the economic structure, a point we socialists have been emphasizing but which doesn't allow of easy solutions. Now, add to these facts that support for the Negroes in the white community seems to be decreasing, and that the passage of the Civil Rights Bill will not greatly affect the life of the ordinary Negro living in a Northern city — and you have a genuine dilemma. What,

* This is a condensed transcript of a discussion held in May, 1964, between a number of leading figures in the Civil Rights Movement and several editors of *Dissent*.

then, do you think the future prospects for, and tactics of, the equal rights movement should now be?

2) You have stressed, and we all here surely agree with you, that the Negro movement needs tremendously to gain and hold allies in the labor movement. Yet my general impression is that the unions have not responded to this crisis with the urgency we would wish. What do you say to your friends and/or critics in the Negro movement who say: "All right, an alliance with the unions would be fine, but how can we have an alliance with organizations that have little interest in forming one, and whose membership is corrupted by prejudice?"

3) There seems to be a genuine crisis of leadership in the Negro movement. It has been obvious all along that there hasn't been a single movement, but rather a loose alliance of parallel and sometimes competing groups. How does this alliance stand now? And something else: I have the impression that there is arising a new kind of Negro militant, in almost all the active organizations. He is fed up with white promises. He has discovered that he is *proud* to be alienated from white society. He has strong "nationalist" inclinations, vague though these may seem. But above all, he is desperate — impatient with the tactics of gradualism, nonviolence, etcetera. In effect, he decides to "go it alone," scornful of the white liberal and labor groups and of those Negro leaders who prefer to work with such groups. He has, it would seem, little faith in the possibility of changing American society, and consequently he is determined to shock and assault it. In a way, though he shows no inclination toward practicing individual terrorism or anything of that sort, he acts out of motives somewhat like those of the late-nineteenth-century Russian terrorists, who tried to substitute their intransigent will for the slowness and sluggishness of history. Is there anything to this description?

4) Finally, I want to ask you about the internal condition of the Negro communities, especially up North. It becomes clear that the struggle for equality will not be won very quickly; it will be a long and hard fight. That means having a community that is ready for a sustained struggle. But many of the activists seem, on the contrary, oriented toward short-run action to the exclusion of virtually everything else. And within the Negro community there seems also to be a very serious process of social disintegration, shown through many symptoms of pathology and demoralized behavior. Doesn't this raise, then, for the Negro movement and leaders the problem of trying to effect an internal self-mobilization in the Negro community, not merely for struggle on the outside but for social, cultural, and morale purposes within its own ranks? I know that the comparison between the present-day Negro community and the Jewish community of thirty or forty years ago can easily become a facile one, especially if it is used too easily as a way of criticizing the Negroes.

Yet, making all due allowance for the ways in which the Jews, even at their most exploited, were in a more favorable position than the Negroes, isn't there something to be learned from the way in which the Jewish world, especially the Jewish labor world, built up a highly complex and rich association of schools, societies, movements, etc., all of which helped sustain morale and provide vision even when objectives could not yet be realized?

BAYARD RUSTIN: A number of the circumstances you pose in the questions are definitely there, but I think the important point is that the civil rights movement, because of its limited success, is now confronted with the problem that major Negro demands cannot be met within the context of the civil rights struggle. The frustration in the Negro community is not merely the result of difficulties in the struggle, but also of the fact that these demands are made in a context where the *Negro alone* is in motion. So that the major problem before us is how to relieve the Negro of this isolation. If there were a democratic Left in this country, the Negro movement would be in it along with labor, liberals and intellectuals, and people from the churches.

But now the Negroes have to deal not only with discrimination but also the problems of the whole society. While many Negroes would not so analyze it, they know in a visceral way that this is true. They know there is really no way to get jobs for Negroes unless something else happens. And they also know, and I know, that the labor movement, affected by automation, is itself unable to provide jobs for the people already enrolled in the unions, that the only way labor can handle this thing is if it allies with the Negro in a bigger struggle in which it can then afford to be an ally because its problems are simultaneously being met. Without this overall political program, the Negro and the labor forces are antagonistic and will remain so. The unions will give money and pass resolutions but they will not act. That, I think, is the problem — not Galamison, not PAT, not Malcolm X — none of the things mentioned as being crucial are really crucial unless *this* is made crucial first.

NORMAN HILL: A related problem is that the usual tactic of direct action which here and there has produced an integrated lunch counter does not seem to be answering the demands of larger numbers of Negro people. The civil rights movement has therefore been forced to dig deeper, just to hold its own as an established part of the Negro community. In its very thrust, this movement poses questions that get at the basic problems of society. It is faced with a situation where, like it or not, it inevitably is driven toward making serious judgments upon society.

EMANUEL GELTMAN: I think Rustin and Hill are right so far as the long haul is concerned, but before you get there, you must face some problems right now. When Bayard speaks of the importance of integrating the civil rights movement with a revitalization of the trade union movement that for us is a familiar context and we, so to speak, know what to do about it. But before we get to the trade union problems, we must come to grips with PAT. I think it's almost easier for us to deal with the broader social problems raised by Bayard than to provide answers to local ones. After listening to a television broadcast where these PAT people were talking, I felt that I could not contain my impatience or even discuss with them. Yet that's the level that willynilly we're compelled to deal with now.

JACK RADER: In the school integration struggle in Queens, one of the things that strikes me about the reaction of the whites is that they act as if the question were one of special privilege for Negroes. There is tremendous irritation and misunderstanding. The postwar period saw the rise of new middle-class elements, typified by the white suburbs. These people who have recently arrived at this middle-class status feel threatened in a personal and direct sense. "My kid, what kind of education is he going to get?" They say, "I was brought up in a ghetto" — an ethnic ghetto, or a slum. "I made it, and I didn't go on any protest. Now, what the devil do these people want?" It seems to me that this threatens the possibility of a labor-Negro alliance. You have a tremendous privatization of life in this country, and the Negro movement arises when there are no other movements to coalesce with.

IRVING HOWE: Let's see if I can focus what's been said so far: In principle we're all for a Negro alliance with the labor movement, but that idea is too general, and doesn't provide guidance for what has to be done tomorrow in Queens or the next day in Birmingham or the third day in Chester, Pennsylvania.

RUSTIN: When I talked about an alliance, I did not mention the labor movement as such. I'm talking about trade-union people. I certainly do not look for any alliance which would include the AFL-CIO per se. Secondly, I think we have to think about what I call a political movement, not as a movement of the thirties or even the sixties, or anything else we've been through, but something new. To me it is programmatic-political; that is to say, I think now, today, around questions like total employment, limited planning, work training within planning, and a public-works program. There are many elements in labor, in the Negro community, and among liberals who can move on such a programmatic base.

I am not concerned fundamentally with the level of argument which has to be made with PAT. If we concentrate on that level, we are lost. PAT and the people it represents "have" to be anti-Negro as long as we are in the objective situation of declining schools. We have got to lift the school problem from integration to that of quality schools, which has to include, we say, integration secondarily. You must make a totally new approach, and it is only then that people can be brought into a broader movement. It is the broader social movement which educates them, while the civil rights movement keeps things stirred up.

HOWE: The question that must then be posed is: What *meanwhile* happens with the Negro movement, when it has to survive in relative isolation, under increasingly difficult conditions?

MICHAEL HARRINGTON: Well, I'll take off from that question and say that the Negro movement will simply lose; there is no happy answer if you posit it that way. This discussion points up that we're not talking about the Negro question, we're talking about the American question. If the American labor movement continues to take the John L. Lewis approach to automation, that is, to bid farewell to the workers who are kicked out, to re-form their organizations on a narrow but highly skilled, fairly well-paid base, to accept a smaller role in this society but to keep their structure intact on that base, then you can say that instead of an alliance there will probably be a war between white and black at the bottom of American society. Second, if the American labor movement does that, not only will there be a war between white and black at the bottom of society, but neither the American labor movement nor any force for social change will be able to answer *any* of the questions, the automation question, the school question, the hospital question, the whole shooting match. But I think the trade-union movement, out of its self-interest more than concern for the Negro, will be forced to start doing some things that will move it into a position of alliance with the Negroes.

The idea we've discussed around *Dissent,* and which is now being discussed at the UAW, of the trade union movement organizing the working poor both as a means of expanding its membership and of reaching Negroes, Puerto Ricans, Mexican Americans and other minority workers, is one proposal. Here I agree with Bayard that in a context of full employment, or in the context of the type of proposal just suggested by Senator Clark's committee in Washington, of a five-billion-dollar additional annual social expenditure for construction, that even the building-trades unions, if they were enabled to double their available jobs and memberships, wouldn't care if fifty percent of that increased membership were Negro, as long as they paid their dues and didn't unduly upset the hierarchy. The possibility for successful action is dependent on these big questions. The answer to what we do meanwhile in the specific situation is — improvise, probably unsuccessfully, so long as so many of the massive determinants are loaded against us.

TOM KAHN: The Negro movement arose at a "wrong" time, when there are no supporting mass movements in the society. But to conclude that the Negroes have to face all issues on their own is to accept all kinds of things which the movement cannot accept. First of all, it means to accept defeat. Now there *is* a certain romantic strain in the Negro movement that's almost willing to do that. A segment of the Negro leadership and perhaps among the rank-and-file seems almost to want the movement to have a tragic ending which would somehow illuminate the human condition in all of its frailty. But the consequences of failure of the Negro movement would really be catastrophic. If you take automation and technological change into account, and if the rate of Negro displacement through automation continues, you get a picture of a class-color society. This will provide the basis for all kinds of extremely reactionary political developments. If that prospect is kept before us, and it's not a matter of hundreds of years, but in the decades ahead, I would maintain that the labor movement even in its present state represents a certain social ballast against such a development.

RUSTIN: Because we have gone so far but haven't come to the final step, we end up with the fact that we find ourselves without sufficient allies, and the Negroes are turning to tactics which are not commensurate with what they're trying to achieve. This is what always happens when a group attempts to achieve more than it has the power to. PAT would not exist if other elements were in the movement, and if it did we wouldn't care, because then it would be of no consequence.

HOWE: In other words, PAT and certain kinds of "extremism" in the Negro movement are both evidence of the absence of a vital major participation by the liberal-labor white world. They form symmetrical phenomena.

RADER: Both Bayard and Mike propose massive public works. But massive public works, government engineered and lopped off the defense budget, is a *substitute* for economic integration. It might succeed in admitting a given number into the building trades, but it will not succeed in allowing the Negroes to break through the normal pattern of employment in this country.

What we come to is that a whole new approach to social priorities is needed. What shall the wealth of the country be used for and how shall work be directed? Posed in these larger social terms of social priorities and the expenditures of the wealth and the energies of the country, I don't think you have anything on the horizon at this point which is concerned with this type of question.

RUSTIN: We're talking about our lives. If the labor movement is concerned now about full employment, it is concerned about public works. So are a lot of liberals. So are church people. Therefore you start with that point. Down the road they will see the logic of what you are saying. But let us start where we're talking about our lives, where our lives can in fact move. On the question of Negro strategy for now, I think we have not to be so pessimistic. In my mind, there have been many more successes of the civil rights movement prodding the society in the direction I want to see it go, than there have been successes in the civil rights movement *per se*. The churches are moving around the civil rights bill as no church groups have ever moved in this country and they cannot stop at civil rights, but must go beyond to the question of full employment.

Number two: There would not be any war against poverty had it been left to white workers. The Negro workers moved out of a sense of Negro dignity, and they stimulated Mike's book, they stimulated Johnson's program, which was in part stimulated by Mike's book, etcetera. It has an accumulative effect.

Three: We got rid of McCarthyism on the American campus in 1960 because Negro students moved in the sit-ins. Whites were touched and some of them had to move also. This made political discussion possible on the campus.

Now concluding: I think that the civil rights movement has two fundamental strategies to follow: First, stay in the streets, winning little victories, and sometimes none, but stay, for the very reason that you stimulate other segments of the society, limitedly, to move. Second, the civil rights movement now has an obligation to carry the question which I discussed earlier under full employment, planning, training, and so forth. They must now begin to carry that message into the streets. When they go to sit down in front of the building trades, or to climb a crane, they have to say, "We are doing this as a symbol of the fact that we want jobs. We want ten jobs *now* in the building trades. And further, we insist that America hear and act on this program for dealing with our real problem." I think the civil rights movement is just about ready to move in that direction.

HARRINGTON: I agree with what Bayard said. But to go back to something that Jack Rader said, not so much in contradiction, but, I think, an extension. When Jack said that this public-works plan Bayard has been talking about would not allow the Negro to break through to the normal employment pattern, that's true. The reason is that the normal employment pattern in the United States is partly being revolutionized out of existence by technology. Nobody's breaking through to the normal employment pattern — not just Negroes, but whites and Negroes, which again points up how radical the American problem is.

HOWE: And to interrupt you, Mike, public works may itself become a normal work pattern.

HARRINGTON: Right. But let me go on to just a couple of statistics I came upon recently which indicate how extraordinary the situation is. According to the House Labor Committee which investigated the functioning of the Manpower Development and Training Act, fifty-seven percent of the Negroes twenty-four years of age in the United States were school dropouts. According to the Secretary of Labor, you need a high school education to really function in this economy. Therefore, presently, fifty-seven percent of the Negroes in the United States cannot hope to break through to a normal employment pattern. At the same time, the committee pointed out that about twenty-eight percent of the whites at the same age are dropouts. This means between a quarter and a third of all youth are unfit for present technology.

In a sense the Negro alone has been facing the entire American question and that's what a lot of the problem stems from. But we can't be too pessimistic, because someday American society is going to have to face the American question, and when it does it can't help but ally itself with the Negroes.

STANLEY PLASTRIK: Unfolding right before our eyes is a beautiful illustration of what Bayard and others here have been talking about; that is, the way in which the so-called Negro question is really the question of the entire future of American society. Until a few weeks ago the concept of the educational park was largely unknown. Now the Board of Education has put it on its agenda. It's posed before the entire population of New York City. I don't want to discuss the merits of it now, but obviously it transforms the whole discussion of education and integration. Or, to take another illustration: Some years ago, a few people — I remember Bruno Bettelheim, for example — raised the question of the effects of a kind of *de facto* segregation within the schools, that is the homogeneous grouping of children. That discussion didn't get anywhere, but obviously the question must come up again.

RUSTIN: Neither of these things could possibly have burst into the picture had it not been for the movement of the Negro. And already the Negro struggle for quality education has forced the school board to do something which is of tremendous benefit to every child regardless of color, and that is dropping the so-called I.Q. tests.

GELTMAN: I find myself annoyed by the pessimism that frequently issues from the civil rights movement. A great deal of progress has been made which may ultimately be a lot more important than whether some particular person got into the sheet-metal workers union or not. Other civil rights leaders do not talk, at least publicly, the way Bayard does, not even the socialists, or the trade unionists like Randolph, or the educators like Kenneth Clark. Clark, for example, speaks in terms of quality education; it is *our* function to give it the broader context. If you tackle slums you find they are not just problems in housing. You have to tackle the slum as a problem in education, and in health. It is really our function as socialist intellectuals to portray the total picture.

And I seriously believe that the problem is not one of just working out some accommodation between the trade union movement and the civil rights movement. Even in terms of self-interest, the leadership cannot stick with the status quo.

HOWE: Let me inject a "pessimistic" note here, just for the sake of stirring up the discussion. It seems to me there's a terrible discrepancy between the general, programmatic, ideological level on which we all really agree and the immediate practical reality. In New York City you have the following situation: a white middle class which favors integration in Birmingham but faced with changes at home has really hardened. For the first time a large section of the Jewish middle class, traditionally liberal, is also hardening, and is simply holding out in behalf of its own narrow interests. And this middle-class reaction has shown itself to be more resourceful than the whole liberal-labor movement in New York City. On the other hand, as far as I know, neither the ILGWU, the main trade union in New York City, nor the NMU sent anyone to the conference on integrated, quality education which was organized by David Livingston and Reverend Donald Harrington. Not only have major unions not participated in this effort to weld a rough sort of alliance, but the intellectuals have also been disgracefully absent. Yes, it's essential to work out the broad programmatic conception. But in terms of concrete politics the immediate situation cannot be confronted only through that general program. Locally the situation is extremely tough and rather bad.

ROCHELLE HOROWITZ: What makes the problem so difficult is that there are reasons for both optimism and for pessimism.

There is the Allen report. And Bayard's right about the churches. But the Negro in the street has not seen one gain, and you have to be an intellectual to see the larger perspective.

The March on Washington raised a whole series of demands in a way that was able to pull in the white community on the programmatic level that we're discussing now. It's interesting —

HOWE: Let me interrupt you, Rochelle. The March on Washington was general, it was humane, it was brotherly, but it didn't affect what happened in the white guy's job or neighborhood. Now suddenly it's come home, and it's hit him, and he's nervous.

HOROWITZ: You have to work out a broad programmatic base to involve the white community. It is possible to march to City Hall, for instance, for quality, integrated education and to get white people involved in this. It would have been possible for Galamison to have structured his demands, before the first school boycott, in a way that would have brought the white community along with it and not have terrified them.

There is a certain type of leadership which does thrive on defeat, a lazy, opportunistic leadership. They not only don't have a program, they are opposed to a program. This can be very demoralizing. Temporarily it results in publicity and an easy style of leadership. It's much easier to be a Milton Galamison than a Bayard Rustin.

HOWE: There are people in or near the Negro movement who say that Bayard's program is certain to fail, that it must fail, that the very nature of American society is such that the idea of a Negro-labor alliance is doomed to failure, that it puts too much trust in the white community. Consequently it seems to me that there must be forming a sentiment which is roughly equivalent, to make an historical analogy, to that of certain kinds of revolutionists in Russia in the late nineteenth century who turned to terrorism, not because they believed in terrorism in principle, but because they believed there were no longer any positive social forces which could act. Therefore they tried to substitute for a static history their own sacrifice and desire. The consequence of such terrorism almost always is to exhaust the best cadres, and to lead to isolation and defeat.

I suspect one of the feelings such people, the "desperadoes" in the Negro movement, have is that they may never have allies in America, but they do have allies in Cuba, China, and in such places. And this is really a terrible illusion.

RUSTIN: I have a little anecdote which bears you out. Norman Hill and I were investigating the set-up at the World's Fair before we went out to have the sit-downs. I called a friend who works for the delegation of a new African nation and asked him if he could get one of the African countries to let us come in early with their officials to look over their pavilion. When I called the next day, he said, "Look, the boys are scared. The last thing they will do is to take you or any other Negro out there to see this fair. These boys are so economically dependent on the West that the only thing they will do is debate South Africa in the UN but they will never touch anything regarding the United States and its internal questions."

KAHN: There is some justification for the comparison with a nineteenth-century Russian-terrorist type of psychology. On the positive side, there are changes in consciousness yet no changes in the basic situation. There is a movement for integrated schools in New York but no signs that major breakthroughs will be made. We talk about the ecumenical movement among the religious groups and the changes in consciousness that result. The liberal ideology spreads over the country but at the same time, underneath, certain regressive trends are going on that clash with it.

The economic situation means certain things for the Negro and unless a massive change takes place, it looks very bad. Demographic changes are crucial. A new consciousness about the New York school situation may arise, but it can make no difference as long as Negroes continue to make up a larger and larger proportion of central cities, while white people continue to move to the suburbs. Therefore, it is bad to have so much activity without visible results, because the democratic ethic may suffer from the disillusionment.

Two years ago I was saying that you have to have a sympathetic attitude toward the Negro extremist because he suffers a great deal of frustration. To an extent, that may still be true. But I am much stronger in my opposition to those elements now, simply out of the realization that it is a tremendous disservice to the masses of Negroes to lead them to expect that their needs can be articulated by a voice in isolation.

HILL: It seems to me that we're in for a very rough period. The leader who is likely to emerge in every local situation is the demagogic type rather than the type who is going to articulate anything of what Bayard says in his speeches. And not only because the Negro movement exists in the absence of any democratic Left, but also because no matter how you put what we've been saying in this room it sounds to the average Negro like "Wait." Galamison can say, "Tie up the schools." Now we can't say it because we're too honest to pretend that that alone would achieve much. Still, we can say all kinds of other things which to the average Negro sound like, "This is for real." As long as his alienation persists and as long as we don't really build some kind of secondary cadre, then we will have to confront the emergence of the demagogic or "nationalist" leaders. The young Negro militants pay attention to them.

HARRINGTON: What Norman is talking about could, by way of historical analogy, be something akin to what took place among the coal miners in the 1920's when they waged a bitter struggle in isolation from the labor movement as a whole. I would only point out on the other side that eventually that struggle did pay off.

I think that the report of the Clark subcommittee calling for five billion dollars extra expenditures annually, the growing consciousness in this society that *something* has to be done, is already leading, not yet at the bottom of society but at the top, to the possibility of some changes which could help the civil rights movement.

HOWE: In all past major social and revolutionary movements there have been ups and down, but the important difference here is that we're speaking about a minority movement, only ten percent of the population. Given a society which is fundamentally cut off from that minority, large parts of which are hostile to it, and large parts of which are cosily affluent, we have a new prospect, namely, a minority becoming more and more desperate, but without the possibility of a major upsurge such as previous social movements have had.

RUSTIN: It's important to point out that one of the problems is that in the civil rights movement we have no literature, no history, no former revolutionary movement that has ever taken place in the context you have just described. Certainly, India where I have worked is not the same because even the untouchables do not have high visibility. The government of India from its very inception, largely because of Gandhi's spiritual approach to revolution, made a tremendous reconstruction effort in India. Gandhi's death did not cut it short as Lincoln's did here. Now I think we have to be very thankful that things have even gone as well as they have. Those who talk about the use of violence and so on, also have to face the fact that no minority is going to get away with guerrilla warfare in the United States. It's just impossible. Therefore we must realize that we are dealing with a situation which is far different from any we have ever been through.

KAHN: I have a question to put to Bayard. Numbers of young people in the movement seem to regard the stall-in and similar tactics as logical extensions of your theory of social dislocation. Where does your theory of social dislocation end and the stall-in tactics begin?

RUSTIN: I think it is, in a sense, a logical deduction. Many of them have come to me and said, "We thought we were doing exactly what you were proposing." I don't think that one can ever think of the theory of social dislocation in the abstract. One must always, when developing tactics, think of the exact situation one is in, the reaction one is going to get, and certain tactical problems. Now, I was opposed to the World's Fair stall-ins for a number of reasons. One, it is a tactic which can only be successful if it is secretive. Once the police know about it, they will do what they did. Second, they can get injunctions against the leadership, isolating them when they should be organizing the masses. Anytime you call upon two thousand people to do something, it could not possibly be secretive and therefore they stepped into the government's hands. And further, it was wrong, because it did not leave an adequate alternative. A tactic which just harumscarum ties up everybody is wrong. Not that in principle I'm against people being alienated. In social change there is always alienation. But if you're trying to win allies, you want to reduce that alienation to an irreducible minimum. Also the tactic was not good because it did not pinpoint the objectives that were to be achieved. No one could have said: "What can we give you to call off this project?" Therefore certain principles have to be applied if social dislocation is to be reasonable.

GELTMAN: Isn't that also true of the sit-in in which you took part?

RUSTIN: No, it was not. Several times I got up to let women and children pass through.

GELTMAN: No, I mean the specific objectives. Could they say, "We'll give you this, we'll give you that . . ."

RUSTIN: Oh yes. If the Mayor of New York City had said, "We will have round-the-clock discussions on the school integration problem. I'll call everyone to my office and tell them to stay there until this problem is settled," we would have left.

HOWE: Norman Hill says that the problem is the incongruity between the long-range political program that Bayard proposes and the difficulty of keeping the Negro movement going in a constructive way right now. Bayard, you ought to talk on this.

RUSTIN: I think we've got to have a political movement, in the sense that the civil rights movement is now a political movement. It's a matter of broadening that. Regardless of people's politics, regardless of what church they belong to, or union, thousands and millions of people are contributing to the civil rights organizations, are getting into the streets. They came to the March on Washington. This is the kind of movement I see as a political movement, around such things as full employment, some planning, training within that planning, a public works program. I think without setting up a political structure or a party we can carry this to the people and get the kind of enthusiasm that you now get around the civil rights bill, or that we got around the March on Washington.

But it has to be spelled out so people can understand it. Meany has already called for public works. Let's take him up on this, not damn him. Men like Ralph Helstein and Reuther are prepared to go even further. Let's get a simple program now around which we can organize. While people may be bound by certain political allegiances and the like, these things can be broken as the need is seen. Then you ask for a deeper program and you proceed in that way. I don't know what else there is except getting the Negroes to carry that program in their demonstrations and saying to them, "Continue to demonstrate. We now have not only an objective of getting a few jobs here but of spelling out a political program."

HOWE: Could you say something about the question: What is the present mood of the more important sections of the Negro leadership in regard to this program?

RUSTIN: I think the Negro leadership out of its own frustration is having to look in two directions. One, organizing the grass roots, getting down to some block organization in the ghetto; and, on the other hand, seeing the limitations of this method alone and thereby increasingly following the Randolph notion of seeing the problem as an American social problem. They will be forced into this, by the fact that they can't deliver what needs to be delivered by merely looking at the problem as a civil rights problem.

HOWE: Question four. Rustin should answer it.

RUSTIN: I agree with what is implied in the question. I don't think there's much of a comparison. Jews were an ingrown group themselves, with a very long history and culture, and this had an effect. They also could become invisible as many of them did. But on the major question I am one of those who has a very dim view of being able to patch up the ghetto. There is a ghetto psychology, and this cannot be eliminated. There is the filth of the ghetto; and the ghetto has its own logic. However, I am very much for mobilizing the community to deal with their immediate problems. If there are rats you help people get rid of them, and the same with roaches and triple-sessions. I am for approaching the problem on this level as a means of doing a basic educational job with these people.

GELTMAN: We're touching on a much broader problem than may be apparent. There has begun very serious consideration not merely for Negroes but for society as a whole, of various kinds of self-mobilization programs. You will see the idea put forward in connection with jobs. If you have so many young people who cannot find jobs, who are not trained, you can employ them in helping themselves. The whole proposal with respect to self-mobilization is going to get attention precisely in the terms in which you originally spoke, that is, of coping with general problems of society, from poverty to narcotics addiction, and anything we can do in this connection with respect to the Negro problem obviously is relevant. There is one point I want to throw in on the Jews and that is that what everyone forgets is that the Jews, in moving forward, had a very important and unique connection. Apart from their invisibility and so forth, their progress was largely tied on the economic front to the unions in New York, especially the ILGWU.

HOWE: Granted, the ghetto has a bad psychology of its own which can't be abolished without abolishing the ghetto itself. I accept that. Granted, too, that the analogy with the Jews has its obvious weakness. My point is this: Given the present situation, school dropouts in Negro communities, and various kinds of social pathology, it is not sufficient to try to involve such young people in political and social struggles. Necessary, but not sufficient. One of the responsibilities of the Negro leadership is to work within its own world, morally, socially, educationally, psychologically, for purposes of sustaining morale, of inculcating values and vision. This kind of thing must be done, and here the comparison with the Jewish world makes some sense because the internal richness of its own community was one of the great sustaining factors of the immigrant Jewish world where there was poverty, alienation, unemployment, and all the rest. Am I wrong?

HOROWITZ: There is a way in which a stereotype produces a certain kind of person, and you have to think about the stereotype of the Jew and of the Negro and the kind of pressure that the Negro community has been subjected to. Never have you heard about Jews being inhuman. That is, they were shrewd, businesslike, etcetera. For Negroes, to conform to their stereotype is to be . . .

HOWE: Why can't one of the objectives of the self-mobilization within the community be to break down these stereotypes?

HOROWITZ: That is what the sit-ins are about, right?

HOWE: Of course, the sit-ins are one way of realizing the objective at a time when you have to have a prolonged struggle, but it seems to me that there's a great need for internal education.

KAHN: There has been a great deal of self-help in the Negro community, and I bet there's been more intensive effort at this among Negroes than among Jews. The whole emphasis on self-help, on Negro solidarity and economic uplift, is accentuated in times of social discouragement. There is a whole Booker T. Washington tradition, that's self-help. Negro fraternities, mutual aid societies, etcetera.

HOWE: But what I'm talking about is self-help toward the objectives of winning the revolution.

KAHN: You find that the fight for integration is pushed by the middle-class, "assimilationist" Negroes and not by the nationalist-oriented Negroes; and that contrasts with the Jewish community. The fight for integration did not come from those Negroes who felt that they had some cultural heritage to preserve. The self-help movement broke up on the shoals of the ghetto. I'm not so interested now in seeing a self-help movement among Negroes, because I know the form it's going to take. We want equality; I want Negroes to get *out* of the ghetto, not to be helped within it.

PLASTRIK: I can understand the fundamental objections on this self-help issue. It seems to conjure up images of small business operations and small capital accumulation, which of course is a very important part of the Jewish background.

A couple of weeks ago, two French intellectuals from the *Esprit* group were here and they asked me to accompany them on a visit to Harlem. They had expected to see, as you do in Paris, a small Algerian quarter. They had absolutely no idea of what was there and when they saw the reality and extent of it, they were dumbfounded. And I realized at that point that if I talked to them in terms of the sort of thing we talk about, self-mobilization, they would have felt the utter inadequacy of that kind of response. They wanted to hear me say, as a representative of the Left, something to the effect that this whole thing has to be smashed to smithereens.

When we talk about self-mobilization, I think perhaps what we have in mind is the struggle against the spiritual and psychological demoralization that one finds in Negro communities.

HOWE: Tom, I mean by self-help the kind of thing that your group has been doing with those young kids — educating them, trying to give them some perspective, so it isn't just a matter of demonstrations but some understanding to build their morale.

RUSTIN: But what you're talking about is that you get these people to realize the nature of life, of the economic system, what dope really means and why it should be overcome, what prostitution really is and why it must be rooted out. You can get this in one way and one way only, not by preaching and not by inculcation, because Negro mothers have always told them this; but in the struggle to destroy the ghetto.

GELTMAN: An illustration of the lack of conscious social aspirations was presented by the coal miners in West Virginia when they were earning twenty dollars a day, and lived in the most miserable shacks, worse than many in the ghettos — because the union and the miners did not have the social aspiration that they should escape. Other workers have associated economic gains with social achievements.

HARRINGTON: There is practically no analogy between the Negro poor and any other poor there have ever been in the United States. There's a danger of looking for a repetition of the forms of the Jewish or other immigrant experiences in terms of the Negro movement. The form of self-help imposed upon the Negro, his past and present, is the civil rights movement itself.

HOWE: What you're saying, Mike, is very interesting. There is a whole aspect to the Negro movement that doesn't get into the papers, which consists of the sustaining educational and cultural work.

HOROWITZ: People in the East River CORE will tell you that they have two alternatives. They can either be in the streets or in the movement, and to be in the movement means to be a man. But if you called it self-help, they would punch you.

HOWE: I'm talking about self-mobilization as part of the way in which leaders lead a movement.

HOROWITZ: But there are things which are intrinsic to people in motion. Something wonderful happens to people when they are somehow determining their own destiny and beginning to control and change their own conditions.

1964

# THE MINERS:
# MEN WITHOUT WORK

## HARVEY SWADOS

The miners have been called in the past the backbone of the
American labor movement. Never yet broken in to the abject
life of the workers in the industrial cities, they have still a
tradition of resistance and a habit of joint action.

EDMUND WILSON, *Frank Keeney's Coal Diggers*

ST. MICHAEL, PENNSYLVANIA

It is a strange thing to come to a town and find it full of grown men. They
stroll the narrow, shabby streets, chat at the corners, lean against the
peeling pillars of the town saloon, the St. Michael Hotel & Restaurant,
and they look more like movie actors than real human beings, because
something is wrong.

Then you ask for one of them by name, in this town where it is obvious that everyone knows everyone else, and you get the reply, "Oh,
he'll be along any minute. Today's sign-up day." And it is borne in upon
you that these men are subsisting on unemployment insurance checks,
that this is a community where practically all of the able-bodied men
have been out of work for many months. Where are the children? In
school, although most of these people are older and no longer have
small children. Where are the teen-agers? Looking for work, moved
away, trying their luck elsewhere. Where are the women? Working,
many of them — which is a story in itself.

St. Michael is a company town (of the Berwind-White Coal Mining
Co.) tucked into one of the many folds of the mountains of western
Pennsylvania. It is as American as any town you could want, by any
standards you could name. But the menfolk are practically all out of

work, and have been ever since the 24th of April, 1958, when Maryland Shaft #1 closed down. This may be why there is not much travel agency business for Caribbean cruises. In its own way, however, it is a tourist attraction, or would be, if tourists could ever find their way to it over the winding, rutted, poorly-marked roads that tie it to all the other little mining communities of the region: for it was here thousands drowned in the Johnstown Flood. Today the old boathouse then used by wealthy summer residents from Johnstown and Pittsburgh stands high and dry on the St. Michael hillside — now a weather-beaten saloon, it is one of the four hangouts for the miners of St. Michael, who are proud of the tragic story of the area, just as they are proud of the tragic history of their calling.

Six hundred and fifty of these men were working at Maryland #1 when the company started to mechanize. The number was gradually reduced to 400; then, after two layoffs and six months of part-time operation, there came a day which none of the miners had really believed could really come, even though there had been signs, hints, warnings. The mine shut down.

It is not practically relevant whether the closing was a result of there being too much coal or too many men. What matters is what is happening to the people. Later on we shall return to the larger issues of increased productivity resulting from mechanization and concomitant shifts in fuel usage. For now let us stay with the men.

It was only a couple of years ago that the coal dust problem was so bad in St. Michael that a civic committee was formed to cope with it. "I was used to not recognizing my husband, to say nothing of the other men who'd come out of the mine and wave to me," says one miner's wife. "But the coal dust got so bad that it lay over the town like a pall. Everything was covered with it, and we got worried, not just about silicosis down in the mines, but about what it was going to do to all of us right out on the streets."

The dust too was a by-product of mechanization, a result of the automatic miners chewing away furiously hundreds of feet under the earth, and the company informed the committee that there was no point in investing the large sum that would be necessary to abate the nuisance, since it was already losing money on every carload of coal being taken from Maryland #1. All too soon thereafter the mine closed down, and the dust stopped sifting through the streets. The committee was disbanded. . . .

Most of the miners have been used to seasonal operations, working winters and taking off summers, and for quite a long time they assumed that this was to be just another layoff. But then the summer was over, fill-in jobs elsewhere in the area did not seem to be available, and the company took out its expensive automatic equipment and moved some of it down to Maryland Shaft #2, half a dozen miles away at Wilmore. At that point the miners and their families began to face up to the reality of their prospects, and habits began to change. The first item to stop moving at the general store was dog food. After the dog food gathered dust, it was the bottled baby food in the little glass jars that stayed on the shelves. A while after that, the shopkeeper himself gave up and locked his doors forever.

The saloons are still going in St. Michael's Hotel, the Workers' Educational & Social Club, the American Legion Hall, and the old boathouse, but many of the whiskey drinkers have switched to beer, many of the beer drinkers have switched to Squirt, and even more do not show up at all nowadays in the saloons.

"I used to spend between forty and fifty dollars every two weeks in the saloons," says one miner. "Now I never go anymore. It's one thing to be a good fellow when you have it — it's a little different when you have no job."

The town barber, a horn-rimmed young man in a starched white shirt who is on the school board and looks startlingly middle-class in a community that is overwhelmingly working class, stares at his cigar and muses over his beer at the Legion Hall. "I bear no resentment to the miners who don't come in anymore to have me cut their hair. I guess if I'd been out of work as long as they have, I'd ask my wife to cut my hair too."

Some of the miners have managed to get jobs elsewhere. Hampered by the fact that their skills — and even more than their easily acquired skills, such intangible assets as courage, fortitude, esprit de corps, and insouciance in the face of continuous danger — are not readily transferable to other trades, they have been absorbed only in lower-paying jobs. Those who came from other communities and only boarded in St. Michael have gone home. A few have gotten into the steel mills, but not many. A few more have gotten construction work and jobs with the State Highway Department, but again not many; the men point to the million-dollar addition to the high school plant now going up with only seven miners among the construction crew, and they claim that it is impossible to get such a job without "politics." A number of the miners are now working, often for a third or less than what they used to earn, as orderlies in hospitals and institutions, and as janitors and stockmen in big stores. Some have tried to relocate — at least one man has been back and forth to California twice tracking down rumors of steady employment there — only to return to home grounds when jobs haven't materialized. Practically everyone, they say, would come rushing back to St. Michael if Maryland #1 were to reopen, even those few who have gotten good-paying jobs elsewhere (a man with seniority is allowed up to three weeks to reapply for his job). Mining is something that gets in a man's blood, and a coal mine is a man's world in a way that a department store or a mental hospital can never be.

It is truly ironic that a substantial proportion of these men, who pride themselves on their ability to live with danger, to work hard, fight hard, drink hard, love hard, are now learning housework and taking over the woman's role in the family.

What happened was terribly simple. When it became apparent that the mine was not going to reopen, the men signed up for unemployment insurance and their wives began to look for work. Committees were set up — as they have been, hopefully, sometimes pathetically, in similarly depressed areas in Kentucky, West Virginia, Illinois, and Michigan — to see what could be done about bringing in new businesses that could provide employment. The ones that did come to the western Pennsylvania area were those that could benefit not only from tax rebates, low rents, cheap utilities, and other enticements, but also from a substantial pool of people hungry for work — almost any kind of work at almost any kind of wage. Now there are in the area a scattering of small garment factories, brassieres, shirts, shirtwaists, children's wear, all employing not men but women to bend over their sewing machines.

So the women go out to work in the new factories at minimum wages and the men stay home, running the washing machines and the vacuum cleaners, doing the shopping and the dusting, often babysitting, occasionally cooking and scrubbing. There are variations. Some wives hire themselves out as cleaning women to middle-class homes in other towns while their husbands serve as cleaning women at home. There are rebellions too. One husband sits in the saloon waiting for his wife to finish her shift and come after him at midnight, which she does, standing in the doorway in her pedal-pushers, her arms folded, smiling tiredly but firmly until he shoves back his chair, finishes his beer, and walks her home. He insists on playing his role as a man even if he cannot do his work as a man, and one can only guess as to whether his wife loves him any less than do those women whose husbands have taken to drowsing in front of the TV after they have finished the dishes and await their wives' return from the factory. But these are for the most part younger women; it is hard for a woman in her fifties to keep up with the production pace in a factory, and a number of them have had to give it up and reluctantly rejoin their husbands on the rockers or the porch steps.

What else does a man do besides keep house and rock, and hang around the saloon, after he has been out of work for fourteen months? One miner says, "I've been going from town to town, city to city, every place within a hundred miles of here, looking for work. I know it's a wild-goose chase. I'm too old. My own boy is thirty-two, or maybe thirty-three, with three kids of his own, and *he* can't find work. One or two places where he could have had work as a carpenter, he couldn't get a journeyman's card in the union. So what chance do I stand? Just the same, I keep trying — it keeps me occupied."

Those men who have given up looking, or are working sporadically here and there, now and then, put in a lot of time hunting and fishing in the neighborhood. The miners of this area are as fanatical a lot of fishermen as you will find anywhere in the United States; and they also like to come home with deer, pheasant, and sometimes even bear. This is not the least of the ties that bind these jobless men to their home place. There are others, which have to be understood if the men and their problems are to be fully understood.

The miners of St. Michael have banded together and purchased (with money borrowed from their local union) the huge old home of the former mine superintendent, on a bluff overlooking the valley, and have christened it "The Sportsmen's Club." Here, in addition to over sixty acres of wooded recreation and picnic grounds and a *boccie* court, they have a big screened-in run that they built themselves to hold more than five hundred baby pheasants which they acquired from the state conservation authorities and will release for hunting when they are grown. The Sportsmen's Club is one more social center that is their very own, in addition to the Legion Hall and the Workers' Educational & Social Club, down the street from each other and from the St. Michael Hotel. Most of the big social events are held in the Legion Hall, which is decorated with blownup photographs of the local boys — all with Slavic or Croatian names — who have played football at the great state universities, some of them in the Rose Bowl. (The football scholarship is not a joke in St. Michael: it is a very practical way for miners' sons to get a college education and so move on and out into another world.)

It doesn't take much of an excuse to throw a party either; and whether it is a testimonial for a local hero, or a blowout with the one hundred dollars the company gives when the mine operates for a year without a fatal accident (not too often, unfortunately), a sheep is roasted, a pig is spitted, the liquor flows, and, as one miner who has the scars to prove it says, "You get twenty-six miners together and you have twenty-seven fights." The oratory is as pungent as the food. "You women," the toastmaster is fondly remembered as having said to the wives last Christmas, "went and voted for Eisenhower. Well, now you've all got jobs!" Lithuanian slugs it out with Ukrainian; Pole battles with Welshman; and they all stick together against owners, outsiders, and union bureaucrats.

Over at the Workers' Educational & Social Club (also refurbished and enlarged with a loan from the union local') there are, in addition to the bar and the miniature bowling alleys, a meeting hall, kitchens, a library, and a parlor where those miners are laid out who choose to die and be buried without the consolation — or interference — of organized religion.

This is a very special kind of life, and a miner knows what he is missing when he tries his luck in the cities or the suburbs.

"More than one of our boys has gone off to Pittsburgh or Cleveland and come back because he couldn't stand those cement lawns."

"In a big city, you have to pick a fight with a stranger. Here in St. Michael, you can fight with your friends."

"Seriously, here we all know each other, we're clannish, we stick together, we help each other out. It's a good place to live."

It's also a cheap place to live. The company houses, put up during the depression, are comfortable and have pleasant yards, even if their plumbing is simple and the roads around them are sooty and potholed; they rent for from $9 to $14.25 a month. When you consider too that water and sewage are provided directly from the mine's pumps at a nominal price, as is 25-cycle electricity (even with the mine shut down), you can understand why $25 a day is a first-class wage for a miner in a company town, even if the mine only has orders enough to run three or four days a week. Naturally mine families are reluctant to trade in all this — in addition to fish and game and the produce of all the farms that checkerboard the mining country — for the inflation of the metropolis and the suburb.

There is an even more compelling economic reason for the unemployed miners of St. Michael not wanting to leave the industry or the community. According to the United Mine Workers' contracts, a miner must have worked for twenty years out of the last thirty in order to be eligible for a one-hundred-dollar-a-month pension at the age of sixty. You can't live, much less support a family on that sum, but when it is added to social security, savings, and life insurance, it can make the difference between a comfortable old age and a miserable one. Seniority leading up to pension eligibility, however, cannot be transferred from one company to another, or even from one mine of a company to another, unless there is such a shortage of miners that you can move onto a panel and directly into another mine without going to the bottom of the list.

Thus if you are forty-eight years old and have worked in the mines for thirty years, you are not going to receive any pension at all unless you can get in two more years before you reach the age of sixty. It is hard to believe that somehow, some time during the next dozen years you will not be able to get in two more years in the mines to qualify for the pension. There are a lot of these borderline men, desperately hanging on — much more desperately than the younger men who have seen their pension hopes go glimmering and who are ready to sell out and move away, even though they discover that their possessions too have become as worthless as their retirement plans, with their 25-cycle electric stoves and television sets quite unsalable in a community which may never again use the mine's power lines. And of course there are quite a few men safely past fifty, who have the twenty years under their belts, and now have nothing to worry about beyond surviving and supporting their families in one way or another for the next decade, until they reach pension age.

Meanwhile, unemployment insurance is running out.

As these lines are written, most of the miners of St. Michael have six more checks (of about thirty dollars) coming to them. When these lines are read, the checks will have stopped. What then?

"After the last check," says one of the younger men, "comes the revolution."

Well, maybe. But probably not. In order to hazard some sort of guess as to what lies in store for these hundreds of Americans, and for many more thousands like them, from Illinois to West Virginia, we shall have to leave St. Michael for a moment and consider the problem of coal nationally.

For the past decade the coal miner has been squeezed from two directions: by mechanization and by the introduction of increasingly popular substitute fuels. While output per man per day has almost doubled in that decade (from 6.26 tons per day in 1948 to 11.3 tons per day in 1958), the number of men employed in the mines has been more than halved, from 441,631 to 218,600. And as a result not only of slumps but of competition from gas (whose production has increased 365 percent in the last fifteen years) and fuel oils, coal production has receded from a peak of over 600 million tons in 1947 to less than 500 million tons.

The railroads, once major consumers of coal, have now practically converted to diesels; household heating, formerly fueled with the coal-stoked furnace, has lately converted so largely to gas or oil that anthracite mining — confined to three Pennsylvania counties — is all but moribund; when we speak of coal nowadays, for all ordinary purposes we are speaking of bituminous.

It is electricity (in addition to steel, stationary at about 100 million tons) that is expected to take up the slack. With the production of energy from mineral fuels and water power already doubled in the last twenty years, it is now forecast that coal production will have to increase by 50 percent to meet the expanded energy demands of 1975. Does this mean that more men will be needed to mine coal, or even that most of the currently unemployed miners will be put back to work? One would have to be a professional optimist (or a union official) to think so.

For one thing, the development of alternative sources of energy has not ended. Atomic power may not be presently economic; that does not mean that it never will be. For another, the inexorable development of mechanization has not yet come to a halt, even though it is true that it is nearing the saturation point: mechanical mining machines which can mine up to eight tons of coal per minute, and other new equipment, now cut about 85 percent of all underground coal production. The development has been truly fantastic, as extreme perhaps as in any other industry. It would seem a logical inference that those mines which for one reason or another are not susceptible of economic mechanization will have to give way to those that are.

We need hardly be surprised that the National Coal Association is both proud of its adventure in mechanization and enthusiastic about the prospects for coal. But it does seem a trifle unusual — particularly in a period of mass unemployment in the industry — that the United Mine Workers should refuse to yield precedence to the operators in their eagerness to welcome the man-displacing machine and their Rotarian optimism about coal's future.

Indeed, the visitor to the Mine Workers' somber and dignified headquarters in Washington is bombarded by the union's research men with data and statistics arrayed to buttress what is obviously the John L. Lewis line: mechanization benefits the miner, and new uses for electric power will vastly increase the need for coal in the years ahead. One thing is sure, no one can charge Mr. Lewis with being soft on featherbedding. His aides are anxious to demonstrate that the union has gone along wholeheartedly with mechanization. (In 1930, 10 percent of coal production was mechanically loaded, in 1956, 85.4 percent; in 1930, 8.3 percent was mechanically cleaned, in 1956, 61 percent; and by now nearly nine tenths of all mined coal is mechanically cut.) True, facts are mixed with foolishness, as in current efforts to beat the drums not only for heat pumps and coal by wire, but also for electric automobiles and coal-fired home furnaces. And Mr. Lewis's propagandizing for technical progress seems to stop short when it comes to projects like the St. Lawrence Seaway, the economic development of atomic energy, and the mechanization of competing fuel industries.

Nevertheless the figures pour forth from the Research and Marketing Department of the UMW. It is only when the visitor asks for a figure on the number of coal miners out of work as a result of mechanization and competition of other fuels that silence suddenly descends.

The conversation is shifted to the 65,000 men on pension. But no, the visitor insists, that is not what he meant — it is rather the men of working age in the union who are not now working. Finally, with extreme reluctance, there comes an estimate of perhaps 50,000 men.

And what is to become of these men?

Once again there is great enthusiasm expressed for electric power, the increasing amounts of coal it will demand, and the great proved reserves of coal — estimated at 1,900 years' worth — waiting to be dug. But by the unemployed miners?

Probably not. The price of progress. Some must fall by the wayside as others progress. It's a cruel world.

Several inferences seem inescapable. First, that the union's estimated figure on unemployment, about which it seems to prefer not to speak, is very likely as deflated as its membership figure is inflated. (On the same visit, actual working members in anthracite were estimated at 30 to 40,000, and in bituminous at around 300,000 full and part time miners. Both figures bear no relation to those released by the U. S. Bureau of Mines or by the Bureau of Labor Statistics, and would seem to be based less on reality than on the growing need to prevent the UMW from being tabbed as numerically a second- or third-class union.)

Second, that Mr. Lewis has more or less decided to cut his losses, concentrate on consolidating the solid gains of a steadily shrinking membership — while maintaining the facade of an enormous organization — and trust to time and mortality to resolve once and for all the problem of the unemployed workers in the coal fields, and so erase them from the agenda of the union and from the public conscience as well. Certainly Mr. Lewis has not recently been devoting himself as passionately to pressing the case of the displaced miners as he has to furthering such concerns of the operators as aiding the career of one of the most conservative and sanctimonious men in public life: "Senators of long service," observed Marquis Childs in a recent syndicated newspaper column, "are saying they have never experienced such pressures as are being applied to bring about the confirmation of Admiral Lewis L. Strauss as Secretary of Commerce. The pressures come from a wide range of sources, indicating an extensive and thoroughly prepared campaign. Several Senators have had telephone calls from John L. Lewis. . . . Lewis' theme is that Strauss, as Secretary of Commerce, would be helpful to the coal interests. . . ."

One long-time critic of the Lewis leadership in Washington is particularly bitter in his condemnation of the failure of the UMW (which he estimates at little more than 160,000 actual members) to take positive measures to protect the interests of the unemployed. With labor displacement in the coal industry greater per 1,000 employed than in any other industry, no program has yet been proposed for the vegetating displaced miners. He attributes this in part to the fact that 90 percent of the union's executive board are appointees, in part to the fact that the delegates who attend the union's quadrennial conventions are *working* miners, with no substantial grievances if they are getting from three to five days' work a week, and with the laid-off and the pensioners unrepresented. At the last convention, a delegate who arose to discuss the plight of the unemployed and to suggest that perhaps the shorter work-week might be explored as one way to spread the work among the membership, was very coolly received by his fellow-delegates, and then was verbally torn to pieces by a buckshot charge of oratory from John L. Lewis himself.

Not only is seniority meaningless in an aging industry; in effect, this critic observes, the UMW is being subsidized in areas like western Pennsylvania by the garment unions, with their lower wage rates.

It would be unfair, however, to assume that the UMW is doing nothing at all for the welfare of its unemployed members. The Washington headquarters is at pains to point out that the UMW is cooperating with "area development organizations" wherever they are being set up by local businessmen and chambers of commerce in the hope of attracting new industry (including, presumably, more garment factories) to blighted areas. It is also campaigning for revision of mine safety regulations — which at present apply only to operations employing at least fifteen miners — so that they will include all working miners, even those in the most marginal strip mines; it points with justified indignation to the fact that these little operations are by far the most dangerous, with only 2 percent of coal production accounting for 25 percent of all fatalities in the industry.

What does this matter of safety have to do with unemployment? A lot. In an area which we have not discussed so far, the coal mining country of Kentucky, West Virginia, and Tennessee, the operators had leased the land in which they drilled their mines from local people who had owned it for generations. As the mines were worked out, or were proved unsuitable for mechanized operation, the operators pulled out and turned the land, and the mines, back to the men from whom they had leased it and who had often been working for them.

These men too have been existing on unemployment insurance and government surplus food. Since the mines are on their land, a good many of them have gone back to digging on their own, trying to pull out enough leftover coal to eke out a living. In a way it is as if unemployed steelworkers or auto workers were to club together to turn out steel or automobiles in competition with the big corporations. In this peculiarly American form of free enterprise one man can have as many as 92 mines on his property, with each mine being picked at by from two to four men scattered along the worked-out mountainside. Naturally their productivity is terribly low, as low as two tons per man, and since they are at the mercy of the brokers to whom they must sell for whatever they can get, they very often wind up with a couple of dollars for a day's dangerous and backbreaking work.

These are the men, digging away in the dogholes, as they are called, who are not covered by mine safety regulations, and whom you may read about from time to time in little newspaper items, either in connection with the odd and complicated Harlan County strike, or with the all too frequent cave-ins (last spring an entire family of nine men was entombed in a doghole). If the UMW is successful, the dogholes will have to be certified by inspectors before they can be worked. And what will happen to the men, who will at least be prevented from taking so many chances in hacking away at the only thing they know now to do? Their strange senseless heroism in the year 1959 can perhaps be seen as analogous to the bravery of soldiers dying in a war which cannot possibly benefit them, their families, or their heirs — to say nothing of the entire social order of which they are a part.

One would think, as one gets closer to the workers themselves than Washington, D. C., that there would be a greater awareness of their problems and a deeper searching for possible answers. The office of District 2 of the UMW, which includes the miners of St. Michael, is located in the county seat of Ebensburg, Pa., about seventeen winding miles from St. Michael. It has taken over an old mansion in the better part of town and it is staffed by Lewis appointees.

A visitor walks in and asks why so many men are being laid off in the district. Because they were unfortunate enough to be stuck in uneconomic low-seam mines which do not adapt to mechanization as well as the mines of District 5 or West Virginia. But even with a 6 percent increase in tonnage nationally, men are being laid off everywhere. Then what is the answer?

"I don't really know."

Once again, there is the story of efforts to attract new industry, with its usually turning out to be light industry, employing women. As for the men in District 2 who are still working, with the exception of the captive mines, working hard to stockpile metallurgical coal in expectation of a steel strike, they are averaging three days a week, and glad to have jobs, with the prospect of occasionally picking up a fourth or fifth day of work. The fact is simply that with three days of work the operators take out all the coal they can sell: which is one more reason for the cutbacks.

What about the men who aren't working?

"They don't come in here, so we don't get any complaints at the office. We're not in touch with them."

And what will happen when the unemployment insurance runs out? "I don't know how they'll get along."

The truth is that no one really does know. The barber of St. Michael may be as close to the truth as anyone when he observes that the men were so stunned by the closing of the mine that they are still in a state of shock, and unable to face the reality that they may never again be able to work at their chosen trade.

Until you go down the pit, it is difficult to sense how much mining can mean to a man, or how strange and unlikely it can seem that you are not going to work when others near you are working. The men who work at Wilmore, in Maryland Shaft #2, are friends and neighbors of the St. Michael men; they have worked together in the past, and they still hunt and fish together. But the men at Wilmore are still working, proud — as the miners of St. Michael are proud — of the fact that they take out the finest coal in the country. Early in the morning, as the sun is just coming up over the nearby hills, they straggle into the big grimy locker room and strip to the skin, depositing their street clothing in wire baskets which they then haul to the high ceiling and secure with long double chains.

The impression is strong that the men have packed away their humor and lightheartedness with their street clothes; at any rate they seem brooding and thoughtful as they foregather in their dark neck-to-ankle working outfits, adjusting the lamps on their helmets and the big batteries that power them from the wide belts at their waists. They wait patiently for the elevator that will take them down to the other world. Here danger begins.

Down in the mine, the men clamber aboard the hooked-together cars pulled by electric locomotives, and clatter off to their separate work centers, starting down the main heading and then cutting off on the various spurs that dart away into the darkness like so many veins. You travel for perhaps a mile, then get off at the end of the line and plod along in a bent-necked stoop until you come to an extensible belt conveyor. Here you hitch a ride, stretching flat on your belly on the rattling leather belt-line. The increasing roar of heavy machinery tells you that you have arrived at the mechanical loader, and you move on crabwise, the glow of your lamp picking a path through the thick cloud of coal dust as you squat forward on your haunches.

You are at the face of the mine. You come alongside the mechanical miner, and you rest on your knees, watching the great continuous mining machine chewing its way into the coal seam with a remorseless roar. There is only the monstrous machine, and a handful of men. One of them shouts, "How far to go?" and the answer comes back: "Twenty feet."

You bend forward to cry into the superintendent's ear. "How long will it take to break through those twenty feet into the next chamber?"

"About forty-five minutes."

"How long would it have taken the men, without the machine?"

He answers laconically, his face already black and preoccupied as he squirts chewing tobacco. "Three shifts."

The slate roof sags, and the men use the machine to swiftly hoist a timber hydraulically into place before they press on. In this world without light and without women, the men are quick, daring, decisive. Formerly they could hear the roof starting to give so that they could quickly install timber props or run for safety; now the roar of the machine drowns out the little telltale sounds, and they must watch even more carefully. The dust, too, that used to rise all the hundreds of feet to the surface and rain down on the streets of St. Michael, is a thousand times thicker from the slashing machine than it used to be when the men attacked the seam themselves; you can taste the silicosis in the air as the thick particles parch your nasal passages and clog your lungs. Roof falls have been many and serious in this particular mine. They are a delay and a serious annoyance to the supervision, a challenge to the men, who must crawl about the too-low passages like dwarves or hunchbacks, shoring up the timbers and building cribs to protect the right of way.

Back on the surface the dirty coal rises in smoking carloads to the tipple. There you follow its course as it is cleaned, washed, sorted, through the towers high above the ground, and there too it seems impossible that the attack on the bowels of the earth will ever stop. How can a man who has been a part of it, who still lives within sight, sound, and smell of the consuming drama, believe that he will not again be permitted to be an actor in it?

In the saloons, the saying goes, the miners love more women than they ever did above ground, and dig more coal than they ever did below ground. At St. Michael, they brag about their narrow escapes, and about their friends' past heroism, as well as about the quality of their coal and the quantity of it they have taken from the mine. And they wonder whether they will ever do it again. In the meantime, they wonder about the meantime.

"In 1922," the president of the local says, "I lived through the winter in a tent on top of that hill with my family. My father was out for eighteen months and we had nothing to live on, nothing. I can tell you one thing: we'll never go back to 1922 again."

"My family will never go hungry," another man says. He stares down into his glass of draught beer, and then looks up defiantly. "Not as long as I've got a rifle and two shotguns at home, they'll never go hungry. Maybe it's not a nice thing to say, but it's how I feel."

Others say the same, but it does not look as though it will come to that. When unemployment insurance runs out, the miners will be eligible to go on DPA (Department of Public Assistance). They will have to sign over their property to the State of Pennsylvania, and give up their insurance, but they will be allowed to keep their cars — as long as they demonstrate that they are using them to look for work.

They will do it, an old militant of the area believes, because they will have no alternative. They will cash in their policies and turn over their property in return for the dole and the opportunity to go on as they are now, waiting and hoping, some waiting for the pension, others just for their social security. They will continue to eat molly-grub, the federal government food surplus parcels so weighted with rice that, as one man remarks wryly, "You can get slant-eyed from eating so much of it."

"I am not disillusioned," the old radical insists. "But I am very tired. Even now, with the checks running out, they are apathetic, and willing to go on DPA. Yet if there were some leadership . . . Right now the officers of at least ten locals would come out for nationalization of the mines. With leadership, many more of the 184 locals certainly would. You heard them curse the old parties — they are looking and waiting for new leadership, and it doesn't seem to be forthcoming."

Even recognition of their problems does not seem to be forthcoming. It would seem axiomatic that the future of the miner is tied up with the future of the whole economy, and that any progress for the labor movement — as for the rest of us — will have to come through political action. The UMW vision of a new coal miner, mobile, no longer tied to the company town, living in a suburb and driving forty miles to work in a mechanized mine where he will be a technician operating a piece of machinery — this may not only be the ultimate reality, it may already be coming to pass. But surely we must think hard about what values of the declining generation will be transferred to a young man who will go into the mines not because it is as thrilling or challenging as going to sea or riveting a skyscraper, but simply because it is a job that, although dirty and tiresome, has a good wage scale and a better pension plan; and about what his relations will be with his fellow-workers, whom he will not fish with, fight with, or drink with, but will see merely as anonymous black faces below the earth and anonymous white faces on the suburban-bound highways above the earth.

Only a romantic fool, and an ignorant one at that, would bewail the loss of backbreaking, torturous, dangerous, poisonous drudgery, and its replacement by impersonally effective machinery. But the loss of fraternity, solidarity, and the comradeship of courageous accomplishment — these are all too precious and rare in the moral landscape of America, and if we allow their transmitters to rot and fade we commit an act even more criminal than the spoliation of the physical landscape for personal gain.

1959

# THE REVOLUTION IN BERKELEY

## PAUL GOODMAN

The dominant system of society is critically dependent on the schools, especially the universities. Schools provide the brainpower for the scientific technology. They are wistfully expected, beginning with age three, to bring everybody into the mainstream of economic usefulness; and more realistically, they process the professional personnel to control the increasing scores of millions useless to the economy, the outcaste poor, displaced farmers, people over 65, unemployable adolescents who must be regimented. Just as part of the Gross National Product, I have heard the estimate that more than 40 percent of the cash is in the Knowledge business.

The organization of all this, however, is calculated by the powers-that-be amazingly without regard to the thoughts or feelings of those who are to be "educated." (50 percent of the total population is under 26.) Establishment forecasts of the future almost never mention the response of the young as a factor; yet that response, whether as anomie or as insistence on more freedom and meaning than the system allows will be crucial. And if we take it into account, we see that the dominant system is probably unviable. Simply, it is not moral enough to grow up into.

The education has become mere exploitation — the abuse of the abilities and time of life of school youth for others' purposes. As I have put it elsewhere, it is the first time in history that a dominant class has imposed on its free children the discipline of slaves. And the exploitation itself is of a peculiarly difficult and deadly kind, for it involves not merely forced time and labor, but active intellectual participation by the exploited, in learning and even in being original and creative under duress.* This is not viable. There must be both breakdown and revolutionary breakthrough; and recently I have come to hope that *freedom and meaning will outweigh anomie*. Needless to say, I am in love with that, and with Berkeley in February.

In my opinion, the situation at Berkeley is historical and will not be local. The calm excitement and matter-of-fact democracy and human contact now prevalent on the Berkeley campus are in revolutionary contrast to our usual demented, inauthentic, overadministered American society. This ordinary freedom had to be won by risky commitment, finding solidarity, living through fear; and its ferment will spread not only to other campuses but finally to other institutions of society.

The movement of the Negroes and their wise white friends, mainly youth, has been encouraging toward change; and probably our society cannot incorporate its outcastes without revolutionary changes in structure. Nevertheless, the shape of reconstruction cannot, in my opinion, appear among marginal groups; they do not have enough culture, science, and technique to work a good modern society, though plenty of spirit and justice. But the rising of students and of professors recalled to manhood occurs in the best of the middle class itself and in the center of the economy; the shape of reconstruction *can* appear here. Not accidentally, the movement for the outcaste has sparked and energized this more central revolution, and we will finally come to the real issues: the revival of democracy, the human use of technology, and getting rid of war.

As a university man, let me put it this way: Our society has been playing with the fire of mass higher learning; it is our duty to let it feel the blast of university truth.

During their troubles last winter, Berkeley students kept phoning me — at 3 A.M. Eastern time — in various states of fever, alarm, and de-

---

* I am using the word "exploitation" strictly. It is hard for people in the labor movement to understand this term as applied to students. Harry Bridges, e.g., seems to feel that the Berkeley students were pampered brats; they never had it so good. We would do well to recall Marx's description of the nine-year-olds picking straw, not because this was economically valuable but as training in work-habits. Besides, we must notice that nearly 50 percent of the young are now kept in schools till 21 and 22 years of age; previously most of them would have been in the factories, etc., for four or five years by that age.

spair; but then after a single shout of "Victory!" after the Faculty Senate decision in their favor, I heard nothing further. (Except for a New Year's Eve visit from Steve Weissman, one of the most thoughtful leaders of the Free Speech Movement, who was now interested in "University Reform.")

My expectation, on visiting in February, was that there would be deep depression. They had won their demand to advocate political action, like any other citizens. The Civil Rights energy, which had obviously been strong, could hardly continue animating them, since it was not essentially a campus issue at all. The election being over, Senator Knowland had subsided. And most important, they seemed to have no future goal to grow toward, to inspirit them. Indeed, reading the FSM's voluminous broadsides and pamphlets, I was appalled at the low level of analysis by such bright people. There was little ideology — which was good — but there was also almost no economics, history, or philosophy. Rather, endless pages about the First and Fourteenth Amendments, gripes about the violation of due process, and proofs of the ambiguities of Clark Kerr, all relevant but not newsy.

I was wrong. Instead of depression, I found what I have called "calm excitement" — the phrase belongs to a youth in the establishment-oriented student government. (During the troubles, the Associated Students were rather unfriendly to the FSM, but part of the "calm excitement" is a *spreading* among the students of the insistence on freedom and meaning.) My error was that I did not realize that every step of the students' fight was desperately immediate, unchartered, and uncharted. But therefore the fruit of it was character-change, the first opening of new possibilities. Beautifully, a moral struggle has given the students a *habit* of good faith and commitment, and their solidarity has turned into community, like the auroral flush of a good society.

The existential language that I am beginning to slip into is entirely the students' own. It is the lingua franca of the revolutionary campus, and is used with simplicity and conviction. (When, on another campus like Ann Arbor, I listen to even a fine group like the Students for a Democratic Society, their talk of "strategy" etc. is grating by comparison.) At Berkeley, there is a sprinkling of neo-Marxist lingo but it is noticeably heavy and dispiriting, except for an occasional Maoism, which is Chinese.

On February 10 occurred a curious dialogue between Jerry Byrne, the special counsel of a committee of the Regents of the University of California to investigate "the causes of student unrest," and a group of students from the government, newspapers, religious organizations, and leaders of the former FSM (now FU, movement for a Free University). Byrne is a frank and likable guy, a lawyer, and I had previous evidence that he was earnest and somewhat unorthodox. He explained to students his mandate and the questionnaire and interview methods that he intended to employ. He intended, he said, to be objective; he had chosen assistants from outside of Berkeley; he had no ax to grind; he meant business. He would present his recommendations to the Regents in three months. Were there any questions?

A slim dark-eyed youth spoke up: "Mr. Byrne, we have been through an existential moment. A composite picture of 'public' student opinion will not reveal our meaning." I take it that this meant that so-called objective methods would get him nowhere. "Yes," another student said. "Ideas don't pop out of data."

Byrne did not seem to grasp this epistemological subtlety; he assured the young man that he had "found students able to dissociate themselves from events last fall and simply work to future improvement." Later, however, the counsel said to me privately, "When that boy looked up at me, his eyes pierced to the bottom of my soul — there was no use in trying to lie to them. The discussion rose to another plane."

Another student (Mario Savio) asked a down-to-earth question: Was there any guarantee that the Regents would release the Byrne recommendations? No, said Jerry, they were the Regents' property. (But the Regents, gasped somebody else, were notorious for *falsifying* scholarly work, specifically a report on *braceros* made by the University.) Savio persisted: "How can the students cooperate with a report for the Regents, if the Board of Regents is itself a morally illegitimate body? How can *it* be the judge?" The bother was that the Regents consisted almost entirely of multimillionaires in aircraft, oil, banks, shipping, etc., with Max Rafferty representing education!

The question now was whether they ought morally to be talking to Byrne at all, since his mandate was inauthentic. It was not that they questioned *his* integrity, a student assured him kindly. About this time, the counsel's unfailing friendly smile began to tighten, so that it became increasingly impossible for him to get into contact with them, unless he wiped off the smile, which he couldn't do. Unluckily, none of the students knew enough psychosomatic medicine to point this out to him, and I kept my mouth shut. "Yes," said a student, "it's the genius of administration to turn a nice guy like you into a fink." "How do we know that the student opinion we give you won't be subpoenaed for the trial?" somebody asked ominously. Jerry firmly and believably declared that this would not happen.

A bright idea suggested itself. They could publish the interviews in progress, while they were still the students' property, so to speak; they could make tapes! Jerry vetoed this with alarm. "Then what *can* you suggest for us to do, what *action,* beginning *right now,* that will put pressure on the Regents and guarantee some results?" — a student asked this very earnestly.

*"How was I supposed to answer that!"* Jerry complained to me later. "In one corner was a reporter from the *Chronicle,* in another a reporter from the *Examiner,* and they ask me to suggest an action to coerce the Regents —" Some more *action* from the students of Berkeley was not, exactly, what the Regents were after! "Oh, why didn't you just explain that to them, Jerry — with a smile? They're hip kids."

"Why," asked a young lady, "is Unrest something that must be 'remedied'? " "How far will the inquiry probe? Might the report suggest that government of the university should be given over to the students and faculty? Would the range of questions include whether UCAL should accept war contracts?" "Why," asked a young fellow, "not let a Thousand Flowers Bloom?" — to my ear this question was entirely innocent, without desire to shock.

The Counsel fielded the questions well and generously. But he did not seem to satisfy. "Don't you see, Jerry," I said finally, "they want you to show a burning zeal to improve their school, and you're not showing it." "I don't feel any burning zeal," cried Jerry, "I just want to do a good honest job, and I intend to do it." "There you are," said Savio, "why don't you quit?" — But to my ear, this was said without hostility, even affectionately. It meant, quit them and join *us,* and put your talents to an authentic use.

My total impression, indeed, was that the students, including the stars of the former FSM, intended to cooperate with the counsel in his further study. They would follow the maxim of Gandhi: Always Cooperate. But they would be exquisitely simple in what they are doing and therefore far brighter than Jerry Byrne; and in the long run he would learn more from them than he, with his auspices, would be able to do for them.

It is vividly clear on the Berkeley campus that there has been a breakthrough into communication, community. The causation seems to have been classical: justified protest, risky commitment, surprising solidarity, and the development of mutual trust, shaking fear met with uncalculating courage, and then the breakthrough into the joyous feeling that "we have a say in the university," "it is our home," "we are free human beings."

They even speak of a founding Event, presumably the Faculty Senate vote that "justified" the students. (Correspondingly, Professor Wolin speaks of the "faculty's finest hour," as if the faculty had been revived and "justified" by the students!) "There occurred on this campus the first human Event in 40,000 years," Michael Rossman assured me — I did not press him for the predecessor. Savio told me with scorn and amazement of a registrar who *after* the Event still tried to enforce a petty rule: "Don't you realize, I told her, that something *happened* yesterday?" The existential theory seems to be that by acting in freedom they made history, and conversely, the historical event made them free. (In a letter to the new Chancellor, Martin Meyerson, John Seeley of Brandeis speaks of the students' action as "the Boston Tea Party.")

An unknown professor came up to me and said, "Since those kids acted up, I feel twenty years younger."

So far as the essence of a community of scholars is the personal relation of students and teachers, Berkeley has already accomplished university reform and Jerry Byrne's inquiry need go no further.* But in fact, in freedom, there is a buzz of activity toward legislating new institutions. Let me give a few examples.

The "Free University" is a para-university of voluntary study-groups off-campus, in which the collaboration of a teaching-assistant or assistant-professor is invited. (Typical subjects, *Moral Responsibility and the Sciences, Marx and Freud, History of the Oppression of Women.*) At a session I attended (*Anarchism*), a young lady complained rather tearfully that if they invited a professor to the next meeting just because he knew a lot about the subject, it would be just like the ordinary university; but the others, who were mostly graduates and undergraduates in History, assured her that the professor was very young. FU plans also "to launch projects for the general welfare of the larger community," e.g. a summer project to organize migrant farm labor; and not least, "to look into the nature of the University of California's financial connections, controls imposed on funds, indirect pressures on professors."

To lighten the student load, I asked the new Chancellor — or Acting Chancellor, it is hard to know † — if academic credit couldn't be given for the para-courses, if they met certain standards. He could see no objection. A Regent, however, thought that the reactionaries in the Legislature might balk at some of the titles. . . .

Faculty proposals for university reform — e.g. by Profs. Tussman and Trow — tend to small voluntary colleges within the university. In one model, 150 students and 10 professors will agree to study some Area or Issue that transcends departmental lines (as a gimmick to get around the entrenched chairmen?). Professor Searle tells me that he had already

---

* A former student of mine at Sarah Lawrence explained to me: "When Amy and I first came out, we didn't know anybody, so we invited our professor to tea. The other students thought that we were simply weird. But now it wouldn't be unusual." — This illustrates, by the way, that student-faculty estrangement is a two-way street. The paranoia of the students toward the grown-ups is probably stronger than the indifference of the professors toward the young.

† Since I wrote this, Kerr and Meyerson "resigned" and were retained apparently as a bid for a vote of confidence against the reactionary wing of the Regents.

tried such voluntary seminars last year, but the *students* didn't come —
they needed the support of Credits and the Official Syllabus; but perhaps
it would be better now.

I discussed these faculty proposals with a Regent, who declared that
they would cost too much. I think he is wrong. In my opinion, administrators misestimate by applying to a different, decentralized system, the
costs that belong to the present over-centralized system. At present the
Multiversity operates by tightly holding together essentially disparate
parts; inevitably a tremendous amount of money is spent on administrative cement. This process, as I have shown elsewhere, usually leads to a
mark-up of 300 to 400 percent over actual educational costs. Of course,
from the Multiversity point of view, the inflation is more than paid for by
rich contracted research, no matter what, and government and foundation grants.

Professor Leggett, the sociologist, has already instituted (I think) an
ingenious form of democracy for a lecture course. Each section elects
two delegates who sit with him and the teaching-assistants at fortnightly
meetings that criticize the course and chart its further progress. The little
council is called a Soviet.

Chancellor Meyerson told me a good idea. He is after some Ford
money for a community project in Oakland. This could be manned by
students for academic credit as well as pay. In turn I proposed to him the
following: Instead of discontinuing the department of Journalism, as
seems to be in the offing, rather make it for real by putting out a good
daily newspaper which the Bay Area sorely needs. (It is interesting to
speculate how Senator Knowland, who owns the Oakland paper, would
take this competition, while CORE, recruited from the University, pick-
ets his door for unfair labor practices!)

The Chancellor's best idea for university reform, however, is a kind of
tacit understanding between him and the students — at least so I have
been told — that certain idiotic rules, which ought not to exist, need not
necessarily be enforced in every jot and tittle.

I was crossing the campus with a Regent and he suddenly asked me,
"Do you notice much change since you were here a couple of years
ago?" "What are you driving at?" I asked. "Don't you think it's —
more lively, more interesting?" "Oh Bill," I cried, "why can't you say
that publicly? The kids would be so proud." "How can I say that in my
position?" said the Regent. (His name is William Coblentz.) "Don't call
them kids!" he said; "they're students." *

:

---

* Something like calling a Negro "boy." In many a Town-Gown fracas, the analogy
of student and Negro is pretty obvious. At present in the town of Berkeley itself,
there is an urban renewal plan to clean up a street which, to me, seems very pleasant and lively, but it *is* occupied by students and their beatnik cronies.

I have been describing a very simple situation, a kind of Fourth of August when the French barons gave up their feudal dues. (Alas! it probably won't last much longer than the Fourth of August, but let's not yet look into the future.) It is a situation where people talk to one another, mean what they say, and intend to act on it, and therefore could conceivably improve their common lot. Is this extraordinary?

It is said that there was a "breakdown of communication" in Berkeley. There was, but why? The failure of communication is not an isolated cause but is endemic in the structure of American society and in the Multiversity as part of it. There is a limitless amount of information, polling, data-processing, and decision-making by objective computation; yet when the chips are down, it turns out that nobody has expressed himself or been understood. Given its exploiting motives, it is impossible for American education to take the young seriously, except as objects to manipulate.*

It seemed odd that Clark Kerr, who had made a reputation as a mediator in labor disputes, should have failed so badly precisely in communications. But indeed he acted impeccably as a professional mediator; he kept the parties apart in order to negotiate their demands. Unfortunately, good faith and commitment are in principle not negotiable; the students were not making "offers" with the intention of "settling" for something different. And in the context of a community of scholars, the technique suddenly appeared as obscene. When students and professors insisted that he, the mediator, was a party to the dispute and must confront them, Kerr's behavior was sociopathological. There were cases when he would not speak directly to professors *by phone* but insisted on an intermediary. When the students were occupying Sproul Hall, he stayed at home and would not speak to them. Clinging to a petty ruling, he kept Regents and professors in separate rooms at the airport.

More seriously, there is evidence that men whom he involved as his intermediaries became utterly demoralized.

Inevitably, the militant students were caught in the toils and became administrative. Dealing with probably benevolent professors, they had to bring lawyers and speak through them, and they became acute experts in their rights under various Amendments to the Constitution of the United States. Yet what they ultimately wanted was just to be told the truth: e.g., if the tables were banned because of traffic congestion, why, when the aisles were kept clear, were the tables *still* banned? Instead they were told another lie.

Or so it seemed to them. But they were making a naïve metaphysical

---

* This can be so hypocritical as to be nauseating. For instance, while I am writing this there is a to-do at Cornell about a marijuana "ring." This comes under the rubric of paternal concern, yet girls are dragged out of classes and dormitories to be grilled by FBI men without counsel.

error. They imagined that a mediator, one who avoids conflicts and ne-
gotiates, is a human being like you or me and makes propositions that
are true or false. Thus they felt lied to and tricked and they got enraged.
But they were really dealing with a juggling robot. Now, for a spell,
disabused of their error, they can be serene — armed.

To be fair to Kerr, I doubt that it is possible, with honor, to avoid
conflict among the forces working at the University of California: Birch-
ite legislators, racist newspapers, Max Rafferty, the Atomic Energy
Commission, Civil Rights, professors who might suddenly recall the
Western tradition, students who might be naïvely moral. The only honorable alternatives are to quit, as Buell Gallagher did, or sometimes to
take a stand and fight.

A Cuban student, not a Castroite, said to me, "Kerr made the same
mistake as the U.S.A. with regard to Cuba. By refusing to talk, he left a
vacuum. The extremists moved into it. Through the extremists, the mass
discovered it had a community."

Besides the calm excitement and community, there is a third property of
Berkeley in February that I, at least, found overwhelming: the fantastically expert organization of the students, as if for instant action *en
masse.* Yet there does not seem to be top-down domination. The "leading figures" are rather easygoing, there is no jockeying for position, there
is no party line, and it looks as if new faces easily come to the fore. But
as soon as there is an activity, the guerrillas are out in force. There is an
evident discipline to attend meetings — naturally many students lost
academic credit for the fall term. The Free University sponsored a
speech of mine and 3,500 students attended. When it was known I
wanted to write this report, at once I received a list of key names and
contacts all arranged: "he will phone you at 3:45" — one expected
15:45. They have put out phonograph records: Joan Baez songs, *FSM's
Sounds and Songs of the Demonstration,* and a remarkable long-player
of the Sproul Hall sit-in and the meeting of the Faculty Senate. The
quantity of printed material is simply appalling. And a related aspect is
the careful sociological research — one can learn immediately that 53
percent of students in FSM favored sit-ins before the movement started;
there are precise political-science analyses of contending forces, legal
briefs, property-holdings of each Regent. Never in history, I guess, has a
spontaneous uprising been so meticulously polled. The students might
object to the factory-University, but they have certainly mastered its arts
and sciences.

It is a remarkable phenomenon, a kind of hyper-organized anarchy.
Perhaps it is a way of creating a Free University in the conditions of high
technology; if so — I am speaking seriously — it is a major social invention. Myself, I find it oppressive. My opinion is that when they begin to

reach for positive cultural goods, rather than engaging in resistance and defense, they will have to become shaggier. But maybe I am prejudiced against social sciences — a writer — from the twenties.

The proper function of such a disciplined student body, I think, is not to be the Free University, which must consist in piecemeal voluntary associations between teachers and students, but to be the Student Government, responsible for social and political rules; collective bargaining agent on food, housing, tuition and other finances; guardian of *Lernfreiheit* against administrative encroachments like grading, excessive courses, unreasonable policies of admission and transfer; mutual aid and self-protection against the local police.

Let us turn to a broader question: what is the relation of a liberated university to social change in the general community?

It was evident in the fall that the movement for the Negroes was a major background cause for the Free Speech Movement. It was part of the immediate bone of contention, the banning of recruiting; and more important, leaders who had taken their risks in Mississippi were not afraid to sit in against Clark Kerr.

Yet in February I did not hear a *single* spontaneous mention of this struggle. Testing, I raised the issue provocatively and was routinely put right and turned off. One of the leaders, Rossman, then explained to me that interest in Civil Rights was simply part of one's commitment, and it was exactly equivalent to the problem of making a classroom for real. (Rossman himself is a section-man in mathematics; he teaches "intuitive" mathematics — I did not have the chance to pursue whether this meant school of Brouwer or something else.) "Don't get me wrong," he said, "I picket *seriously;* just the same, it's a place to see the girls and sometimes we have a great time. It's our way of living." * He had a thing about Abstract Values being entirely dead for his generation, though they had had meaning for "my father and grandfather." I tried to show him that, for some of us, Social Justice with capital letters was not abstract but a concrete property of a tolerable environment, just like unpolluted rivers; and he was visibly impressed by the idea that a three-year-old divides the candy bar with another child for symmetry. (Maybe this was "intuitive" mathematics.)

In my opinion, the matrix of a community in which political action is a custom is essential for the American future. And it is different, in both genesis and meaning, from the Solidarity engendered by fighting for political Causes. Those hostile to FSM have emphasized the number of off-

* None of this was news to me. Several years ago I noted that students of Fair Play for Cuba had no "political" interest in Castro, but were enchanted by a young leader who spoke to everybody on the street and wrangled on national TV with conspirators against his life. To speak proleptically, he was not like — Clark Kerr.

campus participants, who are then called outside agitators, Maoists, Castroites, etc.; contrariwise, the champions of the students then prove that the outsiders are mostly alumni, wives, temporary dropouts. But historically, it is better to consider these university-centered politically active communities in terms of a "withdrawal" from the absurd System and its problems, and a return on more authentic premises.*

Consider the history of Beat youth as a type. The withdrawal into voluntary poverty, the community of the Illuminati, kicks On the Road, and finger-painting did not provide much world. Yet almost from the beginning there were social needs that *were* taken for real, especially banning the Bomb, thwarting the Fuzz, and supporting Negroes and Spanish because they were friends and equally outcaste. In California specifically, it was hard not to join in the rage at HUAC; but even more important was the horror at the Chessman execution: here *was* the threatening Machine literally destroying human life, just as Camus had said.

Inevitably, in this return to involvement, there was joining with proper politicals. But *the event has been not that the young exiles have been politicalized but that politics have been "existentialized" and brought into the community, even containing the dreadful sex and hasheesh.* And this is not because philosophy and pleasure have seduced people from the realities of life, but because *the thoughts and feelings of the young have been more relevant to the underlying realities of modern times,* the drive to rationalization, the abuse of high technology, and the hardware GNP, statism and the Bomb. These abuses occur in every modern country and ideology, whether U.S.A., U.S.S.R., China, or even the emergent African states; and Great Society, Neo-Marxism, and even moral Pacifism do not fundamentally address them.

Come now to the university. A basic trait of the young is that they don't know much, but also, beautifully, that they want to learn something and they hang around hopefully relevant teachers. The young Beats, of course, made a thing of voluntary ignorance like voluntary poverty; and the young Hippies boringly went in for tip-top expertise — they knew all about Black Boxes and Motivational Research — without knowing anything. But pretty soon young people were bound to gravitate, or gravitate back, to the university, as cronies of students, or as auditors, or unmatriculated students, or as diffident and choosy students. To have a chance to learn something was a great advance for the dissident community; and it was certainly a vast advantage for the university to be infiltrated by a new breed of students who demanded authenticity and practical application. Yet, genetically and persistently, this fringe

---

* I suppose this is what these young people mean by their abuse of the word "Alienation." Certainly in Marxist or psychiatric terms they are less alienated than most other people. Hopefully, if they continue a path of commitment, they will discover they are "alienated" in Luther's meaning!

university community — with its own readings and music, political actions, free sexuality, and hasheesh — is not identical with the *in loco parentis* and late-adolescent American college community. And administrators, incidentally, have heightened the tension by dissolving the fraternity system. Some of the young are then penned up in rule-ridden dormitories (built with federal funds but rented at high rates); but the more spirited go off-campus and get lost in the fringe community.

The new community, returning to the university and magnetizing the collegians, is by its genesis and nature not simply economically exploitable, unlike the ordinary college community which is at the top of the sixteen- to twenty-year ladder of school-processing. In principle, it has dropped out and returned. And it resists in the university the identical Organized System that it resists outside. It is suspicious of being "vocationally guided" — though unfortunately it does not yet have much sense of true Vocation. Correspondingly, it is resentful of the jet-set faculty busy with contracted research; and it correctly interprets the so-called "orientation to the discipline rather than to teaching" as nothing but careerism. Unfortunately, again, however, there is not yet any sense of what a real university of professionals would consist in. (I shall return to this.)

In the circumstances, there is an uncanny reemergence of the primitive medieval university, with its fat-cat professors lecturing in the central halls, a ragged student community living in its own neighborhood, and, astoundingly, a new student leadership by the graduates and teaching-assistants, the very Masters of Arts who used to cause all the trouble in 1200! One would have expected, in the era of the Organization Man, that precisely the bright graduate-students, the junior-executives, would be the most conformist, to protect their status and advancement; yet we see at Berkeley that the teaching-assistants provided leaders and almost unanimously went on strike.

But as well as being a medieval fringe, the students *also* want "personal contact" with the dignitaries, as in a small American boarding-school. On the one hand they distrust everybody over thirty; on the other, they want the professors to become part of the fringe community, to give it intellectual structure and self-assurance. And finally, as American citizens, they want self-rule, not only of their own social life like the medieval student-government, but also to have a say in the administrative and curricular doings: that is, the distant Regents are regarded as illegitimate. This novel amalgam, then, of a fringe community of the young and masters of arts; "personal relations" between the students and the professors; and student membership on the Board of Regents — this amalgam is the Free University.

On the campus, this ramshackle constitution proved to have political power. The organized guerrillas sat in. Then, "When the teaching-assistants went out," said a professor, "it was all over, for we can't run the school without them, and if we fired them, we'd never get another good graduate in California." And then the faculty, as Professor Wolin has put it, "stirred to ancestral memories of the ideal of a community of scholars bound together in the spirit of friendly persuasion and pledged to truth rather than abundance." — So the Governor had to send his troopers and for a couple of days Clark Kerr's Multiversity ceased to exist.

The question is: if such a Free University exists in the offing, to whom, to what government, will the federal government, the foundations, and the corporations channel all that money that is the fuel of modern education? It's as bad as dealing with Saigon.

The enigma remains the faculty.

Let me recall a scrap of conversation with the new Chancellor. He was pointing out to me that the chief obstacle to university reform was the teachers, inflexible, narrow, specialist, status-seeking. I cut him short impatiently: "Administrators have parroted this story to me verbatim at fifty colleges across the country. The fact is that for a hundred years you have cut their balls off and now you say they are impotent. Delegate power!" Meyerson reddened; he is himself a strong and broad mind, a professor, and, I suppose, an excellent teacher. A couple of days later he said to the counsel of the Regents, "Goodman is right. Administration turns them into eunuchs and then complains that they are eunuchs."

The overwhelming faculty vote for the students seems to have been a reaction of nausea at the administration's lies, its subservience to outside pressures, its pathological avoidance of contact, and finally the presence of the cops. This is the kind of nausea that recalls decent but self-centered people to their plain duty. Professor Wolin says, the faculty was "shocked out of its shameful neglect of teaching, its acquiescence in the bureaucratization of the university," and it recovered its "collective conscience." These explanations must be substantially accurate for they lead to the evident February situation of friendly contact with the students and cooperation in "university reform" toward *Lernfreiheit,* student democracy, faculty resumption of counseling, and so forth.

Nevertheless, although this breakthrough is splendid for the teachers as human beings — if professors don't like to associate with young people, why in the devil do they hang around schools? — in my opinion it does nothing for them as men. The revival of manhood can occur only if they come on again in the world as the university, as the protector of civilized standards, the professors of truth that makes a difference, and, in our country, the blasting critic of social baseness and lies. Every division and department is falling short. For instance, the University of California has "classified research," but this is entirely incompatible with the tradition of Western science and its theory as consensus. (Some great universities have refused such contracts.) There is, in the country, censorship and managed news in utter contradiction to the principle of the Humanities. The sex and narcotics laws of the community are grounded in superstitions that it is the business of the biological and social sciences publicly to expose, just as the Eastern professors exposed the hoax of the Shelter program. The engineers and architects do not speak as Faculties about the community-destroying Urban Renewal; and the education department does not speak as a Faculty about the compulsory miseducation, or at least Max Rafferty.

I don't think that the students can much help their professors to remember *these* ancient duties. The professors will have to come to their own resolve. But if they do, I think that the students of Berkeley will be proud of them, and I think the students will begin to understand what it is to have not only a free university but a university altogether.

I have tried to point out that the Regents and the new Chancellor could easily accept a more flexible, decentralized, and human "free university." (I don't mean that they *will*, for the Bourbons never learn and never forget.) But I don't think that university truth is acceptable in our society, any more than the democratic action of the Free Speech Movement is *finally* acceptable.

I mentioned these things to a couple of liberal Regents and they turned pale. The new Chancellor didn't seem to relish them either — maybe I am wrong. And since the students asked me to address them, I talked about them at a mass meeting on the campus. (It was an unnerving scene: the planes kept roaring over my head on their way across the Pacific to Vietnam.) To my judgment, the students did not dig what I was saying; they do not have much memory of the tradition of the West. They know what freedom is — yes, they do — but they don't really know what a university is. Kind of to encourage them, I told them of two ancient examples, where revolt in the university led to great social revolutions. First, the Averroists, the new science, the rediscovered Aristotle: this was squelched and "harmonized" after a fierce struggle at Paris, yet it persisted and brought on, at Padua, the heroic age of modern science; it took less than 400 years! And it took only 250 years for the university revolt of Wyclif and Hus to bring on the university-led Reformation.

The Berkeley students didn't much relish the thought of Hus at the stake, but they were crazy for the Wyclifites at Oxford standing on the ramparts and fighting off the king with bows and arrows.

1965

# MALCOLM X:
# THE APOSTATE MUSLIM

## STANLEY DIAMOND

The murder of Malcolm X cannot be reduced to an incident in an under-world conflict over material loot or social spoils. The sophisticated and intelligent ex-con who had been rebaptized Malcolm X by the Black Muslims was publicly killed for ideological reasons, that is, he was assas-sinated. This culturally symbolic murder of the apostate apostle rever-berates throughout American Negro society, bemuses the whites, and is viewed abroad, particularly in Africa and Asia, as another spectacular ex-ample of the American habit of self-defeat. Why does the death of Mal-colm thrust the issue of the Negro, like a lance, into the American body-politic?

First, it is necessary to understand the Black Muslims, not as racket-eers, but as revivalists who readily become racketeers when their pro-grams prove socially absurd. Revivalism, nativism, messianism, are generic expressions of the American Negro community. Christian reviv-alism, often oddly combined with African elements, is a familiar Ameri-can Negro activity. Fundamentalist congregations, idiosyncratically splin-tered, sometimes ritualistically repressive, sometimes ritually expressive of the holy and profane passions of a crucified people, helped keep American Negroes alive.

No segment of our society has been closer to an understanding of evil, that is, to the sense of being seduced by an uncontrollable other; has so thoroughly explored the meaning of salvation, nor so realistically read the signs and symbols that identify the social maze in which we wander. Any colored kid of twelve has a tougher sense of how it is with us than many a white academic type of fifty, whether technically in or out of the academy. To be a Negro in America, to be an *ex-slave,* even if now a new bourgeois, is to see society as tactic, to laugh up the sleeve, to put on the front when necessary, but to know where it is, to know the score, to know the domestic habits of the *master.* The only cure for this inevitable disease in a society that celebrates statuses instead of men (and it is not a true cure but a nostrum) has been the many forms of religious revivalism, those bizarre efforts at transcendence that we patronize or laugh at, from the slowed-down jazz beat of the spirituals to the wonderful peace of Father Divine. So as a revivalistic movement, the Muslims are not new, not to the Negroes.

But Christian revivalism was incomplete, too much had been borrowed from the immediate white environment which, moreover, rejected the Christian message of fraternity. Christian revivalism was expressive but insufficiently disciplined and inadequately symbolic for an increasingly disorganized people. It produced its tin-horn messiahs, who became confidence men in no time at all; and it was an air-plant; it had no strong nativistic root.

But the Black Muslim movement is as close to a full-dress nativism as people without pasts can generate. Unless we see it that way we do not see it at all. The nativism, the messianism, which link the Muslims as a social species to the Plains Indian Ghost Dance religion, the South African Bantu prophets, the Cargo Cults of New Guinea, the Iroquois Handsome Lake cult, can be broadly defined as a logical *reversal* of the usual course of assimilation, since assimilation in such situations is accurately conceived as the emasculation of the social and personal integrity of the members of the lesser by the more powerful group. When a people goes nativistic, its energies turn inward; it gives up the impossible effort to unite with the conqueror (may, indeed, try to become a conqueror); it cries out in defense of what it can rescue, invent, rationalize, or mobilize of its own culture. But that cry is also one of agony; it is the sound of a people dying to the world as it exists and it is in this sense, above all, that nativistic movements rising within or on the margins of the expanding West, are descendants of Judaism, Christianity, and Mohammedanism. For in each of these original instances, there was also a turning away from the world, a denial of mundane problems, a scourging and etherialization of conscience by *prophets* and, on the other hand, the contrapuntal erection of a worldly establishment, sanctifying power and even pleasure by the *priests*.

It must not surprise us to find this same tension in the descendant little movements, no matter how grotesquely resonated. They are means of resolving adversity, although they cannot be reduced to that function. When an immoral magazine like *Time* chatters piously about the sexual tastes, personal crimes, and peculation of Black Muslims, or of Malcolm, we should always bear in mind the grand example of the Renaissance clergy, the business activities of modern church and ancient temple, the Pharisees, the youth of how many saints, and the questionable or false prophets who have graced the major religions. The religious establishments have always taken good care of themselves and they have always held out the gaunt hand of charity to the laity; the Black Muslims crudely show us how. But this philistine form of churchly corruption is always shallow. It is the corruption of the spirit that interests us, the Passion not according to the Hierarchy, but to such a one as Kazantzakis, wherein the temptations and weaknesses of Jesus are explored to their most excruciating point and wherein every degradation that we are heir to is experienced as a prelude to transcendence. Here, too, we find a dwarfed reflection of the larger in the smaller, of the ancestral in the descendant messianisms.

Now let's examine more specifically how the Black Muslims, as a member of the species, logically reverse the blocked, typically persistent thrust towards assimilation. First of all, a new social myth of the Negro past is invented or, to put the matter more precisely, Negro settlement in the United States is regarded as a negative diaspora, in much the classic Zionist sense, and the center of historical gravity is conceived as Africa; but even Africa, ravished by the whites, is relatively impotent, so Muslim Africa, facing Mecca, becomes the source of spiritual pride. The symbols white-Christian-European are blotted out, and Black-Muslim-Afro-Asian are substituted. The personal names of members of the Movement are shifted from those bestowed in slavery to either Islamic names, apparently for those who have made the pilgrimage, or the given name is maintained and the surname reduced to X, symptomatic of a degraded and anonymous patrimony.

There is also a reversal of racism. Caucasians are regarded as inferior; there is even a myth of racial origin to account for it. Correlatively, the idea of integration is regarded as contaminating of the Negro, and a purely formal demand for a self-governing tract of land for Negro resettlement is made.

There is a logical reversal of the locus of responsibility for the Negro condition. Although the whites are considered guilty forever and damned for their crimes against the Negroes, only the Negroes can emancipate and regenerate themselves. Only the Negroes have *that* power, here the whites are impotent. Whites are barred from the movement and cooperation with white agencies is forbidden, although all public facilities are used. It is conceived that only the Negroes can reformulate a Negro personal and social identity which is held to be degenerate. From this self-hatred arises yet another logical reversal — the manifest Puritanism of the movement, forced like sweet milk from the body of Negro amorality. The historically violated Negro woman is considered sacrosanct; she is secluded and protected, and her formal dress, at least, is designed to cover rather than display her sex.

Similarly pursuing the Islamic model, which is so usefully antithetical to the American Negro past, drinking, smoking, and, of course, the habit of drugs are forbidden. This Puritanism also has the effect, at least in abstract, of reversing the roles of the sexes. The men, conceived to be on the road to rehabilitation, regain their positions as heads of families. The intention, if not the result, is to obliterate the more or less typical husbandless, fatherless, mother-centered, lower-class Negro family, that minimal rung on the rope ladder of Negro society. Within the movement, men are supposed to find psychological "security," and it is expected, in return, that they will find steady jobs so as to make both their families and the movement viable. Therefore, many Negro women, dreadfully burdened for generations with the basic responsibilities of sheer survival, look with favor on the movement. These sometime wives, grieving mothers, and thwarted lovers want men whom they can respect, and who will respect them.

Another effort to cauterize the wound of slavery, to embrace the alienation of the Negro from American life, and thus to reverse the process of assimilation is the doctrine of militant self-defense. This is not only a denial of the power and good intentions of the polity at large, the white police state, but also reverses the passive aggressive character of Negro social response, with its collectively nonviolent, symbolic, evasive patterns of resistance. A disciplined troop supposedly replaces the random, opportunistic violence and the patterned evasions with which Negroes customarily confront whites. Self-hatred, self-regeneration, self-defense, compose a logically and historically derived progression, common to all nativistic movements, in the effort to achieve social and personal identity. The Black Muslims, with little loss in meaning, and some increase in irony, might as well be called Black Zionists.

At the pinnacle of the movement stands the *Prophet,* the underwriter of the chosen people's divine fate, reader of signs, and, simultaneously, disbursing favors, as his own chief *priest,* since the immediacy and novelty of the movement do not permit the separate, if linked, growth of faith and church. The Prophet is the movement incarnate, the voice of its inevitability, the recreator of its past, the interpreter of the future, the scourge of its enemies, the holy avenger, the source of spiritual good, which is black; the leader into the promised land. In the person of the Prophet, the climactic reversal occurs; Caliban and Prospero exchange roles, and the notion of the *white* devil takes its logical place alongside the black and yellow devils.

Surrounding the Prophet are the disciples, an elite within an elite movement, which is, in itself, the ordained instrument of a superior people. In all such movements, whether historical or contemporary, the original nucleus of the faith is small. Its significance is to be measured, not in formal allegiance but in what the movement symbolizes to the people at large, in whose name it functions, and in how faithfully it represents the world as experienced by them. For this reason, the defection of Malcolm X was more than a schism that could be contained within the ranks. It was heresy. The heresy lay in Malcolm's cast of mind, and in his capacity to grow, to change his mind. When that became clear, this tough and charismatic man who drifted through the Negro landscape over ground so familiar to them and "shocking" to us, either had to be controlled or done away with. The details are of no importance, but it should be noted that Malcolm was not killed, although he *had* been threatened, until he had begun to change his attitude toward the enemy. A Muslim in the traditional sense he became and remained, but he was ceasing to be a nativist, and was becoming a universalist. That could only have been the ultimate secular heresy in the view of the Black Muslims. Malcolm had graduated from a sect to a great tradition and at one stroke thereby revealed the distinction between Islam and the Black Muslims, while in his traffic with the black and white enemy, he had begun to explore solutions beyond cultism. Malcolm was obsessed with the Negro condition, with the Negro being, with being a Negro, but he was not compulsively restricted to a single pseudo-solution. His real religious faith would seem to have matured when he felt free to experiment with other answers.

At that juncture he had to be executed, because to the degree that Malcolm won his identity, the Black Muslims lost theirs. This man of inbetween color who rose out of the Negro world, our underworld, to confront us could have been born out of the head of Genet. We dare not disown him for we are his creation and he is ours. We need him to understand ourselves; his mere existence publicly illuminated Negroes in a way that drove the liberals back to respectability. And do his life and death not reveal how obtuse white Americans are in failing to see that all they have to do to pull the sting of the Negro as Negro is to accept him, without socio-economic reservations, into our lives? The real problem that will then emerge, is now emerging, is not one of color but of a self-divisive, mutually created cultural being. And even that can be transcended if we are willing to plunge into the depths out of which Malcolm was rising. But first we must learn to swim, white fish in his, in our, dark sea, learning what he learned of us.

1965

# THE IMAGE OF THE ADOLESCENT MINORITY

## EDGAR Z. FRIEDENBERG

In our society there are two kinds of minority status. One of these I will call the "hot-blooded" minorities, whose archetypical image is that of the Negro or Latin. *In the United States, "Teen-agers" are treated as a "hot-blooded" minority.* Then, there are the "long-suffering minorities," whose archetype is the Jew, but which also, I should say, includes women. Try, for a second, to picture a Jewish "teen-ager," and you may sense a tendency for the image to grate. "Teen-agers" err on the hot side; they talk jive, drive hot rods, and become juvenile delinquents. Young Jews talk volubly, play the violin, and go to medical school, though never on Saturday.

The minority group is a special American institution, created by the interaction between a history and an ideology which are not to be duplicated elsewhere. Minority status has little to do with size or proportion. In a democracy, a dominant social group is called a majority and a part of its dominance consists in the power to arrange appropriate manifestations of public support; while a subordinate group is, by the logic of political morality, a minority. The minority stereotype, though affected by the actual characteristics of the minority group, develops to fit the purposes and express the anxieties of the dominant social group. It serves as a slimy coating over the sharp realities of cultural difference, protecting the social organism until the irritant can be absorbed.

Now, when one is dealing with a group that actually is genetically or culturally different from the dominant social group, this is perhaps to be expected. It is neither desirable nor inevitable, for xenophobia is neither desirable nor inevitable; but it is not surprising.

What is surprising is that the sons and daughters of the *dominant* adult group should be treated as a minority group merely because of their age. Their papers are in order and they speak the language adequately. In any society, to be sure, the young occupy a subordinate or probationary status while under tutelage for adult life. But a minority group is not merely subordinate; it is not under tutelage. It is in the process of being denatured; of becoming, under social stress, something more acceptable to the dominant society, but essentially different from what its own growth and experience would lead to. Most beasts recognize their own kind. Primitive peoples may initiate their youth; we insist that ours be naturalized, though it is what is most natural about them that disturbs adults almost.

The court of naturalization is the public school. A high school diploma is a certificate of legitimacy, not of competence. A youth needs one today in order to hold a job that will permit even minimal participation in the dominant society. Yet our laws governing school attendance do not deal with education. They are not *licensing* laws, requiring attendance until a certain defined minimum competence, presumed essential for adult life, has been demonstrated. They are not *contractual,* they offer no remedy for failure of the school to provide services of a minimum quality. A juvenile may not legally withdraw from school even if he can establish that it is substandard or that he is being ill-treated there. If he does, as many do, for just these reasons, he becomes *prima facie* an offender; for, in cold fact, the compulsory attendance law guarantees him nothing, not even the services of qualified teachers. It merely defines, in terms of age alone, a particular group as subject to legal restrictions not applicable to other persons.

Legally, the adolescent comes pretty close to having no basic rights at all. The state generally retains the final right even to strip him of his minority status. He has no right to *demand* the particular protection of *either* due process or the juvenile administrative procedure — the state decides. We have had several cases in the past few years of boys sixteen and under being sentenced to death by the full apparatus of formal criminal law, who would not have been permitted to claim its protection had they been accused of theft or disorderly conduct. Each of these executions has so far been forestalled by various legal procedures, but none in such a way as to establish the right of a juvenile to be tried as a juvenile — though he long ago lost his claim to be treated as an adult.

In the most formal sense, then, the adolescent is one of our second-class citizens. But the informal aspects of minority status are also imputed to him. The "teen-ager," like the Latin or Negro, is seen as joyous, playful, lazy, and irresponsible, with brutality lurking just below the surface and ready to break out into violence.* All these groups are seen as childish and excitable, imprudent and improvident, sexually aggressive, and dangerous, but possessed of superb and sustained power to satisfy sexual demands. *West Side Story* is not much like *Romeo and Juliet;* but it is a great deal like *Porgy and Bess.*

The fantasy underlying this stereotype, then, is erotic; and its subject is male. The "hot-blooded" minorities are always represented by a masculine stereotype; nobody asks "Would you want your *son* to marry a Negro?" In each case, also, little counter-stereotypes, repulsively pallid in contrast to the alluring violence and conflict of the central scene, are held out enticingly by the dominant culture; the conscientious "teener" sold by Pat Boone to soothe adults while the kids themselves buy *Mad* and *Catcher;* the boy whose Italian immigrant mother sees to it that he wears a clean shirt to school every day on his way to the Governor's mansion; *Uncle Tom.* In the rectilinear planning of Jonesville these are set aside conspicuously as Public Squares, but at dusk they are little frequented.

One need hardly labor the point that what the dominant society seeks to control by imposing "hot-blooded" minority status is not the actual aggressiveness and sexuality of the Negro, the Latin, or the JD, but its own wish for what the British working classes used to call "a nice game of slap and tickle," on the unimpeachable assumption that a little of what you fancy does you good. This, the well-lighted Public Squares cannot afford; the community is proud of them, but they are such stuff as only the driest dreams are made of. These are not the dreams that are wanted. In my experience, it is just not possible to discuss adolescence with a group of American adults without being forced onto the topic of juvenile delinquency. Partly this is an expression of legitimate concern, but partly it is because only the JD has any emotional vividness for them.

I would ascribe the success of *West Side Story* to the functional equiv-

---

* A very bad — indeed, vicious — but remarkably ambivalent reenactment of the entire fantasy on which the minority-status of the teen-ager is based can be seen in the recent movie *13 West St.* Here, the legal impotence of the "teen-ager" is taken absolutely for granted, and sadistic hostility of adults against him, though deplored, is condoned and accepted as natural. Occasional efforts are made to counterbalance the, in my judgment, pornographic picture of a brutal teen-age gang by presenting "good" teen-agers unjustly suspected, and decent police trying to resist sadistic pressure from the gang's victim, who drives one of its members to suicide. But despite this, the picture ends with a scene of the gang's victim — a virile-type rocket scientist — beating the leader of the gang with his cane and attempting to drown the boy in a swimming pool — which the police dismiss as excusable under the circumstances. A Honolulu paper, at least, described this scene of attempted murder as "an old-fashioned caning that had the audience cheering in its seats."

alence in the minds of adults between adolescence, delinquency, and aggressive sexuality. Many who saw the show must have wondered, as I did, why there were no Negroes in it — one of the best things about Juvenile Delinquency is that at least it is integrated. Hollywood, doubtless, was as usual reluctant to show a member of an enfranchised minority group in an unfavorable light. But there was also a rather sound artistic reason. Putting a real Negro boy in *West Side Story* would have been like scoring the second movement of the *Pastorale* for an eagle rather than flute. The provocative, surly, sexy dancing kids who come to a bad end are not meant realistically. Efforts to use real street-adolescents in *West Side Story* had to be abandoned; they didn't know how to act. What was depicted here was neither Negro nor white nor really delinquent, but a comfortably vulgar middle-class dream of a "hot-blooded" minority. In dreams a single symbolic boy can represent them all; let the symbol turn real and the dreamer wakes up screaming.

Adolescents are treated as a "hot-blooded" minority, then, because they seem so good at slap-and-tickle. But a number of interesting implications flow from this. Slap-and-tickle implies sexual vigor and attractiveness, warmth and aggression, salted with enough conventional perversity to lend spice to a long dull existence. Such perversity is a kind of exuberant overflow from the mainstream of sexuality, not a diversion of it. It is joyous excess and bounty; extravagant foreplay in the well-worn marriage bed; the generosity of impulse that leads the champion lover of the high school to prance around the shower-room snapping a towel on the buttocks of his teammates three hours before a hot date, just to remind them that life can be beautiful.


When a society sees impulsiveness and sexual exuberance as minority characteristics which unsuit the individual for membership until he is successfully naturalized, it is in pretty bad shape. Adolescents, loved, respected, taught to accept, enjoy, and discipline their feelings, grow up. "Teen-agers" don't; they pass. Then, in middle age, they have the same trouble with their former self that many ethnics do. They hate and fear the kinds of spontaneity that remind them of what they have abandoned, and they hate themselves for having joined forces with and having come to resemble their oppressors.* This is the vicious spiral by which "hot-blooded" minority status maintains itself. I am convinced that it is also the source of the specific hostility — and sometimes sentimentality — that adolescents arouse in adults. The processes involved have been dealt with in detail by Daniel Boorstin, Leslie Fiedler, Paul

* *cf.* Abraham Kardiner and Lionel Ovesey's classic, *The Mark of Oppression* (New York: Norton, 1951), for a fascinating study of these dynamics among American Negroes.

Goodman, and especially Ernest Schachtel.* Their effect is to starve out, through silence and misrepresentation, the capacity to have genuine and strongly felt experience, and to replace it by the conventional symbols that serve as the common currency of daily life.

Experience repressed in adolescence does not, of course, result in amnesia, as does the repression of childhood experience; it leaves no temporal gaps in the memory. This makes it more dangerous, because the adult is then quite unaware that his memory is incomplete, that the most significant components of feeling have been lost or driven out. We at least know that we no longer know what we felt as children. But an adolescent boy who asks his father how he felt on the first night he spent in barracks or with a woman will be told what the father now thinks he felt because he ought to have; and this is very dangerous nonsense indeed.

Whether in childhood or in adolescence, the same quality of experience is starved out or repressed. It is still the spontaneous, vivid, and immediate that is most feared, and feared the more because so much is desired. But there is a difference in focus and emphasis because in adolescence spontaneity can lead to much more serious consequences.

This, perhaps, is the crux of the matter; since it begins to explain why our kind of society should be so easily plunged into conflict by "hot-blooded" minorities in general and adolescent boys in particular. We are consequence-oriented and future-oriented. Among us, to prefer present delights is a sign of either low or high status, and both are feared. Schachtel makes it clear how we go about building this kind of character in the child — by making it difficult for him to notice his delights when he has them, and obliterating the language in which he might recall them joyfully later. This prepares the ground against the subsequent assault of adolescence. But it is a strong assault, and if adolescence wins, the future hangs in the balance.

In this assault, adolescent boys play a very different role from adolescent girls; and are dealt with unconsciously by totally different dynamics. Adolescent girls are not seen as members of a "hot-blooded" minority, and to this fact may be traced some interesting paradoxes in our perception of the total phenomenon of adolescence.

Many critics of the current literature on adolescence — Bruno Bettelheim† perhaps most cogently — have pointed out that most contemporary writing about adolescents ignores the adolescent girl almost com-

* Daniel Boorstin, The Image (New York: Atheneum, 1962); Leslie Fiedler, "The Fear of the Impulsive Life," WFMT Perspective, October, 1961, pp. 4–9; Paul Goodman, Growing Up Absurd (New York: Random House, 1960), p. 38; Ernest Schachtel, "On Memory and Childhood Amnesia." Widely anthologized, cf. the author's Metamorphosis (New York: Basic Books, 1959), pp. 279–322.
† In "Adolescence and the Conflict of Generations," Dædalus, Winter, 1962, p. 68.

pletely. Bettelheim specifically mentions Goodman and myself; the best novels about adolescents of the past decade or so have been, I think there would be fair agreement, Salinger's *The Catcher in the Rye,* John Knowles' *A Separate Peace,* and Colin MacInnes' less well known but superb *Absolute Beginners.* All these have adolescent boys as heroes. Yet, as Bettelheim points out, the adolescent girl is as important as the adolescent boy, and her actual plight in society is just as severe; her opportunities are even more limited and her growth into a mature woman as effectively discouraged. Why has she not aroused more interest?

There are demonstrable reasons for the prominence of the adolescent boy in our culture. Conventionally, it is he who threatens the virtue of our daughters and the integrity of our automobiles. There are so many more ways to get hung up on a boy. "Teen-agers," too, may be all right; but would you want your daughter to marry one? When she doesn't know anything about him except how she feels — and what does that matter when they are both too young to know what they are doing; when he may never have the makings of an executive, or she of an executive's wife?

For this last consideration, paradoxically, also makes the *boy,* rather than the girl, the focus of anxiety. He alone bears the terrible burden of parental aspirations; it is his capacity for spontaneous commitment that endangers the opportunity of adults to live vicariously the life they never managed to live personally.

Holden, Finny, and the unnamed narrator of *Absolute Beginners* are adolescent boys who do not pass; who retain their minority status, their spontaneous feelings, their power to act out and act up. They go prancing to their destinies. But what destiny can we imagine for them? We leave Holden in a mental hospital, being adjusted to reality; and Finny dead of the horror of learning that his best friend, Gene, had unconsciously contrived the accident that broke up his beautifully articulated body. The Absolute Beginner, a happier boy in a less tense society, fares better; he has had more real contact with other human beings, including a very satisfactory father, and by his time there is such a thing as a "teen-ager," little as it is, for him to be. On this basis the Beginner can identify himself; the marvelous book ends as he rushes out onto the tarmac at London Airport, bursting through the customs barrier, to stand at the foot of the gangway and greet a planeload of astonished immigrants by crying, "Here I am! Meet your first teen-ager."

There are still enough Finnys and Holdens running around free to give me much joy and some hope, and they are flexible enough to come to their own terms with reality. But the system is against them, and they know it well. Why then, do they not try to change it? Why are none of these novels of adolescence political novels? Why have their heroes no political interests at all? In this respect, fiction is true to American life; American adolescents are notably free from political interests. I must maintain this despite the recent advances of SANE kids and Freedom Riders; for, though I love and honor them for their courage and devotion, the causes they fight for are not what I would call political. No controversy over basic policy is involved, because nobody advocates atomic disaster or racial persecution. The kids' opponents are merely in favor of the kind of American society that these evils flourish in, and the youngsters do not challenge the system itself, though they are appalled by its consequences.

Yet could they, as adolescents, be political? I don't think so; and I don't know that I would be pleased if they were. American politics is a cold-blooded business indeed. Personal clarity and commitment are not wanted in it and not furthered by it. I do not think this is necessarily true of all politics; but it becomes true when the basic economic and social assumptions are as irrational as ours.

Political effectiveness in our time requires just the kind of caginess, pseudo-realism, and stereotyping of thought and feeling; the same submergence of spontaneity to the exigencies of collective action, that mark the ruin of adolescence. Adolescents are, inherently, anti-mass; they take things personally. Sexuality, itself, has this power to resolve relationships into the immediate and interpersonal. As a symbol the cocky adolescent boy stands, a little like Luther, an obstacle to compromise and accommodation. Such symbols stick in the mind, though the reality can usually be handled. With occasional spectacular failures we do manage to assimilate the "teen-age" minority; the kids learn not to get fresh; they get smart, they dry up. We are left then, like the Macbeths, with the memory of an earlier fidelity. But Lady Macbeth was less resourceful than ourselves; she knew next to nothing about industrial solvents. Where she had only perfume we have oil.

This is how we use the boy, but what about the girl? I have already asserted that since she is not perceived as a member of the "hot-blooded" minority she cannot take his place in the unconscious, which is apt to turn very nasty if it is fobbed off with the wrong sex. Is she then simply not much involved by our psychodynamics, or is she actively repressed? Is she omitted from our fantasies or excluded from them?

It may seem very strange that I should find her so inconspicuous. Her image gets so much publicity. Drum-majorettes and cheerleaders are ubiquitous; *Playboy* provides businessmen with a new *playmate* each month. Nymphets are a public institution.

Exactly, and they serve a useful public function. American males are certainly anxious to project a heterosexual public image, and even more anxious to believe in it themselves. None of us, surely, wishes to feel obligated to hang himself out of respect for the United States Senate; it is, as Yum-Yum remarked to Nanki-Poo, such a stuffy death. I am not questioning our sincerity; the essence of my point is that in what we call maturity we feel what we are supposed to feel, and nothing else. But I am questioning the depth and significance of our interest in the cover or pin-up girl. Her patrons are concerned to experience their own masculinity; they are not much interested in her: I reject the celebration of "babes" in song and story as evidence that we have adolescent girls much on our minds; if we did we wouldn't think of them as "babes." I think, indeed, that in contrast to the boy, of whom we are hyperaware, we repress our awareness of the girl. She is not just omitted, she is excluded.

The adolescent heroine in current fiction is not interpreted in the same way as the adolescent hero, even when the parallel is quite close. Her adolescence is treated as less crucial; she is off-handedly accepted as a woman already. This is true even when the author struggles against it. Lolita, for example, is every bit as much a tragic heroine of adolescence as Holden is a hero — she isn't as nice a girl as he is a boy, but they are both victims of the same kind of corruption in adult society and the same absence of any real opportunity to grow up to be themselves. Lolita's failure is the classic failure of identity in adolescence; and Humbert knows this and accepts responsibility for it; this is the crime he expiates. But this is not the way Lolita — the character, not the book — is generally received. Unlike Holden, she has no cult and is not vouchsafed any dignity. It is thought to be comical that, at fourteen, she is already a whore.

A parallel example is to be found in Rumer Godden's *The Greengage Summer*. Here the story is explicitly about Joss's growing up. The author's emphasis is on the way her angry betrayal of her lover marks the end of her childhood; her feelings are now too strong and confused, and too serious in their consequences, to be handled with childish irresponsibility; she can no longer claim the exemptions of childhood. But what the movie presented, it seemed to me, was almost entirely an account of her rise to sexual power; Joss had become a Babe at last.

One reason that we do not take adolescent growth seriously in girls is that we do not much care what happens to people unless it has economic consequences: what would Holden ever be, since he never even graduates from high school; who would hire him? He has a problem; Lolita could always be a waitress or something, what more could she expect? Since we define adulthood almost exclusively in economic terms, we obviously cannot concern ourselves as much about the growth of those members of society who are subject from birth to restricted economic opportunity. But so, of course, are the members of the "hot-blooded" minorities; though we find their hot-bloodedness so exciting that we remain aware of them anyway.

But girls, like Jews, are not supposed to fight back; we expect them, instead, to insinuate themselves coyly into the roles available. In our society, there are such lovely things for them to be. They can take care of other people and clean up after them. Women can become wives and mothers; Jews can become kindly old Rabbis and philosophers and even psychoanalysts and lovable comic essayists. They can become powers behind the power; a fine old law firm runs on the brains of its anonymous young Jews just as a husband's best asset is his loyal and unobtrusive wife. A Jewish girl can become a Jewish Mother, and this is a role which even Plato would have called essential.

Clearly, this kind of discrimination is quite different from that experienced by the "hot-blooded" minorities, and must be based on a very different image in the minds of those who practice it and must have a different impact upon them. Particularly, in the case of the adolescent, the effect on the adult of practicing these two kinds of discrimination will be different. The adolescent boy must be altered to fit middle-class adult roles, and when he has been he becomes a much less vital creature. But the girl is merely squandered, and this wastage will continue all her life. Since adolescence is, for boy and girl alike, the time of life in which the self must be established, the girl suffers as much from being wasted as the boy does from being cut down; there has recently been, for example, a number of tragic suicides reported among adolescent girls, though suicide generally is far less common among females. But from the point of view of the dominant society nothing special is done to the female in adolescence — the same squeeze continues throughout life, even though this is when it hurts most.

The guilts we retain for our treatments of "hot-blooded" and "long-suffering" minorities therefore affect us in contrasting ways. For the boy we suffer angry, paranoid remorse, as if he were Billy the Kid, or Budd. We had to do our duty, but how can we ever forget him? But we do not attack the girl; we only neglect her and leave her to wither gradually through an unfulfilled life; and the best defense against this sort of guilt is selective inattention. We just don't see her; instead, we see a caricature, not brutalized as in the case of the boy, to justify our own brutality; but sentimentalized, roseate, to reassure us that we have done her no harm, and that she is well contented. Look: she even has her own telephone, with what is left of the boy dangling from the other end of the line.

This is the fantasy; the reality is very different, but it is bad enough to be a "Teen-ager." The adolescent is now the only totally disfranchised minority group in the country. In America, no minority has ever gotten any respect or consistently decent treatment until it began to acquire political power. The vote comes before anything else. This is obviously true of the Negro at the present time; his recent advances have all been made under — sometimes reluctant — federal auspices because, nationally, Negroes vote, and Northern Negroes are able to cast a ballot on which their buffeted Southern rural fellows may be pulled to firmer political ground. This is what makes it impossible to stop Freedom Rides; just as the comparative militance of the Catholic Church in proceeding toward integration in Louisiana may have less to do with Louisiana than Nigeria, which is in grave danger of falling into the hands of Black Muslims. People generally sympathetic with adolescents sometimes say, "Well, it really isn't fair; if they're old enough to be drafted, they're old enough to vote," which is about as naïve as it is possible to get.

Can the status of the "teen-ager" be improved? Only, presumably, through increased political effectiveness. Yet, it is precisely here that a crucial dilemma arises. For the aspirations of the adolescent minority are completely different from those of other minorities. All the others are struggling to obtain what the adolescent is struggling to avoid. They seek and welcome the conventional American middle-class status that has been partially or totally barred to them. But this is what the adolescent is left with if he gives in and goes along.

In the recent and very moving CORE film, *Freedom Ride,* one of the heroic group who suffered beatings and imprisonment for their efforts to end segregation says, as nearly as I can recall, "If the road to freedom leads through the jails of the South, then that's the road I'll take." It may be the road to freedom; but it is the road to suburbia too. You can't tell which the people are headed for until they are nearly there; but all our past ethnic groups have settled for suburbia, and the people who live there bear witness that freedom is somewhere else.

I am not sure there *is* a road to freedom in America. Not enough people want to go there; the last I can recall was H. D. Thoreau, and he went on foot, through the woods, alone. This still may be the only way to get there. For those with plenty of guts, compassion, and dedication to social justice, who nevertheless dislike walking alone through the woods, or feel it to be a Quixotic extravagance, a freedom ride is a noble enterprise. Compared to them, the individual boy or girl on a solitary journey must seem an anachronism. Such a youngster has very little place in our way of life. And of all the criticisms that might be directed against that way of life, this is the harshest.

1963

# ARE WORKERS MIDDLE CLASS?

## S. M. MILLER AND FRANK RIESSMAN

Are workers becoming "middle-class"? Is *Fortune* correct in describing workers as a "salariat" rather than a "proletariat"? A belief is spreading among social scientists and unionists that in their middle age unions are becoming middle class. But an evaluation of a number of sociological studies suggests that the extent of "middle-classization" among workers * is, to recall Mark Twain's comment on rumors of his death, "grossly exaggerated."

We shall deal here with three arguments for the view that workers are becoming middle class: 1) objective conditions of life no longer distinguish workers from the middle class; 2) workers have the same desire for success that middle-class people have; and 3) the ho-

* By workers we refer to manual or blue-collar wage-earners. We do not include white-collar or agricultural workers; nor the "lower class" who are irregular members of the labor force in unskilled and service occupations. Unfortunately, in contemporary social science the all-inclusive term "lower class" is generally used to refer to both workers and the true lower class. This leads to much confusion in both empirical and theoretical studies. We use information about this "lower class" only when we think it applies to the working class and not merely to a statistical agglomerate of lower and working classes. In citing various studies we do not necessarily defend their methodology or implications; what we wish to emphasize is the weight of the evidence.

mogenization of attitudes and values which occurs in a mass society obliterates class differences.

## Objective Conditions

For many craft workers income levels are good, especially when compared to those of lower white-collar employees. Yet the wages of large groups of workers, in the South, in New England, and in "sick" industries are still very low; among workers who suffer most from discrimination — Negroes, Mexicans, and Puerto Ricans — poverty is often extreme.

Many wage earners work far more than a forty-hour week; indeed, high earnings in manufacturing industries are due largely to time-and-a-half overtime. And about one worker out of twenty "moonlights" — that is, holds more than one job. Nor should we forget that the "high" wages in manufacturing are not really so very high: an average weekly pay in 1959 of $90 is not a luxury income if one considers present prices and taxes.

Unemployment occurs more frequently among wage earners than among white-collar workers, especially during the kinds of recessions we have come to know in recent years. In the steel industry between the middle of 1956 and the fall of 1958, semi-skilled workers had a 20 percent, and unskilled workers a 25 percent drop in employment; but no office employees were laid off during the same period. Workers always have a nagging fear of unemployment, for even during boom times many plants shut down temporarily or are closed because they cannot compete with newer, more efficient factories. Daniel Bell has reported that "the most bitter complaint of auto workers is that they have no way of knowing, from one week to the next, how many hours they will work in any given week; through the year, a man may get as many as twenty 'short work weeks.' "

Harvey Swados has described the exhausting and dehumanizing quality of assembly work, even in modern plants. Ford workers fought in the 1955 collective bargaining negotiations for a provision that would permit assembly line or production workers to cut their wages 35 cents or more an hour by taking a sweeper's job. In this way they could hope to free themselves from the exhausting rhythms of the assembly line.

To be a member of a worker's family still means to live a "different" life. In education, for example, working-class children do not fare well. In a wealthy state like New York, about half of all children entering high school don't finish, and most of these dropouts are from the working and lower classes. Since the Russian success with their Sputnik, Americans have been made painfully aware that many of our most talented youngsters don't go to college. But the fact that most of these children come from working-class families has been widely overlooked. Studies demonstrate that workers' children are rarely encouraged and accepted by school personnel in the way middle-class children are.

Data on social mobility show that only 30 percent of working-class sons rise to middle-class positions. On the other hand, about 70 percent of the sons of middle-class fathers stay in the middle class. If a middle-class job is your goal it is a tremendous advantage to have been born middle-class. Moreover, the "mobile" working-class son is much more likely to end up as a poorly paid white-collar worker or the owner of a marginal small business, than is the middle-class son who stays in his own class.

## A Profile of Success

The available information indicates that the objective conditions of middle- and working-class life continue to differ. But at least as important is the subjective outlook of the workers themselves. Do workers absorb middle-class values and strive for "success" as middle-class people do? A desire to get ahead, for "success," most certainly does exist in the working class. But the content of this desire must be carefully clarified, for although the same terms are used by middle-class people, they may have entirely different connotations in working-class usage.

Middle-class striving on the part of workers, if it existed, would have the following characteristics: 1) it would be central to their total pattern of behavior; 2) it would include a desire for prestige rather than merely for improvement in living conditions; 3) it would be individualistic, directed toward a personal rather than a group or collective achievement.* These three conditions would have to be met before we could say that workers strive for middle-class status. We would also have to ask a fourth question: Do workers strive *consciously* to imitate middle-class attitudes and behavior? †

The information necessary to answer questions about these conditions is not fully available. But enough is known to cast doubt on the thesis that most workers strive for a middle-class success and the way of life associated with it.

---

* Two objections to these criteria are that middle-class individuals living in an "other-directed" world do not pursue success, and that group means of achieving improvement are increasingly accepted by white-collar workers. We do not agree with the first point, which stems from the work of Riesman and Whyte, for it is the style and not the fact of success-striving that has changed. As for the second, there has indeed been a tendency toward group improvement, but it has met with much criticism and is limited to occupations that are poorly paid or of a civil service type.
† An important warning: The so-called "middle-class psychology" of workers which we have been describing cannot be taken as an adequate description of the actual psychology of the middle class.

On the problem of how central is the success-drive among workers, the findings of Herbert H. Hyman are very striking:

> The components of this value system, in our judgment, involve less emphasis upon the traditional high success goals, increased awareness of the lack of opportunity to achieve success, and less emphasis upon the achievement of goals which in turn would be instrumental for success. To put it simply, the lower-class individual doesn't want as much success, knows he couldn't get it even if he wanted to, and doesn't want what might help him get success.

Hyman's analysis of public opinion data revealed that workers do not tend to value education — a major vehicle for advancement — as much as do middle-class persons. He discovered also that workers and their children favor a job that provides steady employment and low income over a risky but more promising job.

In a very important study Richard Centers observed the same tendency. He found that a majority of manual workers thought it more important for the government to guarantee every person "a decent and steady job and standard of living" than to make "certain that there are good opportunities for each person to get ahead on his own." Business, professional, and white-collar groups disagreed; they rated "opportunities" much higher. Among personnel managers, it is a generally accepted view that factory workers tend to rate security above other elements in a job, while white-collar employees tend to prefer "opportunity for advancement."

Centers' most significant finding was that more than three-quarters of the workers in his sample of white males identified themselves as working class when given a choice of "upper class," "middle class," "working class" and "lower class." The oft-cited *Fortune* survey which reported that most workers identified with the middle class had unfortunately neglected to include the choice of "working class" on its questionnaire.

Joseph Kahl has written an article in which the difference between middle-class and working-class goals is explored. Of the boys (in a group from Boston wage-earner and lower white-collar families) whom he studied carefully, at least 60 percent had families which were concerned with "getting by" rather than rising into the middle class. Some even expressed the idea that "the competitive game [to rise higher] was not worth the candle."

In a study of Michigan auto workers, Ely Chinoy found that half had "never thought of becoming a foreman or failed to mention foremanship" in discussing plans for the future. Twenty-five percent claimed they would definitely not want to be foremen; and a few had actually turned down the chance to move up to such a position. Only 25 percent admitted to ever wanting "advancement." Charles R. Walker discovered that in a Pennsylvania steel mill there was "a resistance to promotion [that] was striking"; at least three-quarters of the men were not interested in promotion; 25 percent had turned down the opportunity to advance.

Bennett Berger found among workers moving to a suburb (a locale that is regarded as a hotbed of status-striving) that relatively few sought or would accept promotion.

Different kinds of studies — some more reliable than others — all point to the same conclusion: *"getting ahead" does not play as crucial a role in working-class life as it does in the middle class.*

### Consumer Goods or Values?

The desire to improve one's economic position does not necessarily involve subscribing to middle-class ideals nor to the American mania of perpetual upward mobility. One can simply want to enjoy more of the good things of life for oneself and one's family, apart from matters of status or prestige.

We must therefore distinguish between the actual goods and the symbols which become attached to them. A worker may want a bigger income so that he can afford a more comfortable home. The possession of that better home may, in turn, give the family higher prestige among neighbors and friends. But we cannot assume that the status which goes along with the improvement in living standards was a dominant reason for wanting it. In American life, living better — having an easier, more enjoyable life — simply involves having the things many middle-class people have. But for a significant portion of the middle class it is the prestige-value of these goods which is most desired. Workers, by contrast, do seem to seek these goods mainly for their usefulness, not for their prestige.

This contrast in attitudes is nicely illustrated in a story that circulated some years ago. In suburbia, so the story went, many middle-class families, wanting to keep up with the Joneses, were putting up television antennas when they didn't have sets. On the other hand, working-class families, despite low incomes, were among the first to buy television sets, not for the prestige-value but because TV was a highly economical and exciting form of entertainment.

That mobility strivings can have a varied content was demonstrated to us in a small-scale study of workers we conducted a little while back. One respondent, for example, answered "yes" to the question, "Are you trying to get ahead?" But in reply to the follow-up question, "What does getting ahead mean to you?", he said: "Having a steady job so that you can pay your bills. Being able to manage, that's getting ahead." This concept of success is rooted in a desire for stability, not social position.

These divergent attitudes toward status are illustrated in an odd but insightful pamphlet called "The American Worker" by Paul Romano and Ria Stone. They contend that middle-class and working-class people want to become independent businessmen for very different reasons. For both, of course, there is the expectation (frequently unrealized) of a higher income. The middle-class person is likely also to be concerned with gaining in prestige and social status. But for the worker, this is much less true; he wants to start his own business in order to become his own boss, to get away from a foreman's controlling demands and to go his own way, free from factory pressures.

The fact that workers now possess some of the things which were once thought to be exclusively middle-class property (e.g., automobiles, vacuum cleaners, high school education, etc.) does not mean that they really have a middle-class standard of living. Havighurst and Neugarten have pointed out that as middle-class goods become more accessible to workers, middle-class standards and prestige symbols change to include such new items as high-fi equipment, dishwashers, and a college education.

It is also true that the means used for getting ahead are different in the middle class and the working class. Workers improve the conditions of their life mainly through the collective action of their unions. Middle-class individuals do not use, and often frown upon, collective action as a means of self-advancement. To the middle class, if everyone is advancing then no one is bettering himself, since success is measured in relation to the progress of their immediate peers. Many workers, however, accept the union as their vehicle for getting ahead. Sol Barkin of the Textile Workers' Union has summed up this point very well:

> The union seeks to advance the worker as a member of a group rather than as an individual competing with others. It establishes rules of conduct and conditions of employment for all, instead of special terms for individuals. . . . The individual worker reared in our culture looks for personal achievement, not by violating the interests or mores of the group but by taking advantage of the expanding employment opportunity within the plant or the economy as a whole.

Evidence to support the contention that workers seek to emulate middle-class standards is scanty. There is, however, work done some time ago by Useem and Tangent which shows that while workers would like more money and better living conditions they dislike the anxiety and competitiveness which goes along with their attainment. Drake and Cayton report the contemptuous attitude of lower- and working-class Negroes towards "strivers and strainers."

The most interesting conclusions on this subject have emerged from a recent study of the voting behavior of Detroit members of the United Automobile Workers. In their report, Kornhauser, Sheppard and Mayer carefully depict the pattern of attitudes of the most highly skilled, best paid and best educated workers. This group is closest to middle-class standards both economically and socially. We would expect these workers to imitate middle-class life and to adopt important middle-class symbols, for they come closest to the middle-class pattern of living. If they fulfill our expectation we might conclude that there is some tendency for workers to become middle class.

But of all union members, this privileged segment is the most pro-union, the most likely to participate actively in the union, the most likely to vote Democratic and the most likely to think in liberal terms. If one were to develop a scale of class-consciousness, this group would be the closest to the fully class-conscious pole.

The suburban workers studied by Berger had not developed a middle-class style of life. Their basic pattern was not changed by having a little grass in front of their homes.

These findings reveal a false assumption in the salariat argument. Values are supposed simply to follow income: raise income and values will change; lower income and revolt occurs. But this mode of analysis is much too mechanical. Pierre Martineau, market research expert of the Chicago *Tribune,* has cited a number of investigations to demonstrate that at the same income level (even a relatively high one) wage-earners have different tastes, styles, and modes of reaction than middle-class people. Income alone, when considered separately from occupation, does not seem to be crucial in determining attitudes and behavior; educational differences among workers are much more important than income variations.

A counter argument maintains that the spread of mass culture, inundating all classes, has caused common life styles and "homogenized tastes" to prevail in the United States. This is again an example of the environmentalistic fallacy: a description of influence is accepted as an adequate description of behavior.

Much more important than TV and the mass media in shaping life-styles are family, education, and occupation (though all of these are in turn affected by mass culture). The synthetic popular culture of today seems to have a rather deep effect upon youth, but later experiences on the job and in the family may well outweigh the influence of the taste-makers.

Many studies reveal that workers and middle-class people differ in both crucial and noncrucial aspects of attitudes, beliefs, and behavior. This is true no matter what indices of class are used. Although great confusion prevails in interpreting results, considerable divergence in the modes of child-rearing are reported in working-class and middle-class families (Bronfenbrenner). Kinsey and his co-workers have documented differences in the sexual behavior of the American male which follow class lines. Miller and Swanson have concluded that workers and middle-class people have strikingly different basic life-styles and ways of defending themselves psychologically. Their book is constructed around the differences which social class creates in personality. Workers are less likely to become neurotic and a little more likely to become psychotic than are middle-class people, according to Hollingshead and Redlich. Religious behavior also differs: Protestant workers are much more likely to prefer active church services than are middle-class Protestants (Lipset). A great number of studies demonstrate that workers are much less likely than members of the middle class to join associations. Attitudes toward politics and civil liberties also differ importantly in these two social classes (Lipset and Stouffer). Almost every issue of a major sociological journal will add to the list of class differences in attitudes and behavior, although the interpretation is often unreliable.

While fewer workers than middle-class individuals are deeply concerned with the problem of success, there are undoubtedly some groups of workers who are intent upon such goals. And at the same time it is not true that everyone in the middle class worships the bitch-goddess success. Many workers do share a major part of the middle-class orientation. Many other workers share a desire for advancement or education for their children and yet remain uninvolved in the total middle-class value system. A small percentage of workers has an outlook that may be called class-conscious. These, we suggest, are the shadings of actuality, as distinct from the formulas of preconception.

We think that the outlook of the majority of workers is neither that of a class-conscious proletariat nor that of a middle-class salariat. In the 1930's there was a tendency to idealize and sentimentalize the worker. Today, there is a feeling that the should-be "noble proletariat" has succumbed to the attractions of middle-class life and no longer demands our special concern. Neither view is adequate.

What one may gather from current research is that many workers have a distinctive way of life: it centers on the family, and the family is group-centered rather than child-centered; "getting by" is more important than "getting ahead"; a lack of involvement in formal associations and political groups is widespread; an awareness of class differences exists but it is not traditional class-consciousness. The recognition of class differences is not tied to any specific political ideology or platform and most often is implicit (bring a group of college students to an auto plant, and the awareness of class differences on both sides will electrify the air). Workers with a strong "class-awareness" can be quite conservative or uninterested in politics. The socialist expectation of the worker as class-conscious does not describe reality, nor does the new cynical view that he is as much a complaining fat cat as anyone else in the Racket Society. All of this may provide only moderate comfort to liberals and socialists, but at the very least it ought to create a good deal of skepticism about the notions concerning American workers which one finds, unexamined and cheerfully propounded, in almost every speech, book, or magazine.

1961

REFERENCES

Daniel Bell, "The Subversion of Collective Bargaining," *Commentary*, March, 1960.

Bennett Berger, *Working Class Suburb*.

Urie Bronfenbrenner, "Socialization and Social Class through Time and Space," in Maccoby, Newcomb and Hartley, eds., *Readings in Social Psychology*.

Richard Centers, *The Psychology of Social Classes*.

Ely Chinoy, *Automobile Workers and the American Dream*.

St. Clair Drake and Horace Cayton, *Black Metropolis*.

Robert Havighurst and Bernice Neugarten, *Society and Education*.

Charles H. Hession, S. M. Miller and Curwen Stoddait, *The Dynamics of the American Economy*.

August B. Hollingshead, *Elmtown's Youth*.

August B. Hollingshead and Fredrich Redlich, *Social Class and Mental Illness*. Also review by Miller and Mishler, *Milbank Memorial Fund Quarterly*, 1959.

Herbert H. Hyman, "The Value Systems of Different Classes: A Social Psychological Contribution to the Analysis of Stratification," in Bendix and Lipset, eds., *Class, Status and Power*.

Joseph Kahl, "Educational and Occupational Aspirations of 'Common Man' Boys," *Harvard Educational Review*, 1953.

Arthur Kornhauser, Harold Sheppard and Albert Mayer, *When Labor Votes*.

Seymour M. Lipset, *Political Man*. See Miller and Riessman, "Working-Class Authoritarianism," *British Journal of Sociology*, 1961.

Seymour M. Lipset and Reinhard Bendix, *Social Mobility in Industrial Society*.

Pierre Martineau, "Social Classes and Spending Behavior," *Journal of Marketing*, 1957.

Daniel Miller and Guy Swanson, *Inner Conflict and Defense*.

Samuel Stouffer, *Communism, Conformity and Civil Liberties*.

John Useem, Pierre Tangent and Ruth Useem, "Stratification in a Prairie Town," in Wilson and Kolb, eds., *Sociological Analysis*.

Charles R. Walker, *Steeltown*.

# 3

*The world and the United States*

# THE DESTRUCTION OF CONSCIENCE IN VIETNAM

## MARSHALL SAHLINS

### Tea in Ambush

Villages in the Delta are laid out mainly along the canals and rivers. "Village" may be the wrong term. The houses stand side by side, strung out for hundreds of yards along a road or path paralleling the water course. Besides, one community virtually runs into the next; so that the line of settlement extends sometimes for miles, punctuated periodically by a short stretch of forest, a pagoda, or a focal marketplace town.

It is often said of South Vietnam that the day belongs to the Government, the night to the "Viet Cong." Perhaps it is better said of An Phu district that the day belongs to the Neolithic, the night to the Cold War of the mid-twentieth century. Driving that day to the South Vietnamese Popular Force outpost at Khánh An, I was in Samoa or New Guinea again: the thatch-roof houses on stilts in endless procession along the road; the shaded front verandahs overlooking decorative tropical shrubs; the big clay pots in the yard and mats spread out for sunning; the solid fishing boats drawn up on the shore; here and there a woman placidly tending kids or a man mending nets — hardly anything to suggest a civil war, an invasion, and least of all a social revolution other than the neolithic one that brought man from the mobile hunting condition and allowed him to settle down and accumulate a modicum of simple wherewithal. These people, I thought, are historically out of it. Probably they have had little conception of it for centuries, and that mainly in the form of a more or less alien landlord or tax collector, a monk, and the few goods from elsewhere they got at market. They have been more subjects than participants in the cultural evolution of the archaic civilizations of Southeast Asia, of the state but not in it, a petty agricultural existence which civilization has rested upon but not incorporated. The Neolithic is here joined as a tributary to the Bronze and Colonial Age, yet preserves its character; so the state is an historic medley of incongruent and opposed nations: the one urban, wealthy, sophisticated, and latterly comprador, the other seeking to perpetuate against exaction "the idiocy of rural life."

But at night, in this war, the two historic epochs join in a ballet which, when it is not a dance of death, is a moment of high comedy. Our Popular Force, platoon strength in black peasant clothes, took stealthily to the road for an ambush position at a river crossing several kilometers from camp. There was something of a moon: one could make out the man several yards ahead and perhaps the man ahead of him, and then one or two others in the parallel line on the opposite side of the road. Somewhere in the middle were two American advisers. Somewhere ahead was a scout with a walkie-talkie; toward the rear was another. We went quietly, watchfully, a little afraid, hunched forward with carbines at the ready. A few hundred cautious steps, then you stop at a signal from the man ahead, crouch down, look for something, go down on one knee. Then off again on the all clear. Thus we moved, armed black phantoms. Toward what? Last night the platoon had been ambushed just near here. You could never tell.

Certainly not from the incongruent setting. We were carrying guns in the midst of life, where the people live: house by house, family by family, casually going on with it, all along the road we took so seriously. Our antics seemed to make a difference only to the dogs, and then the racket they raised made even our silence ridiculous. (I understood then that whoever controls "the hearts and minds" of the dogs will win the war.) Still their howls brought no response from the houses. The people stayed just so, arranged around their hurricane lamps in peasant set-piece: a sequence of lighted dioramas in a darkened museum, before which passed beings of such *papier-mâché* purpose and expression as to raise the question of who was the imitation of humanity. Sometimes an old woman would peer out and say something to us. She was kibitzing the war. For the most part, the family went about its domestic business: an old man working over some tools, a grandmother fussing with crying grandchildren, younger men and boys talking and laughing softly, a woman singing; in one house a transistor radio blaring Vietnamese music at a spellbound family — and all their neighbors hundreds of yards around. Life went on, and why not? The Neolithic (transistor-ized) was the human occupation; while the black gang with carbines and recoilless rifles and walkie-talkies and Americans seemed as meaningful to this existence as the court ceremony of the Inca emperor.

Around here — in this "loyal" area — it's not a civil war, I thought; nor a revolution, nor an invasion from the North. It's the latest thing in warfare — a medieval war. The feudal barons with their kept knights ravage through the countryside to engage in mortal combat for forty days. The peasants go back and forth between the lines, unconcerned except to see that they don't get ravaged, or to sell a few things to either or both sides. The peace will certainly affect them, but is it their war — as war?

Last night the platoon had gone through a similar performance. They settled carefully into an ambush position at the river. Waiting tensely, one of the American advisers was startled by an arm softly placed over his shoulder. Fortunately, before he could react the thin voice of an old village-woman penetrated his senses. It was Mother Courage. "You boys want some tea?" she asked, with plaintive ingratia-tion. "Go 'way," he said, "we're waiting for someone."

I had got to this district, An Phu, by courtesy of the U.S. Information Service (now part of the Joint U.S. Public Affairs Office). It was rather a model-village tour: an area of Hoa Hao, a Buddhist reform group now solidly (for the time being) with the South Vietnamese Government. But An Phu may have been a perfect model, complete with all the flaws of its political virtues. The Hoa Hao allegiance is probably more prac-tical than principled and based fundamentally on "to thine own self be true." Subject for years to opposition and oppression, the Hoa Hao have fought everybody: the Viet Minh, the Diem regime, the Viet Cong. Today they accept the *Realpolitik* — and the weapons and good payoff — of the American presence, decisive in this province where there are no Arvin (Army of Viet Nam) regulars. It seemed to me quite clear from conversations with the Hoa Hao commander that it was the Americans with whom they were now allied, not the Government to whom they were loyal.

The late intensification of this war between Good and Evil seems to bring no decision between them so much as it throws into relief a sub-merged third term of incommensurate value: life. Recalcitrant under pressure, life insists on manifesting itself in all manner of ways — refu-gees in the cities, revolts in the mountains, desertions in the army, or perhaps just as studied indifference at An Phu. The involvement of the peasant must always have been uncertain and incomplete, *particularly on the Government side*. It is difficult to see how the peasant can be "on" the side — "for" the cause — of a world from which he has been structurally excluded. Historically, peasants have their *own* side: their family, their fields, their village. Saigon surely offers little alternative to this allegiance. It is allegiance to oneself as a human being, to what one knows as the right human condition. Outsiders must appear as only more or less damaging — or beneficial — to this condition. Foreign warriors in the land may open a new, complicated calculus of alternatives. Even so, what appears to us as a choice of sides may present itself to the peasant as a tactical choice of masters — with a meaning culturally incomparable to the American who is "for" America, or even the Republican party.

### Piastres de Resistance

At the Saigon airport I handed over the immigration form to the Vietnamese officer. In the space next to "Purpose of your visit" I had written "tourist." On August 5, 1965, it was an irrelevant purpose. But was it any more irrelevant than the things other Americans were doing in Vietnam?

Actually, I am an anthropologist and an academic critic of the war. Neither is a qualification, in the view of Administration supporters, to speak on Vietnam: one ought to have been there. I always thought it a weak retort, if only because the critics were as a rule better informed than the tropismatic adherents of official policy; for another thing because the record compiled by Americans who had been in Vietnam making and implementing mistakes suggested they had no understanding of Vietnam or of their own existence there. To have been in Vietnam does not make one an expert but perhaps something of a fool, or a victim.

Nevertheless, as an anthropologist if not as a critic I had to accept the argument: one should go into the field. I spent six days in Vietnam: mostly in Saigon, one day in Chau Doc Province (An Phu District) and half a day at III Corps Headquarters, Bien Hoa. Much of the time I passed with U.S. Information Service people, to whom I had offered the proposition that they try to convince me they were right. They accepted — "only in America!" — and put me in touch with others, civilian and military (though not with the gung-ho types I asked to see), and with the war (such as it was) in An Phu. These six days did not make me an expert — and I hope not a fool or a victim.

It is difficult to become an expert anyhow on things that aren't what they seem. Every day I saw something or learned something that made the country appear irrelevant to what was happening to it. After all, we are fighting Chinese there. There are no Chinese there. So *Vietnamese* die by way of demonstration. War is the continuation of Madison Avenue by new means; death becomes an advertisement — and "we mean what we say." The single most important and general condition of the American war in Vietnam is its irrelevance. But to kill irrelevantly is a contradiction in terms. All the compromises and the self-deceptions of Americans, and all the brutalization, originate in this contradiction.

But the most obvious incongruity is that we are defending the "freedom" of South Vietnam. The absurdity of the statement is not fully manifest by the existing Government [?]. To speak of the Government disguises the issue of the class of "brave and determined people" we are involved with, of who are our natural allies, who our enemies. It confronts you as you drive into Saigon. The rich men's big houses are protected by great iron gates and barbed wire deployed along the tops of thick walls. At the American Embassy and other U.S. establishments the same architectural motif is repeated — with variations as minor in social meaning as the differences between the Mercedes and the Mercuries that jostle aside pedicabs in the crowded streets. Together with a large number of Saigon friends who are doing well while we are thus doing good, we are under siege.

The defense of freedom in a lately colonial country takes on elements of a class war. I met a few of our lesser collaborators; also a former enemy:

> The district chief at An Phu was established, with servants, in a well-guarded headquarters; the exterior decor was barbed wire again, and a guard detachment of Regional Forces. A mandarin, proclaimed by the long nail of his little finger; a captain in the army, graduate of a French secondary school. His father was a businessman and a landowner who left an estate of some sixty hectares in Long Xuyen Province. He appearently is joint heir with his brothers, and maintains a home in the provincial seat. The estate, he said, is occupied by sixty tenant farmers. Officials at this level and above are appointed from Saigon.
>
> Mr. B. works for the Voice of America as a researcher and occasional broadcaster. Born in Saigon, his father was a clerk in a French company. Mr. B. was educated in a French college and then embarked on a life-long career of collaboration with foreigners. He worked before the war and through 1944 as a clerk for a French lawyer. In 1945 he was employed by Mitsui (Japanese). During the French Indochina War he worked for local newspapers and a French periodical. Now, for the Americans.
>
> Mr. L., a radio broadcaster for VOA for the past eight years, was born in Haiphong and came south after the peace of 1954 because he "could not live with the Communists." During the French-Indochina War he had deserted from the Viet Minh and gone over to the French Army, where he served as an interpreter. Mr. L. interviews VC defectors and refugees from VC areas for broadcast materials. He related some interesting cases: a VC regular who defected because he saw a comrade killed for reading a Government leaflet; a farmer who fled

from Long An Province because he saw his relative, a rich farmer, killed by the VC for refusing to pay taxes; a VC captain, "an intellectual," who defected because, as he told Mr. L., " 'The Communists only served one class!' "

"What class was that?" I asked.

"The poor," said Mr. L. — the captain was angry because "intellectuals" were not treated well.

I later discussed this conversation with an American employee of USIS. He warned me that there are Viet Cong everywhere in Saigon!

I, myself, interviewed only one VC defector, an instructor of anti-Communist revolutionary cadres at Khánh An (Chau Doc Province). He was from a Central Vietnamese middle peasant family. As a Viet Minh he had lied to the authorities about his background, saying he was of poor peasant origin. He was terrified by the North Vietnamese land reform of 1955–56, when middle peasants were axed. He said he decided then to get out as soon as he could. Infiltrated South in 1963, he immediately defected.

I asked all these people at the end of the interview if they would like to question me. They put it in different ways, but everyone expressed concern that the Americans might lose patience and withdraw.

Critics of the war point to the contradiction between our announced defense of "freedom" and the character of the South Vietnamese Government. The criticism does not go deep enough. It is not a question of what Government, but what ruling class, what *power* we are supporting — and creating — against "Communist aggression." It becomes in general a question of what type of society we offer as an alternative. A massive amount of American money is poured into Vietnam. Part of this money corrupts, breeding prostitutes and vendors of "feelthy pictures"; the larger share is simply corrupted and a Vietnamese elite becomes the latest beneficiary of American affluence. The colonial comprador outlives colonialism. He enters into symbiosis with the Cold War. Marshall Ky says the land speculators who drive up prices around the American development at Cam Ranh Bay will be punished. The black marketeers and other profiteers will be punished. But under what constraints does the Government of Vietnam operate? Large Chinese merchants have a major influence on the Government, a senior USOM (U.S. Operations Mission, the AID program) officer told me, an influence that increases in direct proportion to their wealth. He said too that the contracting business was the going swindle. The still uncontrolled black market is testimony to a large flow of U.S. dollars out of the country, for safe deposit in foreign banks and the import of prohibited luxury goods.

Meanwhile, back at the village —

The scene that day at An Phu was reminiscent of the colonial payday described by Aubrey Menon in *The Prevalence of Witches,* with overtones as degrading and cynical. Through the good offices of the local U.S. Special Forces Detachment, ten selected families of a hamlet several kilometers from the base were ceremoniously to receive food doles, and the children of the hamlet school to get new school kits (though there weren't enough of these to go around). The goods had come down through USOM. Everyone was waiting around when I arrived — it turned out they were waiting for me; it made the most propaganda of a limited supply. The American commanding officer and some non-coms were there, and the commanding officer of the Vietnamese Regional Forces with his bodyguards. A little hollow near the school made do as a ceremonial ground. We stood back on a rise above: it was not an American function; "we're only advisers here." The masters of ceremony were a VIS (Vietnamese Information Service) officer, a Vietnamese nutritionist and the hamlet chief. They were down in the hollow with a portable loudspeaker system shouting to the assembled forty people who were standing several feet from them. Ten heaps of food lay in two rows on the ground. The VIS officer spoke first. He made it clear to the people what the food meant: as one of the recipients told me later, now they would turn in any Viet Cong they saw. The nutritionist spoke briefly — too briefly, I thought, considering the exotic character of the foods. Then the hamlet chief proceeded to dole out the food heaps, calling each family by name and insisting the family representative — many were widows — come over and stand next to his or her food pile. Everyone was so conscious of us on the hill, especially the shy women being given food.

These families had been selected by the hamlet chief and a local committee. I don't doubt they were deserving — the man I talked to was a landless peasant, unrelated (he said) to the hamlet chief — it's just that they deserved better. The ten families had been selected from a community of two thousand people. According to the Sergeant in charge of it, this food program had begun about nine months ago. A settlement of two thousand people could expect to be visited with food packages about every two-three months, although this hamlet had been given food only once before, if that. And what was the benefit of years of American expenditure in Vietnam? Each family received 100 lbs. corn meal, 5 lbs. bulgur wheat, 5 lbs. maple syrup, 6-7 lbs. powdered milk and 1 gallon of cooking oil. The Vietnamese eat rice and prefer it — with corn only on occasion.

The motivation and dedication of American AID people is beyond question and not at issue. Many, I understand, work tirelessly under dangerous conditions to bring a modicum of betterment to the countryside. Likewise the small Special Forces Detachment I saw at An Phu was committed to a program of medical and economic aid for the people — the Peace Corps of the War Corps. But these slim measures of good intention have to be put in the balance against the huge, unplanned subsidization of decadence in the cities to determine a final reading on the American presence. It is not simply that much more goes to bad

causes than to good. Hijacked American dollars in the cities capitalize
a whole social system, and one in which just this unequal distribution of
wealth is proper, a constituted condition. The compradors of Saigon express nothing of the Delta and the Mountains and feel nothing of them;
economically and ideologically they are counterposed to the people and
the resources of the country. The fate of the people, therefore, is not
mitigated by small aid in the countryside; it is sealed by big robbery in
the city.

Saigon, one cynical American said to me, is full of Kennedy idealists
who have discovered the facts of life. I thought it a good *mot* as far as
it went, but incomplete. He might have added that crossing Kennedy
idealism with the facts of life produces a curious political hybrid: a
hard-headed surrealist. I spoke with several of the tribe, middle to
senior officers mainly, in their air-conditioned sanctuaries at the Embassy, USOM, USIS. I wanted to know how they related, morally at
least, to the Saigon cats growing fat on American aid whose interests
rather contrast with the dying people. I was reproached for my naïveté:
"Every Eastern country is full of graft and corruption; it's just like that
and always has been" [and therefore always will be?]. One or two said
that conditions were improving because the present Government included dynamic young leaders who took the people's well-being to heart.
The most general sentiment was that if the Government could somehow
be stabilized, the problem of "corruption" would somehow be solved. I
had come up against standard American innocence of society: "who is
the matter" — as if it were just personalities and not a political structure
of economic interest; that the accumulation of wealth is a mere question
of "graft" and "corruption" rather than an economic formation of
society, a matter of excess rather than a constituted relation to the national economy and the underlying population; that, despite the circumstances, a government could be established on some basis other than the
prevailing distribution of wealth and power, apart from its constraints,
and become more the executive committee of the people than of the
comprador.

The last is anyhow ruled out by the "advisory" role of American personnel (civilian as well as military) in Vietnam. In the decisive sense it
is an American War: it is Vietnam's tragedy to have been chosen the
battleground for America's stand against the forces of evil. Technically,
however, we are just "advisers." I had always thought this was put out
for international and home consumption, to make the American intervention palatable for whoever might be inclined to swallow it. But I
misunderstood. The "advisory" capacity is taken very seriously by Americans within the country, especially by civilian officials, and it has internal functions much more meaningful than the international propaganda
effect. At one level, it is a concession to Vietnamese national feeling; and

Americans have a complementary need to believe and practice it. As a denial of any colonial status or intentions, it provides for Americans an acceptable meaning of their existence in the country. Beyond that, it serves as a convenient institutional means of personal dissociation from the sufferings of Vietnam, sufferings largely inflicted by the American presence—which is one's own presence. To be an adviser is to be involved yet free of the place, to indulge a sense of duty yet disdain responsibility; so it becomes a prefabricated barrier erected wherever and whenever the ugliness intrudes into consciousness, a denial that one is implicated by what may be going on. It is a moral anesthetic. (And I venture to say that the necessity for moral anesthesia is one reason there are so many versions of truth, why it is so difficult to determine just what is going on in Vietnam.

At the institutional level, which is perhaps the critical level, the function of the "advisory" role must be judged from its effects. The effect at every order of organization from hamlet to nation is to interpose obstacles to American direction of Vietnamese affairs, and so give free play to indigenous forces and interests — especially self-interests. Thus even as America generates powerful economic and political force in Vietnam, it turns around to deny itself the leverage. The free floating resources are appropriated instead by local collaborators for construction of their own version of Vietnamese society. We give them the advice to do good and the power to do as they please. We say we are "helping the Vietnamese to help themselves," and that's exactly what they're doing — helping themselves.

The "advisory" capacity is a new chapter in the relations between the West and the underdeveloped world. It is a Cold War epilogue of nineteenth-century colonialism. For all our anti-colonial protestations we perpetuate a colonial condition in the country.

A serious argument against American withdrawal is the bloodbath that would ensue in South Vietnam when the NLF gains control. But against this one might consider the bloodbath without foreseeable end going on now, and the ruling class of South Vietnam to whose tender mercies we would confine the peasant. The escalation of war may be narrowing the alternatives for the people to an end with misery or a misery without end.

Refugees are streaming *en masse* into Government camps — where they live, newspapers say, in unspeakable conditions. Many Americans I met in Vietnam are convinced the Viet Cong have been lately violating their own principles, stepping up economic pressure and terror in the countryside, for their very success has bred control and logistic problems. Washington officials have said that VC terror is the simple explanation. I asked one of the Vietnamese who interviews refugees for

Voice of America — principally, however, on agricultural matters — why, in his opinion, the peasants come over to the Government. His prompt answer was the "bombing"; the people, he said, want security for their lives and peace for their work. An American VOA employee present at the interview insisted I get the meaning of "bombing" straight. On my request for elucidation the Vietnamese said "bombing and fighting," the fire from both sides. Then he went on to relate that provincial officials who have accompanied him in talks with peasants have several times "asked" him to erase complaints about "bombing" from the tapes. The refugees are supposed to say they have fled from VC terror to a happy life under the Government, he said. The provincial officials indicated that the "bombing" need not be broadcast. (Charles Mohr writes in *The New York Times* of September 5: "Already more than 5 percent of the population has fled into refugee camps. Although it is popular among Washington officials to say that the refugees are fleeing from Vietcong terrorism, some officials on the scene are quite willing to concede or even to volunteer that the majority are fleeing from the insecurity of the countryside and that air strikes are the largest single cause of that insecurity.")

I had a number of experiences of this kind, times when I heard a Vietnamese or an American in the presence of another American of official position report something compromising to American ideals, policy or the Washington line on Vietnam. The incident must be repeated often, as a circumstance of the American presence in Vietnam. On the occasions I could observe it, I was interested in the reaction of the American who was thus suddenly confronted with damning information on which he would have to make some reckoning — like the American VOA employee confronted with censorship. If not exactly a moment of truth, the American's response gives subtle intelligence of the critical battle of this war: of how much of America, of what America has meant to us, can be consumed in Vietnam. The Americans I have seen in this predicament were good men and intelligent. But they blanked out, every one of them. Intellectually they refused to come to terms with it. Morally, they passed. Some said nothing. Some spoke of Viet Cong crimes, as if to justify our own or our South Vietnamese agents'. Some glossed over the reported incident as exceptional, as not happening most of the time. And some shrugged, referred to the feudal-oriental character of the country, then asked what one could do since "we're only advisers here." It is, I repeat, an important point. If we are whored by our commitment, if we must lose ourselves in Vietnam, we lose the war — whatever the military outcome.

The contradictions of Vietnam may thus reflect themselves in the everyday behavior of Americans. Among military personnel, of course, such translations of big structural events into terms of ordinary existence will take other forms. Still the American military adviser who turns his back on the torture of Viet Cong prisoners by South Vietnamese soldiers is the khaki counterpart of the VOA civilian who closes his mind to compromising information. But these seem advanced stages of moral decay, people now dangerously close to a final plunge into brutalization. Unless one is so disposed in advance, it may take a certain initial disillusionment with Vietnam to reach this point, a disillusionment that undermines local meanings of the war, leaving one either with the Cold War conviction that it is necessary to stop this Chinese-inspired aggression, Vietnam notwithstanding, or else without any conviction at all. I had a glimpse of this earlier phase among American combat troops at Bien Hoa, most of whom were comparatively new arrivals and had seen comparatively limited action. It was enough exposure: Vietnam was incubating in them. Yet, one or two resisted the infection.

> They were eight Army enlisted men — at least some were draftees — with whom their commanding officer (knowing I was "a professor against the war") had generously given me ninety minutes' privacy. And there was also a ninth: an officer of junior rank who came up to the jeep around which we stood, listened to what we said, and asked then if he could have a word with me because there were a few things I ought to "get straight."
>
> Seven of the men did not at all question their purpose in Vietnam. We had to "stop the Communists from taking over here," or else "they'd go on to Hawaii." At the same time, several had experienced the recalcitrance of Vietnam, its disengagement from what was supposed to be its own life and death struggle, and they were disturbed by it. A Negro private brought it up — by his own compulsion, for the discussion was open just then — and others seemed to agree. He didn't see "the people here" getting with the war. They hold bicycle races in the village while he is on a field problem. He wondered angrily why they did nothing while we fought "their war," fought to make them "free from Communism." As for the South Vietnamese soldiers (and this is I think a very common complaint), they aren't worth a damn: poorly trained and undisciplined, they talk and smoke on patrol and cannot work as a unit.
>
> Every war and every army has its complaints. But Vietnam could foster a new type of American military dissenter, an anti-ideologist, a man whose life has been interrupted when it did not seem threatened and yet, come upon the distant scene of emergency, sees there a people not so much involved in a fight for their lives against Communist expansion as a flight from their deaths — perhaps at American hands. I asked these men what they thought of the statement of Lt. ———, who had refused assignment to a Special Forces outpost and expressed the sentiment that the war "wasn't worth a single American life." All disagreed — except one. To that moment silent, he spoke now unabash-

edly: "All the people and all the ground in Vietnam are not worth a single American life." He believed this, he explained, because he has a high regard for human life, American and Vietnamese; and many people are being needlessly killed because of the ideological views of a few Americans, the President and those around him. They say we are here to defend South Vietnam against Communist aggression, which is a threat to ourselves, but for himself he does not believe it. The commitment to Vietnam is all out of proportion to the importance of Vietnam. He waxed Lippmannesque: "If we start here, we'll soon be all over the world doing the same thing. It's not worth it to America." He was a soldier in a Light Brigade: "The people here have been fighting guerrilla war for twenty years; I don't know anything about that kind of warfare." I asked him which he would choose if it came to a question of American involvement or NLF control. He would pull out — "because I'm selfish — I don't think the Communist control of Vietnam will concern me in my lifetime."

The men left and I remained with the young officer who wanted me to get matters straight. He was not new to the war but almost through with it, twenty-nine days to go, and now there were several things he had to say about it. He spoke from notes he had just made, and I repeat his points here. I am obliged to insist that I do not present his views as facts of war, as necessarily true in specific content. But they are unequivocal truth of another kind — they are an American experience of Vietnam:

1. The officer had it from "an informed source in a position to know" that Arvin desertion rates jump from 25 to 40 percent whenever American troops came into an area. He was seriously concerned. It meant to him that Arvin has no inclination to fight; that, neither brave nor determined, they "would rather have us do the work for them."

2. He has heard on good authority — "though it is not confirmed and must be" — that on occasion Arvin units fire upon U.S. units in battle, in order to make the situation look worse and encourage a greater U.S. involvement. "I want to know," he said, "if this is reported to the American people, and if it is reported to the President, and if not, why not? And if it is, what are we going to do about it? Or does it just stay in MAC-V [Military Assistance Command, Vietnam]?" In his opinion such actions as these would have the effect, desired by Vietnamese, of relieving their military participation and increasing direct aid to the local economy through military and other assistance — aid that would find its way to local vested interests.

3. When we were preparing to build up a landing base in [a certain coastal] area, why did we have to negotiate with private landowners for space at so many piastres per acre? This is war; we are defending them. He is sure we didn't pay rent to the French in World War II for the privilege of fighting for French freedom. Nor was this compensation for hardships caused to civilians. Leasing land, he said, is distinguishable from compensations. [Note that the officer did mention a

particular area, but I am unable to pinpoint his transliteration of the
Vietnamese. *The New York Times* reported what seems to be an
analogous incident on September 15, 1965: the U.S. "acquired" thirty
square miles near Ankhe from the Vietnamese Government for the
newly arrived First Cavalry Division.]

4. I had talked with the others about civilian casualties. In that connection, he said, "A lot of officers if given the opportunity would bomb
the shit out of all the villages around here. A great many have the urge
and the mentality." He had "so many times heard it said, 'let's drop the
load on that village.'" He has not seen it yet, however, and thinks it
probably never will happen because the brigade commander wouldn't
have it. But it is a definite streak in an interesting number of officers
— "and," he added, "just what the VC would want."

5. He seemed to know my own position, and since I had talked with
the other men about the criticism of the war in the States, he wanted
to insist that "the criticism of the war is extremely healthy. It concerns
me that many military men are critical of the critics and want to deny
them the constitutional right to dissent." He is "upset" by the career
officers who speak only of "beatniks," and whose response is "those
guys ought to be brought out here and sent on patrol to get shot!" The
career officers fear criticism because they are put in jeopardy by it. "If
we were less militant, they would lose their jobs and have to return to
civilian life, where they are not fit for anything." He wondered, in this
regard, to what extent the situation in Vietnam is accurately reported
insofar as the facts are purveyed through the military.

As we walked slowly together toward the commanding officer's tent,
he said I could draw my own conclusions from all this. I responded
with the obvious: "You mean to say that the war is being escalated
because of the South Vietnamese desire to be relieved and make a fast
buck, complemented by the mentality of the American military?" He
made no objection. In parting he remarked that if Vietnam wants
peace, and if peace means VC control, he for one is willing to accept
it. If the VC are elected in a free election, he said in response to my
question, he must go along with it — "for God's sake, it's the only
honorable thing to do." And he added then: "If they want peace at any
price, not be shot at, the freedom to raise a few crops; let them have it.
These are common wants of everyone, aren't they?"

## Losing the Hearts and Minds of Americans in Vietnam

"China" is indispensable to the existence of Americans in Vietnam.

The fixation has its own internal, Vietnamese dialectic. But it begins
from external conditions, from the Washington Cold War policy and its
confrontations with world events. An outsider can attempt only a superficial and partial analysis of the Washington line and very little on its
fundamental causes. Clearly it proceeds from an injunction of sacred
ancestral ideology, the Dulles demonology, which defined the struggle

against the forces of evil. The evil is the "International Communist Conspiracy," known also in its emanation of "Aggressive Communism" and appearing in Vietnam as "Chinese Expansionism." America, medicine man to the world, is impelled to Vietnam to exorcise the evil spirits. But it was not a simple process of divination that led to this move. The policy for Vietnam seems to have developed from the intersection of the demonology with at least two important events, the Cuban missile crisis and the *détente* with Russia, which have impressed themselves firmly and in certain ways on political consciousness. The missile crisis is understood to have spiked Russia's guns for the foreseeable future. The *détente* is taken in evidence that when a Communist revolution generates an economic stake in the world, and when the revolutionary generation with its heady ideas of world uprising dies off, a Communist power ceases to be aggressive and instead evolves an interest in the status quo. Transferred to China, these understandings dictate a policy of buying time for the revolution — that economic development and generational replacement might exhaust its fervor — and, in the meantime, during all that period in which it is dangerous, cordoning the revolution by a strong military stand and preventing its export. Vietnam is the Asian analogue of the missile crisis; therefore, a critical tactic. The "domino theory," moreover, becomes unsuppressible. Its function is to explain the American action, and as the only reasonable explanation of *that fact* it becomes immune to contradiction by any other fact of life in Southeast Asia.

Such seems to be the hard-headed surrealism. In Vietnam, however, the strategy does not present even so rational an appearance. It has to be discussed in more primitive terms. For one thing, the key decision-makers are not there; one sees only partial intimations of the grand design among the few who can seriously reflect on it, and among Americans in general only a vulgar *idée fixe* about the Red Menace. Besides, the strategy here is refracted through the ugly circumstances of Vietnam, which reshape it into something of an obsession: stopping the Chinese threat is the kind of end that will sanction adoption of any means — even, as I shall tell, Chinese means. We are losing the hearts and minds of Americans in Vietnam. Joining battle with the evil spirits by ritual techniques of blood-letting, we get covered all over with blood ourselves and become ourselves dark forces in the land. It is a classic mythical denouement. Between the medicine man and the spirit of disease there is a close relation to begin with: a set of shared assumptions about the nature of illness, its infliction, and its cure. And as they struggle for supremacy over the inert body, only shaman and spirit can seem real to each other. The body becomes immaterial, something merely that each attempts to possess and manipulate to defeat the other. The horrifying quality is that the evil spirit is a construction of the medicine man, and though his operation prove a brilliant success the patient may die from it. In the end the medicine man is indistinguishable from an evil spirit.

Americans in Vietnam hold it as a basic expression of purpose that there we oppose Chinese Communist expansion. I encountered it among men of fighting ranks and among their officers, among staff members of U.S. civilian agencies and among their senior officials. It is the expert opinion of those we employ as political experts. (Vietnamese collaborators, I found, are apt to put it most directly, almost as if the NLF was Chinese.) The confrontation with China has the character of an unquestionable premise of our involvement. Politically aware Americans find it possible to believe it the higher wisdom even though they are unable to trace the chain of NLF command beyond Hanoi. Everyone knows that Communist China is expansionist. Everyone knows too that we are faced in Vietnam with Communist subversion, which if not contained here will have to be faced again, closer to home. That we are fighting China follows with the force of a categorical syllogism.

Perhaps it is the higher wisdom; still, it gives Vietnam a certain air of insanity. Paranoids are after us. The death of Vietnamese is unrelated to their lives. Do we mean to indicate by these deaths that the Chinese must stop threatening us? Then we are involved in killing people to show other people that they should stop threatening us. Or do we mean to show the Chinese they must stop threatening the Vietnamese? Then we are killing people to show other people that they should stop threatening the people we are killing. The "Chinese Threat" obscures in advance the nature of the enemy. We cannot know who he is, or what he wants. So we destroy in advance the possibility of deciding if he is really our enemy. The counterpart on the political level is the total failure of American policy to support, or even to recognize, nationalism and its human aspirations. Not recognizing it, we succeed in destroying it. Opposing it, we drive it into self-defeating dependence upon major Communist powers — and thus in the end obtain the confrontation we sought from the beginning. In my experience, nationalism is simply not discussed by Americans in Saigon. Vietnamese nationalism is a dead issue, buried and covered over by Communist aggression.

But there is a reason for the madness. Without it one could go insane. Even if "the threat of Chinese expansion" did not exist in Washington it would be necessary to invent it in Vietnam. The objective conditions make it impossible to sustain any other image of the American presence. The lack of freedom mocks our "defense of freedom." The military dictatorship mocks our "defense of democracy." The indifference of the people mocks their "brave struggle against subversion." The thought that these people have been suffering war for twenty-five years must be repressed. And shall we admit our responsibility for the misery of Vietnam? How shall we face the innocent victims of our weapons?

Conscience must be destroyed: it has to end at the barrel of the gun; it cannot extend to the bullet. So all peripheral rationales fade into the background. It becomes a war of transcendent purpose, and in such a war all efforts on the side of Good are virtuous, and all deaths unfortunate necessity. The end justifies the means.

I stood one morning outside the Psychological Warfare office at III Corps Headquarters, Bien Hoa. Clearly I was an alien: a civilian and an academic dissenter. The bare courtesy of the reception I had just had inside did not trouble to conceal it. Now a young officer came out of the building. With a curious politeness he handed me a newspaper, saying that "a compatriot" of his (but not of mine?) wanted to present it to me, and I should especially consider the inside spread of pictures on pages 4 and 5. The paper was the *Observer,* a weekly published for U.S. forces in Vietnam. The officer was a little surprised when I asked if he could spare any other issues. He did not understand my motives, that I wanted to know what the *Observer* seeks to teach those who read it. But that general point is not important. The important point is a specific one, dictated by the man who anonymously gave me a present: the inside two pages of the July 3 edition. It meant something critical to him, and he wanted me to be convinced by it.

The two-page banner read: " 'A New Glorious Exploit,' Broadcasts Communist Radio." Underneath were seven bloodsoaked pictures of the My Canh restaurant bombing in Saigon of June 25. Most of the photographs, such as the one captioned "Evacuating Innocent Child," showed Americans coming to the aid of shocked and bleeding victims, many of them Vietnamese.

Should we share our "compatriot's" understanding of the moral? He might indulge himself in the hate of evil killers at the expense of indifference to human pain and death. But no judgment of these pictures should be made in the absence of memory. The American soldiers who see the *Observer* have already seen certain other pictures. They have looked upon the slaughter of villages, contemplated the civilian victims of American bombs and shells — perhaps not just in photographs. If they are then outraged at the My Canh, it is a cynical lie. They distinguish between "good" and "bad" innocent victims. Human agony has no meaning; the meaning is external, a judgment of those who inflict, not those who suffer. The outrage at suffering is indifference to suffering. The soldier outraged at this deception of Vietnamese misery has been prepared to commit it.

Advanced anti-Communism trades places with the enemy. It becomes opposite-Communism, and "opposites" are things alike in every respect save one. The final stages of American dissolution in Vietnam will be marked by imitation of the enemy's techniques. I have heard it foreshadowed in the talk of Saigon officialdom: *discipline,* a senior American civilian officer told me, is what the South Vietnamese Government needs; *power,* he said, is the only thing the Chinese can understand; *history,* he said, will prove us right. In a remote provincial outpost I found two Americans who had appropriated as their own draconic Chinese methods of interrogation and indoctrination ("motivation" is the American newspeak). The forced destruction of people's beliefs is no longer properly described as something "they" do. Torturously exacted confession and conversion are no longer things we fight against. These are now part of our own arsenal, weapons of our own struggle.

The two Americans were leaders of a "motivation" team working among Vietnamese Popular Forces. The team included four Vietnamese instructor-cadres, two of these ex-Viet Cong. The dominant of the two Americans was a field representative of a civilian agency; he was assisted by a Special Forces officer. Both were highly qualified, competent in Vietnamese language and custom, and dedicated to Vietnam and their vision of its future. Their program was anti-Communist revolution; they were training Popular Forces as revolutionary cadres. The texts were classic Communist handbooks on revolutionary warfare, books these Americans studied and clearly admired; it does not go too far to say they were disciples, or at least revisionist disciples, of Mao Tse-tung, Ho Chi-minh and Che Guevara. The revolutionary "techniques" were copied in fine detail. (I was given a pledge card that the Americans issued to Vietnamese trainees; it listed "The Four Principles and Eight Rules" of cadre behavior, apparently an emendation of "The Three Rules and the Eight Remarks" that Mao developed for partisan warfare against the Japanese.) The Americans insisted, however, on one departure from Communist attitudes: alongside self-criticism they encourage the troops to question their instructors and formulate their own views. The indoctrination team moves from outpost to outpost, living in with the troops while "motivating" them.

I lived in with them for a night and a good part of a day. They briefed me and allowed me to see the work for myself. But it is not of this guerrilla program that I write. It is of a discussion I had with the Americans about torture and the transformation of VC prisoners to anti-Communism. The two Americans allowed they had some experience with it, and some ideas of how it is properly done. I recorded most of that discussion and will excerpt parts of it verbatim. But first allow me to develop the context.

The interrogation methods the Americans described are copied from those used most effectively by the Chinese, as they themselves explained. (Of course, there are precedents — for example, the Inquisition.) The treatment seems a compressed and abbreviated version of the procedures used on American P.O.W.'s during the Korean War. The interrogator has at most four or five days before he must send the prisoner on. Physical torture is precluded. A special type of "mental

torture" (their term) is instead inflicted. But it aims not merely at elicit-
ing military information. The prisoner's disclosures are at the same time
a betrayal of his cause and a confession of his errors, a renunciation of
belief. The betrayal is the first phase of a "cure" of Communism — the
American civilian kept likening the process to the rehabilitation of alcoholics. If the technique really is effective, and the Americans claim
it is, I think it must be because of some rather special qualities of revolutionary warfare and warriors. It has to be understood that a VC prisoner comes in with certain comprehensions and expectations that are
deeply entwined with his revolutionary ("Communist") commitment. A
guerrilla movement depends decisively on secrecy. Its members are visible daily to the enemy but must be unknown to him; they maintain a
hinterland conspiracy of silence; a single traitor wrecks the organization
of a whole village, perhaps a district. The guerrilla thus understands
that secrecy is a first principle of the revolution. But by the same token,
intelligence becomes a first principle of the counterrevolution. The
prisoner, therefore, expects to be tortured for information and ultimately killed if he remains steadfast. He meets his interrogators prepared to resist the worse: it is a test of his revolutionary soul.

But by a carefully calculated approach, the interrogator can from the
beginning disappoint the prisoner's expectations, disarm and confuse
him. Instead of torture the guerrilla finds himself in the company of
an "enemy" who nevertheless treats him with respect, even befriends
him, feeds him, makes him comfortable — which is to say, profoundly
uncomfortable. The relation the interrogator seeks to effect is one between them as against the world. For even as he binds the prisoner's
wounds, he systematically invokes the threat of "the others" — that
there are these others (Arvin regulars) around who want at the prisoner
and have "more basic ideas" of how to interrogate him. (The Chinese
in Korea invoked the North Koreans in the same way when dealing with
American P.O.W.'s.) The interrogator is protecting the prisoner, shield-
ing him against the "big, ugly outside world." Thus the bond between
prisoner and interrogator is forged, the captive caught in a deepening
dependence upon his captor. At some point the latter feels he might
press for reciprocity. The guerrilla yields some minor information. Yet
emotionally it is not slight: it is a fundamental betrayal of himself, his
comrades, and his cause. Still, he is told the information is nothing, not
enough, that he will have to do better or the others will move in on
him. The trap has been closed. The interrogator is now the only one in
the world with whom the prisoner has anything in common. Behind are
the people he has sold out, ahead those who would kill him — and only
the interrogator can help him. The revolutionary is likely to break completely. It is a moment of extreme anguish — "the lowest point in his
life in terms of human meaning and existence" (the American civilian

said). Yet again, in a disorganized and probably unintentional parody of Chinese techniques, the prisoner learns his confession is still not good enough: he cannot unite with his captors; he must have further "processing" at a rehabilitation center. So I understand the procedure.

Something must be said as well of those who described it to me. First — and it is a thing seriously to consider — these two Americans are not strangers, not people who have been metamorphosed by some satanic forces to a point beyond our understanding or recognition. Met on a college campus or in a business office, they would not attract unusual attention. Their attitudes toward Vietnam are indeed more scholarly than demonic. They want to involve themselves in the country. They profess with sincerity their respect for the people — so much that they actively wish them a better fate. For the first several hours of my visit, we had only sparred in a rather formal way. It was not until they saw me sit cross-legged on the floor of a Vietnamese house, and with them eat Vietnamese food with Vietnamese people, that they, these two Americans, accepted *me*. They did not give the impression of evil. On the contrary, they presented the appearance of good.

And now consider this interview, what they said and what they revealed of themselves.

The main protagonist — identified here as "Mr. X" — describes himself as an "agnostic atheist," but clearly he believes in the devil if not in God. In fact, his is a holy work: to exorcise the Communist devils possessing Viet Cong. He undertakes the prisoner's "conversion" for the prisoner's own good: he is "helping" the man, saving him. I asked, "How do you offset the damage to yourself?" "Your belief," he answers.

Why do these Americans so intensely need to crack down the prisoner, to convince him he is wrong, they right? Is it because they need to convince themselves? The officer ("Captain Y") says that if you don't try to break the prisoner, you're admitting he's right. And "Mr. X" makes a curious slip: he speaks of an "emotional *inter*dependence" between the prisoner and the interrogator, where he means to discuss the dependence of the prisoner upon the interrogator. I sense these men are identified with the prisoner, that they have themselves under the knife, that the prisoner's conversion will validate their own integrity. And so inevitably they fall into a hopeless contradiction. For if their own righteousness is at test in the prisoner's response, then they need too to fail. The prisoner's successful resistance is the interrogators' greatest satisfaction: his strength proves their strength, his will their will, his conviction their conviction. There is no question of Mr. X's admiration of the prisoner who will not be broken. "Tremendous," he says, "just tremendous." Then he lies when I ask if he admires this man. And at the end he lies the ultimate lie of Americans in Vietnam. Notwithstanding he had just described a specific prisoner who would not yield, he denies he was ever involved in such an interrogation: "because we're advisers — in every sense."

Here are excerpts from the tape. (A heavy "dot" in the transcript indicates that a portion of the interview is skipped over; three dots, that a portion of an answer is elided; and a word in parenthesis followed by a question mark indicates an imperfect rendering on the tape and my guess of the word involved.)

MR. X: At this time [the prisoner] kind of feels an emotional dependence upon you because for two days you've been protecting him from the big outside ugly world that he doesn't understand: feeding him good chow, talking with him, calling him a (can-bo?) of the NLF, not the derogatory term of Viet Cong . . . Then you indicate that this nice treatment that he's had so far [has] not been disinterested good treatment, that we expect his cooperation. We're cooperating with him in a sense; we expect cooperation from him. This again reintroduces the whole issue of the big ugly outside world. What's going to happen to him now? Well, he might tell you a couple of things, beginning with rather innocuous things. Well, you can imply that you knew that already, what you're really after are better things and this might rather (uncalm?) him. Then you might say, "Jeez, that scrape you got on your shoulder . . . it obviously needs attention; we'll have to give you some penicillin." And while you're giving him the penicillin, you're telling him that, "You know, there are these other types of people who just . . ."

•

MR. X: Actually again, this is the technique that Captain [Y] . . . and myself have been trying to promote in an advisory relationship. Again, it's a technique that's been used most effectively by the Chinese, in which you've pulled the man out of his familiar environment: he's dependent . . . upon you for his continual well-being. And even though the prisoner may (resist?), it's kind of an emotional interdependence that's created, and what you try and do is (use?) this emotional interdependence in such a way that he comes to the point where he *must* tell you what he knows.

SAHLINS: It's in effect brainwashing — is that the point of this?

MR. X: No, what it is, is breaking him down. But . . . once you've broken him down, it comes to the point where he wakes up in a sweat one morning and tells you, "All right." Then he tells you the names of the two people in his cell; or, he gives you the location of the camp that he just recently came from. Then you're through with him, in practical terms. You've got what you needed to continue operating. But at this point, if you really believe in anything yourself, what you've got to do is give him something to hope for before you send him back for further processing. Because you have just brought this individual to the *lowest point in his life* in terms of human meaning and existence. So at that point, that's when you've got to stress that, "Well now we're releasing you for further processing. But for you, what you've just told us is the beginning of a positive affirmation. We just can't process you right into our unit now; because you don't know what we stand for and what we're fighting for, but we hope that some day you will be joining us." See, we don't have time to get any brainwashing. The Chinese can do that because they have P.O.W.'s for months and months and months. If we get a guy, we've got him for two to five days, and then he's out of our hands. In that two to five days, we've got to get the information we need. But we will not get the information we need by physical torture. We've got to get it by an emotional and mental torture. And you can do that because that's what they're least adequately prepared for. It's what Americans are least adequately prepared for when they find themselves in the other side's hands.

&bull;

SAHLINS: What kind of control do you have over Arvin types of interrogation [i.e., physical torture]?

MR. X: Well, again, that's an advisory function. And what you're trying to do is — this is just a traditional, feudal Asian society; Mainland style — and what you're trying to do is change the course of warfare in Asia. To some extent this has been done: the Chinese People's Liberation Army; it's happened probably in the Japanese Army, the Japanese Self-Defense and Home Defense Armies. But until the end of World War II, we always thought of the Japanese Army as a real cruel, vindictive, bunch of cutthroats. Well it turned out in post-World War II analysis that the Bataan Death March was something that they handled to the best of their ability, given the available transport and the way that they would have handled their own prisoners. They just moved them, and they moved them as fast as they could. People who couldn't keep up the pace in some cases were helped and in some other cases — just according to the individual guard — were bashed and thrown aside. Vietnamese to our eyes seem rather cruel sometimes to prisoners, but they're not doing this with any ideological vengeance. They're doing that because that's just been the bent of warfare in Mainland Asia for a thousand years, and what we have got to try to do is sophisticate it, and tell them, "Look, that's just not the way." It's a slow process; we're attempting a reformation of a whole society.

SAHLINS: What practical is being done to discourage this kind of thing?

MR. X: Well, guidance on the spot —

CAPTAIN D (SAHLINS' ESCORT): It's up to the individual advisors —

268 ← THE WORLD AND THE UNITED STATES

MR. X: The individual advisor giving guidance on the spot.

CAPTAIN D: Sometimes it's successful, sometimes not —

CAPTAIN Y: In most cases, it's not.

SAHLINS: From what you say about mental torture, you wouldn't make any distinction in the morality of either kind [i.e., physical vs. mental torture]?

MR. X: Hell, no! I don't make any distinction in morality at all: torture is torture, and when you fuck around with a guy's mind and his whole basic *raison d'être,* you're *really* hurting him — especially when he's prepared mentally, spiritually, for the physical torture.

SAHLINS: Then the attempt to discourage Vietnamese water torture . . . is just because the other type [mental torture] doesn't offend American sensibilities as much?

MR. X: No, it's not because of that. Because we don't concern ourselves here with American sensibilities. We concern ourselves with what will work.

CAPTAIN Y: It's relatively ineffective.

MR. X: It's ineffective. It may sound hard-boiled to say that we don't concern ourselves with American sensibilities — but we don't. We're concerning ourselves with Vietnamese sensibilities.

SAHLINS: What about the sensibilities of the Americans who are involved . . . the person who's torturing?

MR. X: To most of the Americans, to most of the simple-minded Americans who get involved in Vietnam — that's all the *boobus Americanus* that H. L. Mencken spoke about — undoubtedly they think that the mental and emotional torture we're talking about is the least objectionable, because they've never really paused to seriously reflect about it themselves; or perhaps they did not go through the experience of being a P.O.W. in the Korean conflict themselves. And they can probably tell you, "Oh, Jesus, I'd try and stop that physical torture, because I know it's just wrong" — you know. But we think that we're looking into it a little more deeply, and we see that the mental and spiritual torture that we bring a man through to the point where he voluntarily gives you the information is pretty rough stuff to get involved in too. But it works.

SAHLINS: How do you offset the damage to yourself?

MR. X: Your belief. Your belief: you have to sincerely believe that in the long run you're helping this man. It's like an AA cure. If you're just breaking the guy down for the sake of getting a poor helpless alcoholic who's hipped on NLF propaganda to admit that he was wrong and give you the information, then you're going to send him out in the street a crushed derelict, then there's something wrong with you. But you have to really believe, as we do — although we get discouraged sometimes by our [Vietnamese] counterparts — you have to really believe that you're *helping* this guy to something better.

SAHLINS: Conversion from Communism is involved in the torture.

MR. X: Conversion from anything to anything involves a certain degree of self-torture. We just accelerated the process because we need that fucking information.

SAHLINS: This is better for him?

MR. X: He's alive, and you can still help him . . .

•

MR. X: Most Americans, unfortunately, don't bother to think deeply about the stuff they get involved in and they make superficial judgments: "Well, it's wrong to torture this guy physically because we're all part of the same (background?)" —

CAPTAIN Y: If you ask you'll get probably 80 percent of the people [U.S. military] will say, "Well, I didn't get involved in it. When they capture them, when they capture the Vietnamese Communists, I just turn my back and go and have a cigarette."

MR. X: They take a drink from their canteen and light up a cigarette. And that's discouraging . . . I'd rather get — not get involved in it, not in the actual physical torture myself — but I'd rather be right there and see it done, and then laugh like a horse when it doesn't work and they don't get the information. And then in the long run you're affecting the situation when you just laugh at this guy and say: "Look, you think he's gonna break? So you cut up his stomach a little bit and his insides fell out . . . He got the last laugh on you, because he didn't talk a bit." And maybe it'll make the guy think, you know, and ten times later, after ten more people have faded out because he physically tortured them, maybe he'll say: "Okay, wise American advisor, what would you do?" . . . We have a moral responsibility, it seems to me, once we've stepped into this country to involve ourselves in the complete fabric of the country, and to understand it, and then try and help the Vietnamese to look at some different alternatives . . . We should be acting as a catalyst, as a thinking catalyst in Vietnam. But you cannot be a catalyst unless you know the entire fabric of the thing. And lighting up a cigarette when they bring a prisoner in for questioning is, well, that's an immoral —

CAPTAIN Y: It's just like saying, "It doesn't happen."

MR. X: That's just about the height of immorality, I think. To think that you can just absolve yourself. That's saying that every man *is* an island; or at least when it is comfortable, when it's comfortable for me to be an island unto myself, then I am; and the bell's tolling for that poor fucker under the knife, not me. That's real bad. And again, it's a simple-minded approach.

●

[Mr. X had mentioned that one of the rules imparted to the cadres in training was "be kind to prisoners." I asked if that wasn't a rule he disobeyed.]

MR. X: Well, if the final result of it is — it's a cruel process — but the result of bringing him closer to you, of conversion — it's a tortuous process of conversion — but the result is a kind one . . . If you believe in your program, this is what you do . . .

SAHLINS: Do you believe in breaking people down so they agree with your program? And breaking them down justifies the end?

MR. X: No . . . That's why we would not take a guy who's been broken directly into our unit at this time . . .

SAHLINS: Either you will rehabilitate him by converting him to your belief or you're going to leave him a mental wreck . . . Can your ends be so God-given as to give you this right among humanity to do this?

MR. X: I don't know. I don't really believe anybody's hands are God-given. I'm an agnostic atheist.

SAHLINS: No, your ends. I'm not asking you for religious beliefs. What I'm asking is, do you believe you have the right to impose by this method: —

MR. X: I think I've got the right to try. Nobody's got the right to succeed — guaranteed. But everybody's got the right to promote and proselytize what they believe.

●

CAPTAIN Y: If we do not break this guy, if we do not attempt to change his ideas then in essence what have we done? We've said that basically he's right!

SAHLINS: No, that isn't so. One agrees to disagree as a matter of principle in a democratic system.

MR. X: Oh wait, this is [where] we begin . . . I've had some tremendous conversations with these guys, and we begin by agreeing to disagree. But you can soon get this guy so flustered and so shaken up that before he knows it, he's agreeing with you — because his assumptions to begin with were rather vulnerable.

SAHLINS: But that isn't the issue here. The issue here is whether you will impose your will by this technique, which is —

MR. X: We don't know what our will is yet.

SAHLINS: You will impose your ideas by this technique —

MR. X: What ideas?

●

SAHLINS: . . . I asked the question, how do you justify the effect upon yourself of acting in this way? And you said you're doing the guy a service. Now, I'm asking you, do you believe you have the right to impose your will on somebody; impose what you believe —

MR. X: We are not imposing our will. We are not imposing will. Even after you've broken him and gotten the information, he's still a free agent.

•

MR. X: Not impose will — if he fails to accept . . . an alternative. And not *our* alternative; there are a number of alternatives. Because in essence that's what we're trying to show him.

•

SAHLINS: You don't accept that [i.e., that there is only one way of doing things and nobody can dispute it], but you accept the other premise that there are many ways . . . So as a matter of fact by this process you either transform him from that belief into one of a range of acceptable beliefs, or you will leave him a mental wreck —

MR. X: But we don't leave him this way. We have brought him to a point where he realizes that the faith he placed in his previous system was essentially not powerful. He has volunteered the information. At this point he's got to find a new way. He's got to have a way out of his dilemma, and the people at the training centers should be skillful enough to point out to him a number of alternatives.

SAHLINS: We come back to the question: whether you have the right — by these techniques, which are external to him — to deny him [the] belief that he came in with in his hand and only accept a set of alternatives which you propose?

•

MR. X: Listen, I've met guys . . . We had a guy in Phu Yen Province in the summer of '63 who was the Propaganda Director for the NLF in that province; and boy, we just worked ourselves literally ragged in four days trying to bring that guy to the point where he'd tell us a few things, and he was tremendous — just tremendous. Didn't tell us a thing.

SAHLINS: You admire this guy?

MR. X: Tremendous — tremendous.

SAHLINS: So you admire more a person who will not acquiesce to the thing that you say is right than one who does?

MR. X: No, not true. I didn't say that at all. I admire a guy who will tortuously admit — if he really believes — that, "Oh Jesus, I never thought about that before. Those guys [NLF] they told me something else; and you're really doing something else." A guy like that who will examine his previously arrived conclusions and change his mind, I admire that —

SAHLINS: That's very admirable, but it doesn't describe the process you went through, which was to leave him in a situation where either he takes this set of alternatives which you give him, or he is a mental wreck.

MR. X: Remember, this was an act of *affirmation* on his part, where he yields the information voluntarily. But it's only a beginning; it's only a beginning; and it's not fair to leave him at the point where he's just made the beginning.

•

MR. X: It's just like an alcoholic. An alcoholic can attend the meetings and he can see everybody else get embarrassed; and if he doesn't want to join them he can just back out again. But once a guy begins to join this little society of alcoholics —

CAPTAIN Y: These cadres we have [as instructors] — these ex-VC, ex-NLF, ex-Viet Minh — they all in some way or another gave up something in their own mind when they turned, came to the Government.

•

MR. X: . . . what we're trying to show these guys when we're interrogating them, through this tortuous process, is that you're not better [off] under the NLF. "Your whole series of assumptions has got to be reexamined here, and we're here to help you reexamine them. And Jesus, there's some guys here have got some more basic ideas of how they'd like to examine you, but we're just holding these guys off . . . and we'll take good care of you." That's the kind of a dirty trick — [but] when you've only got four days . . .

SAHLINS: Have you done this with Viet Cong?

MR. X: We don't do anything because we're advisers — in every sense.

1966

# THE COLONIAL HERITAGE IN VIETNAM
## JOSEPH BUTTINGER

The heritage of colonialism in Vietnam is Communism. The strength of
the Communist Party of Vietnam is a unique phenomenon in the developing world. Vietnam was the only country where a Communist-led
government was established at the end of World War II without the kind
of outside help the Red Army gave to the Communist parties of Eastern
Europe.

From this follows a still unrecognized and therefore startling truth:
*The loss of Vietnam to Communism occurred in 1945.* All the fighting
that has been going on there for the last twenty years has aimed at reversing this historical fact.

There is no evidence at all for an innate disposition of the Vietnamese people to favor Communist ideas. Communist strength is the
result of historical conditions — economic, social, and political conditions peculiar to Vietnam and created by the colonial regime.

Colonial Vietnam had only a small industrial labor force. The social
basis of Communist strength was the rural masses constituting 85 percent of the population. They were not land-owning peasants interested
in maintaining their status and therefore politically conservative. By
creating, particularly in South Vietnam, a system of feudal landholdings,

the colonial regime had gradually destroyed the traditional class of land-owning peasants. Colonialism transformed the rural masses into agricultural laborers, landless peasants working as tenants for landlords, and poor peasants without sufficient land. All were ruthlessly exploited by the landlords, the moneylenders, and the taxation policy of the colonial regime. Land rents robbed the tenant of up to 50 percent of his crop. Of the price at which rice was sold by the Saigon exporters, the peasant's share was 12 percent. Any movement that promised these people an end to their inhuman conditions of existence was bound to gain their support. For reasons also peculiar to Vietnam, this was done only by the Communists.

Another cause of Communist strength was the conditions of existence which the colonial regime created for the country's educated elite. In Vietnam, education had always been not only the primary source of prestige but also a road to power. Under the colonial regime, the elite of the nation was deprived of both prestige and power. Thousands of young Vietnamese, mostly sons of landlords and mandarins, received a higher education, but were not given an opportunity to apply their knowledge and skills. No opportunities existed for them in business, commerce, or industry, activities virtually closed to the Vietnamese. The modern sectors of the economy, as far as they existed, were in French and Chinese hands. A small number of intellectuals were allowed to enter the colonial administration, but under conditions materially unsatisfactory and morally degrading. Others worked as teachers, journalists, lawyers, and doctors, but many remained unemployed, and all were deeply frustrated because the colonial regime deprived them also of any kind of political voice. Ninety percent of the prominent Viet Minh leaders came from this class of people.

Colonial Vietnam never developed a middle class in the Anglo-Saxon sense, a class of property-owning natives opposed to radical social movements. This too was a result of a colonial policy which held back the development of industry and excluded the Vietnamese from participating in trade and commerce. There was virtually no Vietnamese capitalism, no Vietnamese bourgeoisie. Capitalism was foreign, an alien power engaged in exploiting the land and the people, and therefore opposed by all patriots striving to free Vietnam from foreign rule. The people who most consistently expressed this national sentiment were of course the Communists.

The absence of a solidly conservative peasantry, of a property-owning middle class, and of a socially satisfied intelligentsia meant that the country lacked the social basis for moderate democratic movements interested in maintaining or improving the *status quo*. Whoever was awakened to political consciousness sooner or later aimed at overthrowing not only the colonial regime but also the social order it had created. A political movement based on a strong native middle class would of course also have fought for national liberation, but it would have been opposed to social revolution. Since such a class was practically nonexistent, all nationalist movements tended to embrace socialistic ideas. This was true even for an authoritarian conservative like Ngo Dinh Diem.

Most effective in directly promoting Communist strength were the political conditions which French colonialism created for the existence of all nationalist movements. Only pro-colonial attitudes could be freely expressed. Movements organized by moderate middle-class nationalists were as brutally suppressed as was the Communist Party. No trade unions were allowed. Nationalist movements could operate only clandestinely, in an atmosphere essentially hostile to the development of democratic ideas. The most moderate nationalists, forced underground, hunted by the police, condemned to death or to endless years of concentration camp, ended up by becoming radicals, believers in revolutionary action and in the necessity of fighting the colonial regime with force. No one expressed this necessity more consistently than the Communists, who constantly attracted the most determined elements of all the nationalist groups.

The Communists alone possessed certain advantages essential for the survival of illegal organizations. They had a wealth of experience and skills in underground work, and highly sophisticated theories about it, which had been tested in Russia and elsewhere over a long time. They had schools to train people engaged in secret political activities. These schools were held abroad, where the Communists permanently kept a reserve of *cadres*. They also had support from the Soviet Union. No other group enjoyed any of these advantages. Who in the Western world showed an interest in the national aspirations of the Vietnamese people, let alone supported them? France, the only democratic country that knew about these potentially democratic movements, was engaged in destroying them.

Furthermore, the Communists were the only ones who knew that a successful revolution against the colonial regime required organization of the masses. Nationalist intellectuals who lacked a Communist political training clung to the century-old view of Vietnam's elite, which was that public affairs were matters reserved to the educated; the masses were not ripe for political action, and had no significant part to play in the national liberation of Vietnam. Only the Communists trained *cadres* for organizing the masses. When the revolution broke out in April, 1945, only the Communist Party had people who spoke in support of the Viet Minh to the rural masses in the villages all over the country. They did not speak of Communism; the aims of the revolution were declared to be national liberation and moderate social reforms. In the absence of any organized forces to oppose them, the Communist leaders gained the support of almost the entire nation before one month had elapsed. They were solidly in power when the anti-Communist leaders a few weeks later arrived from their exile in China, together with the unwelcome Chinese armies of occupation.

But the colonial regime went even further in its promotion of Communism. After having reconquered the Southern half of Vietnam, the French, in exchange for permission to station army units in the North, recognized the Ho Chi Minh government at Hanoi with an agreement in March, 1946. When the anti-Communist nationalists, in an attempt to exploit popular opposition to the return of the French army, fiercely attacked this agreement, the French cooperated with the Communists in destroying all nationalist groups opposed to the Viet Minh regime. The French were of course not "pro-Communist"; they knew that their compromise with Ho Chi Minh would end in armed conflict, but they did not want the anti-Communist groups as their opponents in the government of Vietnam. They preferred to present the war against the Vietnamese national revolution as a war against Communism.

French colonial policy, by provoking the Indochina War, again contributed to the popularity of Vietnamese Communism. The Viet Minh government became the symbol of national resistance to colonialism. Most nationalists supported the armed struggle against the French led by the Viet Minh. This is why Ho Chi Minh became Vietnam's great national hero.

During the Indochina War, the French could have helped weaken the Communists' hold on the nationalist movement by granting a non-Communist regime what the Vietnamese people were fighting for, which was not Communism but national independence. Instead, the French colonialists set up a corrupt puppet regime under the former emperor Bao Dai, discrediting the cause of anti-Communist nationalism, and enhancing once more the prestige of the Hanoi regime. This failure to take proper political action led, in turn, to the military defeat of the French at the hands of the Viet Minh. During the war the French had denounced the entire resistance movement as Communist; when it triumphed, the Vietnamese naturally gave the Communists most of the credit. The prestige of the Hanoi government was immense. Its popular support and military strength were such that it could probably have thrown the French out of Indochina and extended its power over the whole of Vietnam. Communist control was limited to the North of Vietnam only by the international circumstances that induced the Western and Eastern powers to conclude, and impose upon the Viet Minh, the compromise reached at the conference of Geneva.

:

Why the government established in the South in 1954 failed to break the power of the Communists is another story. This is a failure not only of Vietnamese anti-Communism but also of the United States. Basically it is due to the fact that in too many social and political areas the Diem regime did not liquidate the colonial heritage. It did not create a land-owning peasantry immune to Communist propaganda; it did not oppose organized Communism by creating democratic mass movements, but decided to fight it with police and army; it treated its democratic opponents as they had been treated by the colonial regime, denouncing them as Communists and throwing them into jail. Instead of turning South Vietnam, with United States help, into a country that might seem attractive to the people both in the South and the North, the Diem regime relied for its survival on force.

Many of these colonial conditions still persist under the tutelage of the United States. It would of course be absurd to impute colonial motives to American intervention in Vietnam. But there are still more than merely shades of the colonial heritage in the views and actions which describe United States policy in South Vietnam. If there is still, as under the colonial regime, a total neglect of social and political reform, the United States must accept part of the blame for this. The present regime of South Vietnam, which could not exist without American support, is politically just as ineffective against the Communists as was the Bao Dai regime under the French. We too, like the French, act as if military force alone could defeat Communism. We too use napalm, condone torture, kill innocent civilians by bombing and burning villages. We treat the National Front for the Liberation of the South as the French treated the Viet Minh — as a solid Communist bloc, and, like the French, we refuse to negotiate with the people whom we are fighting. However, what reminds the Vietnam people more than anything else of their colonial past is that the Saigon regime, like that of Bao Dai, would collapse overnight if foreign armies were not again on Vietnamese soil.

If we rely on force, it must be because we either do not know the means required to defeat Vietnamese Communism politically, or we are afraid to apply them. Our force is probably sufficient to prevent the Communists from winning this war. At the risk of starting a larger conflict, we may even succeed in defeating the enemy, but we can defeat him only under one condition: we must summon up the inhuman determination to destroy the country, wiping out most of its unfortunate people.

As long as the colonial heritage in Vietnam is not liquidated by a socially progressive regime, the people of South Vietnam will continue to expect the Communists to perform this urgent historical task.

1965

# THEORIES OF MODERNIZATION
## MICHAEL WALZER

**I**

Historical concepts always tell us as much about the men who use them as about the events they are supposed to describe. Very little is given in intellectual life; artists, writers, even social scientists, must choose the way they wish to see the world and invariably they choose ideas which suit their needs or convenience. American social scientists use the concept "modernization" first of all for reasons of convenience; it groups together all the complex transformations now going on in Africa and Asia and it suggests useful comparisons with similar transformations presumed to have occurred at one time or another in Europe. Modernization is thought to be a single, long-term historical process in which all mankind is destined to participate, but in which some men already have participated. Their experience provides the basis for a theory about the stages, crises, and turning points of the modernizing process, and about the character of its active agents and still vigorous opponents.

Exciting work has been done with this conceptual scheme, but the concept has serious difficulties and these have seldom been treated analytically.* Nor has anyone suggested that there may be reasons be-

* This essay does not pretend to examine in detail the large number of books and articles in which the theory of modernization is used more or less systematically,

yond scientific utility for its extraordinary popularity. One such reason is probably that modernization theory forecloses a great deal of political debate. Even the casual use of words like "backward" or "developmental process" suggests forcefully that the direction of historical change is not at issue. Modernization theory thus opens the way for a social science as self-confident as was the historiography of nineteenth-century Whigs. American academicians seem as certain as were Whig historians that their contemporary world is the modern world, and the modern the very best world there has ever been.

"Modern" has become a term of self-congratulation; it is a way men have of indicating those aspects of the present in which they take special pride and by which they distinguish their own cultural, political, or technological achievements from those of previous generations. It is not really a historical, let alone a scientific, word at all; it is a word, so to speak, with built-in naïveté, the characteristic naïveté of writers who make the contemporary and familiar into something superhistorical.

When social scientists accept this prideful evaluation of contemporary life, they cut themselves off from historical understanding. Their theory then fails to do what a theory of history and society ought to do: to suggest possible or likely connections between the past and future. "Modernization" is by definition a terminal process; it culminates in modernity. It suggests connections only between the historical past and the unhistorical present, the conventionally admired world around us.

The theory of modernization appears in an earlier form as Weber's "rationalization" — a process culminating in a "rational-legal" society. Rational-legal and modern are terms very similar in meaning, but Weber avoided the word which his followers have chosen, perhaps because he realized the instability of the social system he was describing. Acutely aware of the discomforts of rational-legal civilization, he sensed that there would be future transformations. He warned of revolutions led by charismatic men, calling into question all the achievements of human rationality. But the American social scientists who write of modernization live wholeheartedly in the midst of the modern. Like Hegel in the Prussian state, though with a more catholic sense of human destiny, they view their own achievements as the culmination of historical

---

nor the larger number in which its terminology is vaguely employed. My purpose is to suggest some of the intellectual tendencies fostered by the theory and already visible in those books (by Daniel Lerner, W. W. Rostow, S. M. Lipset, Gabriel Almond, etc.) in which it has been most ably developed. The academic theorists disagree among themselves and the criticisms which follow by no means apply equally to all of them. But modernization, in theory as in reality, has acquired a momentum of its own; its terms inevitably have come to have meanings for which its creators are not entirely responsible — though those meanings more often than not are true to the logic of the theory. (It should be said that a critique of the theory has been begun by Professor Wilbert Moore in his book *Social Change*.)

development. Theirs is a theory of progress, but of *progress realized*. Unlike the eighteenth-century French doctrine, it does not point beyond the present. "Modern" men decline to speculate on their future, but absorb themselves instead with their heroic and painful past — confident that masses of men in other parts of the world are now reenacting that past. Complacently they wait for their straining, backward fellows, as if they had no more history of their own to act out.

## II

Marxist theory was constructed around the notion of two revolutions: one had already occurred when Marx wrote, though not yet in all countries; one had not yet occurred in any country. These two revolutions linked three stages of human history: feudal, capitalist, and socialist. The theory of modernization, by contrast, rests on the idea of a single revolution which has already occurred in some but not yet in all countries. This revolution links two historical stages: traditional and modern. The current doctrine, then, represents a major act of intellectual reduction, an act not without some empirical justification. For no country has had more than one revolution, or at any rate, no country has had two revolutions which can usefully be described as bourgeois and proletarian. Marxist writers have struggled to explain why it is that "proletarian" revolutions have occurred only in countries which have never had "bourgeois" revolutions. Theorists of modernization have no trouble in avoiding this difficulty, for in effect they argue that only one revolution is ever to be expected. That revolution marks the final crisis of the old order: a vanguard of modern men bursts through the trammels of tradition and establishes the new society. Because of the complex processes through which ideology and technology are imitated and diffused, however, this crisis occurs at different times in different countries and draws different groups of men into its vortex — businessmen, factory workers, peasants. The character of the emergent society will be determined by the point in economic development at which the crisis takes place and by the social classes which respond to its turmoil. That society can be *either* capitalist or socialist.

Modernization theorists (here following Weber) tend to deny that there are significant differences between capitalism and socialism. The two are equally the products of the revolution against traditional order. Their sociological and psychological foundations are thought to be identical. They both require, for example, the same work-ethic: thus recent writers have rediscovered Weber's Puritanism among the Bolsheviks. They both foster the conjugal family and shatter the ties of extended kinship systems. As against traditional passivity, they both generate mass activism and participation (though neither requires that that participation be meaningful or democratic). They both depend for efficiency upon an impersonal and bureaucratic rationality.

Marxist writers were not, of course, blind to these aspects of social life, but they did center their analysis upon the ownership of property, an issue which now seems secondary. For them, feudalism and capitalism, where property was privately owned, seemed more closely related to each other than either was to socialism, where private property was abolished. In other areas as well, however, socialism was thought to involve significant transformations precisely of modern, that is, bourgeois life. Socialist writers, for example, foresaw the transformation of work into a kind of play or, at any rate, into esthetic creativity; they thought the Protestant work ethic with its overtones of compulsion characteristic only of capitalist society. They looked forward to changes in the conjugal family, for the household with all the inhibitions it placed upon the freedom of women had clearly survived the breakup of the extended kinship system. And so on: they wrote also of changes in the character of political participation; they advocated the radical decentralization and simplification of bureaucratic structures. Yet none of this is integrally connected with socialism in modernization theory — nor, it need hardly be said, in the modern world as we know it. According to our theorists, all these proposals are merely the utopian effervescence of the crisis period, quickly enough forgotten when the time comes for socialists to take over governments and begin the hard but rewarding work of modernization. The theory thus predicts the failure of socialist aspiration insofar as it points beyond the modern world, even while admitting the possible success of socialism as a modernizing ideology.

Once again, there is historical justification for this view. The two forms of contemporary socialism can both be accommodated better by modernization theory than by Marxism. Social-democracy (in, for example, its Scandinavian form) seems indeed a modern social system, far closer to welfare state capitalism than to the Marxist vision. Similarly, Bolshevism is probably best described as a modernizing ideology, its adherents driven to act out that repressive and disciplinary role currently thought necessary to social progress. And the society which the Bolsheviks have produced certainly bears striking resemblances to that modern world which has emerged in the West — there also without the benefit of a second revolution. Socialists, in fact, have not anywhere produced societies conforming to their own aspirations. In the name of progress and of that efficiency and bureaucratic rationality which progress seems to require, they have set aside one by one precisely those purposes whose achievement would have resulted in a radically new form of modernity and would also have required major changes in the theory of modernization.

If such changes are not required by anything which has yet happened, however, one can at least insist that they may yet be required. The aspirations expressed during the "crisis" period are indeed not fulfilled by modernity; but neither are they abolished. For this reason, the Marxist writer has one decisive advantage over the academic theorist of modernization. He is unalterably committed, living as he always does *before* the second revolution, to search in his own society for those "contradictions" in social, economic, and political life which are manifest in human discontent. He quickly becomes aware of the way in which historical problems, like those seemingly outmoded social classes in Marx's *Eighteenth Brumaire,* accumulate through time. He discovers the unevenness of historical change and senses the troubles of the men left behind. Most importantly, perhaps, he understands how historical unevenness fixes group interests and social structures into patterns of conflict which are extremely difficult to overcome. And he sets this overall view of society against the possibilities which the future holds and toward which the aspirations of actual men point. Now, none of these insights are in any way unavailable to the theorist of modernization *so long as* he studies premodern societies or societies which are in some sense in transition toward modernity. The theory of the single revolution, however, commits the social scientist who holds it to view the problems of "rising expectations" or historical unevenness as susceptible to definitive solution through the completion of the modernization process. As that process nears completion, he tends to talk of "areas" of backwardness and "pockets" of discontent and then to call for political or economic "mopping up." He is singularly blind to the anxieties and frustrations which seem endemic precisely in the "modern" life he unquestioningly accepts and which are the result, in part, of that very failure of socialist aspiration which he claims to understand. And he surely does not see the way in which the structure of modernity, like any other structure, may become an impediment to further progressive transformations.

## III

A theory with one revolution is a theory with one revolution too few. However useful it is in explaining the past, it fails to alert the men who use it to that which is transient in the present. But there is another difficulty in modernization theory: *it fails to provide any very interesting means of distinguishing among different presents.* All sorts of distinctions, some rather obvious and some very subtle, can be made among societies which are on their way to modernity, but it is hard to avoid the conclusion that modernity itself is singular in form. Modernization theory, then, lies behind the widely shared view that the United States and the Soviet Union are evolving toward one another and eventually will develop very similar social systems. This is a view which suits men of different political persuasions: it can provide the basis for arguments about Soviet liberalization or incipient American totalitarianism. The bias of the theory, however, would appear to favor a forecast of Soviet liberalization, both because the idea of the modern has been shaped in the image of Western experience, and because the Russians being less recently modern presumably have further to evolve.

If Bolshevism is seen as a modernizing ideology, then Russian totalitarianism can be described as an institutionalized arrangement appropriate to a certain stage in the modernization process. Such a description has a certain plausibility, especially if one ignores or deemphasizes the purges of Stalin's time which seem without historical "appropriateness." Alternatively, totalitarianism, with the purges, can be conceived as a "disease" to which nations are peculiarly susceptible during the crisis period — a view which justifies efforts to prevent the disease and has therefore been favored by American writers. Now either of these views represents an advance over the Cold War conception of the Soviet system as permanent and monolithic evil. Both of them provide a historical framework within which totalitarianism can be better understood than it has been until now. At the same time, however, both of them do us (and the Russians) the acute disservice of suggesting that the future of Soviet society is somehow not a problem (only the past is a problem): the modernizing process will go on; the disease of Stalinism will be shaken off and the patient brought to a condition which, it is assumed, will be healthy simply because it will be modern.

Of course, totalitarianism is bound to be transformed as the historical process of which it is the product, proceeds. The question is, transformed in what way? All processes arrive and are always arriving at the modern, but this is always a particular modern, determined by its history. Not even the spread of a single technology or the increasing interrelatedness of the various divisions of mankind seems likely to produce in the near future a single history and a singular modernity. We will continue to live in significantly different societies. And for the moment, at least, it is useful to argue that some of these societies will be totalitarian. That word need not retain its apocalyptic overtones; its use is only to suggest, in the language of modernization theory, that while the "crisis" may be comparatively brief, the particular ways in which it is met have lasting effects.

Eighteenth-century theories of progress were characterized by a curious notion that the past might be abolished: each new advance in science or politics not only overcame the obstacles which older men had erected, but literally annulled the darkness in which they had lived. So men continually escaped the consequences of their own history. Something of this odd notion survives in modernization theory: at a certain point in the process of development, it is thought, men loose themselves from their parochial pasts and, after one or another sort of social trauma, enter a universal present. There is some truth to this, perhaps, if it is expressed with sufficient caution. The immediate past is more parochial, the present more universal, chiefly because of the worldwide diffusion of ideas and artifacts, itself an aspect of modernization. But this very diffusion evokes from each country a particular response, leads to a special form of social unevenness and eventually to a distinct political creed and a cherished independence. The first result of diffusion is to increase the number of sovereign states, the number of arenas in which political decisions are made. And insofar as parties and politicians make different decisions, they or their descendants will find themselves living in different worlds. This remains true even after one admits that the range of choices is not always wide and that the word "choice" does not always indicate debate and deliberation.

The Russian people thus are likely to endure their modernizing party as an inescapable incubus for years to come, long after its presumed historical function has been fulfilled. Soviet modernity does not depend first upon the activity of the party and then upon its withering away. Instead, the party creates a particular form of modernity, a form to which it is itself integral and not incidental. Similarly, the Western experience of Puritan repression and bourgeois egotism is not simply one pathway into the modern world. Repression and egotism give rise to modern capitalism and are to an extent embodied in their own creation. They form the ever-present past and become our own incubi when we struggle to adjust to (or deny) the possibilities of abundance and automation. Neither the institutional structures of individualism nor the Communist Party, of course, are necessary parts of modernity. On the other hand, one cannot discover the essence of modern life by excluding them from one's conceptual scheme. That excludes too much: modernity always appears in particular historical forms, in which Americans and Russians, Chinese and Indians struggle with the past, adjust to it, evade and endure it, but never escape it. When modernity is turned into a sociologist's ideal type, it suggests that impossible escape and then does not provide any clear way to analyze or understand the particular forms of the modern — where the encounter with the parochial past is as essential as is the universal present.

## IV

These criticisms of modernization theory apparently have more relevance in the "advanced" than in the "backward" countries. The nearer one is to the fully realized modern, the more disturbing is the idea that radical social change is a thing of the past. The theory is most success-

ful in explaining the experience of backwardness, that is, the new awareness of men living in traditional societies that they are in some sense
"behind" and must quickly "catch up." Indeed, the major purpose of the
theory is to facilitate the business of catching up. Large numbers of
American social scientists have suddenly become defenders of social
change — in the backward countries. They have developed a healthy
sensitivity to the human misery upon which traditionalism rests. They
approach the problems of development with a lively pragmatism which
is often appealing. There is a "job-to-be-done" air about modernization theory and the theorists may well feel that the pressure of poverty
and hunger are so great that there is no time for complicated analyses
of modernity. Somber warnings about the inescapability of the past —
and especially of that past which is being made today — must sound to
them like superfluous moralizing. The activity of the modernizers requires a goal which can be assumed; modern life must appear as attractive as it is inevitable. Then the human price for rapid social change
will be gladly paid; all costs must seem worthwhile if modernity itself
is the purchase.

Most American social scientists, of course, do not believe that all
costs are justified; they study modernization at least in part to learn
how coercion can be minimized and totalitarian terror avoided. Thus
they have tended to see modernization as a process whose *means* require
further study and debate, but whose *ends* are given. In fact, however,
the givenness of ends limits and inhibits the debate over means. Given
the character of contemporary backwardness *and the character of contemporary modernity,* it is probably correct to argue that modernizing regimes will always be authoritarian and their methods always
coercive, if not terroristic. All debate is then reduced to questions like,
how authoritarian? how coercive? But this reduction is only necessary
if the model of modernity imitated in the backward countries is not itself subject to change and if there is only one possible end to the developmental process. *The alternatives in the backward countries depend
upon the alternatives in the advanced countries.*

In theory, at least, a thoroughgoing critique of the modern world
would offer men everywhere a wider range of choices. It is in this sense
that the criticisms suggested above are relevant even to the politicians
and economic planners in Asia and Africa who are "doing the job."
So much of what they call modern is already outmoded, vestigial, inadequate to human needs! With automation so near a prospect, for example, how necessary to the job they are doing is the discipline of a
"Protestant" work-ethic? Or again, now that decentralization is technically more feasible than ever before, how necessary to that job is the
creation of a bureaucratic hierarchy? So long as modernity is conceived
in a singular and narrowly contemporary image, with "Protestant"

workers and a centralized bureaucracy part of that image, there is only one historical pathway and it culminates in the American present — or in that immediate future which Khrushchev promises the Russians. Presumably men must struggle along that pathway as quickly and with as little pain as possible, and since the end is preordained, theorists can only distinguish between forced marches and voluntary advance. If, by contrast, modernity is seen as having a multitude of forms, then there are a multitude of paths, and all sorts of choices to be made and opportunities seized.

But contemporary social scientists seem unwilling to confront the modern world in a critical way. They are content to view social problems as functions of backwardness and to offer modernization as a single cure. Thus they become social critics and even revolutionaries — abroad — out of sympathy for their fellowmen, in a good cause, and with admirable energy and skill. If only modernization offered some solution to the problems of the modern! And if only these men were revolutionaries at home!

1964

# PROSPECTS FOR THE NEW NATIONS: TOTALITARIANISM, AUTHORITARIANISM, OR DEMOCRACY?

## LEWIS COSER

The sudden emergence of new nations in Asia and Africa poses crucial problems for our age. No longer is it sufficient to applaud the demise of imperialism. We have also to discard any previous reliance on simple ideologies of progress. And we have to recognize that some or all of the new nations will present features deeply distasteful to men of a libertarian vision. There is no guarantee that the new will be desirable or appealing. Nor can we assume that the end of colonial servitude will necessarily usher in an age of democracy. We must ask bluntly, What are the chances that a democratic polity can ultimately win over authoritarian and totalitarian politics?

Owing partly to the rapidity with which they have gained independence, most of these new states are characterized by fluid and ill-defined social and political structures. Many of them have a political structure boasting the paraphernalia of the modern state while their social structure is composed of essentially tribal or semi-feudal units. In many of these new nations a thin veneer of twentieth-century ideology is superimposed on a community in which magical rather than rational modes of thought predominate. In most of them the cultural distance between the intellectual elite and the underlying population is so wide that the two strata seem to live in entirely different worlds.

None of the new nations outside of the Soviet orbit has achieved even relative social and political stability. All are in flux, open to various courses of development. This very openness poses a challenge: Is it possible to isolate at least some crucial factors which will help determine the structure of these nation-states? This essay will focus attention on a few such variables without claiming that these are the only ones needing consideration.

## Three Societal Models

The difficulty inherent in the fact that political systems differ in a great many ways, so that comparison seems almost an impossible task, can best be overcome by constructing theoretical models against which particular units can be measured. I shall describe three such models, the liberal, the totalitarian, and the authoritarian, and then discuss their applicability to the new nations. The forces likely to push toward one or the other model in the years immediately ahead can then be analyzed and an attempt made to assess the long-run chances for democracy.

Any society beyond the relatively undifferentiated tribal level can be broken down, for purposes of analysis, into major institutional orders of which the political, the economic, the military, the religious, and the family or kinship orders may be considered the most important.* These institutional orders must be integrated in some way if the society is to function. But the way integration is brought about may differ very significantly. Three "ideal typical" models of social integration, derived from a variety of concrete instances, will be outlined. No claim is made, of course, that any of them is fully embodied in any society or nation-state. The three were chosen because they have all been associated with the course of industrial development in a variety of historical settings. The democratic socialist model is not discussed here because, as Marx foresaw, it has been approximated only in those nations which have already gone over the hump of development.

### THE LIBERAL MODEL

In the classical liberal model of society, the structure is unified, yet leaves a high degree of autonomy to the various institutional orders and minimizes the dominion of the State. Conflict and competition between the various orders, far from endangering integration, help to "sew society together."

In the liberal model, economic agents are relatively free from political

* cf. Hans Gerth and C. Wright Mills, *Character and Social Structure* (New York: Harcourt, Brace and Co., 1953), esp. Chapter XII.

or religious interference, and so are religious organizations, which are usually not dominated by economic agents; the family also is protected from political interference. Only the military order has limited autonomy; it is firmly controlled by political agents. All orders are interrelated and influence each other, yet each maintains a high degree of autonomy.

In the nineteenth century, when the liberal model was most nearly approximated in parts of Europe and North America, non-governmental forces such as kin groups, autonomous religious organizations, owners of landed or mobile property, succeeded in restricting and limiting governmental action. The political order thus never achieved a large measure of dominance over the other institutional orders; nor did it dominate the individual. Neither did any other order achieve dominance. By being pitted against each other in competition and conflict, and struggling for the loyalty and allegiance of men, they furthered individual autonomy.

To be sure, the freedom thus made possible was a negative freedom only, freedom *from* rather than freedom *to*. To the extent that the various institutional orders limited each other they allowed individuals a certain interstitial leeway. The full flowering of positive freedom was precluded in the liberal model if for no other reason than that it could function only if internalized repression among its citizens domesticated drives and energies into institutionally approved channels. The liberal society assured that, to use Erich Fromm's term, the great majority of individuals wanted to do what they had to do.

Some political compulsions did in fact face the individual in such liberal societies. The State may have been a "night-watchman" state, but it nevertheless imposed, even if hesitatingly and sparingly, compulsory military service, education, and taxation, and it held firmly to its monopoly over the legitimate exercise of the means of violence. Yet the State's recourse to its power of compulsion, that is to political means, was only thought of as a last resort; the major decisions within the society were preferably brought about through bargaining, conflict, and competition between the agents of the various institutional orders. The State claimed primacy during situations of emergency or stress, but in the ordinary course of events limited its impact on the other orders.

What has been said about the relations between the various institutional orders in liberal society applies even more strongly to relations within these orders themselves. In none of them did a single interest dominate the whole. Even where a State church existed, other organizations served to balance and limit its power in the religious sphere. The competition for souls between proselytizing religions furthered the freedom of the individual; the competitive struggle for scarce resources between a great variety of economic interests prevented the preemption of economic chances. Competition for marriage partners prevented the domination of the marriage market by kinship groups and enhanced the chances of free marital choice. Within the political realm, different political parties competed for power and thus maximized the chances for the citizen's democratic participation in the political process.

Liberal society was crisscrossed by many conflicts and antagonisms between, as well as within, institutional orders. As individuals affiliated with a multiplicity of groups and as these multiple affiliations crisscrossed each other, they welded society together. The multiple antagonistic and diversified interests which found expression within such social structures served as a balancing mechanism, preventing the cleavage of society along one line. At the same time the multiple affiliations of individuals in a variety of groups and associations served to enhance personal freedom.* The individual came, so to speak, to stand at a point at which many conflicting or nonconflicting groups and institutional orders intersected. Such a position in social space helps to minimize the chance of individual autonomy.†

### THE TOTALITARIAN MODEL

In comparing the liberal with the totalitarian model one can apply Max Weber's distinction between individual and collective appropriation of power.‡ Individual appropriation takes place through conflict and competition among the members-at-large of those strata which have a legitimate claim to power; in collective appropriation all positions of power have been appropriated by a single ruling group which then allots shares to individuals and groups according to their status.

The totalitarian model may be considered the antithesis of the liberal model. Here integration is attained through deliberate coordination of all institutional orders and the suppression of conflict among them. The essence of totalitarian regimes is that their claims are total; i.e., that they aim at the control of all institutional spheres. In such regimes we witness an apotheosis of the political order. Political power has been appropriated by a political elite which suppresses all rival claimants. The political order has unquestioned primacy over all others; no independent organization even of an utterly nonpolitical character is allowed to exist. Every social unit must be *gleichgeschaltet;* i.e., coordinated with the governing apparatus. Insofar as different institutional orders still continue to exist, activities within them are heteronomous; they do not follow laws of motion of their own but are impelled by

* *cf.* George Simmel, *Conflict and the Web of Group Affiliation,* transl. by Kurt H. Wolff and Reinhard Bendix (New York: The Free Press of Glencoe, 1955).
† *cf.* Lewis A. Coser, *The Functions of Social Conflict* (New York: The Free Press of Glencoe, 1956).
‡ Max Weber, *The Theory of Social and Economic Organization,* transl. by A. M. Henderson and T. Parsons (New York: Oxford University Press, 1947), pp. 139–43 and 245–50.

forces emanating from the political order. Economic agents act in accord with the demands of State and Party, religious institutions become adjuncts to political institutions, and even the family is pressed into the service of political goals.*

Totalitarian societies destroy traditional social groups, communities, or self-conscious classes and then replace them by new units which are subject to coordination and control by State and Party. Deprived of the support of nongovernmental structures, the individual faces alone the immense tutelary power of the Party and State. Though in such societies he has multiple affiliations with a great number of groups, these do not conflict with or crisscross each other; they follow the same impelling direction. Social forces are no longer antagonistic, the various interests are no longer diversified; indeed, their pressures are mutually reinforcing. The distinction between public and private spheres, central to the liberal model, disappears in totalitarian society. Just as the totalitarian state cannot tolerate autonomous organizations, so it cannot tolerate individual withdrawal into a private — and hence uncontrolled — sphere. The engineering of souls is as essential as the engineering of the social structure. The private as well as the public man must be caught in the seamless web of control. To the totalitarian powerholder anything that is not controlled will seem a fatal flaw.

Monopolistic control of the means of violence and of the channels of communication, as well as an official ideology covering all major aspects of a man's existence, characterize totalitarian societies. No claims of family, property, or religion counterbalance or limit the actions of the State and the Party. All social life is "politicized"; society is integrated by fiat of the State.

THE AUTHORITARIAN MODEL

The authoritarian model may be said to stand midway between the totalitarian and the liberal models. Where totalitarian societies suppress all forms of autonomous organization and all independent sources of information, the authoritarian regimes suppress organized opposition and public criticism. Where liberal society fosters the autonomy of the various institutional orders, the authoritarian society limits and confines activities within these orders but does not attempt to control them completely. While totalitarian societies suppress all conflict among component parts of the social structure, the authoritarian society channels and deflects such conflicts without, however, eliminating them altogether.

* cf. Hannah Arendt, *The Origins of Totalitarianism* (New York: Meridian Books, 1958); *Totalitarianism*, ed. by Carl Friedrich (Cambridge: Harvard University Press, 1954); William Kornhauser, *The Politics of Mass Society* (New York: The Free Press of Glencoe, 1959).

In such societies the political power-holders may recognize no constitutional limitations of State power, yet in practice they do recognize *some* limitations. They may try to make the Church into a pliant instrument of their rule, yet they will not attempt to deny the religious order a measure of autonomy in regard to otherworldly concerns. They may limit the exercise of proprietary rights and channel the allocation of scarce resources, yet they will not attack the legitimation of property as such. In authoritarian societies the military order is typically somewhat independent of the political order; it may even tend to dominate it. Where totalitarian societies have "politicized armies," authoritarian societies often have a "militarized polity." Authoritarian regimes will attempt to mobilize the citizen in the pursuit of their political goals, yet they will not obliterate the distinction between the public and the private sphere — they will leave the latter relatively untouched. The political elite monopolizes political power but it shares social powers with the agents of other institutional orders.

Consequently such societies do not exclude conflicts between the various orders or within them. The Church, the army, economic agents, class interests — all may clash and limit each other. At the same time such groupings and institutions will limit the political agents and prevent them from exercising unchallenged sway. The Church, the army, the family, and property constitute distinct and not always harmonious interests; they compete, and the resultant balance of power among them leaves a deep impress on political decision-making. As distinct from liberal societies, here the nonpolitical orders enjoy no customary immunity from the exercise of political will, but neither are they deprived of all power.

The individual in authoritarian societies does not enjoy the autonomy granted him in liberal societies. He is cribbed and confined by agents of the political order. Yet he can escape from the public scene into the relative autonomy of an uncontrolled private life. To the degree that conflicts between groups and orders mark the social life of authoritarian society — even though they may be channelled and partly directed — individuals have some chance to realize their nonpolitical interests.

The integration of authoritarian society is achieved by a "mixed" process of authoritative imposition on the part of the political agents and spontaneous balancing among the other institutional orders. Shifts in the balance of power between the various groups will find their indirect reflection in political life. Such regimes are likely to lack the frozen rigidity of totalitarian regimes while also lacking, owing to the heavy predominance of the political order, the flexibility of the liberal model. They tend to have a somewhat unstable character. They face two dangers: the rise of liberalism through a revival of the power of temporarily suppressed groups, and the establishment of a totalitarian regime through a *Gleichschaltung* of all orders and interests.

## The Consequences of Underdevelopment

By comparison with the West, all the new nations are "underdeveloped" economically. Their productivity, national product, and per capita income is low and this is reflected in low standards of nutrition, housing, education, and health. The bulk of their populations live in traditional rural communities; most of them have not yet reached the take-off stage in the process of industrialization. This underdevelopment is due to a complex of historical circumstance which can only be hinted at here. Colonial exploitation both through unilateral transfers of wealth from colonial countries to Western Europe and the seizure of peasant-occupied lands for plantation purposes, played a major part. The destruction of rural handicraft industries through the competition of cheap industrial goods from Europe and America was another significant factor. Imperialist domination hindered the development of a class of indigenous industrial entrepreneurs, though it often favored the emergence of a partly Westernized class of *comprador* traders and middlemen.

But quite apart from the impact of imperialism, the traditional cultures of Asia and Africa in themselves did not foster strong and independent middle classes — the classes which in the West were the main promoters of capital accumulation, industrial enterprise, and rational work discipline. The gradual development of a "Protestant" work-ethic and a peculiar pattern of repression and self-control has been a precondition for the development of capitalist industrialism in the West. Individual autonomy, discipline, methodical application to work, characterized the early entrepreneurial middle class, and this "innerworldly asceticism" was a powerful stimulant for that energetic pursuit of rational domination over the world and of industrial creativity which has characterized the West since the seventeenth century. There are no equivalents to this entrepreneurial ethos as yet discernible in the new nations. This relative absence of a work-ethic and a tradition of individual self-control and autonomy accounts also for the fact that nepotism, corruption, and the like do not encounter institutional or internalized obstacles to nearly the same degree as in the West.

The underdevelopment of economic resources has significant consequences for the system of stratification. The poorer a country, the greater the differences between the rich and the poor; i.e., the steeper the stratification pyramid. Not only are the poor in underdeveloped countries poorer in absolute terms than those of the West, but they are relatively poorer within their own class system. The social and economic distance between them and their own upper class is greater than that between the poor of the West and their upper class. In other words, not only absolute but relative deprivation characterizes the mass of the underlying population in the new nations. Moreover, with the growth of modern mass communication and transportation, the poor of the underdeveloped countries increasingly have occasion to compare their lot with that of the population of the developed countries of the West.

So long as the ideology or mystique of a society continues to hold the allegiance of the masses, they will endure the grossest inequalities of wealth, status, and power. But when the traditional legitimations for the status quo break down — and they have broken down to a greater or lesser degree in all underdeveloped countries — then a new standard of judgment seeps into the consciousness of the deprived groups and leads them to compare their situations with that of other groups both within and without their own society.* Hence the urge to develop the country so as to reap the fruits of industrialization, raise national product, and reduce inequalities becomes well-nigh irresistible in underdeveloped nations which have broken from traditional moorings.

What social stratum is likely to take the initiative in this development? Since entrepreneurial middle classes have hardly developed in these nations, and the traditionalistic leaders have a vested interest in maintaining the status quo, the partly Westernized intelligentsia is likely to take the lead. This intelligentsia first becomes aware of the backwardness of the country through more intimate contacts with Western conditions than are available to other groups. Given their trained receptiveness to new ideological currents, the Westernized intellectuals are the first to criticize the accepted scheme of things. As gatekeepers of ideas, they are strategically placed to facilitate the penetration of modern ideologies. Cut loose from traditional thought, troubled by a sense of national humiliation, intellectuals in fact have taken the lead in the movement toward independence and modernization.†

When the intelligentsia searched for models to guide economic development, they almost invariably discarded the liberal model. Lacking an independent entrepreneurial middle class and its peculiar ethic, the new nations could not rely on unaided economic development. A liberal order, moreover, requires some ideological preparation. Before a liberal

* cf. Irving Howe and Lewis A. Coser, The American Communist Party (Boston: Beacon Press, 1957), pp. 513–16.
† The process has often been described in Asia; for a fine study of similar developments in Africa cf. David E. Apter, The Gold Coast in Transition (Princeton: Princeton University Press, 1955). See also James S. Coleman, Nigeria, Background to Nationalism (Berkeley and L. A.: University of California, 1958). For an excellent analysis of key political factors in the new nations see Gabriel Almond and James S. Coleman, eds., The Politics of the Developing Areas (Princeton: Princeton University Press, 1960).

politics could make its appearance in Europe a new breed of autonomous, self-governing men had first to develop. But such men are still very rare in the new nations. As Richard Lowenthal has said in an essay from which I have borrowed several seminal ideas: "If conditions were such that a liberal economy would work, the country would not have remained underdeveloped in the first place." * Given the absence of independent economic agents, the task of development had to fall to the powers of the State. While in the West industrialization was mainly the outcome of a process of spontaneous growth in the economic order, "nourished by the enterprise of individual profit-seekers, exploiting new techniques to their own advantage," † the development of the new nations required concentration of economic power in the State. The mopping up of savings to raise funds for investment, the allocation of scarce resources to the strategically most important tasks, the promotion of an intellectual climate favorable to the development of an ethos of work, the breakdown of the traditional barriers to the exercise of disciplined and rational modes of organization — none of these tasks of industrial take-off could be accomplished without public action by the agents of the political order. If the universalistic criteria which are a precondition for industrial development were to prevail, the particularism of the kinship order and the nonrational taboos of religious tradition had to be broken down. Hence the liberal model with its emphasis on the balanced interaction of different institutional orders found little favor in the new nations.

The appeal of the totalitarian model, in particular in its Communist form, was, on the contrary, considerably stronger. Lowenthal so ably summarizes the attractions of Communist totalitarianism for underdeveloped countries that I shall quote him at length:

> In its Stalinist form, the Communist ideology has been specifically adjusted to deal with the problems of forced modernization. It justifies a ruthless policy of forced savings. . . . It proclaims the superiority of planned investment by the state over *laissez faire*. Finally, it furnishes the militant faith needed for the cultural revolution, with its materialist attack on traditional superstition, its glorification of dedicated, disciplined work for the community, its emphasis on production as the highroad to national power and individual liberation from misery. It invests the uprooting of traditional life, the frightening impact of social and technical change, the bitterness of years of sacrifice with a meaning. And, last but not least, it justifies all the privileges a self-appointed but dedicated elite may require.‡

* Richard Lowenthal, "The Points of the Compass," *Encounter,* London, Sept., 1960, pp. 22–28.
† Myrdal, *Beyond the Welfare State* (New Haven: Yale University Press, 1960), p. 121.
‡ Lowenthal, *op. cit.,* p. 25.

While the totalitarian model has considerable attractions for the underdeveloped countries, it also encounters deeply seated resistances. In fact, most of the leaders of these countries are not at present prepared to accept the totalitarian and monolithic state as a precondition for the planning of development.

The adoption of the totalitarian model would necessarily mean that an underdeveloped nation would forego much of the technical know-how available in however slim a stratum of native entrepreneurs and professionals. Nor would the bulk of the native Westernized intelligentsia relish a head-on clash with the traditionalistic elites — a clash which would inevitably occur should an attempt be made to mold the State according to the totalitarian pattern. They may be committed to deep-going agrarian reform, yet shrink from wholesale collectivization on the Chinese model involving the breakup of familistic property patterns. They may hesitate before the application of terroristic means for the extraction of surplus labor from the peasantry. They may harbor resentment against the West, yet shrink from a course which would inevitably cut them off from Western economic aid, both public and private. (I need hardly stress that considerations in regard to the Cold War play an important role in this context.)

There is a more profound reason why the Westernized elite of most of the new nations, though willing to borrow techniques of development from the Communist arsenal, cannot easily accept the totalitarian model: large illiterate populations, strong traditional ideologies, the newness and numerical weakness of the urban population and the elite — these factors preclude the planned mobilization of the total population. Such mobilization, however, is a *sine qua non* of the totalitarian model. The localism, particularism, and traditionalism which militate against the development of democracy also act against the introduction of efficient Soviet-type totalitarian regimes. Recent developments in Touré's Guinea are instructive in this respect. A few years ago Guinea seemed on its way toward a Moscow-dominated "People's Democracy." Today it has moved in the direction of a mixed regime — and has expelled the Russian ambassador. Even when a determined effort is made to centralize political power, this power seems all too often to seep away through innumerable rivulets to village communities and tribal structures, to money lenders or army chieftains, to religious leaders and heads of clans. Myrdal seems correct when he says that "even if they were willing, they would not be able to exert the fanatical discipline implicit in the Soviet system." * We may then provisionally conclude that the totalitarian regime, short of direct military take-over by external Com-

* Myrdal, *op. cit.,* p. 126.

munist powers, is not likely to become the model for developments in the new nations, at least, not before the destruction of traditional power.

There remains the authoritarian model. Though the nationalist intelligentsia reacts against the traditional culture which it holds responsible for the backwardness of the country, it is also unwilling and unable to create a cultural *tabula rasa* through the imposition of a ready-made total plan. It is typically drawn toward an eclectic program in which it strives to counterbalance traditional elements and innovating plans. Hugh Seton-Watson calls such regimes "populist," by analogy to the well-known Russian movement of the nineteenth century, in so far as they attempt like their Russian forebears to achieve some kind of synthesis between traditional culture and the need for modernization.* In these new nations the intelligentsia is likely to exhibit a fierce pride in the distinctiveness of native culture and must hence be extremely reluctant to rupture the continuity with tradition; yet it is also well aware that only a resolute break with major aspects of past tradition will allow a take-off in development. Hence its ambivalence. And hence the chance that, though it will attempt through programmatic planning to shorten the trials of development, it will at the same time resist the temptation of totalitarianism.

The concrete forms of regimes dominated by the intelligentsia may differ widely. In some countries, as in Egypt, Iraq, and Sudan, where standing armies have been available as a source of power, a revolutionary "intelligentsia in uniform" has succeeded, through domination of the military order, in controlling the political order; in other instances, as in Ghana, Guinea, or Tunisia, a civilian intelligentsia, skilled in methods of mass propaganda, has succeeded in appropriating the governmental apparatus and has used mass parties built around a charismatic leader as an effective counterweight to the traditional forces. There are in addition, as in Pakistan or Burma, a number of mixed modernizing regimes embodying in greater or lesser degree traditional and innovating elements as well as civilian and military power, and maintaining these elements in an uneasy balance.

Such authoritarian regimes might move against the claims of the religious order if its representatives attempted to limit the innovating actions of the State through an appeal to religious norms. Yet they will not break with the religious agents or attempt fully to control the religious sphere. They will react against the particularistic criteria emanating from the kinship order or the tribal structure and attempt to displace them with universalistic standards of judgment and performance. Yet they will not try to dissolve the traditional family loyalties. They

* Hugh Seton-Watson, *Neither War Nor Peace* (New York: Frederick A. Praeger, 1960), Chapter VI.

will attempt to lay out economic plans and allocate resources according to criteria of economic development rather than in terms of profitability. Yet they will not destroy the institutions of property. They are intent upon introducing the rational techniques of the West while preserving what they consider viable in native tradition.

In practice, then, whether by design or force of circumstance, the authoritarian regimes in the new nations will not be able in the immediate future to coordinate the various institutional orders. They will rather operate in an environment marked by a high incidence of clash and conflict. Nigeria, Pakistan, even Burma and Indonesia provide excellent examples. In none of these countries have the strong centripetal tendencies of the ruling strata succeeded in breaking down the centrifugal pull of various types of traditional elites. Furthermore, in none of these countries has it been possible for the ruling elite to develop an indigenous ideology and a set of organizations strong enough to attract and hold men suddenly freed from the world of tradition. In all of them, though economic development is ardently desired, the elite encounters most serious obstacles from the traditional powers.

Yet it seems true that while the day of reckoning may be postponed for a considerable period of time, in the long run such innovating authoritarian regimes will inevitably weaken the hold of traditional interests. The very process of modernization, even though it may be cushioned in various ways, undermines traditional structures, be they tribal or feudal, particularistic family domination or religious interests.

But as the checks on power that can be exercised by traditional elements decrease, so do the chances for a drift toward totalitarian regimes increase. When individuals are freed from the dominance of traditional institutions and when they cannot be attracted by authoritarian regimes devoid of a coherent ideology, they become available for a new type of integration along the lines of totalitarian coordination. Where traditionalistic sources of power have dried up and given way to modern universalistic power structures manned by members of the rapidly swollen intelligensia, the chances of authoritarian regimes decline. At this point the new nations will face another set of choices: totalitarianism or democracy.

### The Chances of Democritization

A minimal condition for democracy is the legitimation of regular opportunities for changing governing personnel, i.e., the presence of social mechanisms — political parties, free elections, free press, etc. — permitting the underlying population to choose among contenders for political office.* But in addition to such mechanisms, a democratic polity requires a sufficient dispersion of power. If the community is to have the right to share in the direction of political affairs, the diffusion of power among a number of power centers is essential. Since only power can effectively check power, democracy requires the presence of secondary groups and associations which can be nodal points of power interposing themselves between the individual and the State.

Democracy has historically been highly correlated with relatively high standards of living, with urbanization, industrialization, and education. But the correlation is not automatic, for in Europe democracy grew out of the resistance of various semi-autonomous communities, strata, and religious bodies to the absolutist State which had begun the process of modernization. And in most cases, this was not a gradual growth but a series of revolutions. In feudal times, the immunities of Church and estates, of landed aristocracy or independent townships, prevented the center from monopolizing power. When absolute monarchs attempted to win such a monopoly, democracy was powerfully enhanced by the struggle of new social formations, reformed churches and sects, trade unions, voluntary organizations of all sorts, and local and regional bodies, all of which sought to limit governmental power and ensure their members a voice in the affairs of state.

In the new nations, with their low living standards, their small degree of industrialization, and urbanization, their low standards of education, and their lack of a "Protestant ethic," the basis of a democratic polity is not at present available. These nations are not only underdeveloped in the economic but also in the political sense, since in none of them is there a sufficient degree of development of those key factors that are necessary for secure democratic systems (though in some, notably the Philippines, India, and Ceylon, a number of favorable factors have allowed approximations to Western democracy). Nor have the social groups and classes which made revolutions in the West developed in the new nations. These revolutions depended on the ability of various institutional orders (e.g., the religious and the economic) to modernize themselves, and then to provide opposition cadres — as did the Protestant sects in England or the Third Estate in France. But if modernization at all levels comes to depend on the State alone, if there are no local, religious, or class forces independently pushing in the same direction, then democratic revolutions become unlikely.

With gradual modernization, one can expect a gradual rise in education, living standards, and the like, and this will remove a significant barrier to democracy. But one cannot expect that the other major bar-

* *cf.* Seymour M. Lipset, *Political Man* (Garden City, N. Y.: Doubleday, 1960), pp. 45 *ff.*

rier — the concentration of power — will necessarily decrease and hence allow the expansion of chances for wider participation in political life. And yet the chances of democratization depend ultimately on the degree to which power will be dispersed or centralized.

The modernizing elites, in their efforts to create new collective symbols and a new source of legitimacy as well as a new economic and social structure, clash with traditional centers of power and prestige. They must attempt to undermine and neutralize traditional modes of behavior. They must desire to create citizens free from particularistic loyalties to village, communal groupings, family, tribal chief, or traditional aristocracy. They must attempt to legitimize secular power, even giving it a "sacral" character, so as to free the polity from control by traditional powerholders and representatives of the religious order.

Yet once the power of the Indian princes, the Indonesian traditional aristocracy, the Ashanti chieftains in Northern Ghana, or the emirs in Northern Nigeria has been broken, the new nations still face the problem of integrating individuals who have become freed from traditional allegiance and loyalties.* This integration can conceivably take place in two different ways: the energies and activities of those who have relinquished traditional positions of leadership as well as of those who can be freshly recruited into leadership positions can be channeled into diversified centers of power, or they can be funneled into one center. If the ruling intelligentsia prevent the emergence of new diversified centers of power and loyalty, if they attempt to control all accumulations of newly available power, they move in a totalitarian direction. If, on the other hand, there emerges a diversity of allegiances and a many-sided integration of individuals in a variety of institutional orders, then the chances for a democratic development at a later time are increased. The liberal model has no chance of institutionalization in the underdeveloped countries, if for no other reason than that economic development will require an amount of deliberate centralized planning which is incompatible with liberalism. Yet, if the road toward later democratic developments is not to be blocked, the widest possible diffusion of power compatible with centralized planning is a prerequisite.

The claims of efficiency might appear often to militate in favor of authoritative directives and centralized government. The requirements of struggle against traditional elements lead to the erosion of local centers of feudal and tribal power. National allocation of scarce re-

* For ideas developed in the next few pages I have borrowed considerably from a seminal paper by Professor Samuel N. Eisenstadt of the University of Jerusalem, "Soziale Entwicklung und Politische Stabilitaet in Nichtwestlichen Gesellschaften," *Koelner Zeitschrift fuer Soziologie und Sozialpsychologie*, XII, 2, 1960, pp. 189–203. *cf.* also Bert Hoselitz and Myron Weiner, "Economic Development and Political Stability in India," *Dissent*, VIII, 2 (Spring, 1961).

sources requires central planning. Yet if the population is not in the long run to become totally dependent on the tutelary power of the State, it is essential that the political elite of the center does not control the new forces set free, thus preventing the development of autonomous social and political centers of power.

The chances for greater participation of nongovernmental organizations in the modernizing process will increase if under authoritarian regimes there grows up a new social structure with an autonomous life of its own: modernizing rural cooperatives under the guidance of new members of the technical intelligentsia; trade unions in the industrial centers; local and regional governing boards; autonomous educational and scientific institutions, and the like. If in addition there develops a rich associational life in the nonpolitical orders, the national community may gradually be led to rely on the process of bargaining between groups and individuals rather than on governmental fiat. Under such conditions direct governmental intervention could be kept at a minimum and broad policies replace detailed directives. The very clash and conflict between autonomous centers of power would serve as a balancing mechanism. Whether such a development will come about will depend to a very significant degree on patterns of recruitment; i.e., on whether potential leaders will be attracted mainly by the centralizing state or at least a certain proportion of them will be available for leadership in local and regional centers of power, and in nongovernmental institutions.

Given the dominant role of the state apparatus in the new nations, it is to be expected that it will attract a high proportion of all those who wish to rise on the scale of prestige and to profit from the reallocation of power. The discrepancy in living standards between the elite and the rest of the population which characterizes underdeveloped nations will be an added incentive for joining the elite. Employment in the State or Party apparatus, be it in executive bodies or the bureaucracy, is likely to be regarded as the most significant channel of upward mobility and as the major means of access to scarce power, resources, and prestige. This would lead to the gradual erosion of other, nonpolitical, institutional orders, and the preponderance of the political over the economic, cultural, and educational elites. To the extent that the centralized State would assume predominance and come to constitute in the eyes of the population the major source of power, financial reward, and prestige, the local, regional, and nongovernmental centers of power would be weakened. If other centers fail to attract gifted leaders, the political order will preempt the available supply of scarce talents.

If gifted members of the intelligentsia flock exclusively to the service of the government rather than, say, to teaching positions in schools or colleges, then the latter will be staffed by the mediocre and lose even more prestige. Consequently they will not be able to function as a counterweight to the powers of the political order. Similar consequences are likely to follow in the economic order, be it private or cooperative: the quality of the economic elite will steadily decline and so will its prestige if the more enterprising and ambitious members of the younger generation will be attracted by employment in the central economic administration.* When power and opportunity are concentrated in the center, they act like a magnet, attracting the talented men from the whole society and gradually undermining the resistances emanating from off-center powers.

Tocqueville knew this well when he wrote, "In proportion as the duties of the central power are augmented, the number of public officials by whom that power is represented must increase also. They form a nation in each nation . . . they more and more fill up the place of an aristocracy." In the long run this would lead to an approximation of the totalitarian model. Such a trend can be effectively weakened only to the extent that participation in the nongovernmental sphere will carry no less prestige and influence, and bring psychic and monetary income commensurate with that derived from employment by the State.

Hence, the strengthening of autonomous institutions, such as independent schools and universities, independent trade unions, regional and local power centers, village cooperatives, and the like are of prime importance if the road toward democratization is not to be permanently barred. (This is why India, where such institutions function rather vigorously, seems to have the best chances fully to institutionalize democratic processes.) Not only are such centers of secondary power likely to function as effective checks to central power; they are also likely to struggle with the central power, as well as among themselves, for the allegiance of the citizens. As citizens are drawn into such conflicts they increase their own political awareness and participation. Conflicts with some produce associations with others and provide bonds between citizens, drawing them into a rich social life. Individuals otherwise isolated, mutually hostile, or apathetic are in this way brought into the field of public activities. A multiplicity of associations, a pluralism of power centers, whose diverse purposes crisscross each other, helps to prevent the atomization on which totalitarianism has always thrived. For atomized and isolated individuals are ready to rely on the immense

* It should also be noted here that to the extent that there are tendencies toward closure in the political and bureaucratic structures; i.e., to the extent that they limit recruitment of new personnel from the outside, there is a danger of the creation of strata of disappointed office seekers. Such strata are peculiarly apt to engage in the politics of discontent; they are especially susceptible to the appeal of Communism. Thus both a too exclusive recruitment of the elite into the central political order, and a closure in that order barring potential recruits from access and yet not offering alluring chances in other areas, are likely to have detrimental consequences for the process of democratization.

tutelary power of a State which alone, so it seems to them, is able to provide the satisfactions they crave; men tempered in the struggles and contentions of societies with rich and diversified group life, drawn toward each other in multifarious battles to realize their own goals, are less wont to rely on the tutelary power of the State.

Tocqueville considered the gravest peril for individual freedom to stem from conditions where "the performance of private persons are insignificant, those of the State immense." It follows that the furtherance of democracy requires the strengthening of "private persons" and this is possible only if such private persons can rely on protective secondary powers uncontrolled by the State. They must, in other words, become part of a network of diverse social relationships in a variety of group involvements.

Those who are moved only by considerations of efficiency and consider that only neat and orderly arrangements are likely to permit the new nations to emerge from the sloth of traditional stagnation, are likely to find my suggestions rather unappealing. But they should heed the warning that the most efficient administrations are likely to be found in model prisons rather than in vital human communities. The best chances for democracy may sometimes clash with the optimum conditions for efficiency. Wherever this is the case, the democrat must be willing to sacrifice optimum efficiency.

A kind of vulgar Marxism has again become quite fashionable of late. Many commentators seem to argue for a rigid determinism according to which industrialization in the underdeveloped countries must necessarily bring in its wake predetermined "superstructures." Yet the European experience itself suggests no such easy generalizations. Consider only the immense difference in the "superstructure" of, say, nineteenth-century Germany and England. This is why I cannot subscribe to the theory of an ineluctable drift toward totalitarianism which is now so often bandied about. The new nations, and those who will make the key decisions within them, face a series of crucial choices. Much will depend on their intentions and on the ideology which informs them. They can, if they so desire, deliberately create or at least permit the growth of a dispersed power structure in their countries. They can, though ruling as authoritarians, lay the foundations for a future democracy. Whether they will do so in a significant number of cases it would be rash to predict. All one can say at this stage is that this is possible, and that the road into the future of the new nations, far from being determined in advance, is still open.

1963

# RETURN TO INDIA
## STANLEY PLASTRIK

**New Delhi — July, 1960**

It isn't easy to return to India after a twenty-year absence. So much has
happened and so much changed. There is a whole new generation that
has known freedom since 1947. What will it be like? Will one find the
spirit of national sacrifice and struggle, so striking to a young socialist in
1940, still alive in the country?

On this visit I plan to spend as much time as possible in the countryside.
Despite uncontrolled movement into the cities, close to 80 percent of
the population still lives on the land or tied down to a village occupation. Arrangements have been made to tour villages under the government's Community Development Project. But I plan also to visit villages
developing independently under the cooperative *bhoodan* or *gramdan* program of Vinoba Bhave, disciple of Gandhi, and Jayaprakash
Narayan, former socialist leader. After two days of New Delhi, armed
with a bedroll and food, I leave by train for Jaipur, main city of the
newly formed state of Rajasthan made up by piecing together many
backward princely and petty territories. Leave-takings from Indian sta-
tions were always dramatic events; this is no exception. The old city of
Delhi where the station is located is a packed shambles of humanity;

we plow through the streets clinging to a motorcycle cab. The station, no matter the hour, reflects the condition of the masses who live in the old city. Thousands fill its platforms and crevices, sprawled on covers, preparing evening meals even on the railway tracks between platforms. I notice for the first time the complete absence of foreigners, Europeans, whites; not an English soldier, official, or policeman. This is the most striking and immediate evidence of independence.

It is to be an all-night ride, reaching Jaipur at 6 A.M. The train will leave on time, but certainly arrive hours late. An hour before we leave the cars are packed. I squeeze my way into a second-class car (one per train). Later in the night someone will offer me his "berth," the baggage rack high above the seats. I spend the night trying not to fall asleep for fear of slipping off and crashing down on the heads below. The endurance test of train travel in India has not changed; the train bumps slowly along over a wornout roadbed.

## Jaipur, Rajasthan — Community Development Block

In India 295,004,251 people, forming 82.7 percent of the country's population, are village dwellers. They live in about 558,000 scattered village settlements. Out of a total popula- tion of 357 million, according to the 1951 census, 249 mil- lion fall into "agricultural classes," and of these, 210 million or 96 percent live in villages. . . . Agriculture in the coun- try is mostly subsistence farming; 83.5 percent of all agricul- tural production being foodstuffs. Besides the agricultural classes, the rest of the village population consists mainly of artisan and occupational castes whose economy and lives are largely integrated with the economic and socio-religious life of the peasant communities.

In general, the village presents a picture of poverty, mal- nutrition, poor standards of public health, and illiteracy.*

The train is two hours behind time, but the telegram arranging my visit has not yet arrived! At the government tourist hotel I endure the awkwardness of breakfast alone in a dining room with five mustached and turbaned "bearers" serving. Summer is an off-tourist season, yet employees must be kept on for lack of work elsewhere. The totally un- employed are said to still run close to the 40 million mark; the sea- sonally and underemployed run into many million more. Mr. U., Deputy Development Commissioner, arrives; he is to take me to the out- lying areas around the city of Jaipur.

The Community Development Program, launched in 1952 under In-

* S. C. Dube, *India's Changing Villages,* p. 7. An excellent work on basic problems of Indian agriculture.

dia's first Five Year Plan, is the government's chosen instrument of rural advance through self-help plus government aid and direction. Its formal aims are to increase substantially the country's agricultural production, particularly in foodstuffs, to improve rural communications, health, and hygiene as well as village education. Its long-range aim is no less than a social and economic transformation of the villages. By 1956, the Community Development Program covered one-fourth of India; by the end of 1959, one-half; and by the end of October, 1963, the entire country will be covered, according to the just-adopted Third Five Year Plan.*

By making the former collector of each district its chief development officer, by carrying the program to each village through the training of local workers, it was hoped that a vast number of rural communities would improve their techniques, create village leadership, foster cooperatives for services, mobilize local labor and, in general revitalize village life. From my observations and from other reports I conclude that, despite some successes, the results have been extremely uneven and spotty.

In Jaipur district, maize, *bajera* (for the making of unleavened pancake bread), and winter wheat sown in October are raised. There are two yearly crops; irrigation — we are close to desert regions here — is employed, with widespread use of canals, and tanks for holding water. The land must be worked hard; dry and lumpy, it is not particularly friendly to agriculture. I jeep to the village of B., headquarters village for the Block, population approximately 4,000. Out of the city the roads become narrow, rutted, with the once metallic surfacing worn off. Thus far, what I have seen of North India's railroad, road, and communication infrastructure is not encouraging; the improvement during the last twenty years seems negligible. Gunnar Myrdal, on a recent visit to India, wrote that India's basic infrastructure was still weak and far removed from that of a modern industrial state.

On the way to the village I make several stops. Here a special Block Development school is in progress; I watch a meeting of top representatives from village *panchyats* (councils). These stops are hasty, permitting only an exchange of greetings and a few questions. Several women, it is worth noting, are at both meetings, sitting quietly, with heads bowed and partly covered. Several lower-caste representatives are also present, sitting slightly apart. The bulk of the men present are clearly picked members of the better-off farm families, examples of the Indian "middle" farmer. They are tall, intelligent in appearance, and energetic. Both school and meeting appear to be effectively run by the Development officials, men of experience, special knowledge, and train-

* *Third Five Year Plan,* A Draft Outline, Planning Commission, June, 1960, p. 153.

ing. The atmosphere is friendly, serious, and good humored. The government relies upon these farmers; both state and central government subsidize them and they are to form the backbone of India's progressive, land-holding, market crop-producing peasantry. Receptive and shrewd, these men are far removed from the militant, revolutionary peasant leaders of 1940. Their lessons and discussions deal with improved farming practices, the growing Jaipur market, profit-making, and not the struggle for land. The village I am to visit is theirs.

Like villages in most peasant lands, B. has one main street which winds off into the distance. By Indian standards, it is a large and well-organized village. Only its fringes are unkempt and disorderly. At the *panchyat* building, which also serves as the revenue collecting office, the village cooperative, and the village school, the village head recites the benefits of the Community Development program: in agriculture, better arrangements for procuring seed and farm instruments; advice from experts; facilities for irrigation under local control; increase in crop production (almost double in winter wheat, 60 percent in other crops). In regard to relationships within and without the village, he explains how it had formerly "belonged" to a powerful, absentee landlord, the *jagadir,* a feudal agent of the Maharajah of Jaipur. Now this gentleman, along with his rajah, has been retired to the city. The villagers have since begun to run their own affairs; this is true throughout Rajasthan, once a center of absentee landlordism and feudal exploitation. The chief's eyes shine as he tells his oft-repeated story; clearly, this is the major change that has taken place. He claims significant progress in village integration; that is, the raising of the depressed castes, redistribution of lands, changed status of the landless. But here, when asked to be specific, he hedges a little.

For one thing, apart from redistribution of lands confiscated by the state — at goodly prices — from the landowners, no basic change in land relationships has come about. As throughout India, the privately owned, family farm is the basic unit. The story I am told in this "show" village supports government claims for its program: the end of the *zamindari* system of absentee landlordism, the creation of an elective and functioning village *panchyat;* a ban on public untouchability and a limited improvement in farm productivity. But only the worst and most monstrous inequalities in land ownership have been abolished by government action; the *jagadir* has gone, but an explosive inequality remains.

Before the village leader takes me on a tour of his village I question him about possible *gramdan* villages in the area, based upon one or another form of cooperative farming. This is unfamiliar to him; in his area the land is far too fragmented for any kind of redistribution to include the landless. As for cooperative farming that might involve a pooling of resources, he is not interested. We walk through the village over a newly built, winding road made of stones fitted together. On either side are small shops; at least twenty temples are scattered throughout the town — some substantial in size, others merely a corner for offerings and an altar. On both sides of the main street are homes, occasionally two-storied, in which people are eating. They are not curious and only a few children follow along; evidently, there have been many visitors here. This village is prosperous, the chief affirms it; most proudly of all, he shows us his new store, a kind of dry-goods store stocked with cloth, cottons, woolens. We talk about the building of the new road — it was accomplished through labor donated by the villagers, but the rich again had bought their way out. The Development official admits that this deprives such village projects of their spontaneity and makes them appear in the eyes of the villagers as days given over to forced labor under government supervision. The village leader, of course, is not concerned with this. The vastly improved appearance of his village counts most for him. He feels he has provided energetic leadership, and indeed he has; his reward is both one of status — acknowledged leader of a well-to-do village — and personal affluence, both as a holder of land and a businessman.

### Patna, Bihar State

The plane trip to Patna has been hot, humid, tiring. Since planes must fly under the monsoon clouds, we have had a close look at the spread of the Ganges plain and river valley, observing the endlessly fragmented fields and paddy lands extending miles in all directions, the network of canals, streams, irrigation ditches, tanks, and wells, the thousands of villages that dot the plains.

In the struggle over federal funds for state development projects, Bihar belongs to the group of states that come off second best. This is reflected in its capital, Patna, an old, dirty provincial city that sprawls for miles in all directions. My appointment with Jayaprakash Narayan is for the following day; I go out to find the Praja Socialist headquarters. One of the young socialists — he is an Urdu village poet from the northern part of the state — accompanies me on a visit to the archeological sites and ruins of ancient Patna. As we roll over dirt roads in a rickshaw, he declaims Urdu poetry he has written. His booming voice attracts a crowd. They seem to enjoy it; it sounds revolutionary and sentimental. Later, when we are alone, he recites an English poem he has composed. He is visibly upset by my unresponsiveness and we never meet again. Unsophisticated, provincial, utterly sincere, he is typical of many socialists in India. Such men are unmarried or have cut their family ties; they offer their service to their party wherever it may be. There is no money, and home is usually the floor of the party headquarters where he happens to be.

In the evening, S., an active organizer in the *Bhoodan* movement, comes to arrange our trip to the remote cooperative village we plan to see. It will take at least three days' time and he will be with us constantly. Capable, intelligent, with a touch of skepticism and sufficient doubting to make his opinions more valuable than those of the blindly convinced, his help is indispensable.

## Jayaprakash Narayan

Since abandoning active leadership in the Indian Socialist movement, Narayan has made his headquarters in Patna, in one of the buildings that belongs to the *Bhoodan* movement. This complex man, known to enormous numbers of people in every corner of India, whose life spans every important happening in the last twenty-five years of Indian history, is now engaged in an experiment that has taken him far from the road of traditional Leftist politics: the *Bhoodan* land distribution movement which appeals to landowners to surrender their holdings voluntarily.

In Gandhi were combined the saint and the politician, the two working together harmoniously. But the same, one feels, cannot be said of Narayan. In him saint and politician struggle endlessly. A man who proposes to dedicate himself to the reconstruction of "village democracy" and to improving the life of the village poor must not only renounce his formal political ties; he must renounce all forms of political action. But for a man like Narayan, this is the most difficult of steps. Hence, there are those who claim his withdrawal from active politics is largely strategic, to place himself in the best position at a critical moment. My own impression is that this claim is either cynical or mistaken; Narayan seems incapable of such manipulation.

Narayan has wrestled long and passionately with the great problems: what road shall his country take, the decline of socialism and Marxism, the rise of nameless authoritarian power. All of this is clear in his manner, his way of talking, his hesitations, his latest writings. His wish is to veer away from power, yet his strong concern with it indicates he has not resolved these problems within himself. In the several hours we spend together we cover a range of topics, but primarily those touching upon agricultural matters in general and the *Bhoodan* movement in particular. He is completely sympathetic, his humor gentle but pointed.

Narayan cannot accept the operation of the Community Development Project. Essentially, he feels, it is an attempt to impose an anti-Indian concept of agriculture upon a weak village base. We discuss in some detail a new aspect of this program, known as the "package program," which is about to be launched under Ford Foundation auspices. It is an attempt to stimulate food production through an elaborate system of incentives, including guaranteed minimum prices, and is, of course, aimed at the middle peasant. But Narayan is more concerned with the landless and the village poor. This leads to a discussion of my visit to one of the *gramdan* cooperative villages Narayan himself has organized and sponsored. He sketches the background of the *Bhoodan* movement, his relations with Vinoba Bhave, its founder, and frankly speaks of its declining prospects. Although the movement had an astounding success in its early phase (asking for and receiving donations of land), its subsequent phase (organization and development of the donated land) has met with many difficulties: much of the land proved to be worthless; donations had to be surveyed before redistribution could take place; most important of all, it was hard to find the necessary capital, credits, resources, to develop properly the redistributed lands. Narayan's general concern with political power applies as well to village political organization. For him, the greatest successes of *bhoodan* and *gramdan* lie in intangibles — the new spirit of collective living and working it has engendered.

## Gramdan Village

The *Bhoodan* movement initiated in 1951 by Acharya Vinoba Bhave has grown into the *Gramdan* movement. Under *Bhoodan*, people were requested to donate voluntarily some out of their land for being redistributed to the landless people of the village. Under *Gramdan*, however, in its ideal form, all the people in the village owning land donate all their land into a pool which would then become the property of the community as a whole. Thus, *Gramdan*, today, is the voluntary surrender of individual ownership rights in land in favour of the community. . . . The village community, as a whole, treats itself as a big family. Love and nonviolence will be the basis of all acts of the community. Cooperation and equitable sharing together will be its guiding principles.*

The *gramdan* village of Berain is 160 miles from Patna, and 10 miles from the nearest railway station. There is no choice but to ride a jeep supplied by the local *Bhoodan* organization and take off for the long drive. We follow a road along the Ganges for some hours, an area still closely linked to the city of Patna — the towns even have electricity.

* From a report published by the Department of Community Development, Government of India, 1951.

But once we turn inland, the true Indian countryside asserts itself. Though there are few cars on the road we move slowly, blocked by the constant passage of cattle into the fields. On all sides are the endless paddy fields; the road runs through the fields on a built-up embankment or *bund*. While we are close to the Ganges there are many funeral processions — a stretcher borne aloft on which the body is carried, covered with a red cloth, head uncovered. Musicians beating gongs lead the way; no women are permitted among the mourners as they move toward the burning *ghats*. Within two hours we are in the heart of village India: huts, poverty, nakedness, dirt, misery in every conceivable form, yet borne with dignity.

The next day, we cross a hilly and lightly forested area before coming back to the plain on which is located the *gramdan* village. In this small, wooded area live a primitive, aboriginal people, among the most ancient of Indians. In the early morning their women trot along the roadside, bearing bundles of firewood on their head for sale in the villages. It is the main occupation of these tribal people. Within a short time we pass through the last village of any size, but here the jeep becomes hopelessly mired in mud. We must walk the remaining five miles. The sun is out; it is impossible to even see the village in the distance. It is necessary to struggle on over roads deep in mud and water and find our way across the paddy fields by balancing ourselves on the slippery embankments surrounding each field. At the end of an exhausting two hours, we hear the sound of gongs and conch horns; men from the village are coming out to greet us and bring us in. On the last half mile we are transported on the sturdy back of a village peasant. Hundreds of villagers receive us; it seems I am not only the first American to come, but the first white-skinned foreigner their children have ever seen.

The village of Berain lies not far from an area inhabited by a primitive people. It consists of 83 families (population, 429), most lower caste. They grow some wheat, but have mainly rice paddies. They have been under *gramdan* for two years and consider it successful; they talk of a "collective spirit." Before *gramdan,* the people of this village were notorious thieves who lived by robbing neighboring villages. They worked for property-owning peasants when they were not busy thieving. Of the 83 families, 73 were landless. When they accepted *gramdan,* it signified that those who owned land donated it to the entire village; this, plus land they have been able to rent, constitute their pitifully small acreage under cultivation.

Given their previous economic and social degradation, it is easy to understand the powerful appeal *gramdan* has for them. When Jayaprakash Narayan came to their village some years back, it was in effect to offer them a new way of life. These people cultivate their lands in common and pool both resources and income. Those who work the land receive wages from a common fund in the hands of the cooperative society which runs the village economic life. As a result, not only has agricultural yield risen, but many typically village industries have been started. The average per capita income has risen from 54 rupees per year to 77 rupees.

I learn all this from the leading men of the village who proudly pour out the story of their accomplishments. They now have work for the entire year. Their rice production per acre — using Japanese methods — has increased from 13 to 22 *maunds* (a *maund* = 82 lbs.). They have built a small school for children; over one hundred people of the village now can read and write; drinking and smoking are prohibited; robberies have stopped entirely. Their enthusiasm is matched only by their eagerness to show us everything.

The appearance of the village is poor. Mud huts, with walls almost a foot thick, thatched roofs, dark interiors. No electricity, no village radio. But one of the major projects is to reconstruct all the homes out of brick; in fact, bricks are being accumulated for this, much as a child hoards pennies. We move out to the fields which encircle the village on all sides. This is the season to transplant the rice plant into the paddies where it will remain immersed in water for some time. As is the practice throughout Asia the village women ranged in a row across the field are advancing the length of the paddy, pushing the rice seedlings into the mud as they move along. In other fields belonging to the village, teams of bullocks are plowing; this is the first time we have seen collective plowing in India. There is much singing, good-natured joking and staring at the white foreigner. I attend a meeting of the village *gram sabha* or council; it is planning the program of the following week, practical, constructive, aimed at the fulfillment of simple tasks. In the school that has been built, primary education is offered to the children by day, to their parents at night. They sing, dance, and recite their lessons for us; I, in turn, am called upon to make a little speech. All words sound banal and inadequate here.

The Westerner coming from the lowest sector of European or American society lives in affluence as compared with these people. There are three to four thousand *gramdan* villages throughout India — sufficient in number for state governments to have passed legislation providing them some help — but compared to the total number of villages, they are insignificant. Even if a village like Berain succeeds by dint of enormous effort in accumulating some means, how can it expect to compete in the open marketplace with the more efficient villages dominated by the middle peasant with his credits, superior technique, government support, and — Ford Foundation? Yet, so low and bare is the starting point for such a *gramdan* village that for a time it cannot help but make important progress. A landless peasant now able to purchase a kerosene lamp for his mud hut feels he has advanced into another world; by that lamp he can read.

That night, standing out alone in the humid darkness, listening to the sounds of the village and the surrounding fields, I grasp — insofar as a Westerner can — what the meaning of impoverishment is to tens of millions. Yet these people want no pity or sympathy; on the contrary, *gramdan* has given them hope. Surely Narayan's argument that the Indian countryside can accept many forms of organization and many ways of life is borne out here.

## The Land Problem

The land problem is recognized as the key to the new social and economic order now being evolved. Accordingly, land reforms are under way, though methods vary and results are not easily assessed. In some countries, agrarian reform has been ruthless. In others, the approach has been administrative.

In India, we have adopted the unique combination of lofty ideals, confused thinking, vague promises, and a bias for spiritual force in planning and enforcing land reform. The result is that we have not even scratched the surface of the land problem in the country. We are still in the midst of indecision and confusion. We lack a clear-cut program based on accurate data and we have not evolved any practical line of action. The program is still bogged down at all levels.*

Food is still the most urgent problem. The annual expenditure to make up the food deficit through imports is entirely too great. But the *real* food shortage is many times more. As Professor Desai has said, *"There are millions of have-nots in the country who have no means to produce or buy food. If there is a general shortage of food, the real sufferer will be that class which is most down-trodden in society — the class of landless and agricultural laborers many of whom live on leaves and roots some months in a year. If these sections are to be fed, the total requirements of food will increase and with it the food shortage."* †

Has there then been so little progress in the annual growth in grain production? It is calculated that 3 percent per annum is the rate since 1952. The new Five Year Plan requires an additional 25,000,000 tons of grain or a yearly increase of at least 5 percent. Although, theoretically, a sharp rise was possible because of the low productivity of most Indian

* From an editorial in *The Indian Express.*
† *Janata,* August 21, 1960.

farms, the obstacles have proven formidable. To break up the en-
crusted accumulation of ancient ways and customs and to release productive forces required a leadership not yet forthcoming in India.

The Community Development Program was the government's answer
to the problem of too many people and too little land. Yields were to be
improved through irrigation, better farming techniques, seed, fertilizers,
and equipment. The size of farms could be regulated by abolishing absentee landlordism and encouraging some redistribution while preventing undue fragmentation. The net result is that the farmer holding 25 to
30 acres of land has become the dominant citizen in the village hierarchy. Below him are the poorer farmers, some owners, some tenants,
some with holdings split into scattered strips — 50 percent of *all* holdings in India are less than 5 acres, many less than one. At the bottom
of the peasant scale are more than ten million families who have no
land, agricultural laborers who work for one rupee a day. Most of them
are also untouchables, excluded from rising in the caste-ridden villages.
For them, the only hope is to get away into the cities.

## Toward Calcutta — late July

A city turbulent, jittery, easily upset. Calcutta is the home of Indian
terrorist nationalism, its people quick and volatile, forever dissatisfied
and demanding. The thing to find out would be the effect that partition,
that deep wound separating Bengal into West and East, India and Pakistan, has had upon its people. Never had the Bengali dreamed he would
see his land divided in two, nor had he expected the day to come when
five million of his fellows would be forced to flee and be shunted like
nomads through different parts of India.

Twenty years ago Calcutta was militantly organized behind the ultra-
nationalist leadership of Subhas Chandra Bose and his "Forward Bloc,"
its dissatisfactions centering largely around the failure of the Congress
movement to move with sufficient rapidity toward independence. The
city felt sure of itself in those days. But Bose perished mysteriously
while allied to the Japanese. And the controlling forces and passions
of the war period are, of course, gone.

Waiting for the Calcutta plane at the Patna airport, I overhear a
dialogue of the deaf. An American woman, in her sixties, on a flight to
"visit friends" in Singapore, is describing her husband's wheat farm in
Nebraska to my friend S., the *bhoodan* guide who is seeing me off.
Half a mile wide, about ten miles long, totally mechanized, valued at
about $300,000. S. counters with a description of the average family
farm in the Ganges basin, two to four acres, operated by arm, leg, and
back power, valued at under one thousand dollars. Neither grasps the
other's description. "Why are all you Indians so spindly in the legs?" the

Nebraska lady despairingly demands. S. smiles politely and explains, there are so many of us.

Some hours later we reach Dum Dum airport north of Calcutta. Calcutta is very much alive; it is, in fact, in the midst of a general strike (*hartal*). The *hartal* is a popular protest strike of Bengalis in support of people from West Bengal who now live and work in the state of Assam, over toward the Burmese border. It is caused by the "language issue," a problem tormenting India's unity since independence. The reports from Assam are unclear, but sufficiently detailed to indicate that uncontrollable violence and mob hysteria are on the loose, a violence directed by Assamese groups against the powerful linguistic minority of Bengalis in their state. Of particular significance is the fact that, for the first time to my knowledge, Indians from one part of the country are apparently unsafe in another part of their own country. The *hartal* which has utterly paralyzed the city is due to end late that afternoon; until then no busses or cars dare move.

The continued industrial development of Calcutta, West Bengal, and the sector leading southward toward Madras may ultimately change the picture I have drawn. For one thing, it will become impossible to ignore the deterioration in relations between New Delhi and Calcutta. Further, the new steel centers (Perambur, Bhilai, Rourkela, located close by) give a weight and importance to the area in terms of Indian economic planification. Take the steel industry. Before the second Five Year Plan (1955), India produced one million tons of finished steel, mainly at the Tata Iron and Steel Works, a single privately-owned plant in Jamshedpur, state of Bihar. The Planning Commission decided to set up three steel projects, now in varying degrees of construction and operation in the publicly owned sector and with a production target of six million tons altogether.* At Bhilai, for instance, the steel township already has 100,000 people. Such towns and areas face all the questions familiar in the modern industrial world: the conflict between the Indian Civil Service administering these vast modern projects and the technicians and specialists who build and run them; the conflict between rival Indian trade unions anxious to organize large numbers of new and comparatively well-paid workers; and the difficulties inherent in establishing new industrial centers with reasonably modern living conditions. For the time being, the triangular industrial area whose points are Calcutta to the east, Jamshedpur to the west, and Visagapatnam to the south must remain in a state of chronic restlessness brought on by large-scale industrialization.

* China, 12,000,000 tons; Russia, 60,000,000; U.S.A., 120,000,000.

## Madras — early August

Madras, capital of the newly reorganized new language state of Madras, is South India's largest city, gateway to what historians conceive of as classic India. The people of Madras and all of South India are clearly different. At one time, these people, Dravidians, controlled the entire subcontinent and the South Indian nationalists have never forgotten this. Then came the endless round of invasions from central Asia, from the Near and Far East, and finally, from the West — each invasion compressing these people and their culture deeper into the southern tip of the subcontinent. C. Ross Smith has summed up the differences between North and South:*

> . . . The north's comparatively light skin becomes black; the frame becomes smaller, more wiry; saris and turbans, no longer pale and washed, become deep green and purple and yellow and red; the languages (Tamil, Kanarese, Telugu, Malayalam, etc.) become agglutinative (the average word contains six or seven syllables); the voice becomes louder, more urgent; the head bounces from side to side in the Madrasi waggle; the smile is more quickly there, more quickly gone, superficial.

In the city of Madras the emphasis is on the historical: the Portuguese were here and built the curious Cathedral of San Thome near which I stay; the doubting Saint Thomas is supposed to have been martyred here; Marco Polo on the way back from China in the thirteenth century stopped in the harbor; the East India Company (1639) set up its famous Fort St. George (Thomas Pitt, Warren Hastings). Madras has a rhythm and pace all its own; to enter it is to enter a world quite apart from the northern regions of India. For one thing, its cultural life — largely traditional and classic — separates it from the more diversified north. Classical Hindu music, theater, dance, are pursued with intense passion throughout South India.

The city itself is dry, dusty, overpoweringly hot. My first accidental contact while I am looking for the PSP headquarters is, curiously enough, with an ardent young Tamil nationalist who explains to me he had once been a socialist but feels the "socialists" betrayed South India to the North. He belongs to the DMK (*Dravida Munnetra Kazagham*), a movement favoring South Indian separatism, and speaks a political language which, I confess, was new and surprising to me; separatism, Dravidians are the victims of Delhi and northern economic imperialism, the Congress is run by northern Brahmans, etc. I learn later to evaluate

* *In Search of India,* p. 208.

this movement as a social protest of the poor of South India (above all, untouchable and lower caste people) against the wealthy and ruling Brahmanic elite. While it is easy to overestimate its strength because of the extreme violence of its language, the DMK is symptomatic of the admitted failure to integrate the parts of India into a coherent nation.

My first day at Madras — it had begun at 5 A.M. in Calcutta — ends twenty hours later in the overpowering embrace of a Tamil movie which, having begun 3½ hours earlier, was still moving strongly along when I staggered out into the heavy Madras night. A fantastic mixture of the incredibly bad (posturing and declaiming at its worst) and the incredibly beautiful (*Bharat natyam* classic dancing, natural scenes shot against the stone pagodas, carvings and elephants of Mahabalipuram, the sacred temple area south of Madras). Like most of the interminable Indian pictures, the story was based on incidents from some ancient legend, this from the life of one of the ancient Pallava kings. Sleep was impossible the rest of the night; it is not as easy to make the transition from Calcutta to Madras as, say, from New York to Chicago.

There are numerous discussions with many individuals, socialists, people of long experience and background in the nationalist movement — in general, their political cultivation is broader and more objective than that of the Bengalis. But to me, most important, was a visit to Antony Pillai, an important figure in the Madras labor movement. Originally from Ceylon, Pillai is now thoroughly integrated into the life of South India. In addition to heading a local group of labor unions, Pillai, who received his political training in the Ceylon Trotskyist movement, was elected by a local constituency to the Indian Parliament at New Delhi. He has the reputation of being one of India's most skillful labor leaders. Still, I must confess to some disappointment, for his approach to trade unionism in India seemed to me to indicate the general weakness of labor in a country whose industrial and economic growth ought to be turned to the profit of the unions.

One of the basic and unresolved problems of the Indian trade unions is their relationship to the political parties that frequently dominate them, a relationship that keeps the unions from achieving the autonomy they have in some of the Western countries. Pillai, however, seemed to find no problem here, perhaps because his public role depends upon a continuation of a commonly accepted situation. But I doubt that the hundreds of thousands of newly-trained workers drawn into the new and complex industries India is building up so rapidly can be satisfactorily served by a trade union leadership that is dependent on the wishes of one or another party.

If we accept the figure of two million union members for all of India, about 48 percent belong to the Congress-dominated unions (Indian National Trade Union Congress), about 20 percent to the Communist-controlled unions (All-India Trade Union Congress), about 16 percent to the socialist-controlled unions (Hind Mazdoor Sabha), about 6 percent to unions organized by dissident socialists (Marxist United Trade Union Congress), and about 10 percent independent.

But, and here I follow the analysis of Rohit Dave, an excellent political and economic observer, these figures by themselves signify rather little. They fluctuate rapidly and workers tend to shift allegiance in accordance with their estimate of who is closest to the sources of power. The activities of outside political leaders in the unions ". . . does lead to the phenomenon of exaggerated promises to the workers, one group outbidding the other and creating tensions which are out of proportion to the economic realities." Dave does not oppose the active participation of outside political leaders at this stage of India's trade union development, but he does insist upon minimizing their political exploitation of economic situations. He feels that ". . . much more could have been achieved than what has been by this [labor] movement so far." *

In the future it seems probable, however, that with the number of workers employed in industry rising rapidly, a different type of labor leader will come forward — one trained in the techniques of industrial relations, economic research, the skills of management, and collective bargaining. There will be little place for the transitory politically oriented labor leader, skilled in organizing the spontaneous strike, in militancy, in the fly-by-night kind of union. This will be infinitely less dramatic than in the past, but then the task of contributing to a nation's growth by pursuing intelligent but limited aims is usually not one of high drama.

My few days in Kerala are largely on my own. Although it is a year since Communist rule was removed from the state, I come away with a sense of uneasiness. One feels in the air of Trivandrum and other towns and cities that these people have passed through a harsh experience whose effects are far from shaken off. Although legally elevated to power in the state elections, the Communists deliberately set about creating a situation in which their rule would be perpetuated through extralegal means: the infiltration and transformation of all political and social institutions. In a state where politics is a pastime (over thirty daily newspapers), suffering from density of population and widespread unemployment, and with a highly literate population, it is not surprising to learn there has always been an intense fragmentation of social and political life.

* See excellent discussion article, Rohit Dave, "New Outlook for Indian Trade Unionism," *Janata*, October 30, 1960, and subsequent issues.

:

The upshot of many discussions with officials and political people is that
Kerala still must go far before overcoming the effects of Communist
rule. Most of all, it must establish its own prosperity and stability.
P. T. Chacko, the powerful minister for Home Affairs, Catholic, Congress leader and anti-Communist ideologue, expresses the need for
basic "law and order" throughout the state, with the application of
economic planning and massive capital import from without. More important, he acknowledges the weakness of the present government (a
coalition of the Congress party, Praja-Socialists and the Muslim League)
by stating bluntly to me that the Communists still have the support of
the workers in Kerala, the industrial unions, and "the poor." As so frequently happens in a coalition government, the various political forces
within it draw strength and supporters from one another rather than
from the enemy they have united against. The socialists have grown but
at the expense of the Congress; the Communists, led by the present
compromise national secretary of the Communist Party of India, Nam-
boodiripad, who had been Prime Minister of Kerala, have retained their
popular strength.

V. V. Giri, the New Delhi appointed Governor of Kerala State,
seemed to have the keenest understanding of Keralian problems: this
shrewd and able politician, an old-time leader of India's railway workers' unions, made clear his dissatisfaction with the uneasy alliance in
Kerala and its lack of accomplishments. Ousting the Communists in an
electoral alliance is one thing — desirable and fundamental — but the
disease, rooted in a generalized poverty and unemployment, still remains. I left Kerala with the impression that no definitive settlements
had been reached, that the future of the alliance was shaky and dis-
cordant (there was, for example, much criticism of the socialist Chief
Minister voiced by his own party people) and that only economic measures involving large sums of money from the central government could
bring results which would push Kerala into some kind of economic integration with the rest of India.

Does the Congress-Socialist coalition set a pattern for future politics
in the country? Or is this an isolated arrangement? This, of course, is an
open issue within the socialist movement. It seemed to me that the Kera-
lan coalition is unique, defensive in nature, and that the question of future coalitions between the Congress Left and the socialists, starting on a
local basis and perhaps leading eventually to a national coalition government, is rather a different question, tied to the country's future needs
rather than a rearguard action against a partly discredited Communist
movement.

Before flying out of Trivandrum to return to Madras, I visited the
University of Kerala to meet the students. Monsoon weather has struck

Kerala and many are idling about, classes over, with time on their hands. Like students everywhere, they are eager to talk. They are displeased with their university, with its teachers and classes, with their own prospects. The curriculum is rigid, old-fashioned, and formalistic; the university is comparable to a small-town, mediocre college somewhere in America. Much of the learning is by rote, by mimeographed sheets of notes handed down from "generation to generation"; there is little initiative or encouragement. The political parties naturally have their clubs, but this affects only a small percentage of the student body. Student actions, rather, result from more dramatic and direct situations — rumors of corruption, bickerings with bus conductors, movie managers, exams, and, above all, bad relations between professors and students.

The conservative elder who complains that the Indian student takes too much interest in "politics" is wrong; he's mistaking the demonstrations and protest riots for politics; actually, I found the Indian student even more indifferent to political life than his American counterpart. Since relations between boy and girl students in India is circumscribed by a tradition of puritanism upon which is imposed caste distinctions, it is quite natural that student energies are directed along pleasure-seeking lines. This is frowned upon, and the student must seek his pleasures surreptitiously; that is, tastelessly, without the normal joy of youth, and with much guilt. I spoke to students in many cities who confirmed this rather bleak picture; in Kerala I saw it again.

Yet, there is another, more official, side to this and it ought to be indicated. Humayun Kabir, the Central Government Minister of Scientific Research and Cultural Affairs and a noted educator whom I was to meet later in New Delhi, balances the picture in these words contained in his 1959 convocation address to the University of Kerala:

> In India, there are today about 800,000 students in universities and institutions of higher learning, which gives an intake of roughly 200,000 per year. The number of possible entrants by relevant age group per year would be almost 10 million! In other words, barely 2 percent of the total population of the relevant age group have the opportunity of university education and yet this proportion is itself high compared to many countries of the world. It compares favorably with the proportion in the United Kingdom and most countries of Western Europe and Japan. . . . In India, for every one in the university, 98 have been denied admission. And while they are in the university, they are being supported by the entire community at a cost which is about four times the per capita national income of our people.

These remarks are true, but they have little bearing on the quality of the university education received and they tend to ignore the many complaints one hears from Indian students everywhere.

## Bombay — early August

Bombay means "Americanization," people with problems of leisure time, vacation time, boredom time, money in ample amounts, juvenile delinquency coexisting with cocktail parties that flout the city's prohibition laws, India's only practicing psychoanalysts, art, theater, culture, rounds of movies (the latest) from abroad. For better or worse, Bombay is a modern city facing Europe and the West.

Bombay means wretched housing conditions, gigantic slums to which flock relatives and their relatives from every possible corner of India and numberless thousands who call their small stretch of sidewalk home. It means a proliferation of small-scale industries, from the village-transposed potter and his wheel to the chemical soap factory, an ultra-modern atomic research plant, air-conditioned office buildings and hotels, technical training institutes of high order, and a university bursting with students.

## Nehru

Still elegant and handsome, Jawaharlal Nehru dominates the parliamentary proceedings as, in fact, he dominates the political life of India. Alert and active, articulate in both Hindi and English, Nehru is present for most of the sessions of the Indian parliament, answering questions, participating in the debates, well-briefed and energetic. There is a flow of humor and wit, always a good sign of a healthy parliamentary body, as socialists, Swatantrists, and independents go about their task of questioning, needling ministers, probing. Nehru himself is treated with utmost respect by all. His standing is clear. The level, tone, and rhythm of the debates are serious and impressive, except for the comparative inferiority of many of the Congress representatives, "party" men who rely entirely upon Nehru and his ministers.

This is the nation's supreme body, and the view of Asoka Mehta, chairman of the Praja-Socialists, that the Lok Sabha must continually assert itself as both the top repository of democratic power and the source of leadership in the country is borne out by what I hear. It is in the Lok Sabha that Nehru has attained the peak of his career. I have never counted myself among his admirers; his arrogant and often petulant style is not to my liking and his frequent ambiguity and even hypocritical way of thought repel me. But there is no question that he has held India together since independence, struggled to lay the foundations of a progressive, secular state, resisted bigotry and communalism, and served as the symbol of an all-India effort within a unified country. If Nehru has become more difficult of access in recent years, more touchy to criticism, the response of the crowd to his presence still indicates that this man is India to them.

By the same token, the chairman of the Praja-Socialist Party, Asoka Mehta, a brilliant and forceful personality, embodies the best in Asian socialism. This man became heir to his party at the lowest moment in its history. It is no secret that democratic socialism in India was close to its end some five years ago. The PSP seemed haunted by its inability to find the proper relation to the Congress movement and to the nation as a whole; it existed, largely as a ginger group, but was uncertain about its right to exist. To inherit leadership of such a movement is no enviable task.

But, and here is evidence that Mehta is a man of political stature, the party's progress does not take place at the expense of the country's inner adhesion or even at the cost of other movements. Just as issues of democracy in India (secularism, national unity, language-based states, etc.) cannot be separated from problems of socialism (agrarian cooperatives, workers' democracy in the new industries, social justice, etc.), so the growth of the socialist party must go together with the growth of all democratically oriented parties and institutions, including the Congress itself. In my opinion, this must also include the so-called new caste associations which are, in effect, political parties based upon the awakening of their people, an awakening expressed in demands for more representation, popular education, the breaking down of caste walls which discriminate against its interests. Many have found Mehta reserved and remote (Guy Wint calls him a political expert rather than a national leader), too logical and cool. Perhaps. I find him a man of fine intelligence, broadminded, and, above all, hopeful for his country's future. He has combined socialist idealism and political nationalism into a finely woven texture.

## Summary and Farewell

*The Race:* The Third Five Year Plan, about to be implemented, is based on an assumed population of 431,000,000 people by March, 1961. There are many other assumptions in the Plan, not the least of which is a continuing high percentage of unconditional foreign aid, but this population outburst is fundamental. How shall the race between food production and mouths that consume be run without faltering? The Plan concentrates on the problem of agrarian production, but avoids that of land relations. As for birth control, it is a farce except for middle-class city folk whose issue would go down in any case; a wise socialist doctor in Lucknow put it to me quite bluntly when he remarked, "Until we offer the villagers and city masses some other kind of life than that of endless work, until we can substitute entertainment and recreation in the form of community life, radio, education, theater, etc., for their present entertainment after the day's work, the soaring birth figures will continue. Only uplifting the people and enlarging their cultural horizons will flatten out the curve."

*The Third Five Year Plan* — whose objective is to drive the Indian economy forward so that it henceforth generates its own fresh capital formation — is India's most ambitious program to date. The Plan cannot be taken literally; there are too many question marks built into it. During the past ten years the habit of planned economic development has taken hold in India. Foundations exist for the development of modern technology in steel, power, and agriculture. The infrastructure has been strengthened, but must be completed not only materially (roads, transportation), but culturally (basic education).

The main issue is what rate of development (pressure) can the economy sustain in terms of the general economic situation. National income is expected to increase at the rate of 5 percent annually. This will be the source of new investments, but also new consumption demands. These demands will be fed further by increased population, the movement into the big, consumer-oriented cities and the general demand of people to live better. Therefore, says the Plan, we must be prepared to keep consumption from rising too fast — a classic problem in countries striving for industrialization.

Further, the immediate economic situation is spotty. Strong inflationary pressures, rising consumers' goods price index, no lessening in unemployment and a tendency for seasonal and part-time employment to drop, poor control over the nation's price structure. These factors are so delicate that gains of the past ten years are easily imperiled by inflation.

What have been these gains?

> Since 1951, a 42 percent rise in national income.
> A 20 percent increase in per capita income.
> A 120 percent increase in industrial output.
> A 40 percent increase in agricultural production.
> A $21 billion investment in the Indian economy to which the United States contribution is merely $1 billion.
> Electricity generated by 200 percent, railway freight-traffic by 80 percent, etc.
> Such figures, of course, tend to conceal the low starting point, but the forward movement is indicated.

When one compares this to Communist China, with its superiority in basic natural resources, and the disputed rate of its development as well as the undisputed nature of its total state structure, why should the democrat, the socialist despair? India today is a free and open society with a mixed economy leaning toward increased governmental leadership and control; it is an authentic parliamentary democracy with a maximum of individual freedom; it is an economically underdeveloped country moving steadily toward a viable economy with a better life for its people.

I make no effort to brush aside its difficulties, perils, and shortcomings. On the contrary. But I cannot help thinking of the multitude of Western and European intellectuals who, their eyes riveted in fascinated horror and/or admiration upon China, have consistently neglected and ignored India. In India itself I found the magnetic pull of China to have completely lost its power except for a diehard group of Communist intellectuals.

The attractiveness of India today consists of the fact that its political community is made up of such a variety of associations, both natural and voluntary, all of which play their role in the exercise of political freedom, in formulating some approximate notion of the public good, in influencing the state directly or indirectly, and in protecting the liberties of both the individual and the organizations. This "pluralism" is more alive in India than anywhere I know.

1961

# 4

*Life in the city*

# THE NEW YORK SCHOOL CRISIS

## JEREMY LARNER

### The Circumstances

*UFT Official:* Why is it we can get young people to volunteer for the Peace Corps to teach in Ghana, yet we can't get them to teach in public schools in Harlem? Answer: Because in Ghana, there's hope.

Let me start with some statistics. There are 132 elementary schools and 31 junior high schools in New York City whose students are almost entirely (over 90 percent in the elementary schools; over 85 percent in the junior highs) Negro and Puerto Rican. In the past six years, while Negro and Puerto Rican enrollment has gone up 53 percent, white enrollment has fallen 8 percent, and the number of predominantly Negro and Puerto Rican schools has doubled. Of New York's one million schoolchildren, roughly 40 percent are Negro and Puerto Rican, 60 percent "other." Efforts of the Board of Education in the past six years to eliminate blatant gerrymandering and allow some voluntary transfers have reduced by a third the number of schools where Negroes and Puerto Ricans are less than 10 percent of enrollment. But the problem gets more difficult all the time, as is indicated by the fact that 52 percent — an outright majority — of the city's first-graders are Negro or Puerto Rican.

The increase in segregated schools is due to three factors. First, rural minority groups are moving into the city and middle-class urban whites are heading for the suburbs. Second, discrimination, economic pressures, and lack of effective planning confine the newcomers to ghettoes. Third, cautious whites send their children to private or parochial schools rather than "risk" a neighborhood school where minorities predominate. Over 450,000 New York children attend private or parochial schools, a figure that would represent a staggering percentage even for an exclusive suburb.

Thus New York City suffers from an educational problem which it has come to describe as *de facto* segregation. The Board of Education says the facts are essentially beyond its control; the civil rights groups say they are the facts of a racist society, and must in all justice be eliminated by whatever means possible.

Segregation in ghetto schools is more than racial; there is segregation by economic class as well. Wherever Negro parents reach the middle class, at least some of them send their kids to private schools. Lower-class Negro kids find themselves isolated in schools which are understaffed, underequipped, overcrowded, demoralized, and conspicuously lacking in the mixture of cultural backgrounds which can make life in New York such an educational experience. Many of them are children of parents who are in effect first-generation immigrants from southern and rural areas; for of New York's 1,100,000 Negroes, 340,000 have arrived in the last ten years, 630,000 in the last twenty years. Most of the 600,000 Puerto Ricans have come in the past decade, while the white population has dwindled by 500,000.

Teaching middle-class children the ins and outs of a culture made for them is obviously easier than struggling with ghetto children, most of whom are members of a racial group which has never been allowed to recover from the effects of slavery. Some minority schools have annual teacher turnover rates of over 60 percent. Some teachers flatly refuse to take assignments in such schools; others drop out as the school year proceeds. Not only is one out of every two teachers a substitute, but some classes may stay without a regularly assigned teacher all year, defeating one temporary substitute after another. One can see that the atmosphere in minority schools is hardly conducive to learning. It is estimated that 85 percent of the eighth-grade students in Harlem are "functional illiterates," which means that their reading is not above fifth-grade level — in many cases it is much below.

Though some authorities, e.g. Kenneth Clark, disagree, it is hard to believe that the social conditions under which most New York Negroes live are not responsible for some of the difficulty. According to the Harlem Youth survey, whose figures many observers regard as conservative, only one-half of Harlem children under eighteen are living with both parents, more than one-quarter of Harlem youth receives welfare assistance, and the rate of narcotics addiction in the area is ten times that for the rest of the city.

By the time they reach junior high school, ghetto children are well aware of their social situation, and it does not exactly give them a feeling of unlimited possibilities. Let me quote from two batches of essays which were gathered at different Harlem elementary schools from a sixth-grade class of "slow" readers (S) and a sixth-grade class of "fast" readers (F). I think the language shows as much about the children — their educational retardation and yet their straightforwardness and toughness — as about the conditions they describe.

*6th-grade boy* (F): This story is about a boy namely me, who lives in a apartment in and around the slum area. I feel that other people should be interested in what I have to say and just like me, *try* to do something about it, either by literal or diatribe means. This book is only to be read by men and women boys and girls who feel deeply serious about segregation and feel that this is no joke.

*6th-grade girl* (S): I am not satifeyed with the dope addictes around our block. They take dope in our hallway every night. Another is they break in stores and bars. I am desatifed with the lady that live under us. she set fire to Doris's door. Some dope backs live under us. The lady under us robbed Teddy's aunt for $17.00's. One night a dope addict went cazey in our hally way. They are so many bums in our block. Please help to get and keep them out.

*6th-grade girl* (S): I don't like people going around youing bad Lanugwsh around litter Kide a bearking in Store and fighting and youing dop. And Killing people. And drunk in hallwall. They should stop drink They are teacher the Kide how to Steel I see it alot of tim but I dont pay it no mind I am surrounded by them.

*6th-grade boy* (S): Im not happy about the people who dink. wiskey and go to sleep And I not happy about the peole who come in my hallway and go up stairs and take a neals and. stick there themselve in the arm. I not happy about the people who buy wine and wiskey and broke the bottle in the hallway

*6th-grade girl* (S): the be out there in the hall taking dope and I be freighten.

*6th-grade boy* (S): I deslike the peple being hit by cars, the car crashes, peple fighting, the peple jumping of roofes, stelling paper from the stores, peple picking pocketes, the peple with out thir cubs on dogs and stop peple from taking dop in this naborhood.

*6th-grade girl* (F): (True) *What a Block!* (true)

My block is the most terrible block I've ever seen. There are at lease 25 or 30 narcartic people in my block. The cops come around there and tries to act bad but I bet inside of them they are as scared as can be. They even had in the papers that this block is the worst block, not in Manhattan but in New York City. In the summer they don't do nothing except shooting, stabing, and fighting. They hang all over the stoops and when you say excuse me to them they hear you but they just don't feel like moving. Some times they make me so mad that I feel like slaping them and stuffing bag of garbage down their throats.

The fact that these kids have been encouraged to describe their surroundings is the first sign of hope that they will be able to change them. The school should represent that possibility; it should be a fortress of security in which the children are respected, accepted, and developed. Otherwise they are surrounded, as the little girl says; drug addiction, for example, will begin to appear in their ranks while they are still in junior high school — and addiction is only the most dramatic form of withdrawal and defeat.

Looking around him, the young Negro boy will find few "father figures" to imitate; for the men of his world have not been accorded the honorable work men need to earn self-respect. The families are matriarchal, the children remaining with their mothers while a succession of "uncles" come and go. There is small hope of that masculine self-respect which is the traditional basis of family pride. The little boy is regarded as inferior to the little girl, and has less chance of survival — by which I mean simply less chance of getting through life without cracking up, without sliding into some form of self-obliteration.

Dismal to tell, the schools in many ways duplicate the situation of the homes. The classroom confronts the child with the same old arrangement: a woman with too many kids. Far too few of the elementary schoolteachers are men, let alone Negro men. The size of classes, usually around thirty pupils per class, makes individual attention — and thus the development of positive identity and incentive — as unlikely at school as it is at home.

When lower-class Negro children enter elementary school, they are already "behind" in several important respects. In crowded tenement apartments children are in the way from the moment they are born. While the adults of the matriarchal clan unit work or wander, children are brought up by older children, who have reasons of their own to feel impatient or harassed. According to the teacher whose "fast" sixth-grade pupils I quoted above,

> . . . middle-class Negro kids need integration. But what the lower-class kids need right now is that somehow we conquer the chaos they live in. They have no stability whatever — no family, no home, no one to talk with them. They live in a world without space or time. I mean that literally. Even by the time these kids reach the sixth grade, most of them can't tell time. You can't talk to them about the future — say, about jobs — because they won't know what you're talking about. And when you refer to concepts of space, why you can't talk about "somewhere else," tell how far away another city is, how long a river is, or simple facts of geography. Though they're fantastically sophisticated, more sophisticated than maybe they ought to be, about how adults behave, their mental orientation is almost utterly without abstract con-

cepts. Look: they don't even know who pays the welfare! They don't even know what checks are!

Of course this particular teacher will get his kids talking and thinking about time and space and jobs and where the money comes from. But there aren't enough like him, and one year of a good teacher can dispel the chaos for very few. The class he has taken such pains with finds itself a year later without an assigned teacher, and the boy who last year wrote a brilliant autobiography is in danger this year of flunking at junior high, breaking down, and spending his high school years in and out of institutions.

Why don't teachers make more progress with these children? Because they are woefully short of books and materials, especially good readers based on the facts of urban life. Because they have to spend so much time on discipline. Because they get poor support from their principals and from the rest of the top-heavy school bureaucracy. But the truth is that most of New York's teachers are too middle-class, too insensitive or too fragile to teach ghetto children successfully. Not that they are worse than teachers in other places, they are simply less suited to their jobs. Not all of them are bothered by their failure; some stay in slum schools because apparently it gives them a sense of security to blame the kids for what they fail to teach them. Others, with the best will in the world, are baffled by children who literally speak a different language. One young white teacher, extremely hard-working and perhaps more honest than most, told me after a grueling day,

> I hate these kids. They're impossible. How did they get this way? I never thought I'd become so authoritarian.

Most of the teachers are conscientious: that's one of the hallmarks of the professional person. But the manner in which teachers are trained and chosen — which I will discuss below — is practically guaranteed to eliminate those possessing the imagination and flexibility to get through to slum children.

As for the curriculum, it is hopelessly inappropriate. The readers still current in practically every school are those insipid productions featuring Sally, Dick, and Jane, the golden-haired cardboard tots from Sterility-ville. One could go on by describing a series of tests and achievement-levels, but tests and levels are irrelevant to children who mostly do not pass or reach them. Let me quote Martin Mayer (from his book, *The Schools*) on what our young tenement-dwellers are supposed to be learning by the time they get to high school:

> In New York . . . the major Theme Center for tenth-grade "Language Arts" is "Learning to Live with the Family." . . . The curriculum guide suggests "round-table, panel, and forum discussions" on

"questions relating to allowances, dating, working after school, selecting and entertaining friends, choosing a career, minding younger brothers and sisters, helping with household chores, contributing earnings to
the family, decorating one's own room, choosing family vacation places,
using the family car."

But what difference does high school make? The battle is lost long
before then. Perhaps it's already lost by the time first graders move to the
second grade, when only 10 percent of them are on reading level.

Yet, when all is said and done, are not these conditions surmountable by
individual effort? Is it not possible for the majority of these youngsters to
pull themselves up by their own bootstraps, as so many of their second-
generation American teachers say that they or their parents did? Or is
this problem unique somehow, does it have to do with the unprecedented
oppression and separation of a group that has never in the history of this
country been free? Is it really true, as the 1954 Supreme Court decision
contends, that "segregation of white and colored children in public
schools has a detrimental effect upon the colored children. . . . A sense
of inferiority affects the motivation of the child to learn"?

In the opinion of this observer, no one could sit for long in Harlem
classes without seeing overwhelming evidence of the demoralizing effects
of segregation. These children are treated as inferior, just as their parents
and grandparents and great-grandparents were — and there is no sense
of any possibility that such treatment is ending! In the classroom of a
first-grade teacher who was a militant supporter of the boycott, I was surprised to find cut-out pictures of white children used almost exclusively
as bulletin board illustrations. Later I found the purified faces of Sally,
Dick, and Jane beaming out at me in ghetto classrooms of teachers Negro or white, liberal or not: as if to say, these are what good children are
like.

> 5th-grade Lower East Side boy (F): I have a problem that I am
> colored. I would like to be handsom but I cant because other people
> have strait blond hair and they are handsom.

In a second-grade Harlem classroom the teacher, a lively, intelligent
Negro woman, has her kids acting out a nursery tale. In front of the class
stands a shy, finger-sucking little girl, her hair in pigtails, absolutely
adorable and black. From her neck hangs a large square of cardboard,
on which an adult has painted the head of a white girl with abundantly
flowing golden hair. Caption: "GOLDILOCKS."

In another second-grade classroom, where well cared-for Negro children are industriously and quietly working under the direction of a
Negro teacher, I glance up and see a row of self-portraits above the front

blackboard. I count: of 23 portraits, 1 red, 1 green, only 2 brown, and 19 white as the paper they're drawn on.

The sense of inferiority runs deeper than skin-deep. I remember a junior-high-school social-studies teacher trying to discuss the school boycott with his ninth-grade "slow" pupils. Most of them are long since lost; they look as though they have drawn curtains across the inside of their eyeballs. It develops that they do not know the words "boycott" or "civil rights," and to them "discrimination" is something that happens down South. And oh the tortured embarrassment with which they answer questions! From beneath the embarrassment there slinks a kind of arrogance, thriving it seems on the mere fact that the teacher is trying to teach them — as if to say, imagine this fool, asking *me* a question! Whereupon they laugh. They have to. And we are all relieved.

Whether they know the word "discrimination" or not, these kids know they are not worth much to the world they live in. Some of them, all too many, are not worth much to themselves, and lash out in self-hating violence at the nearest target, usually someone who reminds them of themselves. Already the white people of America are beginning to dread the day when these children, as some day they surely must, will recognize their real enemies. As they are at last beginning to . . .

> *West Harlem 6th-grade boy* (F): Teacher! In the caveman days, if there were Negro cavemen, did the white cavemen use them as slaves?

## The Frying Pan

Almost never has the New York Board of Education voluntarily taken steps for greater integration. The highly-touted Open Enrollment program was initiated in the fall of 1960 only after neighborhood school strikes and the threat of further strikes led by Rev. Milton Galamison and Paul Zuber. Open Enrollment is a voluntary transfer program designed ostensibly to relieve overcrowding as well as to integrate. In Open Enrollment overcrowded schools (mostly minority schools) are designated as "sending" schools, whose pupils may apply — on an individual basis — for transfer to "receiving" schools in other neighborhoods. The responsibility is on the parents of each child, and the response to Open Enrollment has indicated no desire on the part of ghetto Negroes to rush their children to schools in "better" neighborhoods. To date Open Enrollment busses at city expense only 15,000 children each day. Surely, many of these are middle-class Negroes . . . and whites. A teacher on the Lower East Side whose school is over 95 percent Negro and Puerto Rican reports that the only ones who left her school in Open Enrollment were ten of the remaining white kids, who bussed daily all the way to Queens.

Even since the 1954 Supreme Court decision, the Board of Ed has never done much to relieve *de facto* segregation unless pushed. The emphasis has usually been on adding "cultural enrichment" to the minority schools rather than on breaking them up. The missionary approach is well articulated by a writer in *Commentary* (January, 1964):

> The draining away of the white middle classes from the public schools could probably be slowed down by the addition of more cultural opportunities to the curriculum. This, in turn, would still the fears of Negro leaders about racial imbalance.

Easier said than done. The best-publicized program along these lines so far is the Higher Horizons program (since 1959), which grew from the Demonstration Guidance program (1956). Demonstration Guidance provided extra reading and math teachers, guidance counselors, materials, and trips to symphonies, museums, etc., for the more intelligent members of a certain junior high school, with the result that their achievement levels went up considerably, many fewer of them dropped out of high school, and more went to college. But this was only a pilot program which did not reach every child even in the school where it took place. And now that the project is over, that school is depressing to visit: performance seems as low as ever and white children in the neighborhood look for excuses to transfer elsewhere for junior high.

As for the Higher Horizons program, most of the better teachers in the system regard it as a farce. An occasional movie or trip to the museum does not effectively change a child's view of himself or help him learn what he is not learning. And why assume that the official "culture" is truly educational? A Negro teacher told me that the last Higher Horizons film he had taken his class to see was about Jamaica, and every scene depicted Negro servants smilingly waiting on whites. The class didn't like it, though not all of them could say why.

Another enrichment concept is the designation of minority schools as "Special Service" schools. This program involves beefing up school staffs with extra *non-classroom* personnel: psychologists, guidance specialists, and teacher coordinators. The coordinators supposedly gather special materials, brief teachers on the problems of teaching certain subjects, keep records of individual cases, etc. As a rule the Special Service personnel are resented by other teachers. It's hard to believe that they do a lot of good. Students tend to mistrust the motives of guidance interviewers from class backgrounds different from their own, and to put them on. The NE (non-English) coordinators, who are supposed to help teachers teach Puerto Rican kids English, are not required to know Spanish, and many will explain to you that it's *better* they don't.

It is true, however, that New York has done more for school integration than other cities of comparable size. In Chicago, for example, the

Negro sections lie in two long narrow strips, so that it would be easy to pair off overcrowded Negro schools with adjoining white schools. Instead, the school board, as in St. Louis and other cities, prefers to attach portable classrooms to the Negro schools, and this has led to rioting and great bitterness.

## The Aftereffects

What effects did the 1964 school boycott have? In terms of Negro self-respect, undoubtedly positive. In terms of its own objectives, too, it was successful, forcing a more definite integration plan than the Board of Ed would ever have volunteered. But in other areas the effects were moot.

### THE SCHOOLS

Anyone who knows anything about the New York schools cannot help but be uneasy about the gap between the strategy of the boycott and the situation it attacks. The issue is by no means so simple as Galamison often made it out to be:

> We feel that if we desegregate the public schools, these other problems — like overcrowding, low curriculum, etc. — will go away. Like when you have an infection, and you take a shot of penicillin.

One problem that will not go away is that of money. In the 1964–65 state budget, New York City, which has 34 percent of the state's school-children, is slated to receive only 25 percent of total state aid to schools. Due in part to the machinations of a rurally-dominated state legislature, the city and its residents pay 49.7 percent of all state taxes and get back only 37.3 percent in benefits. The rationale for low school aid is that New York has an abundance of taxable property with which to finance its schools; the catch is that the city also has stupendous upkeep expenses.

To be specific, the value of taxable property per pupil in New York City is $31,878, far above the state average of $26,600; and it is this ratio on which state aid is based. But whereas city taxes amount to $54.27 per $1000 of property valuation, the city spends $39.39 of that money for municipal purposes and only $14.88 for schools — which compares poorly with what is spent by surrounding districts. Even though the city tax rate is high, moreover, funds collected are minimized by the gross undervaluation of property holdings. Real estate in New York's five boroughs is currently valued at the bargain total of $35 billion; theoretically Manhattan is worth only $13.5 billion — but don't try to buy it if that's all you can raise. Furthermore, much of the non-school bite on New York's property taxes goes to pay for problems that only large cities have — such as the costs of tearing up streets and assigning extra police to direct traffic when property owners decide to pull down or put up new buildings for their private profit. And since current property taxes don't entirely cover the costs of municipal overburden, the city shifts the load to the public in regressive taxes such as the 5 percent city sales tax.

Financial shortages drastically affect the operation of the schools. According to a study of the New York schools sponsored jointly by the PEA and the UFT, "thirty percent of the daily instructional staff is made up of substitutes and other persons on similar temporary or emergency status." The schools are short by 27,500 permanent staff members, including 12,500 "professionals," who would be required to bring the city up to the *average only* of the school districts among which it once enjoyed leadership. That leadership position was held in the early 1940's, before suburban flight began in earnest, when the city spent more per child than its suburbs did. Now it spends $200 per child less, which amounts to about $200,000 per school and a total of $200 million per year simply to bring the system up to par in staff, materials, textbooks, and upkeep.* The $200 million does not include extra funds urgently needed for new construction.

At present, there is not enough room, time, or personnel to take care of all the children. A major classroom problem is that one or two children can disrupt an entire class and dissipate most of the teacher's energy; and as one might expect, difficult children are more prevalent in slum schools. According to one assistant principal:

> It's the 2–3 percent who are unteachable and uncontrollable — the ones with very deep emotional disturbances — who take so much time and trouble in the lower neighborhood schools. There's no place to put them. We can't even assign them to a "600" [special problems] school without their parents' permission. The "600" schools have no more room anyway. Sooner or later these kids are caught committing a serious crime: you send them to a judge and he sends them right back to school.

There are also curriculum problems which integration will not necessarily solve. One of the most controversial is the practice of grouping the children according to reading level, and later, IQ test, so that fast, "achieving" children are in a homogeneous group entirely separate from the classrooms of the slow, "nonachieving" youngsters. One of the effects of such grouping is that in schools where a small population of whites remains, it is in effect segregated vertically in the advanced classrooms. So transporting kids from their neighborhoods will not by itself

---

* New York City school supplies and equipment are ordered from a purchasing manual through a central department which buys from designated contractors *at list price only* — which is often two or three times the retail price at New York's discount houses.

guarantee them an integrated classroom experience; in fact, since most Negro children lag in classroom skills, it might not do them much good to be thrown in with white children of their own grade level — at least not without drastic changes in the present set-up. Most experts now agree, however, that homogeneous grouping leads to stereotyping of individuals and is not desirable on the grade-school level. To quote Martin Mayer, ". . . in New York, Wrightstone's study of comparative performance showed no significant advantage for bright kids grouped with their fellows over bright kids scattered through the school at random." But experts also agree that heterogeneous groupings cannot effectively be taught unless class size is reduced to no more than fifteen children, a procedure which would require twice as many classrooms and teachers. For the present, boycotters might take some satisfaction in a provision of the February integration plan, wherein the Board agreed to eliminate IQ tests.

Also beyond the reach of the boycott is the teacher herself, who is often unaware of her middle-class attitudes and the damage they do her ability to teach. I remember one young teacher with an all-Negro "slow" first grade, extremely conscientious and worried that she is not more successful, yet unaware that her tone of voice is superior and humorless. At any given moment, only about five of her children are paying attention, and at least three-quarters of the words she utters are devoted to discipline. Let me give some flavor of her monologue:

> . . . well, why did you raise your hand if you had a pencil? I asked for only those who didn't have pencils to raise hands! That's not funny, Wilma! That's not funny! Boys and girls, we're not getting our work done and if we don't settle down we won't be able to have recess today. NOW I WON'T HAVE ANY MORE TALKING IN THIS ROOM! I'll start over again . . . we draw two lines across and that's the big *A*. Now I see that Freddy didn't hear me, Becky didn't hear me, Nicholas didn't hear me, Roger didn't hear me. And you're not looking! You can't learn to make the big *A* unless you're looking! Now can you make a big *A?* Let's see if you can. Raise hands if you need help. You don't have paper? Deborah, where is your paper? All right, I'll give you more . . .

After twenty minutes, a majority of the children are making big *A*'s. As the teacher starts on the little *a,* I do what most of the kids want desperately to join me in: escape.

To give you an idea of these kids six years later, here is the teacher of a seventh-grade English class.

> Now take a sheet of lined paper and write at the top "English notes." I want all of you to copy down right this second the facts I'm going to give you. Norman, would you be so kind as to put your hand down.

Now your assignment is going to deal with this, so get these facts accurately. Hurry up, I haven't got too much time.

### THE WHITES

Naturally the boycott did nothing to ease the growing anxiety of white middle-class parents. If many more of them withdraw their children, there will be no question of integration.

At an open meeting of a district school board, a white mother stood up and shouted hysterically.

> What are you going to give me to keep my child in the public school system? I've worked for the NAACP for years, but I don't want 300 years of wrong to weigh upon the shoulders of *my five-year-old!*

The woman went on screaming while her listeners applauded her. It was some time before she could be quieted. Whereupon Mrs. Thelma Johnson, who was onstage as a representative of the Harlem Parents Committee, made the following reply:

> I offer you your child's future. Because your child's future and my child's future are bound up together. You cannot accept the privilege of being superior because you're white any damn more than I can accept the stigma of being inferior because I'm Negro. How much longer must I prove to be your superior in order to be accepted as an equal? Bussing is worth it for me because I'm on the lower end. You have to decide if it's worth it for you.

Mrs. Johnson, too, was applauded.

### THE NEGROES

Neither did the boycott clear up the confusion among those Negroes who had, as requested, given the civil rights organizations "the benefit of the doubt." Among the children of a certain Harlem school that was empty on boycott day, there was great fear of "integration," for rumor had it that white kids were coming to fight the black kids.

Negro parents, for their part, might well wonder what changes a boycott might make in the depressing economic conditions they face. It would seem, too, that for some the boycott only reinforced doubts as to the value of nonviolent protest in general. Though the Negro in the United States has been historically nonviolent in relations with his white oppressors, nonviolence is by no means the lesson he learns from the life around him.

*6th-grade Harlem boy* (F): *Fable*

Once a boy was standing on a huge metal flattening machine. The flattener was coming down slowly. Now this boy was a boy who loved insects and bugs. The boy could have soped the machine from coming down but there were two ladie bugs on the button and in order to push the button he would kill the two ladie bugs. The flattener was about a half inch over his head now he made a decision he would have to kill the ladie bugs he quickly pressed the button. The machine stoped he was saved and the ladie bugs were dead.

MORAL: smash or be smashed.

Or, as one of the fable-teller's female classmates puts it:

I think the white people should stop taking advantage of the color people before they get punched in the face.

The boycott was a punch thrown off-balance: it brought on all the reaction to a punch in the face without gaining enough of its satisfaction.

## Boycott and Politics

*6th-grade West Harlem boy* (F): How come we don't have no Negro president! We have to strike for president! We ain't gonna pay no more taxes!
*His teacher:* We've got to keep these kids from exploding ten years from now when they grow up and can't get jobs.

One of the conspicuous failings of the boycott was its lack of political content. It was a beautiful example of what Tom Kahn in the Winter, 1964 *Dissent* calls "project-centered provincialism" based on "a middle-class integrationist ideology." When Bayard Rustin made his last-minute entrance into the boycott organization, he tried to broaden the perspective. Speaking at a rally on January 31, he reminded his listeners that the Negro is at the center of all America's problems; for if America is to solve them, "the lowest must come first."

In a country with 50 million poor, only the black people are in movement. But we black people cannot by ourselves solve the problems of housing, unemployment, and schools. The only solution is for the working classes to forge a *political* movement.

The trouble with demonstrations for limited ends is that the "power structure" can easily afford a compromise which will soon be absorbed in the shifting sands of our profit-controlled economy, without much damage to the status quo. No matter how firmly demonstrators insist that they will not compromise within their area of attack, complete change of one institution is not possible unless other institutions are also transformed.

The unemployment crisis indicates a natural alliance between the Negro and the labor movement: they must jointly demand full-scale public works programs to construct race- and class-integrated schools and housing, even whole new decentralized cities. Also, the Negro has a natural basis for alliance with those liberals who fear the military-industrial complex: they must jointly demand that a substantial portion of the annual multi-billion defense budget be diverted for education and social reconstruction. Until the problem is understood and attacked on this scale, the local projects of the Negro movement cannot achieve their full objectives.

And yet there was a "revolutionary" ardor to the boycott that went beyond political programs. I say "revolutionary" because at times the driving figures behind the boycott spoke with that appetite for pure destruction which far exceeds the reasoned desire for social reform. It comes from the feeling that the society one lives in is so hopelessly corrupt that one's only recourse is to tear the whole thing down. Let me quote the girl who warned of "a punch in the face":

> If I could change my block I would stand on Madison Ave and throw nothing but Teargas in it. I would have all the people I liked to get out of the block and then I would become very tall and have big hands and with my big hands I would take all of the narcartic people and pick them up with my hand and throw them in the nearest river and Oceans. I would go to some of those old smart alic cops and throw them in the Oceans and Rivers too. I would let the people I like move into the projects so they could tell their friends that they live in a decent block. If I could do this you would never see 117 st again.

## Society and Classroom

The subject of New York's schools and what's wrong with them cannot entirely be discussed in terms of more cash, more teaching, and more integration. What is needed for the classroom above all else is a free and democratic, truly revolutionary society based on human value instead of compulsive striving, competition, and accumulation. Even at best our schools educate our young to fit into a world where ability is measured by quantity only. Concepts of art, science, knowledge, creativity for *their own sake* survive at kindergarten level only; the purpose of an American education is to replace these values with symbols of measure. What can be said of a society which reduces its culture to True-False and multiple-choice tests even on the college level? Among other things, that this society rewards cheating, and that the more advanced the competitors the more extensive and complex the cheating will become, until the cheaters finally cheat themselves of the knowledge of what they are doing.

Our ideal should be schools in which each child can develop as an individual, according to his capacities and desires. A good teacher is someone with a talent for getting through to children and letting them get through to him. If a teacher doesn't in some way enjoy being alive he has nothing to teach. What we need is to replace the authoritarian teacher who has traditionally plagued and scourged the children, whether black or white, achievers, nonachievers, or underachievers. We need a teacher who will nourish talent and individuality rather than crush it.

Unfortunately, teaching attracts types who enjoy relations where they have undisputed superiority. Thus the effort to "understand the disadvantaged child" turns out in practice to be the science of patronizing the slum-child without feeling guilty about it. For the disadvantaged child, of course, is really not that at all, no matter what it helps one to know about his background: he is a person, and as such something splendid in his own right even before a teacher gets to him.

In every ghetto school I visited, teachers recommended a book called *The Culturally Deprived Child* by Frank Riessman. Reading this book, they told me, had helped them to understand the nature of the children they had to deal with. Sure enough, I found Riessman's book preaching "a sympathetic, noncondescending, understanding of the culture of the underprivileged." But neither Riessman nor the average teacher realizes how un-noncondescending sympathy delivered from the top can be:

> Moreover, self-expression and self-actualization, other aims of education, particularly modern education, are equally alien to the more pragmatic, traditional, underprivileged person.

No! You just can't talk that way about a child entering elementary school. Kids from "underprivileged" homes want to express themselves and realize themselves just as much as anyone else. Maybe the most important thing for them is to have a teacher who will *expect* something from them. The best teacher I met in Harlem had taken a class of bright sixth graders who up to that time were demoralized and undisciplined. Fortunately he did not assume they weren't interested in self-expression. He assumed that they had something to express, the fruits of their own experience, which is in so many ways deeper and more demanding than that of middle-class children. It was a long haul, after eleven years of neglect, but eventually he got them writing and writing well. He read them French translations and they wrote him parables and fables; it seems Negro children are natural-born fable-writers, for — as we have seen — they are not likely to pull their punches when it comes to the moral. He read them Greek myths and stories, and they wrote him back their own myths, classic transformations, and one boy even wrote an illustrated history of the Trojan War. (One of the transformations begins, "I was transformed from a poor little infant into a nice boy, and as I grew I was transformed into a magnificent extraordinary deceiving nuisance to the world.") Most of the children wrote novels, and one eleven-year-old boy, without having read a single modern novel, began a remarkable autobiography with the sentence, "I am dreaming and crying in my sleep."

This was an ordinary sixth-grade Harlem class; there were some high

IQ's, but it was not an "SP" (specially gifted) class and had attracted no special attention to itself. The teacher disciplined them, yes, kept them in order, but did it not to triumph but to show them he cared. He respected them, which is something you can't learn from books. He visited their homes, which is absolutely unheard-of. He worked patiently with each child, and got them to work with each other.

Now it is a year later, the kids are dispersed into a notoriously depressing junior high, and most of them have lost what they gained. Some are flunking; their former teacher bitterly wonders how the life in them can survive. But for that one year they produced a body of work uniquely theirs.

## The Grouping of Groupings

If conditions within the classroom are bad enough, to look beyond them is to find oneself in a jungle of stumbling and makeshift, where stentorian voices boom from the tops of trees, and clusters of officious missionaries rush about distributing memoranda on the cannibal problem.

First of all, there is the school bureaucracy. According to Martin Mayer: "New York City employs more people in educational administration than all of France." I believe I have alluded to the public relations men on the Board of Ed staff, but I have perhaps failed to mention the endless associations, commissions, sub-commissions, advisory committees, deputy directors, associate supervisors, district superintendents, coordinators, directors, foundations, and independent consultants who must be involved in every policy decision. The trouble with such a set-up is that the basic concern on every level points up, toward impressing the higher-ups, rather than down, toward serving the classroom teacher. Would it be heresy to suggest equal salary for every school position? With the present system, the classroom teacher can be in a panic for materials she ordered three years ago, while the assistant superintendent is sincerely assuring the area superintendent that everything is all right in his sub-sector. In such a bureaucracy, the people who move toward the top are the yes-men, the round pegs, whom the public pays to rise away from the children.* They have a priority on operating funds, too; if they could not get their paperwork properly submitted and filed, the system would collapse. In fact, despite the teacher shortage, there are a number

---

* The $915 million school budget proposed for 1965–6 was criticized by Joseph G. Barkan, the chairman of the Board of Ed's business committee, who pointed out that one unit would have five "assistant directors" at salaries of $15,635 and fifteen "supervisors" at $12,929 to oversee a staff of forty-two teachers. Barkan also questioned a proposed increase of $1,474,049 for the "Curriculum Research and Evaluation" division. According to *The New York Times* (Dec. 7, 1964), he asked, "What has this division, which spent $5,140,242, accomplished during the past year?"

of employees listed on the Board of Ed budget as classroom teachers who never report to their assigned schools; they are clerks and typists working in the central offices. Ironically, the policy directives they type, like great portions of our public school funds, may never filter down to the classroom; but they do reach the publicity department, from which they are carefully distributed to the newspapers, which in turn describe to us a school system that doesn't really quite exist. Nevertheless, its paper achievements will be proudly recounted by the functionary flown to a conference of "educators" at public expense.

The gap between theory and practice is nowhere more striking than among the school principals. Many of them know little of what goes on in their own schools and make no effort to learn. The job of the principal is to spend his time in educational conferences, or addressing committees, or preparing reports for higher-ups who never come to check. At the Harlem school where the sixth-grade "slow" letters I have quoted were written, the principal assured me:

> I don't notice any demoralization on this level. The children are happy, well-behaved and eager to learn.

Small wonder that one of the best teachers at this school could not get enthusiastic about the boycott:

> What if the boycotters are successful and get the Board to come up with a plan? Who has to implement it but these same shits!

Then there is the problem of the teachers themselves and their organization, the UFT. It would be unkind to expect too much of an organization so urgently needed and besieged with such difficulties as is the UFT. But it must be said that an excessive concern of teachers black and white is their own respectability. The most pressing practical issues are submerged in the desire to preserve their "professional image." For instance, a teacher's license in New York City cannot be obtained unless the applicant has passed the expensive and utterly idiotic education courses offered at teachers' colleges. I never talked to a single good teacher who claimed to have learned anything of value in these courses. Furthermore, they discourage many of the specially talented people gathered in New York City from seeking employment as public school teachers. Bright, educated people who want to try their hands at teaching children can't, not in New York, not even if they have PhD's, unless they are willing to go back to school for their "education credits." * Yet the union, although ambitious to work out a joint recruiting program with

---

* Education courses are not the only obstacles in the paths of potentially valuable teachers. Teachers from the South or from Puerto Rico with advanced academic degrees may find themselves disqualified on the interview section of the teachers' license exam for "speaking English with an accent."

the Board aimed at attracting Negro teachers from the South, shows little interest in this question. The current teachers' pay scale is based on these pointless credits, and to upset it would invalidate years of useless course-taking.

Finally, there is the conglomeration of civil rights groups, divided and sub-divided within itself, spreading out toward too many separate targets with only the most general slogans to hold itself together. The structure of the rights organizations is chaotic beyond description. Let me say simply that the end effect is too often the mirror image of the bureaucracy they are arrayed against. And the boycott offered no program for the Negro children to realize their own particular talents, no social-action program with which to unite the Negro community in self-respect. Was not the boycott in some sense one more appeal to the great white father to do right by his poor black children?

## No Ending

Have I captured the confusion? Here is New York City with a mass of black people, most of whom have never been allowed to partake of our civilization. Now they must be allowed that dubious privilege, for there is no other place for them. In previous eras of American life, there was some room for a variegated lower class, which took care of the dirty work and was not permitted entrance into the cultural mainstream. Little by little most groups surfaced into the middle class, leaving behind among unlucky remnants of themselves a permanent body of American Negroes, who, handicapped by years of slavery and oppression, remained what a Negro teacher describes to me as "a colonial people encapsulated *within* the colonial country." But now automation is chopping away at the colony; we see the natives in the street, shaking their fists. We must open the door and let them in.

The big question is, Will they come in having truly changed and purified and reformed our social structure, as some say they must? Will we have to chip away at our stone walls to let them in, as the Trojans did for the Greek horse? Or will the Negro scrape through bloody, bitter, and confused, ready to perpetuate the authoritarian ethic he has so far, to his unique credit, managed to evade?

The answer to this question depends in part on our schools. But all school systems are — and have always been — failures. Even Leo Tolstoy, with all his genius, his wealth, his command, and with not a single bureaucrat to hamper him, could not educate his peasants into free men. His failure, our failure . . . the failure is always the same: the failure to educate each man — not for a prestigious "function" or "role" — but to fulfill his own capacities for living, for being alive, for finding and making his own kind of beauty, for respecting the diversity of life without, in his frustration, turning to violence, self-suppression, and the worship of authority.

So what the boycotters are demanding, ultimately (and more power to them!) is a change in the nature of the lives we lead.

> *6th-grade Harlem girl* (S): I wish that the hold city can chage. and that the governor make new laws. that there to be no dirt on streets and no gobech top off and wish that my name can chage and I wish that whether can trun to summer.
>
> *6th-grade Harlem boy* (F): *Fable*
>
> Once upon a time there was two men who were always fighting so one day a wise man came along and said fighting will never get you anywhere they didn't pay him no attention and they got in quarrels over and over again. So one day they went to church and the preacher said you should not fight and they got mad and knock the preacher out.
>
> Can't find no ending.

1964

# REAL ESTATE CONFIDENTIAL

## DANIEL M. FRIEDENBERG

**I**

The most striking fact about New York in the last decade is the realty boom. Wherever one goes — in the heart of old Manhattan or the farther outskirts of the Bronx and Staten Island — construction is seen. Craters yawn in what were pleasant meadows, metallic booms and tiers of steel loom against the sky, overhead bridges span entire sidewalks with scaffolding, and the pressure hammer constantly gnaws at the vitals of the pavement. It would seem that nothing is spared in this massive demolition and rebuilding. Old trees and young buildings enter the same insatiable maw, for neither leafy elms nor elegant Park Avenue structures can withstand the path of progress as conceived by builders.

It must bewilder the senses of the spectator, this awesome chopping down and regurgitation of concrete and steel. Why are stately edifices barely thirty years old uprooted for squat ribbon-windowed office structures? Why are new massive apartment houses crowded jowl to jowl, blocking out air and light, when even the atrophied organs of the city dweller still feel joy at a shaft of sunshine? And, most of all, where do the tenants come from to fill the wave on wave of new apartments and office buildings? With rents frozen at approximately twenty to thirty dollars per room in the older houses, while the new apartments charge an average closer to sixty dollars per room for lower ceilings and cheap partitions; with older commercial space renting at an average of about three dollars per square foot while the newer office buildings demand almost double — what is behind this boom?

The author of this article has participated in the postwar building frenzy from its inception. He has watched its legitimate start, when the city woke from a depression lethargy and war immobility, to erect new housing for the generation of war brides and new offices equipped with air-conditioning, acoustical ceilings, and fluorescent lighting. He has seen the maturity of the boom, as shifts in racial population have altered the residential character of whole boroughs and the needs of expanding business have integrated many out-of-town companies into the financial web of the metropolis. And he has now begun to observe a repetition of the overbuilding of the 1920's in which, like fabled Midas whose touch turned everything to gold, the city will throttle itself.

To understand why the builders have had such a field day in New York City and continue to build without reference to actual space needs, skyrocketing land values, and ever higher construction costs, the economic background must be examined. Building is a favored industry, comparable in some respects to oil drilling from the point of view of accelerated depreciation, and stock market speculation in so far as capital gains are concerned. The tax structure is deliberately keyed to subsidize the rich and acquisitive, who then find themselves compelled by the very logic of this favoritism to expand and expand again without reference to the market needs; and let the devil take the hindmost!

The factors that stand behind this favoritism can be simply enumerated: land appreciation, the leasehold device, tax-free accelerated depreciation, new complex methods of financing, the development of the syndicate, juggling of space measurement, "escalation" clauses and maintenance charges, and the use of capital gains. This study will concern itself primarily with private enterprise and not public housing nor the very genuine activity of organizations like the United Housing Corporation, the nonprofit group run by Abraham Kazan, whose efforts have accomplished more in building decent apartments for the middle class in New York City than all the speculative builders put together.

## II

### LAND

It is undoubtedly true that many of the old American fortunes originated in land speculation. The Astors, Goelets, Rhinelanders, and Schermerhorns profited by the tremendous expansion of New York City in the early part of the nineteenth century. A possibly apocryphal story illustrates the technique. John Jacob Astor offered to sell a Wall Street lot for eight thousand dollars in 1810. A buyer, surprised at the low price, promptly appeared.

"Yes, you are astonished," Astor was reported to have said. "But see what I intend to do with the eight thousand dollars. That Wall Street lot, it is true, will be worth twelve thousand dollars in a few years. But I shall take the eight thousand dollars and buy eighty lots above Canal Street and by the time your one lot is worth twelve thousand dollars, my eighty lots will be worth eighty thousand dollars."

In our time, however, the big money in real estate rarely enters land speculation. The leisurely approach, waiting five to ten years for land appreciation, does not fit the tempo of modern life. Only the very rich, mindful neither of temporary losses nor income taxes, can afford this outlook. The government has taken the position that since buildings age, a certain part of their cost may be allowed as a tax-free deduction each year. This is known as depreciation. But the tax authorities refuse to allow depreciation on land itself, following the sound theory that land cannot wear out. As a result, investment in land for the sake of future appreciation is limited either to very small endeavors or to the extremely powerful who think in terms of generations rather than of their annual tax return.

Certain old estates still follow this approach: the Astors and Goelets are still with us. The Astor Estate, for example, anticipated the development of Park Avenue as a financial community and purchased several large plots between 46th and 59th Streets in the 1940's. The Aramco Building, constructed by the Uris Brothers as the first large postwar building, was erected on Astor land. The Goelet Estate acquired the blockfront on the south side of 42nd Street between Lexington and Third Avenues, on which the Galbreath interests erected the Socony Mobil Building. And, in a continuing process, the Astors are now investing in land to the east of Park Avenue in the 50's, while the Goelet heirs have acquired a large plot directly facing the Lincoln Square project.

No special genius is required to foresee such developments. The future of Park Avenue above Grand Central was clearly understood by most old-time investors, as is the future value of land in areas directly abutting the present midtown nexus. It is still possible to buy land located in proximity to Lincoln Square for about thirty-five dollars a foot, which should certainly triple in value within the decade. But only the very rich can afford to make such investments, for they require enormous outlays of cash, rarely can be mortgaged to a significant extent, and usually show a carrying loss.

Sometimes, of course, land speculation does produce fabulous profits. From the small truck farmer whose lot on Staten Island happens to sit adjacent to the bridge now being built over the Narrows to Brooklyn, to the Bronx junk dealer whose yard abuts the junction of the Hutchinson River Parkway with the Cross Bronx Expressway, we are all familiar with such luck. But there are other examples in which more than blind chance is involved. In one case (the specific location and exact details shall remain nameless for obvious reasons), a speculator netted a cool million dollars in cash for six months of control. A large plot in a key part of Manhattan remained covered with rundown buildings for many years. A speculator bought one part of the plot for $600,000. He held on for almost a decade and then, in disgust, sold at a loss of $200,000 to another speculator who suddenly appeared. One month later a tremendous development was announced for the entire area, which required the acquisition of the part of the plot in question. The man who had stepped in for $400,000 insisted on and received a price of $1,400,000! Even the most charitable spirit has doubts as to the background of this transaction.

LEASING

While the old estates specialize in buying land and leasing it after an appreciation in value, it is the "new money" which concentrates on the acquisition of these leases. Men like the Uris brothers, Erwin Wolfson, and the Tishmans have skyrocketed into multimillionaires within short years by realizing the unique advantages of leased land or what is called a leasehold.

While no depreciation is allowed on land, both the leasehold rent for the land and the depreciation on the building itself are tax deductible when a building is constructed on a leasehold. The overwhelming advantage of the leasehold (until 1958)* was that the person leasing could depreciate or write off the entire building cost during the first term of the lease, usually twenty-one years. The government further allowed accelerated depreciation, meaning that the largest part of the cost could be written off in the early years. Under the 200 percent declining balance method, for example, the depreciation allowance can be doubled (hence 200 percent). If a leasehold runs for twenty-one years, the annual depreciation allowance is thus almost 5 percent — that is to say, the period of years of the leasehold divided into one hundred percent — which when doubled means that the builder receives close to ten percent of his money tax-free each year in the early years!

Nor is this all. Depreciation is allowed against the entire building cost whereas the builder invests at the maximum about one-third of the total cost, the rest being covered by a mortgage or mortgages. In effect, the builder thus receives an annual tax-free return of up to 30 percent; since

* The law has been changed on this point, but the problem can be solved, in the majority of cases, by other methods too complicated to describe here.

10 percent is tax-free and the equity or actual cash investment of the builder is only one-third, the total tax-free amount is enlarged three times. And this is before figuring his actual profit from renting!

It can readily be understood why New York City is rebuilding at such a frantic rate. The builder makes a profit "coming and going": from the government as accelerated tax-free depreciation; and into his pocket as normal profit from rent collection.

The leasehold is fantastically profitable, but there is still another method to increase the return over and above both depreciation allowance and rent income. This is known as the collapsible corporation, a device only recently authorized. In essence, the government allows a builder to liquidate his corporation after holding a piece of property for three years and a day, and then taxes him only 25 percent on his capital gains. He thus escapes double taxation, first on the normal profit and then on dividends.

A certain Mr. X., to take an actual example, built an apartment house in the East 50's several years ago. He set up a new corporation for a sixty dollar fee. He borrowed what seemed 65 percent of the money for the job from an insurance company, but in reality the mortgage represented over 80 percent of the cost; his architect and engineer supported the inflated estimate, for otherwise they would not get his next job. Then, with only a 20 percent investment of his money, he sought and received double depreciation on the completed structure, in this particular case running even higher since he broke the building down by what is called the "components" method and depreciated the elevators, roof, air conditioning, etc., at a still faster rate. Just recently he sold the apartment at a high profit to a syndicate, liquidating his corporation in order to pay a single capital gains tax. The result is that he received an annual tax-free return of over 30 percent, his investment, in effect, being returned in three years through the depreciation alone, above and beside the profit from rent, and then sold at another high additional profit subject only to a tax of 25 percent!

If the speculator can manage to build in his individual name or that of a partnership, the profits are again enhanced, since he can apply the depreciation against his own total income, which is usually taxed higher than the corporate level. Erwin Wolfson, for example, leased land from Columbia University on a short term lease and constructed 100 Church Street. Assuming a 5 percent accelerated depreciation factor (very conservative under the circumstances) on a ten million dollar construction job, Mr. Wolfson had a legitimate tax-free deduction averaging somewhat less than one-half million dollars annually to apply against his personal income tax for the next few years. As the principal owner of Diesel Construction Company, the largest construction company in New York City, and the sponsor of Grand Central City, which will be the largest office structure in the world (now renamed Pan Am Building for its principal tenant), Erwin Wolfson presumably found this deduction of use.

## FEE BUILDING

The classical method of construction is to buy the land outright, called the fee simple, and then build. Its disadvantage is that the builder has money invested in the land as well, a nondepreciable item. This is to a degree compensated for by the fact that mortgages tend to give more money to fee builders than leasehold builders, feeling their investment to be more secure with the former. The variations by which speculators have achieved success with this method are as infinite as the cunning of the human mind. Sam Rudin, an old-time builder whose development of Washington Square North sparked the postwar boom in Greenwich Village, decided to erect a mammoth office building. He bought a plot, now called 80 Pine Street, and projected a structure of almost 900,000 square feet. But he was unable to get financing, because the area was somewhat east of the financial district and the mortgagees had doubts as to its success. The Chase Manhattan Bank, which had sold him the plot, was concerned. They did not want to get back the land. Furthermore, since the First National City Bank and the Hanover Bank had announced plans to move a major part of their operations to the midtown area, the Rockefellers wanted 80 Pine Street to reinforce their tremendous investment in the Chase Manhattan Plaza, only two blocks away. The upshot was that Chase Manhattan rented enough space in 80 Pine Street to enable Mr. Rudin to acquire financing.

Very often the builders end up working for the mortgagees. The Tishmans at 666 Fifth Avenue and the Minskoffs at 575 Lexington Avenue — second-generation builders both, whose families have been identified with midtown construction for fifty years — were staggering under the load of the tremendous equities involved. The Prudential Insurance Company, which had indicated an interest in providing mortgage money, obligingly bought the two buildings before they were completed and leased them back to the builders. The result is that the Tishmans and Minskoffs make large sums operating the buildings which belong, however, to the Prudential Insurance Company.

There is as much skulduggery behind many of these deals as in the most sinister novels; and far more is at stake. One reads that gunmen can be hired to murder individuals for a few thousand dollars; those on the inside of realty laugh at such petty antes. Several years ago, for example, a large financial institution was approached by a speculative builder who thought the institution might be interested in letting him develop a property which it owned. The builder asked his structural engineer to draw preliminary plans for a new building. The engineer, rich in his own right, was a partner in one of the largest realty syndicates. The next week a very important man, of the same social background as the president of the financial institution, arranged a meeting through which the realty syndicate got the job. The speculator with the original idea was left out in the cold, and it was not until several years later, when his structural engineer fired a draftsman, that the truth came out.

Another case of the ruthlessness pervading this struggle for money is one involving a principal corner in downtown Manhattan. An investment builder was going to build on an inside plot when it struck him that a large insurance company, occupying the adjacent corner building, was in need of additional space. He reasoned that by combining his plot with the other, he would create a better structure and satisfy the growing needs of the insurance company as well. But the insurance company refused to sell, offering to lease instead. The deal was arranged but problems arose because of the difficulty of mortgaging a combined fee simple and leasehold. The insurance company refused to sign the lease, though it kept on assuring the investment builder it would honor its commitment. The latter, getting deeper and deeper, without money and unable to arrange temporary relief because of the unsigned leasehold, was eventually forced to sell out at a loss to the insurance company, which then used the same plans and proceeded to erect the structure. This building, when fully rented, will net close to $400,000 per year in profit!

Perhaps the most startling case of banditry in the history of New York City real estate occurred very recently. A tremendous apartment project, occupying a magnificent location in the center of Manhattan's East Side, has just been completed. Its history is unusual. Several years ago one of the city's most prominent builders decided to go ahead with this project. He spent a large sum for the land. By the time he sought financing the money market, in one of its perennial swings, had become very tight. No matter what the builder did, he was unable to raise money.

Finally this builder turned in despair to that private market of vultures that always wheel in the financial air, looking for dying victims. These are the very rich men who for a price save propositions by investing a certain sum of money, taking back a large interest. He found one such gentleman who was willing to give aid. The terms were that the new party would lend three million dollars for a short period of time, until a package deal of financing could be arranged, and in return receive 50 percent interest in the mammoth job.

The new participant thereupon approached his banks and borrowed $3,000,000 at 6 percent interest. This new equity money enabled the job to proceed. The money market soon loosened up and financing was arranged. The terms of this new financing were so liberal that $2,000,-000 of the $3,000,000 was returned to the gentleman who had stepped in. To sum up, the new partner thus obtained a 50 percent interest in one of the largest apartment building projects in the history of New York for what amounted to 6 percent interest on $3,000,000 for several months and 6 percent interest on $1,000,000 for three years (his real equity money). The total interest will amount to some $200,000 and for this money he has obtained a permanent position in a magnificent project which should return his $1,000,000 equity in short years and then show one-third of a million dollars annual return thereafter!

INTRICATE FINANCING

The above deals are comparatively simple. A piece of property is bought or leased and a building is constructed subject to a normal mortgage. The only widely known exception to this rule was the bond issuances that took place during the construction frenzy of the late 1920's. At the time it was common practice to issue bonds instead of mortgages, because more money could be obtained through this method. With the arrival of the depression, most of these bond issues collapsed in value. Certain very smart individuals thereupon proceeded to buy up the defunct bonds at a few cents on the dollar, until they obtained control of the properties against which the bonds had been issued. Some of the "older money" in real estate came about through this technique which, of course, was thoroughly legitimate according to the laws. The Salmon Building, 500 Fifth Avenue, at the northwest corner of 42nd Street, was acquired, for example, by means of this technique.

It took, however, that amazing manipulator of modern times, William Zeckendorf, to improve to its highest degree the procedure of squeezing money from buildings. This wizard decided in the early 1950's that the typical financial operations of real estate men were amateurish. They divided property into equity, the cash they put in, and that money contributed by the mortgagee. Mr. Zeckendorf reasoned that realty could be regarded much like other forms of modern corporate ownership, that is, merchandised in separate units comparable to common stock, preferred stock, and debentures. Thus, he reasoned, an improved property is a unit consisting of many parts: it is land on which a building has been erected; the building itself; the operating value due from rent income; and the additional mortgage value of the rents isolated from the building. He was the first person properly to understand that the land could be sold to one party, the building to another, the operating lease to a third, and that even another mortgage position could be hewed from the rent income separate from the operating lease.

The first building to which he applied this technique was 2 Park Avenue. The structure had a value, according to traditional standards, of something less than $10,000,000. The primary step was to sell an operating lease on the entire property for $5,000,000, composed of $1,500,-000 cash and $3,500,000 lease mortgage. This was reasonable because the building tossed off about $1,000,000 which, even with the very heavy carrying charges of $600,000 on the new lease mortgage, meant that the investors received about $400,000 annually or an 8 percent return. Then Zeckendorf went to a mortgage company and borrowed $6,750,000 at 4½ percent. In a short time the rents went up, serving as additional security against the property, and Zeckendorf borrowed in the form of a second mortgage an additional $2,250,000. He thus received a total of $14,000,000 for a property that was estimated as worth less than $10,000,000 — and still held the fee, on which he turned down an additional offer of another million dollars!

In effect, what Zeckendorf did was to wring 50 percent more money out of the building by dividing it into parts — fee, operating lease, and separate fee mortgages. He perfected and even elaborated this technique in the subsequent purchases of the Graybar and Chrysler Buildings, as well as the Equitable Building at 120 Broadway. A peculiar refinement of the Chrysler-Graybar purchase was that the owning corporation he was going to acquire had several million dollars in its bank account. This money he needed for the purchase. Operating through a new corporation, he borrowed money from other sources to close the transaction and then immediately withdrew the money from the bank account he had now acquired to pay off his borrowing; in a sense he thus bought the building with the building's own money.

The labyrinthine mind of Mr. Zeckendorf is at present engaged in a project which will make even this earlier financing seem childish. Anxious to enlarge the facilities of his Drake Hotel, he is now closing the following proposition. As the first step, he will sell the Drake to a syndicate that will give him $4,500,000 cash over a present $4,500,000 mortgage. He will simultaneously lease back the hotel for a long term and also agree to use the money received to build the addition. The syndicate likewise will agree to lend him another $1,000,000 so that he can proceed with construction, as well as permit him to increase the mortgage by an additional $2,000,000 in order to assure him all the money required for the job. The return to the syndicate (it is reported in the trade) will be guaranteed at approximately 12 percent, with the rent being reduced in proportion to the reduction of the mortgage. At the end of ten years Mr. Zeckendorf will have a six months' option to buy back the entire enlarged property for $8,500,000 over any mortgages then outstanding.

The terms of this type of financing stagger the imagination and are even difficult for experienced realty people to follow. The basis is a continuing market, one which will get better and better. But conservative men with many years of background shudder to think what will happen to buildings laden with top-heavy mortgages and demanding leases if ever there is a downward dip in our booming economy.

SYNDICATES

What has made this rickety structure of building and expansion possible is the syndicate.* The syndicate is merely a group of people who get together and form a partnership, participating in the profits according to their proportionate interest in the total deal. The attraction of the syndicate is its tax position. The corporation is subject to double taxation, first on normal income and then on dividends. But an individual or a partnership is subject only to one tax, the return received directly by the participant. Furthermore, the depreciation on the property, which is a tax-free item, goes to the corporation and not the stockholders when a property is held in corporate form, while it goes tax-free directly into the pockets of the individuals in a syndicate.

This simple equation has transformed New York real estate. Since properties are judged according to their return to the investors, the effect has been quite simply to double values. A building valued at $5,000,000 to a corporation is now worth $10,000,000 to a syndicate. Furthermore, since at each sale a new depreciation allowance is set up based on the new selling price, by raising prices the syndicates in practice add tax-free dollars to the income of their investors. A building formerly worth $5,000,000 might be close to the end of its depreciation deduction. When bought for $10,000,000, the entire difference (minus land value, which is nondepreciable) is credited as additional depreciation. The syndicates then take this depreciation in one of the accelerated forms: presuming, in the above example, that $4,000,000 is additional new depreciation at 4 percent, or $160,000 tax-free money, they take the 150 percent declining balance method (or 1½ times) and pull out $240,000 instead, all of which goes tax-free into the pockets of the participants.

Building after building, hotel after hotel, apartment after apartment, has fallen to the scythe of the syndicates. As buildings get older their depreciation runs out and the owners are forced to sell. When the syndicator offers almost double money for what the owner thought the property was worth, the urge to liquidate becomes irresistible. And the process feeds on itself. The syndicates have been offering between 10 and 20 percent annual profit, part of this tax-free, and the better they do the more money pours into their portfolios. The consequence is that values of New York real estate have soared so high, the market has been picked as clean of purchases as the dead carcass of a cow by ants. This is part of a vicious cycle, because builders feel compelled to erect new structures, knowing that even if they rent only with some degree of success, they can immediately sell at a profit. The whole swollen apparatus of leasehold building, accelerated depreciation, capital gains tax, and syndicate oper-

* The new Real Estate Investment Trust Act extends the syndicate method on an even vaster scope.

ation forces a wild spiral of building and speculation which must load weight on weight until the realty market may collapse in a horrible shambles.

## III

Real estate is subject to other tricks beside tax juggling. It is the perfect medium for the huckster mentality because the cheaper the product the higher the return. Cost of construction has risen to the point that a speculative formula has evolved to substitute tinsel for quality. The result has standardized building to the point that one can identify speculative structures merely at a glance.

It is so obvious that builders cover every inch of land with construction that when rare exceptions occur, like the Lever Building between 53rd and 54th Streets on Park Avenue, and the Seagram Building a block to the south, the news hits the front pages of the newspapers. The fact that crowding massive structures over narrow streets ruins the esthetic effect of architecture is of no importance, because the builders are concerned not with esthetics but with the rent received per square foot. This itself is legitimate in our economy, but when the ultimate desire is *only* the profit as divorced from architectural value and the municipal interest, we have gone a step in monetary perversion beyond all known previous civilizations. The so-called Babylonian or ziggurat effect is merely an extension of this maximum land use on the vertical level, whereby the builder conforms to the city code by the use of setbacks every three stories. A recent adaptation, the block base and tower, has become popular not because the builders underwent some weird conversion to artistic values, but rather because of the rising costs of roofing material and plumbing for the numerous setbacks.

A corollary of the 100 percent land usage and maximum setbacks is the application of glamor to the public parts of the structure. The typical speculator builds a fancy lobby, usually including an abstract mobile or ceramic design as a sop to "modern architecture" — Noguchi is the favorite for this today. The curtain wall facade is made of precast stainless steel cubes or hexagonals, cream plastic plates, or aluminum members anodized in silver or gold. These skin treatments are "modern" too: and also cost less than the traditional brick and limestone. The fact that the thinly veneered facades leak like a sieve is irrelevant since the tenants will have already moved in on long-term leases by the time this is apparent. The elevators are the newest gimmick, playing soft semi-classical music with their operatorless controls that save the builder up to twenty-five cents per square foot in labor cost.

The lobby, facade, and elevators are the center of glamor application. Where the speculator recoups is in the mechanical equipment and in particular, air conditioning. The difference between a good and bad air-conditioning installation runs as much as three dollars per square foot in a modern office building and, since the average structure today is over 300,000 square feet, this item alone can save the builder almost $1,000,000. An adequate air-conditioning system should have zone controls for each face of the building and separate zone controls for the upper and lower parts. It should have air diffusers sufficient to handle each specific area, yet capable of throttling or "balancing." The system must have return ducts for the stale air, extended not only into the different zones but also into the areas subdivided by masonry or ceiling-high metal partitions. And, what is extremely important in the spring and autumn seasons, where there are wide oscillations of temperature in the same day, the installation should be equipped with what is called "100 percent fresh air," or oversized entry ducts, that permit the air to be completely replaced by new fresh air in a short period of time.

A defective air-conditioning system is eminently suited to the purposes of present-day builders because it is something the prospective tenant will not see. One cannot tell the difference between good and bad air flow merely by looking at plans. When more sophisticated tenants call in engineers to review the design of the air conditioning, the builder usually adapts or improves the system for the executive area, still ending up with a large saving on the unimproved clerical areas.

It might be added that the speculators themselves are not solely at fault, since many aspects of the elevator and air-conditioning industries are virtual monopolies. Costs have been pushed so high the builder reacts in natural fashion because of the competition. For a speculator to construct office space according to good standards, he would be forced to rent at a figure much higher than his competition. But again, the question of "fair return" is relevant since most builders feel that a job is losing money if they do not "get their money out" in six or seven years, which means a 14 percent or 17 percent profit before taking advantage of the accelerated depreciation deduction.

Allied with the continued cheapening of mechanical equipment is the new popular theory of large office areas. By a sort of hypnosis unrelated to reality, many tenants have been convinced that tremendous floors are more amenable to modern office layout. This hallucination is fostered by the Madison Avenue publicists who have been hired by almost all the topnotch speculative bidders. Objective studies indicate that between 12,-000 and 20,000 square feet is the ideal layout space for big firms. It is to the builder's interest, however, to convince tenants that huge floor areas are ideal because the larger the cube construction, the cheaper it is to build. The land acquisition is only a minor part of the total cost picture, yet due to the peculiarities of the city code, one can build proportionately more space the bigger the plot. Two stairways as fire exits and one fire tower air shaft are needed in a small building as well as a large. The bigger the floors, the less toilets per square foot are installed and the less sun load is confronted by air conditioning. Also, it is just as easy to build a large building as a small building, since the same number of trades are involved. The success of the campaign on the part of builders to convince tenants of the necessity to rent tremendous floors is one of the most striking phenomena of real estate today.

The speculator not only saves on tax techniques and cheap construction, but on renting and maintenance methods. The Real Estate Board of New York, a non-governmental association dominated by the larger realty interests, changed its method of computing square footage in 1953. Up to that date, tenants did not pay for corridors, toilets, air conditioning fan rooms located outside the premises, slop sink closets, and electric and telephone rooms. Today, the tenant is required to pay for everything on a single-occupancy floor except the stairs, fire tower shaft, and space occupied by the elevators. In effect, this means that the landlord receives between 7 percent and 12 percent more rent for the same space. Since few buildings are constructed on exact right angles and straight lines, the architect usually works hand in hand with the builder, giving him "the benefit of the doubt" on angles when the structure is not built flush with the lot line: for example, on a 8″ skew over 200 lineal feet, the landlord would pick up almost 70 square feet (averaging the skew is 4″ or one-third foot times 200 feet). Assuming two walls skewed in a thirty-story building, the landlord would then pick up over 4,000 square feet! And we are starting on the assumption that the landlord indicates the correct footage to begin with. . . .

Another method by which landlords receive rent for useless square footage is by calculating as rentable area the enclosures of the peripheral air conditioning, a practice universally accepted. Most of these enclosures stick almost two feet into the premises. Assuming a building of 20,000 square feet on a floor of 200′ by 100′, there are 600 lineal feet of exterior walls. This means that the tenant pays for 1,200 square feet additional on each floor! It has been calculated by those in the know that the really shrewd operators, who combine all of these methods, receive a bonus amounting close to 20 percent over traditional measurements. Since the average equity runs less than one-third of the building cost, it is not hard to see why so much money pours into New York construction today.

But the tricks are not limited to space measurement. A standard item of modern leasing is the inclusion of the so-called "escalation clause" which provides that all increases in labor and maintenance costs, as well as taxes, are paid by tenants in proportion as their occupancy or rent is to the total occupancy or rent of the entire structure. Originally created to solve the problem of inflation on long-term leases, this clause has become a bonanza in the hands of ruthless landlords. The technique is simple. Certain common cost items are delayed during the first or base year and then applied later so that they fall into escalated items. The net effect is to increase the rent or landlord profit. For example, a very expensive matter in modern buildings is elevator maintenance. The large elevator companies charge about $2,500 per cab annually. What the speculator does is withhold awarding the contract for elevator maintenance during the first year the new building is open. Thereupon he hires the company and charges the entire amount to the tenant! In the case of a building containing fifteen elevators and some 400,000 square feet, this contract would run about $37,500 annually. The landlord would thus pick up as extra rent a bonus of almost ten cents per square foot.

The escalation clause has been extended to include everything from uniforms and broken windows to toilet paper and soap. The side possibilities are almost too obvious to mention. The landlord needs soap, toilet paper, hand-tailored suits as well. And sometimes he has a dull-witted nephew who then appears as a new mechanic or central control inspector. . . .

Real estate management is singularly adapted to multiple corporations in common ownership. Since each corporation is only taxed 30 percent up to the first $25,000 profit, every new building job is organized under a separate corporate entity in order to avoid the full 52 percent tax at the lowest step. Another common method of "thinning" taxes is by means of creating a management corporation distinct from ownership. Suppose a builder has completed a structure. He can operate the building directly, hire a management company or set up his own separate management. With the last method, he can then charge the ownership corporation a commission for operating the property and deliberately juggle the rent, salaries and benefits to fall into the most favorable tax position. This device is usually employed when the builder has relatives he must put on the payroll; in effect, it means that the government is paying their salaries for the most part.

Another popular aspect of real estate is its fat expense account allowance. The purchase, sale, rent, and general investigation of property is a category so large in its implications that almost any and every expense is legitimate. If one wants to check realty in southern California during the cold part of the winter, and the approach is carefully documented with letters to brokers, etc., this is a legitimate tax deduction. If a syndicate considers buying a property in Venezuela, a trip to that country is only in the line of business, with all sundry expenses allowed. When a potential tenant wants to see the latest show on Broadway or stay overnight at the best hotel or be provided with the consolations of a call girl, these are all reasonable accommodations to the problem of realty advancement. It is only part and parcel of business that expensive Christmas presents must be sent to one's clientele; and some of these presents, like homing pigeons, have a remarkable talent for returning home. Twenty-three-foot Cadillacs with television and telephones, including ship-to-shore yacht connections, are owned by certain well-known titans of realty. How can they do business without being able to contact their colleagues at a moment's notice?

One amusing aspect of the expense account is the expansion of New York realty interests in Florida. This has an obvious background. Suppose an apartment builder in Manhattan wants to spend his vacation at Miami Beach, Boca Raton, or the Keys. If he builds or buys a hotel or apartment house in the city of his choice, it is inhuman of the government to expect him to have all the rooms fully rented for the entire season. The fact that one large hotel or apartment suite stays vacant merely reflects the vagaries of renting. Then again, this same owner must see that his business is going on satisfactorily. It is only logical that he fly down several times during the winter in order to check his affairs. And the transport, meeting with clients at night clubs, restaurant bills, etc., are fairly regarded as legitimate business expenses. . . .

A last aspect of holding real estate bears notice. If an individual invests in the stock market, he must pay a normal tax on dividends. The Internal Revenue Department has decided, however, that after a realty corporation has paid a tax on regular business profits, it is entitled to a tax credit of 85 percent on additional profits if this money is invested elsewhere. The remaining 15 percent is then taxed at the regular 52 percent rate, which means in effect that if a realty corporation goes into the stock market with its undistributed profits, it pays a total tax of less than 8 percent (that is, 52 percent of 15 percent) on what it then makes. Since a like investment of this money in realty over again would be taxed the full 52 percent, the result is that dividends from the stock market are only hit by the Internal Revenue Department at one-sixth the same rate, or less than 8 percent instead of 52 percent!

Let us take an example. Suppose a realty outfit has made $100,000 after taxes. If it takes this money and reinvests it in another proposition, the profit is again subject to full tax at the 52 percent rate. On the other hand, if the corporation invests the money in the stock market and collects dividends at 5 percent, or $5,000 on the $100,000, it then pays approximately 8 percent of this $5,000 as taxes, leaving it over $4,500 after taxes. At the same time the money is fully liquid since the stocks can be sold within twenty-four hours. In a market like that of the last years, where stock values have shot up, this is particularly significant because a sale then would only be subject to capital gains or a total of 25 percent tax on the rise in value of the stocks. Instead of being "frozen in" with their money, as the trade terms corporate realty holdings, investment can be made at minimum taxes both on dividend income and sale profits.

## IV

In trying to analyze the social consequences of the favorable treatment afforded to building, the first thought to strike even the most superficial observer is the resulting architectural mediocrity. In truth, speculative builders with a high sense of product can rarely survive, as the history of Fred F. French at Tudor City well documents. Speculators, obsessed by the gold lodestar, tend to "mortgage out" or reduce the money stuck in a job to the minimum, and then add structure on structure in a dizzy pyramid until the slightest breeze of vacancy may blow it over. This leads to a frantic chase for the cheapest methods, which is evidenced by the mechanical repetition of building patterns. The Uris Bros. have a style: colored bakelite disks behind aluminum fins. The Tishmans have a style: microscopic enlargement of a fly's eye, pasted on concrete blocks. Erwin Wolfson has a style: loft construction of the 1920's, built ten times larger. And New York City might be renamed Rothville for the architectural firm of Emery Roth & Sons, whose monotonous variations on Speculator Style have dotted Third Avenue and Park Avenue with squat boxes. The difference between Levittown and Rothville is only size.

Several of the new buildings, created as home offices for billion-dollar concerns, escape this general pall. The main problem even for these worthy structures is their setting. Leonardo da Vinci observed centuries ago that a building should rise in height only one-half the distance of the free span of space before it, but Municipal Code is based on the exact reverse. For a short time New Yorkers can look from the east side of Sixth Avenue and 52nd Street across a vacant plot, recently purchased by Uris Bros., toward a group formed by the RCA building, the Time-Life Building, and the Equitable Life Building. When the Uris Bros. — the largest single builders of office space in the city today — add another of their hulking masses to this vacant lot, the mighty tableau will be drowned in the total effect.*

But the practical results of the present boom provoke more than merely esthetic objections. New York City is strangling itself. By mass transit 40,000 persons can be transported on the same amount of roadway that will only carry 1,600 persons in private cars: or twenty-five times as many. But buses and the railroads, which the municipal and state governments refuse to subsidize for the public good, have become so expensive, that cars — on an average carrying less than two persons apiece — are used more and more. And the focal points of traffic are two small

* Since the Rockefellers have become partners in this project, the Uris architectural style has been vastly upgraded.

Manhattan zones: from Bowling Green on Broadway to Fulton Street in the downtown area, and the Park-Sixth Avenue complex in midtown. Since the prime rule of building is location first, last, and always, the concentration becomes worse with each passing year. Permitting the construction of the Pan Am Building — due north of Grand Central Station — which will dump 25,000 additional persons in the heart of midtown, is an act of municipal madness.

The rising cost of land has led to a type of economic ghettoization which is the antithesis of democracy. The rich and poor used to live close together, but this is much less true today. Public housing brings the lucky poor together, and high rents keep the unlucky poor segregated in ugly slums. The Protestant whites have left New York City and the Jews are following. By rule of the inverse ghetto, the East Side is becoming the haven for the last-remaining rich. A broker three years ago offered the author a large vacant plot on the East Side at $70 a foot. The price seemed ridiculous but the broker said: "Take it. The East Side is the only place where white people want to live today. The values must go up." Recently the same plot was sold, after two additional turnovers, at over $100 a foot. If the present movement continues, New York City will soon resemble a grotesquely enlarged medieval town, with each caste in its own quarter.

Commenting on this metropolitan concentration over two decades ago, the well-known social critic Lewis Mumford referred to the new Trinity of finance, insurance, and advertising. Certainly, the Rome of this Trinity is New York City and its leading churches the home offices of these industries. The insensate march of Manhattan realty values reflects the disease of modern times, for in this city are collected all the bureaucratic and nonproductive functions of the American economy. The great hive of advertising, design, speculation, publicity, news, television, periodical literature, and insurance buzzes with frantic energy of which the building boom is merely the outer form: buzzing for wild profits and quick turnover, not the production of capital goods or values adding grace to human existence.

As long as predatory cunning and acquisitive lust are the highest social virtues, this state of affairs will continue. The public really admires its dream fulfillment in megalomania; in one sense, the conniver is the embodiment of American Success. A recent survey of the National Bureau of Economic Research showed that since 1949 — which not so coincidentally was the birth of the realty boom — there has been a trend toward more wealth in the hands of fewer people and that already by 1953 only 1.6 percent of the country's population held 30 percent of the nation's personal wealth. Again not coincidentally, the survey indicated that New Yorkers lead the nation in total personal incomes. The report did not indicate that more children die of rat bites in the slums of the metropolitan area than elsewhere. People seem less fascinated by such statistics.

Without doubt, real estate — and its sister, the stock market — are the two provinces where money can be made most quickly in our society. Accelerated depreciation, capital gains, the single tax on syndicate ownership: the entire structure, emphasizing cheap building and rapid sale, is a mechanical milker that pumps out a continual stream of cream from the public cow. As long as the laws deliberately subsidize the rich and rapacious, a frenzy of building and speculation will be a permanent aspect of American life, a frenzy which has robbed America of internal equilibrium and a sane view of the changing world.

These distortions can be resolved simply. Depreciation, like amortization of mortgages, should be *after* taxes, and not represent a tax-free return. This is the method prevailing in many European countries. Home owners even in this country do not get allowances for depreciation and there is no reason why business should be given advantages denied to the home owner.

Syndicates are permitted a single tax denied to corporations on the peculiar basis that no tax ruling has specifically called them to account. Such tax discrimination is neither logical nor does it serve a useful social function; to the contrary, it favors one class of investors against another and is thoroughly "un-American" in the most abused sense of the word. And, most important of all, capital gains should be eliminated; this spacious tax dodge rests on the fiction that capital held over six months is a long-term investment as distinguished from capital invested for less than six months, and hence subject to a maximum 25 percent tax on profits. To this one gimmick alone can be attributed the violent cycles and distortions of the American economy.

But the individuals who take advantage of these legal devices are also the individuals who make the laws; it is their representatives who control the legislatures and sit on the courts. And each obscure voter, who votes for them, dreams of participating in the great rat race of amassing income as a symbol rather than for use. As far as the objective observer can see, only when the whole inflated structure collapses of its own weight — as it must — will reforms such as those touched on above be effected. And then it may be too late, since we shall all, the innocent as well as the guilty, be buried in the falling debris. . . .

1961

# THE VILLAGE BEAT SCENE: SUMMER, 1960 *

## NED POLSKY

Now, it is obviously easier to recognize ideologies wherever
they are strongly institutionalized or highly verbal. . . . The
true meaning of ideology for identity formation, however,
can be fathomed only by descending into those transitory
systems of conversion and aversion which exist in . . . adolescence. Such implicit ideologies are often overtly and totally unideological; yet they often exist as the most vital part
of a young person's or group's life, as a basis for a tentative
and yet total orientation in life, without the knowledge or,
indeed, curiosity, of the adults around them.

ERIK ERIKSON †

This essay is both more and less than a portrayal of the beats of Greenwich Village and its environs. More, because much of it holds good for
beats elsewhere. Less, because I have not depicted some of the Village
beat world's well-publicized aspects, but have tried for completeness
only in regard to the changes that have taken place in that world since
my last acquaintance with it (1957). I use the word "beat" for brevity
and ask readers to note that it obscures as much as it illuminates.

* For criticism of an earlier draft I am indebted to two members of the beat scene
who must remain anonymous, and among the non-beats to John F. Gallagher and
Erving Goffman. In this essay Village commercial establishments frequented by
beats appear pseudonymously, except for one bar now defunct.
† "Identity and Totality," in *Human Development Bulletin, Fifth Annual Sympo-
sium*, Univ. of Chicago, 1954, p. 68. A full psychological analysis of the beats,
which I do not attempt, should in general proceed along Eriksonian lines. But in
view of the significant minority of beats in their thirties and forties, it should place
greater stress on the persistence in more or less chronic form of some psychic states
characterizing acute adolescent pathology.

*"The Village Beat Scene: Summer, 1960" by Ned Polsky. An expanded and revised
version of this article will appear in Ned Polsky:* Hustlers, Beats and Others *(Chicago: Aldine Publishing Company, 1967); the original article appearing here was
first published in* Dissent, 1961, *and is reprinted by the permission of the publishers.*

**I**

The individuals in question resent any label whatever, and regard a concern with labeling as basically square. But insofar as they speak of themselves generically and are forced to choose among evils, they prefer the word "beat." Until recently "hipster" meant simply one who is hip, roughly the equivalent of a beat. Beats recognized that the hipster is more of an "operator" — has a more consciously patterned life-style (such as a concern to dress well) and makes more frequent economic raids on the frontiers of the square world — but stressed their social bonds with hipsters, such as their liking for drugs, for jazz music, and, above all, their common scorn for bourgeois career orientations. Among Village beats today, however, "hipster" usually has a pejorative connotation: one who is a mannered showoff regarding his hipness, who "comes on" too strongly in hiptalk, etc. In their own eyes, beats are hip but are definitely not hipsters.

Although beats are characteristically ignorant of history, even of their own history, most know the oft-discussed origin of "beat" as applied to the postwar disaffected. But all are in the dark about "hip." The few Village beats with any opinion suppose that it comes from the "hep" of early 1940's jivetalk. Actually "hep" and "hip" are doublets; both come directly from a much earlier phrase, "to be on the hip," to be a devotee of opium smoking — during which activity one lies on one's hip. The phrase is obsolete, the activity obsolescent.

As early as 1938 David Maurer noted that due to the rapid decline of opium smoking much of its argot was being loosely transferred to other types of drug taking, "frequently without a full knowledge of the original meanings of the words transferred." * Today's use of "hip" extends this process, for now the word has the generalized meaning of "in the know" and even among beat drug-users doesn't always refer specifically to knowledge of drugs.

**II**

Paradoxically, nearly all articles on the beats neglect the thread that colors beat life: the overwhelming majority of beats are *not* exhibitionists or publicity-seekers but precisely the opposite. Articles by beat writers, who belong nearly always to the publicity-seeking minority, implicitly deny this fact. And square writers, who as often as not simply lift their material from beat writings, don't know this fact, or minimize it because it is unexciting, or explicitly deny it. One of the rare exceptions

* *cf.* Maurer's "Argot of the Underworld Narcotic Addict: Part II," *American Speech,* Vol. 13, Oct., 1938, p. 179, fn. 3. *cf.* also Alfred Lindesmith, *Opiate Addiction* (Bloomington, Indiana: Principia Press, 1947), p. 215.

is Caroline Bird, who nearly four years ago correctly noted of the beat that "his main goal is to keep out of a society which, he thinks, is trying to make everyone over in its own image. . . . He may affect [distinctive dress] but *usually prefers to skulk unmarked.*" * Today, despite the attention given to beats in the mass media, despite the consequence that some beats now resemble professional "angry young men" securing toeholds in the lower levels of our "establishment" (the slicker cheesecake magazines) and yearning for our peculiar version of the aristocratic embrace (*Life*), Miss Bird's observations are still generally valid.

Nearly all Village beats most of the time and most of them all of the time want not even a hostile relationship with squares. They restrict their relations with squares to that bare minimum needed to live at all. Many a beat, sociable enough with other beats, goes for weeks at a time without engaging in a single real conversation with a square, his "conversation" with squares being limited to the few ritualistic phrases required to make food purchases, etc. Moreover, the large majority of beats do not flaunt their physical presence before the public gaze. Most beats dress in an ordinary lower-class manner, distinctive only to middle-class eyes. A substantial minority, between a fourth and a third, also wear various kinds of badges (beards, typically) but usually do so as a ready means of identifying themselves to one another and to promote a "we" feeling, not out of a desire to call the attention of outsiders to themselves. Most of even this badge-wearing minority want to remain quite inconspicuous as far as squares are concerned. Their badges are meant for fellow beats, and were worn long before publicity made the squares aware of them; it will hardly do to call these beats "exhibitionists" just because squares have lately stolen their signals. These fundamental points are garbled or suppressed, when known at all, as more and more writers discover a market for articles on "colorful" beats.

It is indeed obvious to the tourist that some beats need frequently to proclaim their negative identities by costume and behavior designed to shock. But that is no reason for even our social scientists to remain merely tourists and write, for example, as if beats typically were devoted to "conspicuous consumption of the self" — an absurdity comparable to suggesting that most homosexuals are drag queens. To describe only what is more or less deliberately exposed to tourist view is to forget that the cool world is an iceberg, mostly underwater.

## III

There has been in three years a great proliferation of Village coffee shops, chiefly because square patronage makes them profitable. New

* "Born 1930: The Unlost Generation," *Harper's Bazaar*, February, 1957. (My italics.)

York's beat scene has become a major tourist attraction, just as happened earlier in San Francisco.

But an important secondary reason for the coffee shops is that in the last three years the attitudes of beats in their thirties have spread rapidly downward all the way to very young teen-agers (13–15 years old), who need these shops because they are too young to fake their age in bars. About a fourth of those under sixteen are fully beat and have totally abandoned, among other things, such square institutions for teen-agers as parental home and school. The remainder are quasi-beat, not so much because they have doubts about beat life as because they are not yet able completely to escape parental control.

Some newer coffee shops are on the Lower East Side (out of the Village proper) and a couple of that neighborhood's restaurants have also become fairly beat. In part this is the result of low-income Villagers moving eastward in the face of rising Village rents. But these shops cater also to beats from various parts of the city who want to avoid Village tourists. These beats, together with many others who go to Village coffee shops entirely or almost entirely during nontourist hours, and still others — including most older beats — who rarely go to coffee shops at all (a great portion of beat social life takes place at private parties), comprise the large majority of beats.

## IV

Many beats are teen-age runaways, but hardly any are being sought by the police; apparently most come from families that would just as soon be rid of them. But Village beats, teen-agers and otherwise, are not predominantly of lower-class parentage. Roughly 35 percent are from the lower class and 60 percent or a little more from the middle class. There is also a sprinkling (about 5 percent) of upper-class renegades; as a group they seem the most psychologically disturbed of all beats and as often as not are remittance men, i.e., are sent money by their parents to stay away from home.*

The composition of the Village beat population today, compared with that of three years ago, shows several other changes in addition to the greatly increased number of young teen-agers. A dozen or so Italian neighborhood kids are breaking away from Italian community values (always opposed to Village bohemians) and are attracted to the beats. And some Puerto Ricans are beginning to enter the beat scene; previ-

---

* The above percentages are tentative estimates, based on quite sketchy material concerning family origins. I used the following rough-and-ready class definitions: lower-class origin if parents' annual combined income was under $4,500; middle class, $4,500-$9,000; upper class, $9,000 or more.

ously the only "American" group one found them in was the homosexuals.

Although a number of beat writers are of Jewish origin, the proportion of Jews among the white male beats has severely declined in the past three years, and in the Village beat scene they now seem to be considerably underrepresented. Jewish women, on the other hand, are if anything overrepresented. Otherwise there seems nothing unusual about the religious origins of the beats.

A few of the newer beat women are worn-out ex-prostitutes from the Times Square area, in their early twenties, who realized they had nothing to show for several years of hustling — no love, no money, no friendships. They want to escape the hustling scene but of course have difficulty adjusting to a square scene, and hence are attracted to the beats, toward whom they are motherly. Conversely, a few beat men hustle themselves a couple of nights a week in uptown homosexual bars, making enough money to stay straight in the Village the rest of the week. In one way this last is typical of the odd job the beat takes when, despite all his efforts to avoid it, he must work: he doesn't want to be *seen* working by other beats, and prefers a job away from the beat scene (except that it is considered all right to work in a beat coffee shop).

But the biggest change in the composition of the Village beat scene, and in Village life generally, is the far greater absolute number and far greater percentage of Negroes.

Until about three years ago there were few Negroes in the Village and they were forced to have their own bar, Johnny Romero's. Romero's paid off the syndicate after several broken windows reminded the owner of this civic duty, and of course paid the police, but was eventually closed because it got too hot to handle (one of the bar's prostitutes was discovered to be a juvenile runaway from a prominent family).

Today, hundreds of Negroes can be found in any number of Village coffee shops and bars, some of which, e.g., Polelle's, function mainly as places for Negroes who want white girls to pick up same. The Negroes around Polelle's haven't much in common except such desires, and range from very beat to Ivy League types. The only thoroughly beat Negro scene is the Maracanda, where most of the clientele are junkies and Charlie Parker is the squarest thing on the jukebox.

## V

On the increase in the Village and its East Side adjunct are beats with literally no place to live, without even a slum sleeping-room. I'd guess that at any given time these homeless beats number not less than 150.

To sleep, some drop in on friends who live in cheap lofts; often there will be ten or twelve people sleeping on a loft floor. Or they sleep in tenement hallways — the top landing, just inside the door to the roof, being the usual choice for beats (unlike homeless alcoholics, who usually must choose the less secure ground level because they can't make it up the stairs). In warm weather there are rooftops; or parks, where one has a 50-50 chance of not being awakened by the police. And some beats sit out the wee damp hours in Smith's, one of the restaurants in the area.

For several years Smith's has been a favorite place for junkies and marihuana smokers to meet their connections. But it has been very hot ever since the police stationed an informer there and one night arrested eleven people, and since then it has had a fink on more or less permanent detail. The first fink uncovered by the beats and junkies was replaced; but at this writing the police haven't bothered to replace his replacement, and the current fink, who is known to all the regular customers and knows that he is known, often gets baited with stage whispers of "Can anybody turn me on?" etc.

## VI

Naturally, the Italian residents of the Village are going down fighting.* The older ones, upset by the noise and the Negroes, this summer petitioned their political chiefs to do something — whereupon two of the most prominent coffee shops were closed by the Fire Department for violations, one of them later being permitted to reopen at half its former capacity. (The shops selected were of course non-Italian, though hardly any commercial establishment within blocks of the area doesn't have fire violations.) However, contrary to the opinion of some beats, it is doubtful that the syndicate had anything to do with the closings, for long ago the syndicate put aside its anti-Negro feelings in favor of its commercial interests and declared itself in for a piece of the beat pie. Except for a few upper-class places north of Washington Square, every Village coffee shop or bar or restaurant, beat or non-beat, pays "grease" to the syndicate as well as to the cops.†

---

* "Italian" refers mainly to Sicilians, the dominant Village ethnic group whose criminal minority control Village nightlife and who are prominent in the national crime syndicate, not to Neapolitans living south of the Village.
† Syndicate enforcement methods are the well-publicized strongarm ones. Less known are the police methods for handling those who contribute too little or the rare idealist who contributes nothing at all. These methods are nonviolent, flexible, and various. Among them are "disorderly premises" (almost anything will make it stick), "finding" heroin in the place — one astonished response: "Man, don't crucify me, you know I only smoke pot" — and having a New York newspaper columnist blast the place until the owner comes across or the police are "forced" by the publicity to raid him.

Given the system's values, the method chosen usually represents a quite rational police estimate as to how severely the holdout needs to be punished — whether it is best to just scare him, or have him fined, or cause him expensive repairs, or close him for a bit, or have the S. L. A. lift his liquor license, or send him to jail. Occa-

Many younger Italians of course make violent efforts to roll back the beat invasion, especially during summer with everyone in the streets. Most of the violence is directed against Negroes and much of it is focused in and near the main beat crossroads, Washington Square Park. The kids under twelve usually restrict themselves to throwing water bombs and feces down on the beats from Macdougal Street rooftops; but more than occasionally beats are also slugged by junior hoodlums from the local Catholic Youth Organization — described by one beat as America's only juvenile gang with a lawyer on retainer. The daily newspapers, except for the New York *Post,* ignore such things as much as they can, and even the *Post* dare not offend part of the readership by mentioning the C. Y. O.; nor, for that matter, can the *Village Voice.*

I summarize one of many incidents:

> A beat couple are set upon and stomped by the C. Y. O. gang. The police arrest the beats along with some of their attackers. The beats of course can't make bail. As a result of the beating the girl has a miscarriage while in the Women's House of Detention. The cops, discovering that the girl is underage, point out to the couple that if anyone talks about the miscarriage they will have to charge her as a sexual delinquent and him as contributing to her delinquency. At the hearing everyone plays it cool and all are released. But the police have the judge lecture the male beat that he is barred from the Village and will be rapped the next time he's found there, so now he stays east of Third Avenue. This has raised his status in the eyes of some: "A way out bit, man. I mean, lots of studs've been eighty-sixed from bars but he's the first one eighty-sixed from the whole fucking Village."

Some beats have correctly observed that opposition to them is in part displaced hostility toward another "invading" group that the Italians can't fight effectively because it is too rich: the uptown squares who are tearing down low-rent Village housing, moving into fancy buildings that Italians can't afford, and in the process of wrestling local political control from the DeSapio machine.

## VII

Beats avoid work. Contrary to what I expected among the non-junkies, this avoidance is typically not a rationalization for any kind of work incapacity (such as one finds in, say, the neurotic sleeper who can't get up in the morning), but is almost always a matter of conviction pure and

---

sionally irrational factors are involved, such as one cop's invariable method of operation or another's sadism. Much less frequently, there is also an "outside" factor; e.g., public outcry leading to pressure from high brass, or an owner's strong political connections, or the owner of, say, an established homosexual bar being outbid by someone else who wants to obtain the local homosexual business.

simple. This conviction is so strong that many beats are willing to starve for it. Consequently, even among the non-junkies there is widespread malnutrition, and many instances of beat "passivity" owe as much to lack of food energy as anything else.

Since an important factor in some kinds of retreatism is an inability to meet job norms (whether legitimate or criminal), it should be emphasized that beats typically can meet such norms but voluntarily choose not to do so. True, most beats are decidedly neurotic; and because they generally refuse their chances for either job training or college education, they can get only low-skilled jobs. But their intelligence and native talents are likely to be superior when not average, and their neuroses usually do not as such incapacitate them for holding jobs. Furthermore, their ideological refusal to work is not essentially a product of neurosis, even for the most neurotic of them, but is largely cultural in origin. (In this respect beats remind one of professional criminals, who may or may not be neurotic but whose neuroses usually have little to do with the genesis of their criminality.)

Unlike most of their age-mates, beats are keen critics of the society in which they have grown up. Their anti-work ideology is not nearly so much a sign of inability to accept the reality principle as a sign of disaffiliation from particular, mutable realities. Sensible of America's inequitable distribution of income *and* its increasing depersonalization of work and leisure *and* its racial injustices *and* its Permanent War Economy, the beats have responded with the Permanent Strike. This response happens to be tragically mistaken, destructive of the self as well as incapable of provoking social change; but it is a virtuous error, arising out of dismay at things that are rotten in the social fabric.

A few beats live off parents or girlfriends and are "social parasites" as pure as anyone living off dividend checks. Most beats scuffle; they take jobs temporarily when all else fails,* but exist most of the time by combining panhandling, quick moves from one pad to another to beat the rent, a complex round of borrowings and repayments, short cons such as selling marihuana that is heavily cut, etc. This freedom from routine work is bought at an enormous price: not only does scuffling often consume more time and brainpower than a square job,† but its effect on leisure is more stultifying than any job dissatisfaction would be.

* Beats quit jobs as soon as possible, seldom working a total of four months per year. But most beats of several years' standing have at one time or another — usually just once — tried the expedient of working barely long enough in a given year to be eligible for unemployment compensation. Informants recently on the west coast say that because Hawaii is now a state and one can collect unemployment benefits there, it is, among those beats who can scrape up boat fare, becoming increasingly popular as against Mexico.

† This and other intelligent objections to the beat life-style can be found in the anonymous "open letter to the beats from a spy deep in enemy territory," *Beatitude* No. 15, June, 1960 (San Francisco), pp. 17–20.

Beats believe that voluntary poverty is an intellectual gain; they gain by giving up the evil effects of meaningless work, gadgetry, and the mass media. But the net effect on their leisure is that even the most ardent intellectuals among them often can't spare the carfare to get to the better free libraries and concerts and art exhibits, seldom can attend cultural events for which admission is charged, and never can build up reasonable book and record libraries of their own. Their meager amount of intellectual consumption is not only questionable as such, but of course also stunts their growth as intellectual producers. "Holy poverty" enforces comparative poverty of the mind.

A number of times I used the above argument with beats, and got variants of one response: better to have a poorer intellectual life than get caught up in the rat race. And with the rare beat who conceded that the rat race occasionally could, with much prodding, be made to yield up work meaningful in itself, the argument quickly became the old interminable one about the virtues of remaining simon pure vs. "boring from within," with the beat being confirmed in his purity as approaching daylight reminded me to stagger off for a couple of hours' sleep before rejoining the rat race.

## VIII

I looked hard for changes in the beat attitude toward politics, but found instead confirmation of my old impression that it is wrong to describe the beats as apolitical *lumpen* who are potential fascists (Malaquais) or potential socialists (Mailer).

Far from being *lumpen,* beats are more keenly aware of the range of political alternatives than is the average voter. They are not apolitical but consciously and deliberately *anti*political, which is something else entirely, and, as a common attitude, something new in American history. Beats suffer not from political apathy but from political antipathy. They totally "resign" from society in so far as this is possible, not least of all from its politics, and reject extreme political sects with no less vigor than they reject major parties.

It might seem reasonable to call the beat an anarchist, for he objects to representative government on the same ground that Proudhon did, i.e., that no man can truly "represent" another man's thoughts and feelings — but more important is the fact that the beat doesn't want to promote anarchism or any other ism.*

All this has some virtues of its defects. If it means that the beat rejects

---

* In this respect as in some others, it is misleading to rely on the beat literary record, where one can, occasionally, find a quasi-political stance. Those who see the beats exclusively through their literature should remember that over 90 percent of the beats neither write for publication nor wish to do so.

any rational political planning, it means equally that he is not going to be a sucker for any charismatic leader whether of the Right or Left. Of course he is pleased to see beat attitudes spread, but he isn't interested in joining any organized social movement toward that end. Each of the three words "organized social movement" sounds obscene to the beat's ears.* And though naturally amused to see some of his fellows such as Allen Ginsberg achieve notoriety and shake up the squares, he doesn't regard Ginsberg or anyone else as his "spokesman" (much less "leader") in the sense that squares conceive of spokesmanship. The beat's only spokesman is himself.

American intellectuals, and those of European origin especially, misunderstand this because they are prone to see every irrational excrescence in American political life as a sign of fascism round the corner (recall the panicky overinterpretations of MacArthur's "triumphal" return from Korea, etc.). To those who insist on finding a German ancestor for the beats, I would suggest that the proper ancestor is not the storm trooper but rather the philosopher-poet Friedrich Nietzsche, who correctly described himself as "an ardent anti-antisemite," as "opposed to everything that calls itself *Reichsdeutsch*," and as "the last anti-political German."

If the three hundred and more beats I talked with are in any way representative, then many journalistic detractors of them — sometimes misled by ambiguities in "The White Negro" — have made utterly false equations between the teen-age hoodlum and beat worlds. These armchair social analysts need to catch up with current sociological theory and learn the differences between "conflict" and "retreatist" delinquent subcultures. Even more, they need to stop bombinating *in vacuo* and actually meet the people they write about — if only to learn that for every beat who is unusually given to violence there are at least two dozen beats who are sincere pacifists.

---

* In view of my earlier finding (*Dissent,* Winter, 1958) that the beats are not totally atomized individuals but instead form a subculture, they must of course have some social organization. But it is of the most tenuous sort. The beat group approximates the *primitive band* as described by Ralph Linton: a group of fairly constant membership larger than the family, compact, nomadic, but exploiting a fairly well-defined territory, socially self-sufficient and facing inward, without *rites de passage,* without formal governmental machinery, etc.

The last two features (perhaps the last three) distinguish the beat group sharply from the gang. Although Lewis Yablonsky in "The Violent Gang" (*Commentary,* August, 1960) claims that today's gang "lacks all features of an organized group," he goes on to contradict himself by describing types of gang officers and their duties, etc. The very concept of office is nonexistent in any beat group.

## IX

In the Village beat world, as in all bohemias by definition, the socially disapproved forms of sexual behavior are tolerated if not encouraged. And as one would expect in the current bohemia, interracial intercourse is particularly frequent.

What one would not necessarily expect is the peculiar pattern that homosexual behavior takes among the beats. Proportionately, the amount of such behavior is as high as in the non-beat world even though the beat whose outlets are entirely or almost entirely homosexual is proportionately very much rarer than his non-beat counterpart. In other words an extraordinary number of male beats, whites as well as Negroes, are fully bisexual or in some cases polymorphous perverse.* They accept homosexual experiences almost as casually as heterosexual ones. Even beats with numerous and continuing post-adolescent homosexual experiences typically do not feel the need to define themselves as homosexuals and create some sort of beat wing of the homosexual world. Nor do they give up heterosexual involvements. Beats not only tolerate deviant sex roles but, to a much greater extent than previous bohemians, display a very high tolerance of sex-role ambiguity.

Most likely this subcultural trait was originally transmitted to the white beats by Negro beats, for not only do Negroes set much of the tone of beat life, but Negro culture has always had a higher tolerance of sexual ambiguity than white culture, and also the non-beat white groups showing high tolerance (e.g., seamen, ex-convicts) have had a special conditioning factor — prolonged absence from women — that is lacking in the beat world.

The unusual breadth of beat sex-life is accompanied by very little depth. All types of beats at all age levels fail to establish deep and lasting sexual relationships. Lack of virility, however defined, is a frequent problem among the white males (and a characteristic of all long-time junkies); this substantial minority is essentially passive. The majority of beats, conversely, engage in an endless series of short-term affairs that bespeak much more of acting-out than of action. Their bed-hopping "genitality" comes about precisely because they too are sexually impoverished — "orgastically impotent" in Reich's terms — and have yet to discover that in sex life there is no automatic passage from quantity to quality. Consequently, even among the oldest beats it is uncommon to find a couple who have been living together more than two or three

* In terms of the Kinsey heterosexual-homosexual rating scale from zero to six, beats show an unusual clustering at points two, three, and four. *cf.* Alfred Kinsey, Wardell Pomeroy, and Clyde Martin, *Sexual Behavior in the Human Male* (Philadelphia: W. B. Saunders, 1948), pp. 638-641.

years; and as often as not, such couples have managed to stick together only by replacing sex with the symbiotic cement of mutual drug addiction.*

## X

For obvious reasons beat drug-taking is a furtive affair, and hence few outsiders realize that it is a totally pervasive part of beat life, both as an activity and as a topic of conversation. The illegal use of drugs is one of the handful of things that characterize all male beats with very rare exceptions, and a good majority of the females. But contrary to some popular views, (a) the majority use nonaddicting drugs exclusively and (b) the majority of such users do not eventually go on to use addicting drugs and become junkies.

I talked with about 285 male beats and directly or indirectly queried about 205 concerning their possible illegal use of drugs, of whom only 14 denied any such use whatever; of about 25 female beats queried, out of about 40 I talked with, 9 denied illegal use of any drug.† Some beats who denied such use were doubtless lying. Although for most beats I did not obtain data on frequency of use, it seems certain that the majority use drugs at least once every couple of days, whether the drugs are addicting or nonaddicting or a combination. Many younger beats have been thoroughly socialized to drug-taking without ever having been socialized to drinking, and are teetotalers when it comes to alcohol.

Beats do not constitute the majority of those who use drugs illegally, but their lives often intersect with that majority at the points of supply. Consequently much of the information below, though gathered from Village beats, deals with general New York drug distribution.

ADDICTING DRUGS

Heroin is the drug of choice among beat junkies, though a few are hooked on barbiturates. The other addicting opiates and synthetics — morphine, codeine, demerol, dolophine, pantopon, etc. — are all used freely by junkies when available, but in the Village they are available less often than heroin or barbiturates, and no beat junkie seems primarily addicted to one of these drugs as such; rather, these drugs are used in addition to heroin or as substitutes for it.

---

* This is not to imply that junkie couples achieve long-run stability (the reverse doubtless is true), but rather that in its *initial* phases mutual addiction "helps keep the family together."

† The figures are exact for those denying illegal use of drugs; the other figures are estimates, as I didn't start keeping strict count of these until part-way through my investigation. My talks with beats were no formal interviews and varied considerably in length. With some beats in the sample I spent less than five minutes; with others, more than thirty hours.

Opium itself is often available. However, it is expensive ($15-$20 for a *toy,* a ball about the size of a large pea) and beats regard it as something to try once for kicks but otherwise not worth the price — partly because it is less powerful than its main derivatives and partly because there is rarely an opium layout and experienced preparer available. A few beats claim there is still one old-style "opium den" in Chinatown, to which no whites or Negroes and very few Chinese are admitted. Although disappointed at being barred, they admire the Chinese for playing it so cool.

Apart from questions of secrecy, it is hard to estimate the percentage of junkies among the beats because there are marginal cases (those who use addicting drugs occasionally but have not become addicts) and because some addicts cannot yet admit to themselves, much less to an outsider, that they have been hooked. I counted as junkies not only those who indicated they were, but all admitted users of addicting drugs who indicated they had ever experienced withdrawal discomfort — whether or not they indicated that drugs had been taken to relieve such discomfort, and regardless of frequency of use.* By this criterion, among Village beats under twenty, about 1 out of 15 is a junkie; between twenty and twenty-five, about 1 out of 11; over twenty-five, about 1 out of 9.

Off and on during the past year — though not at present — there have been in the Village severe shortages of heroin. Users unanimously state that this has not been due to an increase in Village arrests but entirely to another factor: the syndicate some time ago decided to pull out of the drug business at least temporarily — this is partly what the Apalachin meeting was about — because of successful government prosecution of some very big shots (Stromberg) and harrassment of others (Genovese).

Negroes and Puerto Ricans controlled some distribution in their neighborhoods but were not equipped to fill entirely the hole that the syndicate pullout left in their own supplies, much less take over distribution elsewhere. Apparently Negro and Puerto Rican areas at first felt the pinch as much as the Village, not merely because of the syndicate pullout but because many more white junkies began trying to score from them. Indeed, some white Village pushers and users of heroin moved to the more racially mixed areas of the Upper West Side and Lower East Side.

When the syndicate pulled out, for some junkies there was at first total panic; their connections simply had no junk. Now all junkies can obtain heroin regularly again — a few believe that syndicate members previously unassociated with the drug traffic are entering it — but complain that the

---

* A partial justification for this procedure is the statement of Lindesmith, *op. cit.,* p. 75: "The writer has never heard of a user who, having experienced the full intensity of the withdrawal symptoms in full knowledge of their relation to the absence of opiates, did not become an addict."

price has risen steeply in the form of greater dilution. (In the absence of actual analysis of drug samples, such statements should be treated with caution. Complaints about increasing dilution are always common among junkies, the main reason being the junkies' increasing tolerance of drugs.) Three junkies say that there have been a sharply increased number of sick junkies unable to support their habits at former levels, trying to taper off on such things as Cocinil, and hitting drugstores so often that some stores have been totally "burned down," i.e., refuse to supply even nonprescription items to known junkies.

NONADDICTING DRUGS

Beats frequently use nonaddicting and nonhallucinatory stimulants, such as dexedrine. But their use of nonaddicting drugs focuses invariably and overwhelmingly on the hallucinogens. Among these, marihuana is the drug of choice. Marihuana smokers also use peyote, hashish, and synthetic mescalin in that order of frequency. Recently a few marihuana smokers have experimented with using peyote exclusively for extended periods. Cocaine is seldom used because it is expensive and the "high" it produces does not last long; beats say it is an upper-class drug, used mostly in wealthy show business and criminal circles.

Beats who use no illegal drugs are few. To estimate the proportion using marihuana, it would not be far wrong to simply reverse the above estimates concerning beat junkies. Thus, among beats under twenty, marihuana smokers would outnumber junkies nearly 14 to 1; between twenty and twenty-five, nearly 10 to 1; over twenty-five, nearly 8 to 1.*

* These estimates differ astoundingly from those usually found in the literature on narcotics, where it is typically estimated that about 91½ percent of all New York drug users known to authorities use addicting drugs and about 8½ percent use nonaddicting drugs such as marihuana. cf. Second Interim Report of the State of New York Committee on Narcotic Study, Legislative Document (1958), No. 16, p. 12.

There are several possible reasons for the discrepancy, all of which seem to be operative here: (a) Though I tried to secure a representative sample of beats, junkies may have been slightly underrepresented. (b) Some beats who are junkies doubtless kept this fact hidden from me. (c) Beats are somewhat unrepresentative of New York drug users generally, because nearly all the junkies attracted to New York from the rest of the country (New York is now estimated to have between one-third and one-half of America's junkies) probably go to non-beat circles. (d) The number of New York marihuana smokers may indeed be several times the number of junkies, but the latter pose such a severe problem that narcotics police must give them near-total attention, and hence marihuana smokers rarely come to the attention of the authorities. (This would follow from the beat testimony cited below, which there seems no reason to doubt, concerning the pattern of narcotics arrests.) (e) Additional support for the view that marihuana smokers may greatly outnumber junkies is that the latter often must turn to crime to support their habits and/or turn themselves in for treatment — both of which bring them to the attention of the authorities — whereas marihuana smokers do neither.

The one other comparative survey of drug use I know of that does not depend on arrest rates also finds that marihuana smokers outnumber heroin users, though the

About a dozen men and two women stated that most beat women smoke marihuana but few are real "potheads" (devotees of marihuana) and that most smoke it mainly because their men do.

Although beat heroin users and beat marihuana smokers are part of one subculture, they tend to split into two separate groups when it comes to the specific activity of taking drugs, each developing its own customs.

As Howard Becker has shown, marihuana smoking is a group activity in which the psychic response to the drug in large part has to be *taught* to the newcomer.* (It appears that marihuana is a drug in which tolerance not only does not go up, but as a result of learning actually goes down.) Beat marihuana smokers not only confirm this, but indicate that even after the user has internalized the group norms and thus can get high alone, his drug-taking continues to have a much more social quality than that of the heroin user. One made a remark that would be almost inconceivable from a heroin user: "Sometimes it's okay to get high by yourself, but then I always like to go out and bounce it off other studs." Beat statements about group marihuana-using sessions and group heroin-using sessions consistently indicate a far greater degree of mutuality in the former, particularly with regard to both verbal and nonverbal sharing of drug-induced psychic states.† It is possible that this mutuality has a strong latent homosexual component and that this is what bars most female beats from full participation; the four beats I asked about this thought there was something to it.

Narcotics police in the Village, say the beats, used to spend all their time chasing junk (addicting drugs). Marihuana users were safe if they stayed on their own scenes, and were arrested only if they were discovered accidentally — typically if they were on a junk scene when the police came looking for junk. This is still generally true, but beats note that in the past year there have been two major Village raids on strictly marihuana-smoking groups. And the police forced the one coffee shop that earlier this summer was selling peyote openly (not against New York State law) to discontinue sales, by invoking a city health ordinance concerning potentially poisonous foods.

During the past four months (May through August) there have been recurrent shortages in the Village marihuana supply. These shortages have been more frequent and of longer duration than heroin shortages, a situation the beats say is truly extraordinary: "Man, there's never been

---

differences are not nearly as startling. *cf.* Charles Winick, "The Use of Drugs by Jazz Musicians," *Social Problems,* Vol. VII, No. 3, Winter 1959–60, especially p. 242.
* Howard S. Becker, "Becoming a Marihuana User," *American Journal of Sociology,* LIX, Nov., 1953, pp. 235–242.
† This psychic sharing among marihuana smokers reaches its peak in the "contact high." *cf.* Winick, *op. cit.,* p. 244.

anything like it. All the smack you want and a complete pot panic." * To obtain marihuana at all, beats have sometimes been forced to buy it in a form (already rolled into "joints," rather than loose) and at a price (75 cents or $1 per joint) that they say are usually reserved for the rich college crowd. There are many stories about marihuana being cut with bay leaves, oregano, etc., and about an increase in the number of "burns" (in which someone who claims he can obtain drugs takes money in advance and never returns).†

Beats feel that the marihuana shortages, unlike those of heroin, have little to do with the syndicate lying low, for the distribution of marihuana has always been only slightly syndicate and mostly independent. The consensus is that marihuana supplies have not significantly decreased but in recent months have had to be spread over a suddenly expanded market.

The horde of new teen-age beats, many just arrived in the Village this summer, nearly all use marihuana. Moreover, while the Village beat market has been expanding, some of its normal supplies have been deflected to new markets elsewhere. Beats say that the use of marihuana in white non-beat circles was until recently pretty much restricted to jazz musicians and theater people, but that in the past year it has been spreading rapidly in the worlds of advertising, radio-TV, college students, etc. — the *Playboy* readership essentially — and that some suppliers formerly in the Village have shifted to the favorite hangouts of these groups because they pay more. It is said that some ex-Village pushers of marihuana and hashish now work the uptown East Side bars, and that earlier this summer two Village pushers took off for Provincetown when they discovered that what would be a five dollar bag of marihuana in the Village was selling for fifteen dollars to the Provincetown sports car set.

* "Smack" is one of several terms for heroin. Marihuana is usually "pot," though "boo" and other terms are sometimes heard. "Panic," usually in the form of "there's a panic on," means that there is a drug shortage. The argot is of course subject to rapid change. For humorous effect, beats will sometimes use a term that is no longer current except among square writers: "Got a reefer, man?"
† Some older drug users say the greater number of burns is due to the increased mobility of today's beats. Beats are in fact more mobile than old-style hoboes. Not only do they shuttle between New York and California, but they have their own "international set" whose principal stopping places are in Mexico, the Balearic Islands, and Paris.
In the opinion of some beats, which I share, the new teen-age beats will end up producing proportionately fewer junkies than older groups have done. This is *not* because they are aware that "just fooling around" with heroin almost always leads to addiction, for there is hardly a heroin addict alive who didn't know that to begin with. It is rather that among beats today the use of heroin has lost much of its glamor, is less often considered a requisite of being hip, and frequently is even considered "uncool." A similar change seems to have taken place in the ideology of jazz musicians. *cf.* Winick, *op. cit., passim.*

## XI

Almost all Village beats technically are literate, and some whites have even attended college, but at best a sixth are habituated to reading (none seem addicted) and far fewer are concerned with writing. (Most square articles on "the beats" go astray because beat writers, being highly visible, get all the attention and thus a small and atypical part is taken for the whole.) Among the minority who could be called regular readers, the "literary" materials consist almost wholly of writing by romantic hedonists, much of it third-rate or worse and nearly all of it contemporary.

Interest in Zen passed its peak over a year ago and has radically declined. In the Village at least, Zen now appears to have been a beat fad whose only lasting significance in American intellectual history is that it (along with jazz-cum-poetry) marks the first time that a West Coast bohemia exerted a major influence on an Eastern one. About the only carryover from earlier mystical concerns is that some beats continue to take an interest in divination; but formerly beats used the *I Ching, or Book of Changes* for this purpose, whereas now one finds the use of Tarot cards or some Harlem-derived routine.

Insofar as most beats, whites and Negroes alike, can be said to have a dominant intellectual interest, it is jazz music. And the jazz world is the single non-beat segment of American society that often attracts beats. (Their admiration for it is not requited, to judge by musicians' complaints.) The nature and depth of the beats' relation to jazz have remained unchanged over the past three years, except that these years have produced some new heroes (e.g., Ray Charles) and a new villain (for some beats, Ornette Coleman has replaced Dave Brubeck as the archfraud).

Although the white beat's attraction to the jazz world is often the very core of his "white Negro" role, there is little uniquely "beat" about all this. Such involvement is socially not very different from the relationship of adolescent whites to Negro jazz in several American non-beat and pre-beat bohemias. For example, nearly twenty years ago, when I was v. p. of my high school jazz club, a thirteen-year-old zoot suiter, we often used to make the Harlem "balcony scenes" — boosting old Bessie Smiths and Hot Fives from the balcony of the Rainbow Music Shop before the war-time scrap drive wrecked the supply, going wild in the Apollo Theatre's sweet-smelling second balcony — odoriferous from pomade and pot, though we didn't know about the latter at the time — to a Basie-Millinder two-step. And we traveled Swing Street when it still swung (where half the time we'd get kicked out despite our borrowed I. D.) to hear Billie Holiday at the Onyx Club or Tatum at the Three Deuces. Today, the big boosting scenes are Goody's and the Colony instead of the Rain-how; Swing Street has been replaced by scattered Village clubs; the white intellectual jazz mentors are Nat Hentoff and Martin Williams instead of Ralph Berton and Gene Williams; there are goatees instead of twelve-inch peg pants, etc. But apart from the music itself, and the fact that now one merely listens to it at Birdland instead of stomping to it at the Savoy, not much has really changed.

## XII

A few beats, invariably among the youngest, are not so much interested in jazz as in the folk music of the "ethnic" set. But all beats reject the folksy-artsy group as people because in fundamental attitude the latter, despite the number of Negroes among them, are un- or anti-beat.* The Village devotees of ethnic music are historically minded, scholarly, middle-class youths, mostly Jewish, who are trying to disown their parents' culture not by becoming beat but rather by proving that ancient proverb, "New York ain't America."

The intersection of beat and "ethnic" circles, and indeed of Village social circles generally, can be seen at its warm-weather wildest in the hundreds of people who on Sunday afternoons gather round the children's wading pool in Washington Square Park. The circles here are as much concentric as intersecting.

The inner circle consists of people who arrive by 1 P.M. and thus get seats on the rim of the pool and on the steps leading down into it; this circle is a mixture of early-rising square Villagers, many of whom have brought their children to wade, and beats who get there early because they've been up all night. (The beats used to get high and roll around in the pool with the kiddies, fully clothed, until the Park Department erected signs restricting the pool's use to those under twelve years of age.) Surrounding this is a second, standing circle of clusters of folk and hillbilly performers and their listeners: uptown tourists and new-style rich Villagers, "ethnic" teen-agers, Italians, a few beats. Around this is a third circle, also quite mixed but consisting mostly of beats asking each other what's happening, tourists with cameras trying to elbow their way into the second circle for a good shot, and tight-trousered Village homosexuals walking their dogs and cruising each other.

[Section XIII, omitted here, examines beat literature and beat literary theory.]

---

* When the Fire Department raided beat coffee shops, the proprietor of The Folklore Center on Macdougal Street went so far as to issue a mimeographed broadside (dated June 12, 1960) praising this action and condemning the beats. Shortly thereafter he had his window broken.

## XIV

Both white and Negro beats are notably given to calling a spade a spade. One would never catch them describing race relations as "intergroup" relations even if they knew the term, nor describing the lower class as the "working" class or old people as "senior citizens." But this forthrightness of speech and attitude, laudable as it may be, is not accompanied by much clarity of vision. Nowhere is there greater disparity between beat theory and practice than in the role that Negro beats, wittingly or unwittingly, are forced to play for white beats.

The several white beats I met who knew my earlier critique of them — unfortunately I met no Negro beats who knew it * — all disputed my claim that they accept the Negro only for his "Negro-ness" (as bringer of marihuana and jazz, etc.) and thus practice an inverted form of "keeping the nigger in his place." According to them, they really do accept the Negro in his totality. Maybe so; but I doubt it. White beats should be given credit for the best of conscious intentions, but it is disheartening how regularly their actions confirm that old Negro proverb, "Whenever you see a white man with a colored man, the white man wants something from the colored man."

To see that Negroes living in the interracial beat world are still "invisible men" means to become sharply aware of something that white beats characteristically dodge: no modern urban Negro — raised as he is on white movies, white comic books, white television — can avoid internalizing white ideals, most especially can he not avoid internalizing white ideals of physical beauty, and on one level or another of his consciousness he puts himself down every time he looks in a mirror. (Hence the enormous Negro hair-straightening and skin-lightening industries, the profound discrimination among Negroes themselves on the basis of skin color, the high-yellow beauty on the cover of *Ebony* who gives the lie to the magazine's title, etc.) Contrary to what many white beats believe, there is hardly a Negro alive who in his heart of hearts doesn't want to be white, and the various kinds of Negro chauvinist movements invariably represent a reaction formation against the forbidden desire to be white.

The modern American Negro's need to be white is one culture trait that the white male beat, like most of his square white brethren, cannot emotionally accept. This comes out most clearly, though not exclusively, in beat sex-life; the Negro's desire for white girls is continually and subtly opposed by the white males, whatever their conscious beliefs may

---

* Some material that follows is touchy if not downright offensive to most Negroes, beat or non-beat. As I was able to explore all of it with only three Negro beats (two agreed completely, the other hedged on some parts), it should be regarded as subject to further proof or disproof.

be, *not* merely in the terms with which one usually opposes a sexual rival but with such remarks as "X is too hung up on balling white chicks" or "Y's trouble is that he's too fay-oriented," etc. Thus miscegenation in the beat world is essentially a conspiracy between white females and Negro males, that triumphs over strong white male opposition only because the latter can never become fully articulate since it contradicts the conscious ideology.

In addition to the remarks of white beats quoted above, there is evidence from the Negro side that all is not well.

Every Negro knows that the white man, though he dislikes all non-whites, has especially hostile feelings toward American Negroes; he knows experientially the truth in Max Weber's remark that the difference between the white man's attitude toward Indians and toward Negroes is that the Indians were never slaves. So the Negro who finds his status intolerable sometimes concludes that if he can't change his skin, at least he can try to escape his status as an *American* Negro — can try to enter some halfway house by pretending to be a Jamaican or Haitian or whatever. Recently the most influential halfway house among Negroes has been Islam.* These halfway houses are part of what Franklin Frazier calls the Negro "world of make-believe" — few Negroes or whites are really fooled by an American Negro's claim to be somebody else — but they do ease the pain somewhat. Now, it happens that several prominent jazz musicians have been converted to Islam. Statistically speaking, they represent a small portion of either American Negro Moslems or jazz musicians; and yet their presence has a real meaning, which is this: even if you're a very successful Northern Negro and move in circles that include many hip white admirers, and make it with some cool white chicks, you're still expected to play it like a spade and it's still a drag.

The hip attitude toward Negroes is, to be sure, not only better than the usual square rejection of them but is superior to the phoney some-of-my-best-friends-are routines (which at best let in special performers of the arts, scholarship, and politics under special conditions). And this ideology does mean that white beats meet with Negroes more often than white squares usually do. What is still questionable is the nature of these relationships.

Although the white beat grants the Negro a fuller role than other white "pro-Negro" groups do, he does it merely by compounding the limited roles those groups demand. For the white beat, the Negro fulfills the liberal's demand that he entertain plus the radical's demand that he sym-

* However, the emergence of West African nations is causing a shift among some Harlemites from a North African Moslem orientation to a West African non-Moslem one. *cf.* for example, Priest Ofuntola Oserjeman, *Orisha: A First Glimpse of the African Religion of Brazil, Cuba, Haiti, Trinidad and now U. S. A.* (N. Y.: Great Benin Books, African Library Series, n. d. [1960]), available from The Shango Temple, 71 East 125 Street.

bolize the results of reactionary oppression plus the Harlem thrill-seeker's demand that he act out the primitive in all of us. One thing the Negro must *not* do is try to be white.

Instead of worrying about the Negro becoming "too fay-oriented" the white beats might consider accepting him in his inescapable aspect of Negro-wanting-to-be-white. They might even encourage it, for surely the only real solution to the psychological problems peculiar to the American Negro is the very solution that so worries our Southerners: miscegenation on a grand scale, the production of more and more Negroes who can pass, and ultimately the total "mongrelization" of the two races.

## XV

I found it relatively easy to talk with beats, though the talk often had to be literally in their terms and representatives of the nonexhibitionist majority had to be sought out: first, because they are typically more tolerant than political sectarians, more willing to accept an outsider who makes an honest attempt to understand them; second, because I agree, as any socialist must, with many of their criticisms of modern society; third, because from the onset of my own adolescence until a couple of years thereafter (at which time I enlisted in the death-struggles of Marxism), I and some of my friends went through a "white Negro" phase similar to that of many young beats today. However, if one makes it clear to the beats, as I did, that he is essentially a square, he will run into some who will give him a rough time, he will occasionally be put on (a combination of being conned and being baited). This was overcome in nearly all cases.

Generally, the only real hindrance proved to be that the beats, who by definition avoid work, are nightpeople. With respect to drugs there was the special problem that anyone investigating this area must of course convince the people involved that he is not a fink or a plain-clothesman, and I was not always able to do so. Thus the material on drugs, full as it may seem, is actually the thinnest part of my essay.

Nearly all beats I talked with at any length were told that I would write about them, and with four exceptions fairly easily accepted this. Nor was it necessary, except with a few paranoid-homicidal types, to keep from them my disagreements or the fact that what I wrote would in good part be critical.

1961.

# HARLEM, MY HARLEM

## CLAUDE BROWN

At the age of nine I had already acquired the reputation of being the worst boy in the neighborhood. And in my neighborhood this was no easy accomplishment. My frequent appearance in juvenile court was beginning to bother the judges. By spring of 1946 I had been placed in four juvenile detention centers by the Manhattan Domestic Relations Court. However, during my travels through New York City while truant from school, I had become exceptionally well acquainted with the city subways. As a result, I was usually back on the streets of Harlem within two days, from wherever the court had placed me. A year earlier, I had acquired the habit of staying away from home for several days and nights which occasionally lengthened into weeks. Due to my skill at living in the streets, it would sometimes be many days before my parents learned of my unofficial departure from the places to which I had been confined by the courts.

While roaming the streets at night with one or two other boys who were also afraid to go home or disgusted with home life, I was often arrested for breaking into stores and stealing. I only stole items that I could sell to my private customers or to one of the neighborhood "fences." And I knew a large number of the latter. Among my many customers and associates were prostitutes, pimps, dope peddlers, stick-up artists, professional thieves, and other petty criminals with great ambitions.

My favorite fence was Miss Eileen. She was not the highest paying fence; in fact, there is no such thing. Any thief will tell you, they are all a bunch of crooks. But Miss Eileen had such a nice way of robbing me. She would put her arm around me and beg me in a very sexy tone while she played with my ears. I thought she was the prettiest lady in the world. I think she was the first woman I ever knew who had red hair. Miss Eileen was also something more than a fence, and I would have discovered this much sooner had it not been for my youth. Many times when I came to her house at night she would be in her slip and a new husband would be there. As time went on I heard the older fellows talking about selling Miss Eileen something for a "piece of loving." I too began to dream of the day when I could sell her something for a piece of loving, but to my regret I never got the chance. A year later Miss Eileen went to jail for three years, and when she came out she wasn't as pretty as she used to be. As a result, she changed her "game" to selling drugs. For three years she was very successful in the "horse trade," but gave it up and did seven years for her troubles at the insistence of the Narcotics Bureau. The last time I saw her she was profitably engaged in one of Harlem's more legal vices; the "numbers" racket.

These were the people I admired and wanted to be accepted by. People like Miss Eileen and my other teachers from the streets of Harlem.

By June, 1946 I had been expelled from not less than six public schools in New York City, and refused acceptance by as many others. The Board of Education would tolerate my numerous absences from school, and even my fighting with teachers. But they refused to have a boy in the school system who had attempted to push another boy out of a five-story window.

Following a thirty-day psychiatric observation period in Bellevue Hospital, I was ordered out of the state by a juvenile court judge. After enduring what seemed at the time a miserable year on a small farm in South Carolina, I returned to New York. When I arrived in Harlem on August 10, 1947, I was also returning to a familiar way of life. Less than two months later I was standing before Judge Bolyn diligently trying to look pathetic. She appeared to be a woman devoid of any emotions, especially pity. From Judge Bolyn, to whom I am deeply indebted today, I received my first sentence.

My first court sentence was actually not a sentence at all, but a commitment to Wiltwyck School for Boys for an indefinite time.

Wiltwyck is an interracial institution which accepts delinquent boys from eight to twelve, committed by the courts of New York or by social agencies. Only children are considered who can profit by its program of individualized treatment in the regulated and planned environment of a children's community.

Following a two and a half years' stay at Wiltwyck, I returned to my dear old Harlem. I was then thirteen. In a few weeks I became uncomfortably aware of not being able to fit in anymore. There were many new vices to learn, but somehow I just could not pick up where I had left off. Having no alternative, however, I set out to reestablish myself in the old community.

Things were somewhat different now. The dope fad had hit New York, and all of my old gang were using heroin. I wanted nothing to do with drugs, but the problem was very disturbing. Either I could continue my relationship with my old cohorts or get in with a younger gang of delinquents, my own age. The younger group was stealing and making much less money than my former partners. I would have chosen my old friends, but I was handicapped by parental restrictions. So I became leader of a gang of fellows mostly my own age. There were many things I could teach them, such as how to pick locks, how to rob a subway slot machine, how to pick a woman's pocketbook, how to bargain with the "fence," and how to roll "pot." Also, I knew how to organize a gang fight and hold a gang together.

I didn't have to steal for money, because Butch, Kidd, and Danny were doing good, "pushing horse," and money was mine for the asking. I think they preferred that I steal it from them. So, that's how I usually got it. Butch, Kidd, and Danny were all at least four years older than I was, and for many years we had all lived in the same tenement building. These guys whom I considered to be "big time," were like older brothers to me. They fought the bigger guys who tried to bully me. It was they who had taught me how to steal, how to live in the streets of Harlem. It was Danny who had taught me most of the street ways. He taught me by cheating me, taking me along on "scores," and showing me my mistakes whenever I lost a fight.

Whenever I lost a fight Danny would always say you should have stabbed that punk. To Danny, everybody was a punk. It was Danny who had first taught me how to use a knife in a street fight. I remember him showing me how to get the knife out of my belt without my opponent seeing it. Danny would say, "A cat should never know that you have a knife until he has been cut or stabbed." And this is usually the way it was when he stabbed a guy.

Butch was the most loyal guy I knew, and also the best thief. Butch had taught me how to hitch rides on street cars and buses. He also taught me not to run when I stole something. Butch would never admit that he was the best thief in the neighborhood. He would always say that Sol was the best because Sol had taught him many things about stealing. Sol was much older than Butch and had been stealing much longer, but he had been caught while Butch had not yet been "busted." In my opinion that made Butch the better thief.

Kidd had taught me how to play hookey from school. I was about six years old when I first heard about "hookey" and I pleaded with Kidd to teach me the game. He promised me he would teach me on the first day I went to school. This promise had to wait until the second day, because on the first day my mother took me to get me registered. Once I learned how to play hookey, I seldom went to school, and this often led to staying away from home. I would look in the mailbox and could always tell if there was a card from the school. The yellow truancy card in the mailbox meant that if I went home that night, the razor strop awaited me. When I played hookey I would either go on a stealing tour of the city or sneak into a movie. Kidd had also taught me how to sneak into a movie.

Stealing had become a part of me and I became very adept at this art. After Wiltwyck I felt lost whenever I was not stealing or "rumbling." Perhaps that's why I began to spend more time with my new gang and less time with my old cohorts.

Less than three months after my release, I was arrested for gang fighting, but was released in my mother's custody. Three weeks later I was in a backyard stealing some sheets off a clothes line. Turk, a member of my new gang whom I had become "tight" with, was with me. At my house there were festivities taking place because mama had hit the number. I had to get away from it and when I reached the street, the first person I saw was Turk. He was always ready to do whatever I suggested. Turk's favorite words were "Sonny, what are we gonna do?" That cold night in December, when I said to Turk, let's go steal some sheets, he seemed to be waiting for the suggestion.

When we had been in the backyard for about fifteen minutes, Turk shouted, "Foot it, Sonny!" I stood there waiting to see what he wanted to run from. I didn't see anybody, but after the first shot was fired I decided to run. By the time I reached the top of the stairs leading from the backyard I was feeling unusually tired. But I kept running even after I felt the blood streaming down my leg and realized I had been shot. I panicked and started yelling, "Turk! Turk! I'm shot." I ran into a fish-and-chip joint where I collapsed. As I lay on the floor of the dirty joint, my fear of dying began slowly to diminish.

I found myself wishing that mama would stop jumping up while she cried, because she was shaking the shabby floor and it made me feel the bullet more. I never gave a second thought to Turk's question when he bent over me as I fell to the floor, and asked me if I were going to tell the cops that he was with me. This was all very normal in Harlem where somebody was always getting shot, stabbed, or his throat cut. However, I found it disturbing to have it happen to me. As the pain began to ease up, I starting thinking how lucky I was to die this way. I thought about the boy whom I had watched two members of my old gang throw from the roof of a six-story building. I recalled how frightened he looked when they grabbed him, and I recalled his terrified screams as he went over. Yeah, compared to him I was really lucky.

While I lay on the rolling stretcher in Harlem Hospital emergency ward, I thought the police would never stop questioning me. Danny, Butch, and Kidd arrived shortly after I did. First Butch would beg me to tell him who had shot me, then Danny would start while Kidd threatened to kill Turk if I died. They all had their "pieces" and were ready and anxious to shoot somebody. Fortunately, I had not seen whoever it was that shot me, and could tell them no more than I had told the police.

Three weeks after my two-week stay in Harlem Hospital, and while the surgeon who had operated on me was still marveling at what he and God had done, I was sent to New York State Training School for Boys at Warwick, New York. I stayed at Warwick for nine months. When I returned to Harlem, I had learned many new ways of crimes. I had also become well acquainted with many of New York City's teen-age criminals.

Upon my return to Harlem I no longer cared to steal or partake in gang fights, but I had to steal a few things to show my gang that getting shot had not unnerved me. Two days after I came home, I received my first real pistol, as a coming home gift. After pulling enough scores to get up one hundred dollars, I bought a half pound of pot and went into business. Within two weeks, the word had gotten around that I had the best pot in town. For the next three months — at the end of which I got "busted" — I did a pretty good job of emulating a Harlem "hustler" who was doing good. This included wearing thirty-dollar shoes and giving frequent handouts to old friends who had become junkies. Danny, one of my favorite old tutors in the ways of the street, had now become my favorite junkie; I would always give him a "nickel bill" to get a fix.

Following two more trips to Warwick, I moved out of Harlem and got a job. Most of my spare time was spent in Harlem, taking the ribbing and laughing that my attending evening high school evoked from my old street corner cronies. They laughed for three years. When I entered college there were no more laughs.

Some interesting changes have occurred in Harlem during the past few years. It seems that many of the people who I once thought were merely waiting for something to happen to them, have made things happen. The last time I saw Danny, I could not help but admire him. Danny is making money by the fists full. There is nothing remarkable about a guy making lots of money selling drugs. But in Danny's case the admirable feat was his being able to kick an eight-year drug habit, and then make the stuff work for him. Danny is the only reformed junkie I have ever known to stay reformed for any length of time. And his presence in Harlem is most encouraging to other junkies who dream of kicking their habit and becoming pushers in turn.

I saw Turk yesterday and we talked of his next fight. It was an inspiring experience for me to hear Turk, who has become one of the world's leading heavyweight fighters, explain how he would beat his next opponent. It seems like only yesterday when I was explaining to him the strategy of our next "rumble."

The big changes in Harlem are in the people I know who have changed my sympathy to respect and admiration. If you've ever known a junkie for any length of time you'll understand the struggle he has to go through to get off the poison kick. He can't leave the world entirely, so for him to become master and dispenser of the thing that had ruled him for so long and so destructively is a great achievement. Harlem still has a much greater number of the miserable than any place else I know. This is inspiring also. Where else can one find so many people in such pain and so few crying about it?

1961

# 5

*People in politics*

# THE EXAMPLE OF NORMAN THOMAS
## BERNARD ROSENBERG

Ours is an omnivorous culture. Even the most prickly and apparently indigestible of critics, like Lenny Bruce and Paul Goodman, get cannibalized. It ought therefore to surprise no one that a socialist leader in America should be universally honored as an elder statesman. Such is the fate of Norman Thomas, and not just now as he approaches his eightieth birthday; it has dogged him throughout his career.

Murray Seidler, the more scholarly and detached, if less intimate, of two biographers,* dubs Thomas a "respectable rebel," and sums him up as a "successful failure." The labels fit. We have to do with a complex paradox which tells us perhaps as much about ourselves as about Norman Thomas. Most people who have known him have loved the man while eschewing his principles. They seem largely to have agreed with the H. L. Mencken of 1948 who declared that it was "a rare and exhilarating pleasure" to hear Thomas, the only presidential candidate that year to strike Mencken as being a "really intelligent and civilized man." Whereupon, most of them went out to vote for a Republican or a Democrat, too often neither intelligent nor civilized.

* Murray Seidler, *Norman Thomas: Respectable Rebel* (Syracuse U. Press, 1961). Harry Fleischman, *Norman Thomas: A Biography* (Norton, 1964).

The virtues everywhere ascribed to Thomas are in very short supply among politicians, and we have shamelessly wasted them. Even when leavened by charisma within a big opportunistic party (say, by an Adlai Stevenson), intelligence and urbanity are not conducive to victory at the polls. Still able to exhilarate and even electrify an audience as spokesman for a minority party, Thomas has naturally never held public office.

Six times the presidential nominee of his party, Thomas has withheld his name from the ballot since 1948. Asked recently if he would run in 1964, he replied, "Run? I can hardly walk." Actually, he continues to walk at rather a brisk pace, on and off picket lines, and from one platform to another, still alert, still responsive, still animated by an irresistible spirit of gaiety. Nevertheless, there is just enough poignant truth in his witticism to make it infinitely sad that through all these decades such a man should have been allowed to run for president, governor, senator, mayor, and never win.

That a socialist should be excluded from the formal exercise of power, while being celebrated on all sides, is somewhat less puzzling than why this man should have become a socialist at all — for there can be little doubt that he could have made his mark in conventional politics.

Bernard Kops has said: "Take one Jew and already you have an opposition party." But a middle-class Presbyterian reared in Marion, Ohio? Take one, and already you probably have a more famous Marionite: Warren G. Harding, the cipher who played at being President. Young Norman was an all-American boy, an animal lover, much interested in sports, outgoing, a booster. The son and grandson of ministers, he too was destined for the cloth. There is no recorded rebellion at adolescence, no tempestuous rejection of parental beliefs, neither of the religious orthodoxy nor the conservative Republicanism that Thomas imbibed as a boy. Nor is there a breath of skepticism, let alone radicalism in the college student, Princeton-bred and insulated from hard realities, who does his stint as an old-fashioned social worker, becomes a seminarian and finally, a clergyman — albeit of the liberal persuasion.

What causes someone with such a life history to invite trouble, indeed to court it by defying the gods of his society? None of the usual clichés applies. In his thirties Norman Thomas ceased to be the Reverend Thomas. He chose to embrace socialism and join a dissident little political party that had already seen its glory days. We may say, in the jargon of social science, that Thomas' relatively late change is an example of radical, adult, but not entirely discontinuous "resocialization." His brother and lifelong soul mate, Evan, himself a pacifist, recalls, ". . . We were brought up to be good. Success was not a goal in our family." Thus the hyperactive conscience, if not all its elements, did have roots in a specific background which, when coupled with later experience, flowered into the personality we know.

As both Seidler and Fleischman make clear, the decisive experience took place over a period of ten years in the slums of New York City, where Thomas and his bride — even less of a proletarian than he — devoted themselves to ameliorating the woe around them. Still a Republican, but greatly disturbed by the difference between life as he saw it and as he had been taught to see it, Thomas by 1912 had registered as a Bull Moose Progressive. In a class letter he wrote:

> With all my love for Princeton, I sometimes think, unjustly of course, that my education really began when I left there and that not the smallest part of it has been the life here in this district. It is a sort of school which sets hard lessons and asks some difficult questions. What is our democracy worth? How shall we make it apply to our social, industrial, and political problems? Are we preparing well for national safety in peace or war when so many of our workers cannot even under favorable conditions make the proper living wage?

So the route was classically Fabian: from a privileged position, through "poverty, filth, and vice" in the metropolis, to Christian, or at least a greatly muted Marxist socialism. The vain effort to grapple with overwhelming social problems at a Settlement House level made many a pre-professional English or American social worker conclude that total change was necessary. Later, with the professionalization of social work and the conversion of many "angels of mercy" into "snoopy civil servants," a narrower psychiatric emphasis took over.

Having learned the lesson that "our various reform efforts were, in the words of the familiar simile, like bailing out the tub while we kept the faucet running," Thomas was ripe for socialism. In 1907, shortly after graduation from Princeton, he took a trip around the world; in a quasi-clerical capacity, he was able to see much of Asia, and there, starting with a view of empire much like Kipling's, he learned to despise colonialism. All the while he was reading widely, a habit with which he is still afflicted.

Then came the war which propelled Thomas out of his pulpit for good, and plunged him into pacifism and socialism, movements which that war almost certainly doomed to failure. The Thomas family crisis must have been very acute. Of the elder Thomas' four tall sons, two had no great scruples about military service, the other two conscientiously objected to it. Evan, accurately described by Seidler as "an eccentric blend . . . part socialist, part anarchist, part pacifist, part agnostic," went to prison under barbarous conditions, subsequently became chairman of the War Resisters' League, continued unremittingly to struggle for peace, and flirted with but never joined the Socialist Party. Their soldier brother Ralph wrote to Norman in February, 1918, "I am sorry we don't agree in this, the biggest affair of our lives, but you know I respect your courage of conviction and idealism." Norman Thomas perpetuated this politically permissive attitude within his own family; he never sought to impose socialism on his children; he is dear to them, but they are no more heirs of his legacy than the public at large.

A solid substratum of tolerance, then, underlay all differences among the Thomases over several generations. This quality helps one understand that character which so many find very nearly exemplary. Thomas could always laugh, not least at himself, and though often grim and stern, he has never been subject to fanaticism, the ideologue's occupational disease. It is hard to resist the conclusion that just those elements in his makeup which militated against election to office made it certain he could leave a great impact upon the nation. To an extraordinary degree, he has become what his campaign literature always claimed for him: the incorruptible watchdog of American society.

Not that Thomas is a saint. He points to his own irascibility and impatience (if only to offset the many encomia which sound to him like premature obituaries). A great naïveté in personal relations is the commonest criticism one hears nowadays. Yet this too reflects favorably on the man, for it is said that he too frequently allowed himself to be deceived by assuming that the integrity of others was as great as his own.

What else is wrong with Thomas? Well, both biographers assert that his otherwise superb speeches suffer from over-rapid delivery. Seidler attributes this oratorical weakness to Thomas' habit of talking fast into the telephone during the period when A. Mitchell Palmer's boys might be listening, and Fleischman to the Party's penury which required Thomas to cover everything over the radio in a breathless fifteen minutes.

All the same, Thomas has been taken to task severely enough throughout most of his life, from left, right and center, outside and inside a party historically given over to factionalism — when not engaged in the more serious business of fratricidal warfare. After the First World War, Thomas emerged as leader of a Socialist Party in the doldrums. It had grown steadily and flourished from 1901 to 1912. The year Thomas voted for Teddy Roosevelt, Debs polled nearly a million votes, and in this same year, Seidler reminds us, the Party was able to boast that 1,039 of its members were public officeholders, including 56 mayors, more than 300 aldermen, some state legislators, and a member of Congress. The party had a vigorous youth movement, 13 daily newspapers, 232 English and 36 foreign-language weeklies, 12 monthlies, a copious flow of pamphlets, growing strength among students and in organized labor, where the Socialist Max Hayes gave Gompers a real run for the AFL presidency. And in Debs, Morris Hillquit, and Victor Berger, American socialism could claim an attractive group of leaders.

Then, in 1914, all hell broke loose. In the wreckage of World War I we may find the remains of socialism, a shriveled token of international brotherhood. Soon after war broke out, Thomas recalls, "Socialists were killing socialists as cheerfully, or docilely, as Christians were killing Christians. Democratic Socialism in 1914 missed a tremendous opportunity of a sort which never could return again." That the powerful socialists of Europe betrayed their principles and that Thomas stood by them, isolating himself from chauvinists of every stripe, is a matter of historical record. So is the general collapse that followed. Why did socialism fail to catch fire in the United States? The list of reasons is a long one (the Russian Revolution, Fascism, the New Deal, the Second World War, the conservatism of American labor, its comparative well-being, and so on), but none was as profoundly shattering as the Great War.

That war, to which most Americans rallied with a romantic enthusiasm such as they were never again to know, caused widespread departures from the Socialist Party. Thomas does not exaggerate when he observes, "I entered the party just as everyone else was leaving." And hardly a moment too soon. The War and the Red scares of 1919–20 left their mark. Debs had not long to go, his last years were clouded, and few thought the party could outlive him. A biographer of Debs, David Karsner, intoned in 1924, "It becomes increasingly clear as the Socialist Party steps into the shadows, that it was a one-man organization . . . ," a view interminably repeated since Thomas' formal assumption of leadership in 1928.

As an organization man, it is generally admitted, Thomas was no great shakes. Even his loyal campaign manager in 1944 and 1948, Harry Fleischman, scores Thomas for having been bored by organizational details. The socialist standard-bearer really came to life only in discussing issues. "In public speeches, he would stir his audience and then all too often forget to urge them to join the Socialist Party." Seidler, by contrast, credits Thomas with reawakening the party through personal communication between various locals and national headquarters, and doing "yeoman service . . . on a strictly organizational level." He was a tireless and apparently effective fund-raiser. For years Thomas appears to have known more about local conditions by maintaining direct ties with local activists than anyone else in the party.

And yet, and yet — the party was hideously undone by factionalism. It tore American socialism apart from 1930 to 1940. Was Thomas' incapacity to handle internal schisms responsible for all the bitterness of those years, the dissipation of energy, the scar tissue that would not heal? It would seem that the role he played exacerbated a bad situation. Would another stance (short of Lenin's disastrous "democratic centralism") have helped? Surely not much. Let us glance at some of the prevailing circumstances.

First of all, a millennial spirit and an apocalyptic atmosphere. In the thirties capitalism was actually crumbling; socialists had reason to feel vindicated. It seemed to them that the rest of their vision would also soon unfold, and that, with proper tactics, socialism was within their grasp. Each faction thought it knew best how to attain the cherished goal. Those who at the time squabbled over esoteric dogma can scarcely remember what it signified, but all are agreed that their faction-fighting bordered on savagery.

A second factor, which Seidler and others have emphasized, was generational conflict: younger people in the party versus older people; newcomers, keen on innovation and bristling with verbal radicalism, pitted against a more conservative Old Guard that had long controlled party policy and machinery. With the depression, there was a big spurt in membership, which increased the distance between hotheads and coolheads. These contingents, subtly subdivided in ways that no longer bear recounting, made up the two big factions and produced the great split of 1936 which decimated the Socialist Party beyond hope of recovery.

The conflict, further complicated by tension between foreign-born and native members, and sectional rivalries, as well as Thomas' determination not to be a mere figurehead, had been simmering for some time. At the national convention of 1932, an attempt was made to oust Morris Hillquit as national chairman, and some of the grounds used by his opponents, at least by innuendo, smacked of anti-Semitism. There were murmurings about that foreign-born New York Jew, which prompted Hillquit to tell the delegates: "I apologize for being born abroad, for being a Jew, and for living in New York." This shamed them into reelecting him — without damping the fires of discord. Torn many ways, the party nonetheless did unusually well in 1932, an electoral peak for Thomas which must have thrown a little scare into FDR, who appropriated some planks from the socialist platform. ("Roosevelt carried it out," New Dealers used to say. "On a stretcher," Thomas would add.)

Ferment in the party did not abate. Three factions, "Thomasites," young Militants, and Old Guardists crystallized as they moved toward a painful showdown in the national convention of 1936. Thomas for the most part occupied a centrist position between his party's left-wing and its right-wing. The pamphleteering, the cruel in-fighting, and the passionate speechifying that ensued have been amply documented from every point of view. Controversy swirled mainly around a resolution called "Declaration of Principles," drawn up by a Militant, some of whose passages appeared to be sounding a Bolshevik clarion call. Thomas found himself in full sympathy with neither faction, and failing in strenuous efforts to reconcile them, finally sided with the Militants, an act symbolized by his vote in favor of their Declaration. A majority of the delegates likewise endorsed that misbegotten manifesto. Whereupon, the Old Guard withdrew.

The Thomas of 1936 was a trifle "soft on Communism," although not soft enough to satisfy those of his comrades in the Socialist International who would have liked to support the Popular Front. But in another year or two, with the Moscow Trials, Thomas took the full measure of Soviet totalitarianism — of which he became a principal scourge and to which he consistently offered a democratic alternative.

It cannot be denied that Thomas was briefly, if not very seriously, mistaken about Bolshevism and Stalinism, nor that Louis Waldman and other representatives of the Old Guardists were, in this respect, right. But there is a final fillip to the story that should not be forgotten. The Old Guard no sooner deserted the Socialist Party than it joined the American Labor Party — which was dominated by the Communists, who never managed to infiltrate Norman Thomas' Socialist Party except as spies. And the Militants? Most of them objected to Thomas' moderation — until they drifted to the New Deal, and shyly or ardently espoused it.

How should Thomas have comported himself in this whirlpool? He has been taxed, notably by Daniel Bell, for not going along with the Old Guard (a few of whose remnants rejoined the Socialist Party in 1957) and mercilessly ridiculed as a phony socialist, notably by the Trotskyist intelligentsia that entered his party in bad faith in 1939, only to break off another chunk of the membership (and some of *its* remnants rejoined the Socialist Party in 1957). He is criticized both for his intransigence and for his latitudinarianism, and maybe each in its time was inappropriate. Perhaps. Perhaps he should have been lax when he was firm and firm when he was lax. The only pertinent question remains, Would it have made any difference? There is now no reason to believe that it would. And if the issue is not just tactical but moral, then Thomas' stature is not diminished, while that of his critics is.

In a monograph on American socialism, Bell pinpointed two grave flaws in Thomas as a party leader: he distrusted his own generation and surrounded himself with younger men who allegedly stood in an admiring and uncritical relation to him. To this indictment, Fleischman offers a convincing rebuttal:

> To a certain extent, Bell's charge that Thomas preferred the company of younger men in the Party is correct. But he fails to explain why. In the thirties, most of the older men in the Party were Old Guardists, who elevated inactivity to the dignity of a theory. There were some Old Guard leaders, however, whom Thomas not only respected but warmly liked, such as B. Charney Vladeck and Abraham Shiplacoff. As for the young men, far from being "admiring and uncritical" of Thomas, they

were hypercritical — and usually on flimsy grounds. They considered themselves "more revolutionary" than Thomas and better theoreticians. But Thomas sympathized with their zeal, and felt that time and experience would tone down their left-wing dogmatism. (As one of those youngsters, I can testify that Thomas was right about our development. Most of us agree that he was far more correct then than we were.)

With both wings gone, the Socialist Party could hardly be expected to soar. In the forties, it nearly perished of blows more crushing than those that had already been absorbed. With another World War in the offing, many interventionists dropped away (quietly, in deference to Thomas, as part of a "silent split"). Of those who remained some were pro-war, others anti-war. Thomas had abandoned absolute pacifism by backing the Loyalist cause in Spain. Thus when he opposed American entry into the Second World War, it was not for doctrinal reasons. The handful of socialists who favored war stayed with their few confreres who were against it in a miniature of the "all-inclusive party" that Thomas had once dreamed of creating. His own passion for peace, based partly on a mistaken conviction that war would totalitarianize the United States, led him to his lowest fortunes. He who had spurned common action with the Communists, for a brief time consented to common action with the America First Committee. That there were many liberal isolationists willing to do likewise in no way absolves him of a cardinal blunder. Our pride in him stems very largely from his avoidance of pitfalls constantly trapping liberals. Lending his good name to America First and its bigots only demeaned him, for no cause could justify this unnatural alliance. Fortunately, it was a passing aberration. After Pearl Harbor Thomas adopted a position of "critical support" for the war — thereby shocking and losing pacifists without gaining any new adherents.

If Thomas hit bottom in 1940, he may well have reached his high point four years later. Today, he views the campaign of 1944 as the most satisfying of his career. Not, surely, on account of the votes cast for him, a paltry 80,518, but because of the sensible message he alone carried to the people. Who else was there to excoriate the President for violating the rights of Japanese-American citizens when they were transported to our very own concentration camps? To proclaim that Soviet Russia, for all the liberals' renewed infatuation with it, was still a slave state? That unconditional surrender was an insane policy?

If, twenty years later, the Liberal Establishment could be made to read those speeches and to compare them with the productions concocted for Roosevelt and Dewey, the effect would only be embarrassing, and just possibly, chastening. There is no ectoplasmic presence in anything Thomas ever says, for one reason because he cannot afford ghost writers, and for another, because he finds them morally offensive. The quips he made in '48 about Truman and Dewey (Truman asking his speech writers, "What's it going to be tonight?" and Dewey pictured as a candidate "clad each day in a pair of platitudes") apply as well to scores of political opponents Thomas has bested simply by speaking for himself.

He speaks and he speaks, not only through his miniscule political party, but through the many voluntary organizations he has had a hand in founding. Tocqueville contended that only with a multiplicity of such organizations could democracy be secured and preserved. If so, then in helping to build the Civil Liberties Union, the League for Industrial Democracy, the Post-War World Council, the Workers Defense League, SANE, The American Committee on Africa, Spanish Refugee Aid, Inc., and many more — all intrinsically valuable — we begin to see the magnitude of his contribution.

There is no end to the tributes, and no doubt about their accuracy. Here is Bryn J. Hovde, former president of The New School for Social Research, echoing many others on Thomas:

> His function in our public life has been that of planting doubt where other leaders thought they had implanted certainty, that of arousing controversy about alleged divine inspiration in economics, that of holding up, always with hands of glowing utterance, the shape of a better world than that we have. Norman Thomas, in all his strenuous campaigning, never ran for office. There was never any prospect of his election — to office, that is. He was elected to be sure, or to use the language of his profession "elect," to serve greater purposes than administration. He is "elect" in the way of Isaiah and Micah, a prophet among us to chide us when we do wrong and to show us the light.

But how many of us see by his light? When Thomas insists in 1964 that the basic problems to which socialism addressed itself remain unsolved, he is advancing an elementary truth which few Americans care to face. To face it would be to recognize that he is not a prophet with premonitions of doom for mankind in some vague and indefinite future, but a man devoted to saving us from race suicide right now. The canonization of Norman Thomas is no substitute for the fulfillment of his vision, and celebration of his character no substitute for acting upon his truth.

1964

# ALBERT CAMUS
## NICOLA CHIAROMONTE

A man is dead: you think of his living face, of his gestures, his actions, and of moments you shared, trying to recapture an image that is dissolved forever. A writer is dead: you reflect upon his work, upon each book, upon the thread that ran through them all, upon their vital movement toward a deeper meaning; and you seek to form a judgment which takes account of the secret source from which they sprang and which is now stilled. But the picture of the man is not made up of the sum of your memories; nor the figure of the writer of the sum of his works. And one cannot discover the man through the writer, or the writer through the man. Everything is fragmentary, everything is incomplete, everything is the prey of mortality even when destiny seems to have granted both man and writer the gift of living to the limit of his forces, and of giving everything humanly possible, as in the case of Tolstoy. The story of a man is always incomplete; it is sufficient to think of what could have been different — almost everything — to know that his story can never contain the meaning of a human life, but only what that existence was permitted to be and to give. The truth was the living presence; and nothing can replace it. Immortality is an illusion for thought and art, as for man. They are nothing but relics mutely surviving time's erosion and history's disasters, like monuments of stone. But it is in this very fragility — that equates the humblest existence with the one that we falsely call "great" and is simply one that had the luck to express itself — that there lies the meaning and value of human life. And that value is eternal.

Albert Camus appeared in my life in April, 1941, in Algiers, where I had come as a refugee from France. I met him soon after my arrival, for in Algeria he was famous: the leader of a group of young journalists, aspiring writers, students, friends of the Arabs, enemies of the local bourgeoisie and Pétain. They lived together, passed the days on the seashore or hillside, and the evening playing records and dancing, hoping for the victory of England and giving vent to their disgust with what had happened to France and to Europe. They also put on plays, and in that period were preparing a production of *Hamlet* in which Camus, in addition to directing, played the leading role opposite the Ophelia of his wife, Francine.

He had published a volume of prose poems entitled *Noces,* they told me. I did not read it, because in those days I was not in the mood for prose poems, but chiefly because the company of him and his friends was enough. In their midst I found the France I loved and the pure clear warmth of French friendship. I attended the rehearsals of *Hamlet,* went to the beach with them, took walks with them, talking about what was happening in the world. Hitler had just occupied Greece, and the swastika waved over the Acropolis. I suffered continual nausea and solitude in the face of these events. But solitary and shut off as I was, I was the guest of those young people. To know the value of hospitality one must have been alone and homeless.

I try to recall details, as if through them I could relive those days and learn something more about the young writer with whom I actually spoke little, since he felt no more like talking than I. I remember being totally obsessed by a single thought: we had arrived at humanity's zero hour and history was senseless; the only thing that made sense was that part of man which remained outside of history, alien and impervious to the whirlwind of events. If, indeed, such a part existed. This thought I considered my exclusive privilege; I felt that no one else could be so possessed by it, yet I yearned for someone to share it with. But there was no one. It was not an idea compatible with normal life, let alone with literature — or so it seemed to me.

However, I did have something in common with this twenty-eight-year-old writer — love of the sea, joy of the sea, ecstatic admiration of the sea. I discovered this one day when I was his guest at Oran and we went by bicycle beyond Mers-el-Kebir to a deserted beach. We spoke little even then, but we praised the sea, which does not have to be understood, which is inexhaustible and which never palls. All other beauty does, we agreed. This agreement sealed our friendship. Camus told me then that he was writing a tragedy about Caligula, and I tried to understand what could attract a modern writer to such a subject. Unfettered tyranny? But contemporary tyranny did not seem to me to have much in common with Caligula's.

From Oran I continued my journey to Casablanca from where I had been told I could embark for New York. I said good-bye to Camus and his wife, knowing that we had exchanged the gift of friendship. At the core of this friendship was something very precious, something unspoken and impersonal that made itself felt in the way they received me and in our way of being together. We had recognized in each other the mark of fate — which was, I believe, the ancient meaning of the encounter between stranger and host. I was being chased from Europe; they remained, exposed to the violence that had driven me out. I carried away with me the impression of a man who could be almost tenderly warm one moment and coolly reserved the next, and yet was constantly longing for friendship.

I saw him again in New York in 1946 on the pier where I had gone to meet his ship. In my eyes he seemed to me like a man coming straight from the battlefield bearing its marks, pride and sorrow. By that time I had read *L'Etranger, Le Mythe de Sisyphe,* and *Caligula.* In those black years the young man from Algeria had fought and conquered. He had become, together with Jean-Paul Sartre, the symbol of a defeated France, which because of them had imposed itself victoriously in its chosen domain — intelligence. He had won his position on the stage of the world; he was famous; his books were brilliant. But to me he had conquered in a more important sense. He had faced the question which I considered crucial and which had so absorbed me during the days that I first met him. He had mastered it and carried it to extreme and lucid conclusions. He had succeeded in saying in his fevered way and in an argument as taut as a bow why, despite the fury and horror of history, man is an absolute; and he had indicated precisely where, according to him, this absolute lay: in the conscience, even if mute and stilled; in remaining true to one's self even when condemned by the gods to repeat over and over the same vain task. In this lay the value of *L'Etranger* and *Le Mythe de Sisyphe* for me.

With an almost monstrous richness of ideas and vigor of reasoning Sartre had said something similar. But when he arrived at the question of the connection between man and history today; between man and the choices which impose themselves today, Sartre seemed to have lost the thread of his reasoning, to have turned backward to realism, to categorical obligations imposed on man from the outside, and worse, to notions of the politically opportune. Camus held firm, at the risk of exposing

himself, defenseless, to the criticism of the dialecticians, and of seeming
to pass brusquely from logic to emotive affirmation. It is certain that
what induced him to remain firm was not an ideological system, but the
sentiment, so vehemently expressed in *L'Etranger* and in some pages of
*Le Mythe de Sisyphe,* of the inviolable secret which is enclosed in every
man's heart simply because he is "condemned to die." That is man's
transcendence. That is man's transcendence in respect to history; that is
the truth which no social imperative can erase. Desperate transcendence
and truth, because they are challenged in the very heart of man, who
knows that he is mortal and eternally guilty, with no recourse against destiny. Absurd such transcendence and truth — but absurd as they were,
they were reborn every time that Sisyphus descended "with heavy, but
equal, steps, toward the torment whose end he would never approach.
. . ." This secret, like the "eternal jewel" of Macbeth, can never be
compromised or violated without sacrilege.

Albert Camus had known how to give form to this feeling and to remain true to it. Because of this, his presence added to everybody's world,
making it more real and less insensate. And because of this, not of his
fame, the young writer from Algeria has "grown" in my eyes, worthy not
only of friendship but admiration. It was no longer a matter of literature,
but of directly confronting the world. Literary space, that *trompe l'oeil*
that had been invented in the nineteenth century to defend the individual
artist's right to be indifferent, was broken. Camus (and, in his very
different way, Sartre) by the simple act of raising the question of the
value of existence, asserted the will to participate actively, in the first
person, in the world; that is, to challenge directly the actual situation and
contemporary man in the name of the exigence of a conscience whose
rigor was not attenuated by pragmatic considerations. With this, one
might say, he returned to the *raison d'être* of writing. Putting the world
in question means putting one's self in question and abandoning the artist's traditional right to remain separate from his work — a pure creator.
In the language of Camus this signifies that if the world is absurd, the
artist must live immersed in the absurd, must carry the burden of it, and
must seek to prove it *for the others.*

This was the real and the only valid meaning of *engagement.* Such a
choice carried within itself the threat of the cancerous negation that
Camus called nihilism. One had to go through the experience of nihilism
and fight it. The simplest act of life is an act of affirmation; it is the
acceptance of one's own and others' lives as the starting point of all
thinking. But living by nihilism is living on bad faith, as a bourgeois lives
on his income.

In 1946 Camus was invited to speak to the students of Columbia University in New York. I have kept notes of his talk, and am sure I can

reconstruct it without betraying his meaning. The gist of the speech was as follows:

> We were born at the beginning of the First World War. As adolescents we had the crisis of 1929; at twenty, Hitler. Then came the Ethiopian War, the Civil War in Spain, and Munich. These were the foundations of our education. Next came the Second World War, the defeat, and Hitler in our homes and cities. Born and bred in such a world, what did we believe in? Nothing. Nothing except the obstinate negation in which we were forced to close ourselves from the very beginning. The world in which we were called to exist was an absurd world, and there was no other in which we could take refuge. The world of culture was beautiful, but it was not real. And when we found ourselves face to face with Hitler's terror, in what values could we take comfort, what values could we oppose to negation? In none. If the problem had been the bankruptcy of a political ideology, or a system of government, it would have been simple enough. But what had happened came from the very root of man and society. There was no doubt about this, and it was confirmed day after day not so much by the behavior of the criminals but by that of the average man. The facts showed that men deserved what was happening to them. Their way of life had so little value; and the violence of the Hitlerian negation was in itself logical. But it was unbearable and we fought it.
>
> Now that Hitler has gone, we know a certain number of things. The first is that the poison which impregnated Hilterism has not been eliminated; it is present in each of us. Whoever today speaks of human existence in terms of power, efficiency, and "historical tasks" spreads it. He is an actual or potential assassin. For if the problem of man is reduced to any kind of "historical task," he is nothing but the raw material of history, and one can do anything one pleases with him. Another thing we have learned is that we cannot accept any optimistic conception of existence, any happy ending whatsoever. But if we believe that optimism is silly, we also know that pessimism about the action of man among his fellows is cowardly.
>
> We opposed terror because it forces us to choose between murdering and being murdered; and it makes communication impossible. This is why we reject any ideology that claims control over all of human life.

It seems to me today that in this speech, which was a sort of autobiography, there were all the themes of Camus' later work, from *La Peste* to *Les Justes* to *L'Homme Révolté*. But in it there remained, discreetly in shadow, the other Camus, the one that I can call neither truer nor artistically superior, for he is simply "the other," jealously hidden in his secret being — the anguished, dark, misanthropic Camus whose yearning for human communication was perhaps even greater than that of the author of *La Peste;* the man who, in questioning the world, questioned himself, and by this testified to his own vocation. This is the Camus of the last pages of *L'Etranger,* and especially the Camus of *La Chute* in which we hear his deepest being, the self-tormenting tormentor speak, resisting all forms of complacency and moral self-satisfaction. He wrote, "I was persecuted by a ridiculous apprehension: one cannot die without having confessed all one's own lies . . . otherwise, be there one hidden untruth in a life, death would render it definitive . . . this absolute assassination of the truth gave me vertigo. . . ." With these words, it seems to me, the dialogue of Albert Camus with his contemporaries, truncated as it is by death, is nonetheless complete.

1960
*Translated by* MIRIAM CHIAROMONTE

# C. WRIGHT MILLS: A PERSONAL MEMOIR

## HARVEY SWADOS

I first met C. Wright Mills in 1941 or 1942, when he was a young assistant professor of sociology at the University of Maryland (at that time, at least, a singularly dismal-looking provincial school whose president was one "Curly" Byrd, a former football coach). I was about twenty-one, some five years his junior, and at the time I was either working the night shift in an aircraft factory or had recently left the factory to join the Merchant Marine; in either case, I was aware of what Mills was up to, from certain pieces that he was publishing, and we hit it off at once. He was living with his first wife and baby daughter in a co-op development which he supported on principle but otherwise ignored completely, since he was absorbed day and night with other problems. He might have said the same of the baby, who crawled about at his feet — if indeed she was old enough to — while he explained, to my youthful astonishment, that she was still a vegetable and would only be worth bothering with some few years later.

I last saw C. Wright Mills in 1962, late in January, at the Nice Airport, where I had driven him from my French home so that he could return to America, after many months of fruitless wandering about Europe, to die. His youngest child, who had been toddling about, tripped and split open his lip on the terrazzo floor. Mills was concerned, but unable to cope (fortunately his wife was). We shook hands, for the last time, and I looked back to see him walking slowly up and down with his child, being the dutiful parent because at this terrible moment he had nothing else to do with his time or with his life.

In the two decades between those two encounters, Mills and I were very closely attuned, psychologically and intellectually, so much so that we often quarreled violently, and there were years on end when we had absolutely nothing to do with each other. When we parted with that final handshake in Nice, it was with the tacit recognition that after twenty years neither of us really understood the other. More than tacit: We had just spent the better — or rather the worst — part of a month grappling vainly for clues that might lead us back to the whereabouts of an earlier Mills.

"At those crossroads of one's life," Manes Sperber has written in *Journey Without End* (incidentally, a book which I had tried unsuccessfully a year or two earlier to get Mills to confront), "when one ceases to ask, 'What is still to happen to me?' and begins instead to wonder: 'What has happened to me? What have I done with my life?' — that is a time when it is easy to panic."

There are aspects to Mills which are badly understood or misunderstood, and which my experiences with him may help to clarify. He was an important and a characteristic American, and if I was not always able to predict and hence to rely on his conduct in a given political or personal circumstance, I knew him I think better than anyone else ever did, with the possible exception of my wife. However, if I were to attempt to unburden myself of the complicated tangle that our lives, and those of our families, became during those years, I would have to undertake an exercise in autobiography, a distasteful and impossible task.

Within those narrow limits, then, there follow some reflections on the man who called me his best and only friend (in all honesty I think he said the same to two or three others, depending on his mood and the kind of sustenance he needed from those others), and whom, far from regarding as my best friend, I must say frankly I never loved, often did not like, but always struggled to respond to and to aid. In the end I think that maybe I failed him, but that too is a personal matter.

Mills was a complex man because he was a bundle of contradictions. That is an easy thing to say — it needs some spelling out. In recent years he was perhaps more appreciated abroad than at home; but if the Europeans — and the Orientals and Latin Americans — understood what he was *saying* better than the Americans did, they could not possibly understand what he was *doing*. As a result we already find him described as a battler for the oppressed, which is absurd, or as a crusader without honor in his native land, which is ludicrous. In the United States there is a tendency to think of him as a disinterested clinical observer, which seems to me equally wrong, and to refer back to Thorstein Veblen.

I would suggest that if we think rather in terms of Theodore Roosevelt and Scott Fitzgerald, or if possible of a weird melange of the two, egomaniacal and brooding, hearty and homeless, driven by a demon of discontent and ambition, with faith only in the therapy of creative work, whether intellectual or physical, we will come closer to the mark. In all of his writing, as in his lecturing and his public stance, and indeed in his private existence, it was the blending of these forces that gave his work and life its ineluctable impact, its sense of a powerful mind and a forceful personality at grips not with the petty and the ephemeral but with the profoundly important questions.

My first inkling of the way in which this was to operate in our personal relations came in 1946, when I was living in Brooklyn Heights and Mills in lower Manhattan. I had to leave town for several weeks, and told him not only my schedule but my reasons for going. Yet upon my return I found a note in my mailbox from Mills, informing me that he had walked all the way from his house to mine with his little daughter in tow, in hopes of finding me in (I had no phone). I was touched, of course, that anyone should go to so much trouble to see me; but as I thought about it, and discussed it with him on my return, I came to see that while he was truly anxious to talk with me about a number of problems, he was so absorbed in the problems — his own and not mine (which was almost always to be the case) — that he had no interest in and hence no memory of those of my movements and activities which were unconnected with his.

For many people this utter self-absorption was intolerable, and I must confess that there were occasions when it was for me also. But after a time it was borne in upon me that Mills could not function without the absolute conviction that what he was doing was not only right but was more important than what anybody else was doing. More than that, the unique thrust of his best work — I am thinking of the decade of the fifties, of *White Collar* and *The Power Elite* — derived directly from his egocentricity. These books would have been paltry if they had not been informed throughout with a sense of the magnetic self-assurance of their author.

The contradictions of which I spoke earlier worked in greatest tension during those years and issued in those books, written when Mills was in his thirties. Thus he was simultaneously sociable and aloof, democratic and snobbish, uneasy and bold, generous and close, humble and cocky, rationalistic and simplistic. Although he could still rattle off the Latin he had learned as a choir boy, he tended to make light of the effect upon him of Catholic dogma, and I incline to think he was right about this, for religion in any of its manifestations simply bored him. On the other hand, he insisted more than once that what had made him into a rebel and an outsider was the relentless hazing he had undergone as a college freshman before transferring to the University of Texas. He swore to me that for the entire year he had lived surrounded by a wall of silence, without another student addressing a single word to him. Perhaps. Yet he loved to romanticize his early years, even more than most of us do, and he conned people into believing that his background was such as to make it remarkable that he should have become an intellectual at all. The truth was, as I learned for myself in the course of a visit to San Antonio, that his parents were — and are — sympathetic middle-class people, proud of their son and his achievements.

This was, however, one of Mills' charms as well as strengths. I shall never forget his leading me stealthily to a bureau and then triumphantly pulling out the top drawer to disclose layer after layer of Oh Henry! bars. "I decided to lay in a man-sized supply because I never could get enough of them when I was a kid."

He never could get enough of anything. One afternoon he came upon us drinking a bottle of cherry soda, vile stuff I have always thought. For Mills it was a great discovery, so great that on our next visit we tripped over cases of it that he had laid in and stacked outside his kitchen door.

He worked hard, often twenty-four hours at a stretch, and he relaxed hard. Since he knew nothing of tennis, swimming, skiing, even walking, he took his relaxation in the form of sleeping (he could recharge his batteries like a baby, for twelve hours on end), eating (he was the greatest trencherman I have ever known — one night at the Homestead Restaurant he enjoyed our steak dinner so much that after dessert he called back the waiter and ordered the same dinner all over again, from scratch), gadgetry, and building.

This gadgetry was another form — a very American form — of gluttony. When he found a gadget that pleased him he would seemingly try to corner the market in it; and when he became deeply involved in a mechanical hobby, as with cars or cameras, his passion to possess all the peripheral gimmicks was really unbounded.

Thus he started with an MG and worked his way up through a Porsche to a BMW motorcycle; along the line he acquired driving goggles of every conceivable tint, driving gloves of leather, cotton and wool, and a shelf full of subscriptions to obscure and arcane British motoring journals, the contents of which used to drive us into hysterics — Mills included — when we read them aloud. He never participated personally in races or rallies, he didn't even care to drive fast (although there were times when we commuted down Route 303 at 85 miles an hour, with me riding pillion on the BMW), and he did not enjoy tinkering with motors (although he flew specially to Germany — his first glimpse of Europe! and his favorite country! — to take a factory course in servicing his motorbike).

I believe there were two principal reasons for this particular passion, both of them related to Mills' code, to his political attitudinizing, and to his published work. First was a respect amounting to reverence for the well-made object, its designer, and the man who knew how to use it properly. Among the Americans whom Mills respected most (in truth there were not very many) were a group of mechanics, factory foremen, and such, who had a motorcycle club — a serious one, not of the black-leather jacket variety — and were first-rate riders. His second reason was a hatred, which became more ostentatious as the years went by, of everything marked Made in America. It seems to me that the last American vehicle he owned, before the MG and all the rest, was that masterpiece of ingenious simplicity, the jeep.

In any case, there was a connection between the gadgetry and the love of building, which so impressed those who came upon Mills in the act of putting up with his own hands a house of his own design. In addition to its serving as his greatest relaxation after prolonged bouts of research and writing, it bolstered in his mind the proud belief that he, like the mechanics, drivers, architects, and designers whom he so admired, could do things that were utterly beyond the ken of metropolitan intellectuals who could only write books, or worse, articles about books and articles about articles about books. Although we never spoke overmuch about this, it was a shared assumption, and I am sure that for him it had its roots in profound feelings of uneasiness in confronting dyed-in-the-wool intellectuals, particularly Jewish intellectuals who made him feel the outsider. Just so, I am sure that this was one of the two main links which bound us in our peculiar connection (the other being the fact that we were both constitutionally loners, incapable of fitting comfortably into the *Partisan Review* set, the *Commentary* set, etc., etc.), for over the years we exchanged a good many man-hours of labor on mutually helpful projects, as well as kicking around and even getting involved in a kind of subsistence farming.

I was always ready to pitch in, to the best of my ability, on his outlines, his drafts, his chapters, his galleys; and I spent many weeks working with him on *White Collar, The Power Elite, The Causes of World War III,* and *The Sociological Imagination* (a book which I did not very much like, even in its toned-down final draft, despite the fact that Mills dedicated it to my wife and to me). He for his part was always ready to advise me on problems of my house, and to put in time and labor too.

If I worked for some weeks laying the fireplace for his first Rockland

County house and the footings for his second Rockland house, he showed me how and helped me, over a dozen years, to pull stumps with his jeep, to fit up my gutters, leaders, and drainage pipe, to construct and sink in concrete a new cover for my well, to build a closet in my daughter's room and last of all to tie into my new wing a comfortable typing table and an open file hooked to the wall (he was always appalled at my sloppy filing, particularly in connection with any work in progress). He was so patently my superior in all of these tasks, whether at his house or at mine, that I was perfectly content to do the dirty work under Mills' supervision.

When it came to writing, however, this was not the case, and I must say that I never had any particular interest in his opinion of my fiction. I never reciprocated his imperious demands for help by so much as showing him my work, for his taste in contemporary fiction ran to writers like the late Nevil Shute, whom he regarded in all seriousness as being one of the world's ten best living novelists; and, on the one occasion that I requested that he read something of mine in draft, because I needed technical clarification of some social science stuff, he put me off. I was hurt by this at the time, for I had never turned down a similar request from him, but God knows he had his troubles, and I did not continue to hold it against him. If that was my first request, it was also to be my last.

What I have said thus far has probably been weighted on the Teddy Roosevelt side of Mills' personality, his heartiness, handiness, ruggedness, and seemingly limitless gusto and self-assurance. But when I speak of his unending and humble desire to learn how to commit to paper with precision and fluency all that he believed, I must refer to the Fitzgerald side of his character.

I am not attempting to point up the parallel between Fitzgerald's dashing about France without troubling to learn the language and Mills' wanderings about Europe without knowing a word of any foreign tongue, although that was true enough; nor between Fitzgerald's high living and Mills' living on unwritten books, although that was true enough too; nor even between Fitzgerald's crackup and Mills' terrifying conviction at the same age that he was written out, worked out, burned out, although that was horribly true. What I am thinking of are Fitzgerald's — and Mills' — devotion to their craft and their belief that through it they could express a unique vision of America.

This is what Mills' detractors have never been able to understand. Attacking him bitterly, often with as much venom as he attacked them, for the crudities of his style (of which he was painfully aware and worked unremittingly to overcome), for his unrefined methodology, his grandiose generalizations, his gross inaccuracies about the military or the educational system or whatever, his fascination with the supposed technological efficiency of totalitarianism, they were unable to understand how it was that he was not merely respected but looked upon as spokesman and mentor by many of the best of the young academics and by many thousands of plain readers, nor how it is that he is avidly attended by millions in Japan, in Russia, in Mexico, as a refreshingly different voice of America.

For a long time I have thought — I still do — that it was because all these people were responding to what was at bottom not merely a logical indictment which could be upheld or attacked, but a poetic vision of America; an unlovely vision perhaps, expressed with a mixture of awkwardness and brilliance, but one that did not really need statistical buttressing or the findings of research teams in order to be apprehended by sensitive Americans as corresponding to their own sense of what was going on about them, more truly and more unflinchingly than any other contemporary statement. They were responding, in that unlovely decade, the fat and frightened fifties, to one who refused to compromise or to make the excuses that others were making — excuses mislabeled descriptions or analyses — for what was happening to their country. They sensed correctly that, faulty and flawed as it was, the vision of Wright Mills cut through the fog and lighted their lives for them.

I have deliberately left out much. I must say a word, however, about Mills' fascination with the totalitarian variety of the global shift to what is called socialism. He and I had many sessions, some of them shouting sessions, over this, at about the time when he was writing *The Causes of World War III,* and after his first (triumphal) visit to the Soviet Union. At the end, early this year, we had arrived at what I suppose you might call a kind of truce. The ever-accelerating race of history would demonstrate soon enough where the deeper truth lay, and each of us was wholly persuaded of the other's good-will if not persuaded of the other's correctness.

What happened, it seems to me, is that Mills was caught up by the greatest contradiction of all, that which had carried him so far but was in the end to fall crushingly on his massive shoulders, the impossibility in our age of being simultaneously a Teddy Roosevelt and a Scott Fitzgerald, a public figure-man of action and an artist-thinker. Increasingly, with everything he wrote, Mills found that he was addressing himself to a defined audience. He was becoming a leader with a following. Not merely requests to speak, but pleas for guidance and counsel came pouring in on him, and after *The Causes of World War III* they became a flood. Under such circumstances the temptation to become oracular was almost irresistible; for a man who was absolutely sure of his own insight and analysis it was inevitable.

So was the tragedy. I do not think I am overstating when I say that Mills was never deeply affected by what totalitarianism did to great masses of people. To particular intellectuals, yes; but not to masses. For him Nazism was something that could be comprehended by reading Neumann and some other books; there were no horrible unplumbable depths. Hence he was impatient with my continually reminding him of German anti-Semitism: he regarded the murder of six million Jews as one of the terrible things that can happen when reactionaries take over and nation-states go to war. Nothing more. For him Stalinism in its turn was contemptible not for what it was doing to national minorities, to workers and peasants, to millions languishing in Siberia, but for its political vulgarity and intellectual emptiness. Its standard-bearers throughout the world were crude epigones, parrots incapable of originality or vision, much less of redirecting mankind toward new goals.

For a while it seemed to him as though the Chinese Communists might very well be doing just this. The Great Leap Forward excited him enormously. Eager to be shown that the pro-Communist Australian — and other — Sinologists whom he read, understood, and filed, were indeed right, he itched to be off to China to see for himself. But he was not able to get there because, like it or not, he was an American. Cuba, however, was still available, and people in both North and South America had been asking him what he had to say about the Cuban Revolution, an event far more anti-American in its implications than the Chinese Revolution.

Anyone who knew Mills' admiration for the motorcycle drivers could have foreseen his admiration for the successful Cuban guerrillas; anyone who knew his hurt at being ignored or patronized by his colleagues could have foreseen his reaction to Castro's assurance that he and his fellows had been studying Mills during their long months in the mountains. The result was *Listen Yankee,* in which Mills climbed further out on a limb than he had ever gone before.

For a new generation the Cuban Revolution, together with its aftermath, was a crucial event comparable in magnitude, in resonance, to the Spanish Civil War for an earlier generation. For Mills it was definitive proof (as it was for many of us) of the blind rapacity of the American power elite; but more, it provided him for the first time with an emotional home. When this latter certainty was destroyed, everything was destroyed.

In his last months Mills was torn between defending *Listen Yankee,* as a good and honest book, and acknowledging publicly for the first time in his life that he had been terribly wrong. This would have meant not only caving in to the few whose opinions he valued, which I believe he would have been strong enough to do (I had waited until I believed —

mistakenly — that he was recovered from his heart attack before telling him what I really thought of the book), but returning to the United States and telling not only his enemies on the right, but the hundreds of thousands who had, so to speak, voted for him, that he was not a rough-rider after all, but only a man of ideas who could be wrong, as men of ideas so often are. The tension was too much, the decline of the revolution, atop his personal pains, was too much. I can only add that he declared to me in his last weeks that he was becoming more and more impressed with the psychological and intellectual relevance of nonviolent resistance and absolute pacifism.

When I think of my friends who have died prematurely in recent years I mourn the missing sweetness of one, the incomparable insightfulness of another. I would be a liar if I were to say that Mills was a sweet and lovable friend, or that he understood and cared about many individual humans any more than he understood or cared about many individual artistic creations. But hardly a day passes without my arranging in my mind an argument to present to Mills about this event, that book, this development, that crisis. He was as combatively exhilarating as any man has ever been, he worked with the contagious wild passion of an inventor or a driven idealist, and when he was really dauntless he was the bravest man I have ever known.

1963

# ON DAVID SIQUEIROS: A DILEMMA FOR ARTISTS

## MEYER SCHAPIRO

I have been asked several times during the last years to sign a statement requesting the Mexican government to release the painter Siqueiros from prison. He has been sentenced for a long term because he led a violent demonstration against the government and thus exposed himself to the penalties of a law which classifies such acts as crimes of "social dissolution." From what I have heard of this law, it seems to me unjust; at any rate, the penalty of eight years in prison for leading a demonstration and inciting to violence is barbaric. This law was enacted, supposedly, to strike at fascists and others who plotted to overthrow the Mexican government which prided itself upon being a revolutionary regime committed to the welfare of the Mexican people. Like the Smith Act in our own country, this law was once supported by the Communist Party, which saw in it no threat to its own members. It is like the laws in the Soviet Union that punish severely any public demonstration against the regime.

In calling for the release of Siqueiros the signers of the petition have made much of the fact that Siqueiros is a great painter and therefore deserves a special treatment. Imagine, says the letter, Van Gogh, Michelangelo, and Goya languishing in jail. Most painters would resent as impudent the idea that Siqueiros was one of that company of genius and would feel indignant or amused if they were asked to back that judgment with their signatures. But the issue here concerns the life of a brother-painter, and in such extremes one doesn't hedge over a phrase, no matter how repugnant to an artist's integrity of judgment. The important thing is to oppose an unjust law and to defend an artist who is its victim.

For those who composed the letter, the comparison with Van Gogh, Michelangelo, and Goya is more important, even indispensable. By elevating Siqueiros to artistic greatness, they divert attention from his sinister political role. From the viewpoint of justice Siqueiros is not invulnerable. If one takes justice seriously, one must describe the painter in a somewhat different and less glamorous way. In 1940, he organized and led an attack on the house of the Russian revolutionist, Leon Trotsky, in the course of which his band kidnapped and killed one of Trotsky's guards, the American Sheldon Harte. He has also been accused of a part in the assassination of Trotsky. Siqueiros never denied his role in the attack on Trotsky's house and boasted of his action as "one of the greatest honors of my life." He was arrested, and indicted on nine criminal counts; but with the connivance of a foreign consul, he left Mexico and returned after the tumult had died down. He has never been tried for those crimes.

It is my knowledge of this history that keeps me from signing the appeal in Siqueiros' behalf. To defend Siqueiros as a victim of injustice, without telling the truth about his crimes, is to maintain injustice. To speak of Siqueiros as a great painter who through some arbitrariness of the State languishes in jail, is to play a dangerous game of political double-talk. Those who have lived through the 1930's and '40's when the arts were used as instruments of Communist politics and the fascist threats to the liberty of the artist were arguments for support of Stalin's policies — though Stalin had no respect for that liberty at home and exterminated some of the greatest Russian writers — those who remember the petitions and appeals of that time, signed by artists in perfect good faith, will look more skeptically at the gross formulations of the Siqueiros letter.

I urge those who have approved the Siqueiros letter to read the statement issued by a group of French writers, addressed to the committee of artists that sponsored an Exhibit in Homage to Siqueiros. (It is printed in the Bulletin d'Informations of the Commission for the Truth About the Crimes of Stalin, May, 1962.) They review the history of his crimes and refuse to ally themselves with those who picture the Communist politico Siqueiros as a pure artist, victimized by a reactionary regime. It is their statement, I hear, that led Picasso to refuse to join the sponsors of the exhibition.

The appeal for Siqueiros has also its comic ambiguities. We are told that Siqueiros, a man for whom painting is his life, is being kept from his easel and that mankind as a result is denied all those masterpieces which we would possess if Siqueiros were free. When this argument was presented in Paris at a meeting of the International Association of Art Critics in order to win their support for the appeal, an inquiry at the Mexican embassy disclosed the fact that Siqueiros was able to paint in prison. We hear now that he paints two or three canvases a week and sells them for over three thousand dollars apiece. Never has he been so productive, never has he contributed so much to the cultural patrimony of Mexico and the world — assuming, of course, that his paintings are good. During much of his life he has been a Communist militant, more active in leading demonstrations, planning and participating in murders, and carrying out faithfully the instructions of the Moscow dictators than in painting pictures. In prison perhaps he has at last found himself as an artist.

1963